EICHMANN'S MEN

More than sixty years after the advent of the National Socialist genocides, the question remains: How could a state-sponsored terror that took the lives of millions of men, women, and children, persecuted as Jews or Gypsies, happen? Now available in English, Hans Safrian's pathbreaking work on Adolf Eichmann and his Nazi helpers chronicles the escalation of Nazi antisemitic policies beginning in 1933 and during World War II to the "Final Solution." This book examines a central group of National Socialist perpetrators who expelled German, Austrian, Polish, Russian, French, Greek, Italian, and Czech Jews from their homelands and deported massive numbers of them to the ghettos, concentration camps, and killing centers of occupied Eastern Europe. Safrian reconstructs the "careers" of Eichmann and his men in connection with the implementation of racial policies, particularly the gradual marginalization of their victims and the escalation from stigmatization, divestment, and segregation to deportation, forced labor, and, finally, mass murder.

Hans Safrian lectures in history at the Institute für Zeitgeschichte at the University of Vienna. He was also a Pearl Resnick Fellow at the United States Holocaust Memorial Museum, Research Team Leader for the Independent Commission of Experts – Switzerland – Second World War, and a research historian for the Historical Commission of the Republic of Austria. He is the author of numerous works on World War II and Nazi war crimes.

Eichmann's Men

HANS SAFRIAN

Translated by Ute Stargardt

Published in association with the
United States Holocaust Memorial Museum

CAMBRIDGE UNIVERSITY PRESS
Cambridge, New York, Melbourne, Madrid, Cape Town, Singapore,
São Paulo, Delhi, Dubai, Tokyo

Published in association with the United States Holocaust Memorial Museum

Cambridge University Press
32 Avenue of the Americas, New York, NY 10013-2473, USA

www.cambridge.org
Information on this title: www.cambridge.org/9780521617260

United States Holocaust Memorial Museum
100 Raoul Wallenberg Place, SW, Washington, DC 20024-2126, USA

First published in German as *Eichmann-Männer* by Hans Safrian 1993
First updated, English edition published 2010

Printed in the United States of America

A catalog record for this publication is available from the British Library.

Library of Congress Cataloging in Publication data

Safrian, Hans.
[Eichmann-Männer. English]
Eichmann's men / Hans Safrian ; translated by Ute Stargardt.
    p.   cm.
Published in association with the United States Holocaust Memorial Museum.
Includes bibliographical references and index.
ISBN 978-0-521-85156-5 (hardback)
1. Holocaust, Jewish (1939–1945)   2. World War, 1939–1945 – Atrocities.   3. Antisemitism –
Germany – History – 20th century.   4. State-sponsored terrorism – Germany – History – 20th
century.   5. Eichmann, Adolf, 1906–1962.   6. Eichmann, Adolf, 1906–1962 – Friends and
associates.   7. Nazis – Germany – History – 20th century.   8. National socialism – Germany –
History – 20th century.   I. United States Holocaust Memorial Museum.   II. Title.
D804.3.S24513   2010
940.53′18–dc22   2009034652

ISBN 978-0-521-85156-5 Hardback
ISBN 978-0-521-61726-0 Paperback

For my grandfather Otto Haas,
born 1897 in Břeclav, Moravia,
probably murdered in 1943 in Auschwitz-Birkenau
after being deported from Paris

In memory of Raul Hilberg,
the foremost Holocaust historian,
who taught me to ask the right questions

Contents

Acknowledgments   *page* ix

   Introduction 1

1 Eichmann and the Development of the "Vienna Model" 14

2 The Unsuccessful Beginning: The Deportations to Nisko
   on the River San 46

3 The Development and Initial Activities of Referat IV D 4 59

4 From Expulsion to Mass Murder: 1941 72

5 Controversies over the Deportations to the Occupied Areas
   of the Soviet Union: 1941 91

6 The Development of the Genocide Program: 1942 112

7 Collaboration and Deportations: 1942 134

8 The Destruction of the Jewish Community of Salonika:
   The Cooperation of the SS and the Wehrmacht 150

9 Manhunts in France and Greece: 1943–1944 173

10 Manhunts in Hungary and Slovakia: 1944–1945 194

11 The Postwar Era 211

Notes   225

References   295

Index   311

Acknowledgments

My study of sources would not have been possible without the assistance of the staff members of the following archives: Bundesarchiv-Militär Archiv, Freiburg; Central Archive for the History of the Jewish People, Jerusalem; Centre de Documentation Juive Contemporaine, Paris; Dokumentationsarchiv des österreichischen Widerstandes, Vienna; Leo Baeck Institute, New York; Museum Mauthausen-Archiv, Vienna; Yad Vashem, Jerusalem; YIVO Institute for Jewish Research, New York; and the Zentrale Stelle der Landesjustizverwaltungen zur Aufklärung nationalsozialistischer Verbrechen, Ludwigsburg. I want to thank all of them for their cooperation in locating documents.

Such access to documents from the National Socialist era is by no means a given, even fifty years after the events took place. I had occasion to realize this in the Archiv der Republik Österreich. After publishing *Und keiner war dabei: Dokumente des alltäglichen Antisemitismus in Wien 1938*, with my coeditor Hans Witek, the administration of this archive denied me access to the documents on the grounds of data protection, prohibiting the study of documents of the Vermögensverkehrsstelle, the institution responsible for Aryanizations in Vienna, even though these records had been freely available until publication of the book.

I am grateful to Gabriele Anderl, Johanna Braithwaite, Peter Malina, Walter Manoschek, Gustav Spann, Franz Weiss, and Hans Witek for suggesting primary and secondary sources in the early stages of my work. I thank Randolph L. Braham, New York; Serge Klarsfeld, Paris; Shmuel Krakowski, Jerusalem; Christopher Simpson, Mt. Rainier; Georges Wellers, Paris; Elliot Welles, New York; and Simon Wiesenthal, Vienna, for their conversations and suggestions.

Thanks to the hospitality of Susan Korda and Mark Simon in New York, Marita Dresner in Washington, D.C., and Francine Aptel and Franz Grafl in Paris, I was able to conduct my research in the archives of these cities. I appreciate the discussions, critical comments, and encouragements of

Brigitte Bailer-Galanda, Karin Berger, Florian Freund, Bertrand Perz, Doron
Rabinovic, and Karl Stuhlpfarrer. They were vitally important in sustaining
my engagement in this challenging and emotionally taxing subject.

I thank my son David for his patience with my many hours of working at
my desk, and for his insistence on taking me away from my work from time to
time to play, read comics, or visit the pool.

Finally, for arranging the publication of the English-language edition of
this book, I thank the staff of the Center for Advanced Holocaust Studies
of the United States Holocaust Memorial Museum, where I was generously
granted a Pearl Resnick Fellowship. Among those whose efforts I appreciate
are Paul Shapiro, Center Director; Benton Arnovitz, Director of Academic
Publications; and Patricia Heberer, Staff Historian. Special thanks, too, to
translator Ute Stargardt, to Brewster Chamberlin for proofreading and his
work on the index, and to Anthony Zannino for additional proofreading.
Appreciation is due, as well, to Eric Crahan at Cambridge University Press and
to their production editors and copyeditors at Aptara.

Introduction

The silent transition from falsehood to self-deception is useful: anyone who lies in good faith lies better. He recites his part better, is more easily believed by the judge, the historian, the reader, his wife, and his children.

Primo Levi, *The Drowned and the Saved*

Even more than sixty years after the onset of the National Socialist genocides, the question arises how it could happen that men, women, and children persecuted as Jews or "Gypsies" became victims of a state-sponsored terror that deprived millions of their lives. This book deals with a centrally situated group of National Socialist perpetrators who drove German, Austrian, Polish, Russian, French, Greek, Italian, and Czech Jews from their homes and homelands and carried out deportations into the ghettos, concentration camps, and extermination camps in occupied Eastern Europe. This examination reconstructs the "careers" of Adolf Eichmann and his men in relation to the entire program of racist policies. The National Socialists escalated exclusion from the community of the *Volk* (nation) step by step – from stigmatization, pillaging, and segregation to expulsion, forced labor, and deportation, and all the way to mass murder.

The chronological organization of this study traces this escalation within three main sections:

- the forcible expulsion of Jews from Großdeutschland (the Greater German Reich) and the confinement of Polish Jews in ghettos from 1938 to 1941
- the transition from the policies of expulsion to the policies of mass murder during 1941 and 1942
- the deportation to concentration and extermination camps and genocides from 1942 until 1944.

1

The "Vienna Model" (Wiener Modell) of the forced expulsion of Jews developed in 1938 represents the beginning of Eichmann's and his men's rise in the Schutzstaffel (SS) hierarchy: Simultaneously, it represents a turning point in that phase during which the National Socialist regime disenfranchised, robbed, and forced into emigration German, Austrian, Polish, Russian, French, Italian, Greek, and Czech Jews. Even though various historians have pointed to the intensification of anti-Jewish policies in connection to the Anschluß (annexation) of Austria, the "Vienna Model" is nevertheless frequently equated with the foundation of the Zentralstelle für jüdische Auswanderung (Central Bureau for Jewish Emigration) and discussed in reference to Eichmann's supposed ideas and organizational skills. Such explanations totally ignore the fundamental sociopolitical dimensions of the indigenous antisemitism of the Ostmark (Austria), even though it is precisely the greed for loot and the Herrenmenschen-Allüren, the pretensions of the members of the "Master Race," on the part of the Austrian antisemites, and their participation in racist policies that accelerated the criminal logic of exclusion. This antisemitism in the Ostmark, prescribed in no way from above, provided the foundation upon which Eichmann was able to establish the Zentralstelle für jüdische Auswanderung and soon could report expulsion figures to Berlin that caught the attention of his superiors. The "Vienna Model" looked so successful to the National Socialists that it became the prototype for corresponding institutions established in the Großdeutsche Reich, the German Reich comprising the so-called Altreich and incorporated conquered territories. At the same time, the appropriation of the strategies and structures developed in Vienna served Reinhard Heydrich as a means of expanding the power of the SS-Sicherheitsdienst (SS Security Service, or SD) within the Party and vis-à-vis other government organizations discharging anti-Jewish policies.

This study, following an outline of the social, political, and biographical backgrounds of Eichmann's men, turns to the beginnings of the organized mass expulsions across the German–Soviet line of demarcation in the fall of 1939. During the preparation and execution of these deportations into the Nisko area at the River San, Eichmann and his men were able to demonstrate to their superiors that they could deceive thousands of people with fictive tales about Umschulungslager ("retraining" camps) and freie Ansiedlung (free settlement programs) and so spirit them out of the country within a few weeks without arousing undue attention. More ambitious plans for expulsion operations organized on a large scale in the fall of 1939, however, failed initially because at that time coordination among the SS, the Wehrmacht (Armed Forces), and the Reichsbahn, the national railway, was still poor. In the newly established Reichssicherheitshauptamt (Reich Security Main Office,

or RSHA) Eichmann became head of his own section, which in 1940 organized the so-called Umsiedlertransporte (resettlement transports) into the
Generalgouvernement, the Government General (German-occupied Poland).
The controversies that arose among executives of various administrative units
in charge of the occupation as a result of the development of the policy of
expelling Jews and Asoziale (so-called asocials who in Nazi judgment did
not conform to the norms and mores of the German Volksgemeinschaft, the
German "national community") from all territories under German rule and
their deportation into Reservate (reservations) were to be resolved by the
"Madagascar Plan." The proposals worked out in cooperation among the
Auswärtige Amt, the German Foreign Office, and Eichmann's RSHA section,
however, never advanced beyond the planning stage.

   The foci of this investigation are the transitions from policies of expulsion to the policies of mass murder during the years 1941 and 1942, as well
as the importance of Eichmann's Section IV B 4's involvement in them. One
chapter each deals with the disputes over the deportations to Łódź (renamed
Litzmannstadt by the Germans in 1939) in the fall of 1941, the occupied territories of the Soviet Union in the fall and winter of 1941, and the decisions before
and during the "Wannsee Conference" to pursue policies of mass murder.
During this phase Eichmann's section functioned as a mediating and switch-
ing station. On the one hand it coordinated requests for mass deportations.
On the other hand, in search of locations that could receive the deported, it
accepted, examined, and passed on to superiors more radical, even murderous proposals from subordinate or affiliated departments and, once they were
approved, took charge of implementing them.

   This book reconstructs the decision-making processes in the conflicts
between central government authorities and occupation agencies. It studies
the effects of the savage conduct of Operation Barbarossa, Germany's invasion
of the Soviet Union, on the development of the strategies of mass murder, as
well as the attitudes of the Wehrmacht and German civil administrative bodies
in occupied Eastern Europe. The commonly assumed existence of Hitler's specific order for the destruction of European Jewry in the summer/fall of 1941
is another subject of investigation. The book decodes the meanings that the
policy makers of the Third Reich attached to the term "Final Solution of the
Jewish Question" during these various phases up to the Wannsee Conference,
where it was finally established as the synonym for mass deportations, Selek-
tionen (selections of individuals for killing), and various methods of mass
murder. The Final Solution also involved the differentiation between victims
to be considered arbeitsfähig, fit or capable of work, or arbeitsunfähig, unfit
or incapable of work; the rapid murder of those categorized as "incapable of

work"; and forced labor in ghettos and concentration camps under conditions that for almost all victims "capable of work" would come to mean a slow, protracted death.

The execution of the programs of deportation agreed upon in principle at the villa in Wannsee gave Eichmann's men from Vienna another opportunity to distinguish themselves. Through the progression of the "Vienna Model" to merciless manhunts they already had concluded the mass deportations from the Ostmark in October of 1942. From then on the Austrian man-hunters could be deployed wherever the progress of the deportations had been delayed or had come to a standstill. As a Sonderkommando, a special detachment most frequently under the command of Alois Brunner, they employed all those methods they had developed and practiced in Vienna: in 1942 in Berlin, in the spring of 1943 in Salonika, and, starting in the summer of 1943, in France.

In 1942 the deportation trains from the Ostmark and the Protektorat Böhmen und Mähren, the Protectorate of Bohemia and Moravia (formerly western Czechslovakia), for the most part were bound for Maly Trostinets, a killing site virtually unknown to this day. It was located near Minsk in the Reichskommissariat Ostland, the Reich Commissariat Ostland, which comprised the German-occupied Baltic States and most of Belorussia. At about the same time the trains from France and Slovakia started rolling into the concentration and extermination camps being built or enlarged in occupied Poland. How was it possible that in the years 1942–1944 hundreds of thousand of men, women, and children could be seized, interned, and sent to their deaths by just a small number of deportation specialists, and what kind of support did the SS man-hunters receive from German and local authorities? The importance of the collaboration of non-German administrative agencies in the execution of National Socialist programs of expulsion unfolds by examining deportations that Eichmann's men conducted from occupied and unoccupied France in 1942 and the participation of Slovak and Croat antisemites in the discrimination, despoilment, expulsion, and murder of Jews. In Slovakia as well as Croatia large segments of the population participated in racist policies and profoundly accelerated the exclusion of Jews and specific ethnic groups. The fascist-clerical rulers of Slovakia accepted, with goal-oriented zeal, Berlin's "offers" to deport Jews. The Ustasche (Ustasha), Hitler's Fascist puppet regime in Croatia, also carried out its own genocide programs, and in the infamous death camp Jasenovac. There, that regime butchered thousands of Croat Jews, as well as large numbers of Roma (Gypsies) and Serbs.

As a result of close cooperation of departments of the Wehrmacht, the Auswärtige Amt, and the SS-Sonderkommando in the spring of 1943, almost

50,000 people were deported from northern Greece within a few weeks. Following their deployment in Salonika, the SS-Kommando, consisting of Viennese deportation specialists, was sent to Paris to jump-start the stagnating expulsion there. In 1943–1944, despite brutal manhunts in Paris, Nice, and other French cities, SS-Hauptsturmführer (Captain) Alois Brunner's Kommando was unable to meet the quotas set in Berlin.

Eichmann and his men conducted deportations until the military defeat of the Third Reich. With active support from the army, one Kommando under Anton Burger in the spring and summer of 1944 sent thousands of Jews from the Greek mainland and the Greek isles to Auschwitz. In the fall and winter of 1944 Alois Brunner hunted Slovak Jews who had survived the suppression of the Slovak Rebellion. Eichmann himself organized the deportation of half a million people from Hungary. Not just in Hungary but also in other countries that formerly had been part of the Austro-Hungarian dual monarchy a labor-sharing alliance between the SS and a specifically Central European antisemitism came into being. The latter was indigenous and religiously and materially motivated.

During the postwar period, as this book describes in closing, the traces of many of Eichmann's men dissipated. Very few were arrested at the end of the war and forced to account for their deeds. The rest, like Eichmann himself, went underground, lived with false identification papers in Austria or the Federal Republic of Germany, or with the help of their old associates, were able to escape to South America or the Middle East.

This study has been guided by the determination to examine the activities and "careers" of those SS men, almost all of them Austrians, who with Adolf Eichmann between 1938 and 1945 drove hundreds of thousands of people from their homes and homelands or deported them to concentration or extermination camps. The general public knows little about "Eichmann's Men,"[1] as they are referred to in standard historiographies about the Holocaust. Their names generally appear only when one of them is arrested and tried or when – as was the case with Alois Brunner who may yet be alive in Syria – Western or Central European states demand their extradition.

By examining court records and original documents, struggling with sources, and trying to connect their contents, the historian becomes increasingly aware of inaccuracies and contradictions between these documents and historiographic presentations and interpretations. Were Eichmann's men mechanical parts of a machine, as the social science literature suggests, or did personal initiative determine their actions? Were they dogged bureaucrats blindly following the directives of superior authorities, or did they make personal decisions within the parameters of their assignments? What was the nature of their basic orders in the first place? The effort of characterizing subaltern perpetrators necessitated reexamining the prevalent characterizations of Adolf Eichmann, as well as reexamining the available sources for representations of the ambience and structures within which Eichmann and his men operated.

In the course of the last decades assessments of Adolf Eichmann's role have varied widely. Immediately after the war Eichmann was demonized. Robert H. Jackson, one of the prosecutors of the Nuremberg Trial against the main Kriegsverbrecher (war criminals), describes him as "the sinister figure who had charge of the extermination program."[2] Joe J. Heydecker and Johannes Leeb's book about the Nuremberg Tribunal refers to him as "the Number One Destroyer of Jews,"[3] and Robert M. W. Kempner calls him the "Commissar of the Jews" invested with an "incredible degree of power," the "Lord over life and death of European Jewry."[4] This exaggerated view of Eichmann's power, assessments that dominated the 1940s and 1950s, also informed the indictment brought against him at his trial in Jerusalem.

Since Hannah Arendt's report of the trial, *Eichmann in Jerusalem: A Report of the Banality of Evil*, published in 1963, other evaluations have come to the fore. Arendt opposed overblown imputations and reduced Eichmann's significance within the machinery of destruction. In so doing, however, she placed too much emphasis on his mediocrity: "Except for an extraordinary diligence in looking out for his personal advancement, he had no motives at all.... It was sheer thoughtlessness – something by no means identical with stupidity – that predisposed him to become one of the greatest criminals of that period."[5] It was precisely these arguments that historians following Hannah Arendt adopted in characterizing the attitudes and motives of functionaries of the National Socialist genocide machinery, referring to "misdirected fulfillment of duty," "slavish bureaucratic obedience," and "subaltern mindset." Eichmann had not acted "primarily on account of antisemitic motives," Hans Mommsen declares in the introduction to Arendt's Eichmann Report. He argues in a similar vein in his article "Die Realisierung des Utopischen: Die 'Endlösung der Judenfrage im Dritten Reich'" ("The Realization of Utopia: The 'Final Solution of the Jewish Question' in the Third Reich"), published in 1983, in which he presents Eichmann as a "spectacular example of the mechanism of compartmentalized responsibility coupled with bureaucratic perfectionism and absolute subjugation to the demands of totalitarian state power."[6]

Notable in more recent historicism is that, without exception, descriptions of the perpetrators and reconstructions of the basic decisions for the introduction of genocide are based on the statements that Auschwitz commandant Rudolf Höß and Adolf Eichmann made after 1945. Especially Eichmann's declarations are frequently accepted in a totally uncritical manner. What strategies of exculpation and defense informed Eichmann's and Höß's reports are at best marginal considerations. Historians have neglected even the most fundamental rules of using sources: They have cited, circulated, and constructed, ignoring the "manipulation of memory" in the testimonies of both Höß and Eichmann. "When fate put them before judges ... they built a convenient past for themselves and ended by believing in it," Primo Levi observes about the perpetrators in *The Drowned and the Saved.*[7] Just like Höß and the other accused National Socialist criminals indicted after 1945, Eichmann styled himself as an absolutely obedient recipient of orders who personally had nothing against Jews and adorned this basic statement with bits and pieces of reality. At the same time he fell back on lies and half-truths he had already employed since 1938 whenever he passed orders to the representatives of the Jewish communities in Vienna, Prague, and Berlin to ensure the smoothest possible accomplishment of his measures. Not everything he said in Jerusalem was a lie; he just recast his part and used what seemed advantageous to him.

One of the few extant "private" documents of that time provides an impression of the tone prevalent in Eichmann's circle. At the end of February 1943 the then-Hauptsturmführer Alois Brunner wrote a letter from Salonika to a comrade in Vienna in which his own words provide a glimpse of his activities as well as his personal impressions far from home (errors and idiosyncracies reflect those of the original).

> Dear Rudolf! You are probably saying already that Brunner once more confirms that ingratitude is the way of the world. Not so Rudolf. First I wanted to look around thoroughly before saying what it really looks like here ... The weather is becoming more and more beautiful and our work is progressing terrifically. On February 25 the yellow stars started gleaming here. Many a soldier said, oh no, my girl is wearing a star too. And the Greek population is so delighted with this marking and the ghettoization that I tell myself what a crime that such measures were not taken much earlier. Inflation and the black market could never have achieved such dimensions if the Jews had been watched closely. These days there is hardly a store without the sign Jewish stores hanging outside. And when we take off with them the jubilation among the Greeks will really start.

When Alois Brunner wrote this letter, he had been in Salonika only three weeks but had already drastically affected the life of the Jewish community. "Misdirected fulfillment of duty" and "bureaucratic mindless obedience" – nothing of the sort was happening here. With unmistakable satisfaction and undisguised glee Brunner reports the "gleaming of the yellow stars" and the "terrific progress of his work." He couldn't wait to "take off with them" – to deliver thousands of people to their murderers in Auschwitz – and was so adept at connecting "his work" – the hunt for human beings – to his plans for entertainment and self-enrichment that he wanted his cronies to partake of these amenities as well.

> And now to personal matters. You need to picture the Greek women of antique heritage here as a little shorter and darker. But otherwise they are said to be very grateful. They especially like the Viennese dialect. What luck that I do not speak Viennese. A few days ago I had a deathly cold. I allowed myself to be persuaded to take a Turkish bath and was cured. Rudolf that is something you just have to experience. It's simply fantastic. You know with these baths the Turks got the women in their harems "ready for bed." And with your strength that kind of bath wouldn't hurt you at all. No matter what in addition to your Africa expertise I could here show you a quite nice bit of European orient too. Don't you have any business here? If so you would have to come while I'm still here. Of course everything would be taken care of on this end. If necessary even the Greek ballet will dance for you at dinner. And dear Rudolf I have a personal request too. Don't let the last Jew leave [Vienna] until my black box has been delivered because otherwise my buddy Berger's junk will break in the suitcases. And please write me or tell my wife if the possibility of a crate of dishes for my sister still exists... Greetings to Miss Hilde and all our acquaintances, many greetings to you your Brunner Lois, Heil Hitler!"[8]

By that time Alois Brunner was no longer a neophyte when it came to the persecution of Jews. As Eichmann's successor, or rather as the successor of Rolf Günther in the position of Director of the Zentralstelle für jüdische Auswanderung in Vienna, he and his coworkers between February 1941 and October 1942 already had transported the majority of Vienna residents who, according to the Nuremberg Laws, were classified as Jews, for Aussiedlung "resettlement" or Abwanderung in den Osten "emigration to the East," to use the parlance of the SS bureaucrats.

The style of Brunner's letter, his obvious delight in his "work" and in acting out the racist pretensions of the Herrenmenschen, provide a stark contrast to the Nazi perpetrators' self-justification efforts that have become part and parcel of historiography. This contradiction is one of the main lines of investigation in this study. How could subordinate employees, as Eichmann and men such as Theodor Danneker, Alois Brunner, the brothers Hans and Rolf Günther, Franz Novak, Anton Burger, and Siegfried Seidl were at the beginning of their SS "careers," get to be decision makers whose orders decided the life or death of hundreds of thousands of people?

∞

The contradictory scholarly interpretations and presentations of the development of National Socialist genocide policies led to a further expansion of the original research inception.

One of the main historiographical efforts of interpretation originates in the thesis of linear "execution of a world view" – as states the subtitle of the book *Hitlers Herrschaft: Vollzug einer Weltanschauung* (Hitler's Reign) by Eberhard Jäckel. The British historian Gerald Fleming in *Hitler and the Final Solution* advances this argument most distinctly:

> The line that leads from ... Hitler's remark to his childhood friend August Kubizek, ... "that does not belong here in Linz" ... as the two passed the small synagogue in the Bethlehemstraße in Linz, ... [to] the first mass shooting of German Jews in Fort IX in Kovno on 25 November 1941 and in the Rumbuli Forest outside Riga on 30 November 1941 at 8:15 AM ... [is a direct one. A straight path leads from that day] in April 1908 when Hitler joined the Viennese *Antisemitenbund* (Antisemite Association) ... to Report 51 "addressed to the *Führer*" [to announce under the heading] "campaign against gangs" the execution of 362,221 Jews during the period of 1 September to 1 December 1942.[9]

Jäckel and Fleming are representatives of the so-called Intentionalist School of interpretation, which stresses the direct, immediate connection between Hitler's antisemitic ideology, plans, directives, and the realization of mass murder.

A second interpretive approach proposes the "twisted road to Auschwitz," as it is so characterized in the title of Karl A. Schleunes's study in which he presents his conclusion that the "Final Solution," as it developed in 1941–1942, was not the product of a grand design of a large-scale planning operation. The representatives of this "Structuralist," sometimes also referred to as "Functionalist" School of interpretation, among them historians Martin Broszat and Hans Mommsen, point to a "cumulative radicalization" of National Socialist racism and, by doing so, modify the importance of Hitler's unequivocal directives for the execution of genocides. Origin and translation into action of National Socialist genocide policies, according to this approach, can therefore not be deduced to have developed in a straight line from one specific point, such as antisemitic ideology. Instead, they can only be approximated from the step-by-step radicalization of individual motives and the concentration and interplay of a variety of different elements.

A third interpretive direction espoused by, among others, Herbert A. Strauss points to the absolute incomprehensibility of the Holocaust. Dan Diner, for example, suggests considering Auschwitz as a "black box." "Auschwitz is a no-man's-land of comprehension, a black box of explaining, a vacuum of extra-historical significance sucking up any and all historiographic efforts of interpretation."[10]

The reinterpretation of the central strands of development of National Socialist policies and the formation of the apparatus of genocide necessary for this examination of the "careers" of Eichmann's men is based on the fact that the genocides of Jews and Roma took place in an industrialized society using methodologies involving division of labor. This premise rests mainly on the findings of the research by Raul Hilberg, the author of the seminal work on the destruction of European Jewry. He refers to the apparatus that conducted these genocides as the "machinery of destruction" to which four hierarchical groups of the German power bloc under Hitler provided specific support.

> The civil service infused the other hierarchies with its sure-footed planning and bureaucratic thoroughness. From the army the machinery of destruction acquired its military precision, discipline, and callousness. Industry's influence made itself felt in the emphasis on accounting, penny-pinching, and salvage, as well as the factory-like efficiency of the killing centers. Finally, the party contributed to the entire apparatus an "idealism," a sense of "mission" and a notion of "history-making."[11]

What remains unanswered in Hilberg's work, however, is who actually put this machinery of destruction into motion and what specific interests of National Socialist rulers or specific segments of society informed its decisions. Hilberg is convinced that more than five million Jews were murdered because "it had meaning to its perpetrators. It was not the arrogant strategy for the attainment of some goal but an undertaking for its own sake, an event experienced as Erlebnis, an adventure lived and lived through by its participants."[12] Even though Hilberg does not explain just what that "meaning" was, he is nevertheless convinced that this self-sufficient process could have been initiated only by Hitler himself. During a panel discussion Hilberg, in response to Structuralist interpretations of the genesis of National Socialist genocide policies, pointed to the premise upon which all his research is based: "I was always convinced that there must have been a Führerbefehl, Hitler's express order of genocide; that such a bureaucracy could not have functioned from

Norway to Greece, from France to Russia without central guidance or at least a green light."[13]

With subliminal horror he suggested to his audience and perhaps to himself just what the lack of a central Führerbefehl would mean for evaluating the perpetrators of this extermination machinery:

> But when I hear from Professor Broszat or Professor Mommsen that a Führerbefehl was essentially superfluous, just what exactly does that mean? Was everyone within this National Socialist world philosophy already prepared to do his part to murder these millions of Jews? Was this willingness so advanced already that even without official announcement or order to the Reichsbahn, the armed forces, the party offices, on the part of the *Kreisleiter* (District Party Leaders) so advanced everywhere that nobody needed an order at all?[14]

This statement addresses one of the issues central to the contradictory confrontations with National Socialist genocide. The mere thought of thousands of people having reached a degree of inhumanity such that without specific orders they had done their part in executing mass murder is so intolerable that even a historian who for decades has examined and delineated the process of destruction in minute detail recoils from it. Precisely for this reason one needs to consider whether ultimately the reality of the development of the decision-making process was not far more horrific than those involved and accused after 1945 claimed for obvious reasons and, for the most part, accepted and spread by historiography: Hitler ordered it; the order was carried out – after all, they all had learned to do their duty.

At that same historical conference on the murder of the Jews, Israeli historian Saul Friedländer advanced a basic thesis. According to him "there was no mass movement directed against the Jews, not even a crusade by a fanatical sect," but bureaucracy was to have played the main part, "a bureaucracy indifferent to this destruction but led by a *Führer* who for his part was driven by the most powerful conviction."[15] This assessment is questionable for a number of reasons.

The ghastly efficiency of the bureaucracy was certainly necessary but not sufficient for the successful process of excluding and murdering millions of people. Without support from other segments within the German ruling apparatus and local racists in the various states and areas of Europe occupied or dominated by the National Socialists, the seizure, deportation, and murder of the persecuted would more than likely never have reached these dimensions, and far more people would have escaped their persecutors. The list of individuals and groups who more or less can be considered accomplices of the

SS in advancing racist policies and/or carrying out the policies of expulsion and genocide is long. Not all groups of accomplices, assistants, or beneficiaries will be dealt with in the confines of this study, the main purpose of which is to discuss those who were of importance in connection to the activities of Eichmann and his men: the Wehrmacht and collaborators of all kinds.

Friedländer's thesis that there had been no mass movement against the Jews must be countered. The question of if and how the "little" National Socialists (the "simple" Volksgenossen, the ordinary citizens of the Third Reich) participated in the racist and expansionist policies of National Socialism has been largely excluded from German and Austrian historiography. Accordingly, Konrad Kwiet in a historiographical overview summarizes the state of research, suggesting "the attitudes and modes of behavior of the German population with respect to the persecution of Jews are essentially still shrouded in darkness."[16] Gerhard Botz, an Austrian specialist of contemporary history, takes both the Intentionalist and the Structuralist interpretations to task for underestimating the importance of an "anti-Semitic mobilization of large parts of the population for National Socialist measures of persecution" and for undervaluing the degree to which "the persecution and annihilation of Jews quite concretely satisfied immediate economic and social interests of large strata and classes."[17]

If one consults available sources, the picture of a "Final Solution Machine" being powered, as it were, by one single motor and sustaining its momentum through several transmission belts clearly points in the wrong direction. Without doubt, many perpetrators functioned as mechanical parts, providing service according to regulations, never pausing to consider the consequences. Many not only knew what they were doing but also tried to exploit the misery of the victims for their own benefit; a good number of the often-mentioned little "cogwheels" in the machinery demonstrated a dynamic of their own. There were individuals who, within the framework of their more or less vaguely defined competences, made decisions and scheduled activities for which no direct orders existed of yet and so started and advanced the entire process.

What Günter Anders in *Besuch im Hades* (Visit in Hades) wrote about the "chance of unpunished inhumanity" in respect to the National Socialist murderers applies not only to the Eichmann men but to their accomplices as well.

> For those who were responsible for the production of corpses were not "desk murderers" without exception. After all, those determined to keep their hands clean did need actual, hands-on perpetrators. And there were thousands of those to whom National Socialism offered the opportunity to commit inhumanity without threat of punishment, an opportunity never before offered in

such dimensions. . . . As wrong as it is to see the victims exclusively as a mass of people as incorrect it is to consider the murderers exclusively as cogs in the colossal machinery of murder. The murderers, too, were individuals who seized the opportunity within the machinery to satisfy their personal sadistic urges. They, too, must not be depersonalized, for they, too, though not in the Kantian sense "ethical persons," were individuals who in Hegel's terms have the right to be held personally responsible.[18]

1 Eichmann and the Development of the "Vienna Model"

Shortly after the National Socialists' pogrom on the night of November 9–10, 1938, the Sicherheitsdienst (SD)-Hauptamt (Schutzstaffel [SS]-Security Service Main Office) sent a top-priority telegram to Vienna, addressed to Dr. Walter Stahlecker, the Chief of the SD of the SS-Oberabschnitt Donau (SS Region Danube). The recipient was informed by SS-Sturmbannführer (Major) Erich Ehrlinger that on the following day an important discussion was to take place in Berlin on issues concerning operations against the Jews and a coordinated plan of action to be followed in the future.[1] "Because the plan was to establish a center within the Reich modeled on the one that coordinated such activities in the Ostmark, SS-Gruppenführer (Lieutenant General) Heydrich considers it appropriate for SS-Obersturmführer (First Lieutenant) Eichmann to be in attendance to relate his experiences in preparation for such a plan's implementation."[2] Ehrlinger asked that Eichmann be dispatched to Berlin immediately. He was to present himself to Ehrlinger at the SD-Hauptamt the next morning.

The meeting announced in the telegram took place on November 12, 1938, in the Reich Air Ministry, where the highest dignitaries of the Third Reich – Hermann Göring, Joseph Goebbels, Reinhard Heydrich, ministers, and state secretaries – were discussing pogroms and their consequences and determining the next steps to be taken in the process of discrimination, pillage, and expulsion of German and Austrian Jews.[3] Compared with Heydrich and his rank in the SS, Eichmann was a low-level member of the SD. What experiences of consequence could someone such as Eichmann present to this senior gathering that made Heydrich think it advisable to telegram an order for him to rush from Vienna to Berlin?

On the one hand, the answer to this question lies in the history of Heydrich's SS Secret Service and of a particular SD office. During the first five years of National Socialist rule in Germany, that office had played a rather inconspicuous part in the network of the various state and party authorities involved in the formulation and execution of antisemitic policies. It was Referat (Section) II-112 of the SD-Hauptamt, where Adolf Eichmann had been employed as a specialist from 1934 until the beginning of 1938. On the other hand, Eichmann's summons can be explained through the development of his office in Vienna in 1938. It was originally a branch of the Berlin office, but it soon took on a rapidly growing life of its own in the current of the antisemitic mass movement in Austria. The evolution of Referat II-112 of the SS-Oberabschnitt Donau into the Zentralstelle für jüdische Auswanderung in Vienna and the "success" of this institution that was to serve as a model for the Altreich was also the result of specific sociopolitical processes in the Ostmark. After the Anschluß the new rulers attempted to channel and use outbreaks and consequences of indigenous race-hatred, greed for self-enrichment, and the vicious Herrenmenschentum (Master Race ideology) of Austrian National Socialists and their followers to further their own designs.[4]

The origin, structure, and "success" of the Zentralstelle can neither be oversimplified by crediting Eichmann's organizational talents[5] nor explained through the historic growth of bureaucracies and thus exclusively the work of technocrats of repression or planning.[6] They can be understood only by including considerations of sociohistorical aspects. The example of the Ostmark in 1938 reveals to what extent a number of factors influenced each other. Specifically, there were the participation of many thousands of "Aryan" citizens, non-Jews of presumably "pure" Germanic ancestry, in racist policies, and, conversely, the aggressive activities of institutions in the formulation of such policies and their conversion into political measures.[7] In addition to ideological factors, another reason for the step-by-step radicalization of antisemitic policies is to be sought in "concrete material interests."[8]

Eichmann in Referat II-112 of the Sicherheitsdienst-Hauptamt

Anti-Jewish policies of the Third Reich escalated step by step after 1933 and developed as parallel or successive Bewegung (National Socialist "movement"), party, and government initiatives.[9] Individual acts of violence directed toward Jews and political opponents on the part of groups of Sturmabteilung (SA) thugs, party-organized measures such as the boycott in April 1933, and the burning of books, as well as pseudo-legal steps such as elimination from certain professions, defined the situation beginning in the spring of 1933.[10]

Several ministries were involved in compelling Jewish men and women to emigrate, for emigration, in addition to "lawful" discrimination, was another means of government-regulated exclusion of Jews from German society. The Reichsstelle für das Auswanderungswesen, the "Reich Center for Emigration," was set up in the Ministry of the Interior, and sections of the Ministry of Finance and Economics were in charge of handling the financial settlements attending emigrations.[11] At that time Jews fleeing abroad still could conduct limited transfers of money, mainly because of the Ha'avara Agreement of August 1933, through the Palästina-Treuhandstelle (Paltreu), and similar trusteeship organizations. Between 1933 and 1939 more than 50,000 German Jews emigrated to Palestine. They were able to transfer a total of about 140 million Reichsmarks (RM), a portion of their frozen assets.[12] Altogether, according to a statement presented at a meeting at the Reich Ministry of Economics in November 1938, approximately 170,000 Jews were thought to have emigrated from Germany, a process involving the transfer of roughly 340 million RM, an average of RM 2,000 per person, in the form of foreign currency, release of frozen holdings abroad, portable goods, or Palestine transfers.[13]

Already in August 1931 during the so-called Kampfzeit (the Nationalsozialistische Deutsche Arbeiterpartei's [NSDAP] struggle for power), the SD of the SS had been established as Section I-c at the SS Oberstab (Superior Staff) in Munich. It was organized on a military model and led by then-SS-Sturmführer Reinhard Heydrich, who shortly before had been dishonorably discharged as an Oberleutnant (lieutenant) from the German navy.[14] Initially, the main task of the I-c service of the SS, in competition with other National Socialist intelligence services such as that of the SA, was to ferret out "traitors" and informers within its own ranks. Soon, however, ever more ample files on so-called "opponents" were set up. In the late summer of 1932 the I-c service of the SS was transformed into the SD. Eventually it was to serve as the sole Nazi Party intelligence service, which on a large scale and in a comprehensive manner

> following the model of the British Intelligence Service and the *Deuxième Bureau* was to gather and evaluate factual, precise material about goals, methods, and plans of political opponents throughout Germany; to report defects in National Socialism's own ranks, if necessary; and to provide superiors and the party leadership and later still the National Socialist government with all worthwhile information.[15]

With Himmler's rise to the position of Commander of the Bavarian Political Police in the wake of the so-called Nationale Erhebung (National Uprising) in January 1933, followed by his promotion to Inspector General of the Prussian Secret State Police in 1934[16] and after the elimination of the leadership of the SA in June 1934 during which Heydrich had distinguished himself by personally commissioning murders,[17] the SD continuously was built up to gain a monopoly of intelligence services within all National Socialist organizations. In January 1935 the SD-Hauptamt was established in Berlin at Wilhelmstraße 102. It was organized into three offices: Office I – SD Administration and Organization, led by the jurist Dr. Werner Best; Office II – SD German Internal Affairs; and Office III – SD Foreign Affairs.[18]

A more detailed intelligence investigation of Jewish organizations by the SD began in June 1935. It was, as Eichmann's short-term superior, SS-Untersturmführer (Second Lieutenant) Dieter Wisliceny, phrased it, a "systematic work-up of the adversary Jew." Until that time the surveillance of Jewish organizations had been assigned to the SD Referat II-111 responsible for Freimaurerei (Freemasonry).[19] Before joining Referat II-112 of the SD-Hauptamt, Adolf Eichmann, born in 1906 in Solingen but having grown up in the Upper Austrian city of Linz, had worked as a sales representative in Upper Austria and Salzburg for the Vacuum Oil Co., Inc., of Vienna. In 1933, however, the company had dismissed him, allegedly on account of his membership in the NSDAP.[20] Shortly thereafter he had contacted the Österreichische Legion, the Austrian Legion, in Bavaria and had participated in a two-month military training course at Camp Lechfeld. In October 1934 he was transferred to the SD-Hauptamt, where he started out sorting files in the Section "Freimaurer."

The task of Referat II-112, which in 1935/36 was headed by SS-Untersturmführer Leopold Itz Edler von Mildenstein and, until the beginning of 1937 by SS-Oberscharführer (Sergeant First Class) Kuno Schröder, consisted of investigating Jewish organizations through "constant perusal of the Jewish press" and "surveillance of Jewish assemblies," which members of the SD carried out in cooperation with the Geheime Staatspolizei (Gestapo), the secret state police.[21] Section II-112 was organized into three subsections, one each for "Assimilated," "Orthodox," and "Zionist" Jews, and produced subject indexes and organizational charts. It also created manuals for personnel training. By 1936, reports on the international Jewish vocation training organization World ORT and the Agudas Jisroel-Weltorganisation (Agudas Yisroel World Organization) had been completed; reports on the Zionist movement and the Reichsbund jüdischer Frontsoldaten (Reich Association of Jewish War Veterans) were in progress. In 1937 a network of agents was to be set up. Together with the Staatspolizeistelle, the State Police Headquarters in Berlin, this network conducted "interrogations of prominent Jews," among them Georg Kareski,[22] the leader of the Staatszionistische Organisation in Deutschland, the "State Zionist Organization in Germany."[23]

As a member of Referat II-112, Eichmann was the official in charge of Zionist organizations. What precisely he did in that capacity is made clear in a situation report of March 1937 in which, under the heading "Organizational

Alterations," he listed that the Agudas Yisroel association had moved its office from Frankfurt to Fürth.[24] In addition to such trivialities he pointed out that assemblies of Zionist organizations "had, even lately, not abated at all," that at these meetings the political and economic conditions in Palestine had been the topics of lectures and reports.[25] He studied press releases on the preparations for the International Zionist Congress and kept abreast of the financial situation of Keren Hayesod and its transfers of money and goods to Palestine.

When the recent university graduate Dr. Franz Six[26] took over Department II-1, the Referat II-112 activities, which consisted mainly of observation and registration, were to be changed. Closer cooperation with the Gestapo and increased influence on National Socialist policies concerning the Jews were to be pursued. In the spring of 1937 SS-Untersturmführer Dieter Wisliceny was in charge of Referat II-112. Born in 1911, this son of an estate owner had abandoned his study of theology in the early 1930s, had been unemployed, had joined the NSDAP in 1931, and had become a full-time employee of the SD in 1934. At the same time another member of the SD, SS-Oberscharführer Theodor Dannecker, who had been employed as an expert at Referat II-112 of the SD-Oberabschnitt Südwest (Region Southwest), was transferred to take charge of the subsection dealing with Assimilanten, "Assimilated Jews."[27]

In a note, Wisliceny described the basic aims of his section's tasks. He postulated that "the Jewish Question in Germany" could be solved only through centralized approach and legislation. Although the "elimination of the Jews from the cultural and *völkisch* (national) life of Germany" through legislation by the Nazi government already had been largely accomplished, this was not the case in German economic life.[28] He was convinced that the only possible *Lösung der Judenfrage*, the "solution to the Jewish Question," lay in promoting a "Zionist Exodus of Jews from Germany by any means possible." Accordingly, Referat II-112 was to launch a "systematic survey of Jewish participation in the German economy"[29] and work out issues specifically related to emigration and transfer. Wisliceny proposed the "destruction of all assimilationist associations" and, simultaneously, the skillful promotion of Zionism to "split the Jewish community internally by playing off one Jewish-political philosophy against the other."[30] Under the direction of Herbert Hagen, who succeeded Wisliceny in the summer of 1937, an expansion of activities took place. This mainly involved setting up a file for every Jew abroad who was prominent in politics, economics, and the sciences. In June 1937 such Jews in Austria received special attention: "All important members of the various Austrian Jewish organizations" were to be identified and recorded on index cards.[31]

The recruitment of agents, however, made little progress. Discussions with Feivel Polkes, a member of Hagana who lived in Palestine but who also had contacts with British and French secret service organizations, took place in Berlin.[32] In September 1937 Hagen and Eichmann made a tour abroad; it was to take them to Palestine via Egypt. The plan was to establish contacts with agents and "Arab politicians such as Emir Abdulah and the Mufti of Jerusalem."[33] Eichmann's preparation for this journey consisted, among other things, of asking his superior, Dr. Six, for financial support to complete his wardrobe: "Since my journey includes negotiations with Arab nobility, I need one light-weight, light-colored suit and one dark suit, and a light coat."[34] The head of Office II-1 refused Eichmann's request outright. He did, however, once again consider it necessary to remind Eichmann and Hagen emphatically that they were to comport themselves carefully and discreetly. They were to refrain from committing anything to paper or engaging in any conversations in heavily frequented public areas or rooms. Moreover, "terms such as SS, SD, Gestapa (Geheimes Staatspolizeiamt, the central headquarters of the Gestapo in Berlin), were not to be used" during the entire trip. Equally important, as Dr. Six ordered his scouts, they were not to send postcards to acquaintances housed in the office or to any other acquaintances or members of the SS or the SD.[35] The trip was a failure. In Cairo, Hagen and Eichmann were unable to obtain visas for their visit to Palestine. They could neither negotiate with Arab aristocrats nor conduct conversations with new agents.[36]

Cooperation between SD and Gestapo was expanded. I-112 summoned officials of Jewish organizations to the Gestapa "to organize the entire Jewish Policy in such a way that emigration of destitute Jews would be promoted continuously."[37] Hagen envisioned "handling the Jewish Question in Germany" in a centralized fashion that would give the "SD and the Gestapo sole executive powers," including management of finance and transfer through Jewish trust organizations such as the Allgemeine Treuhandstelle (Altreu), Paltreu, and Ha'avara.[38] Hagen's proposed extension of Gestapo and SD control over the economic and financial sphere of National Socialist politics became reality, however, only through developments in Austria.

Bureaucratic Efforts of Containment and the Intensification of Antisemitic Policies in the Ostmark in 1938

The pogrom-like excesses that were to characterize Vienna's atmosphere through the following weeks and forever to alter the lives of those who were their targets already had begun during the night preceding the German army's entry into Austria, on March 12, 1938. Viennese citizens who considered themselves Arische Herrenmenschen (members of the Aryan Master Race) did not wait for the arrival of the German "liberators" to give free rein to their antisemitic attitudes.

In *Als wär's ein Stück von mir*, Carl Zuckmayer recalls the evening of March 11 in Vienna.

> That night all hell broke loose. The netherworld had opened its portals and spewed out its basest, most horrid, and filthiest spirits. The city changed into a nightmare painting reminiscent of Hieronymus Bosch: lemurs and half-demons seemed to have hatched from eggs of filth, and to have risen from boggy craters in the earth. The air was filled with endlessly piercing, chaotic, hysterical screeching issuing from the throats of men and women alike, shrilling day and night. All faces were distorted, some out of fear, others through lies, and still others in wild, hate-filled triumph. I had seen my share of human dissolution, horror, or panic. I had participated in a dozen battles during World War I, the heavy barrages, death by gas, assaults. I had lived through the unrest of the postwar era, the suppression of revolts, the street battles, the beer hall brawls. During Hitler's Munich Putsch of 1923 I was in the midst of the crowds in the street. I witnessed the initial phase of Nazi rule in Berlin. None of that was comparable to those days in Vienna. What was being unleashed here had nothing at all in common with the *Machtergreifung*, the Nazi seizure of power in Germany, which at least externally seemed to proceed legally and was witnessed by parts of the population with displeasure and skepticism or with simpleminded national idealism. What was being unleashed here was the revolt of envy; malevolence; bitterness; blind, vicious vengefulness – all other voices were condemned to silence.[39]

The excesses of native National Socialists and their nominal followers were directed mainly against persons thought to be Jews. The Viennese variation of *Enrichissez-vous* (get your hands on what you can) started with looting, gang raids, and blackmail. Jewish-owned stores were stripped clean of merchandise, cars were "confiscated," and money and valuables were seized for "safekeeping" during house searches. During these first weeks and months following the Anschluß, the envy and hatred of the Viennese antisemites, which up to that time had been articulated mostly verbally or in writing, exploded. The crop of indigenous, organically grown antisemitism so carefully nurtured by conservative and Pan-German Austrian political parties was bearing fruit. Now antisemitism was no longer just ideology but violence pure and simple, an instrument tens of thousands used to satisfy their own interests at the expense of the now excluded.

Now that the Jews were fair game, anyone who sported a swastika armband or passed himself off as a Gestapo officer could deal with them as he saw fit. The Anschluß immediately triggered a wave of arbitrary arrests. In most instances the victims were unable to determine whether they were confronted by a party or government official or a common thief and blackmailer: The dividing lines between officially and privately executed terror were fluid, the differences minute. Inquiries or complaints to government agencies were useless, even dangerous. One victim described the situation this way:

> At once after the so-called *Umbruch* (regime change) the arrests began. Anyone who had ever made an enemy had to reckon on the prospect of being incarcerated. It was totally sufficient for some Aryan, no matter how bad his reputation, to appear at an SA, SS, or other party establishment and accuse this man or that woman of having said or done this or that. No one ever bothered to check the truth of such allegations. The person so accused was arrested and jailed without further ado. I know of cases where people were released after weeks of incarceration without a single interrogation having taken place. Other people, after spending weeks or months in jail, were questioned why they had been jailed. The authorities simply did not know. Denunciations and blackmail flourished as never before. It became daily routine for a blackmailer to appear, demanding a given amount of money, and in the case of refusal, threatening to lodge a complaint with the NSDAP. Or the blackmailer appeared accompanied by a party official to lend persuasion to his demands. It goes without saying that in most instances such demands were entirely unjustified.[40]

On the street and in apartments and business establishments Jewish men and women were herded together, formed into Putzkolonnen (cleaning "columns" or detachments), and forced to scrub the sidewalks with soap and water, allegedly to remove the propaganda slogans for the Schuschnigg plebiscite. Even if individuals caught in such roundups resigned themselves to such spectacles with gallows humor, these publicly staged rituals of humiliation constituted a social and mass psychological rehearsal of dividing people into Herrenmenschen and subhumans. All participants were made to realize in no uncertain terms that those who only a few days earlier had the same rights and obligations as anyone else were now helpless, devoid of protection, while their tormentors could order them about and insult, deride, and mistreat them at will.

In a contemporary report Leo Lauterbach explained the consequences for the victims:

> Though obviously a minor issue compared to other deeds performed under the aegis of the new regime, the forced scrubbings of sidewalks, cleanup of army barracks, etc. had the most profound impact on the Jewish population. Not only paralyzing fear of being reduced to performing such slave labor but also

the spectacle of gloating, sneering, screaming non-Jewish mobs inspired by such humiliating performances produced a horrific shock in the entire Jewish community. It destroyed any sense of personal security and faith in their fellow citizens' humanity. It revealed to them that they did not merely inhabit a fool's paradise but hell itself. No one acquainted with the average Viennese of those times would have believed it possible that they could sink to such levels.[41]

Among other things, the extreme fear weighing down the victims and the hopelessness of their situation led to increases in suicides.[42] The majority sooner or later decided to escape this horror through flight abroad.

The pogrom-like outrages, and especially the wild lootings and gang robberies perpetrated by Viennese antisemites, were too extreme even for the new rulers. Immediately following the Anschluß, government agencies, however halfheartedly, attempted to curb the grossest excesses. Already on March 14, readers of the *Wiener Zeitung* learned that one of the Viennese National Socialists' main activities was actually against the law: "Confiscations, expropriations, or arrests by party comrades or SA men are strictly forbidden except when expressly permitted by the *Gauleiter* [Nazi Party provincial chief] or SA-Gruppenführer of Vienna."[43] This warning seemed to impress no one.

On March 17, Heydrich sent a memorandum to Josef Bürckel, the Sonderbeauftragte der Partei für Österreich, the special party commissioner for Austria, and later Reichskommissar für die Wiedervereinigung Österreichs mit dem Deutschen Reich (Reich Commissar for the Reunification of Austria with the German Reich), threatening deployment of the Gestapo against party comrades "who in the past several days had engaged in large-scale trespasses in totally undisciplined ways."[44] Heydrich also informed Bürckel about his newspaper publications alerting readers "that Communist party members through misappropriation of official party uniforms are trying to endanger public order and safety by conducting illegal confiscations, residence searches, and arrests."[45]

Internally, it was known and to a degree even acceptable that lootings and arrests were the handiwork of party and SA members; publicly, the responsibility was shifted to imaginary Communists who supposedly were even in possession of the appropriate uniforms.[46] In the March 17 issue of the *Neues Wiener Tagblatt*, the chief of the Sicherheitspolizei, the security police, announced "the state police will counter such criminal behavior in the most strident manner and will proceed with unsparing severity. Mobile squads to be deployed immediately will make sure that these gangs will be taken out of commission."[47] In his letter to Bürckel, however, he made it clear that these publications were not directed toward Communists but rather their own party members and urged him "to instruct all party offices accordingly."[48] Bürckel, too, had to acknowledge that the zeal of National Socialist looters could not be significantly reduced by these threats.[49]

News about lootings in Vienna reached the ministries in Berlin, where it was feared that this kind of Arisierung, the Aryanization of property of Jews, proceeding without any basis whatsoever in existing German law could produce irreversible consequences. So, on March 21, 1938, the Ministry of the Interior issued a call for order. State Secretary Wilhelm Stuckart had learned from the Minister of Economics that in Vienna "Jewish businesses had been shut down by out-of-control mobs while others were reported to be now under the management of NS-HAGO (National Socialist Business and Trade Organizations) and similar organizations." Other types of "wild Aryanizations" were rumored to have taken place as well. At the request of the Minister of Economics, State Secretary Stuckart instructed the Special Party Commissioner for Austria to "take steps against such unauthorized activities and to see to it that Aryanization efforts of this type come to a stop. After the plebiscite the measures necessary for containing foreign domination of the economy will be determined by the Reich Minister of Economics in accordance with the law."[50]

In March and April public humiliations, physical attacks, blackmail, and robberies were daily occurrences. A reduction, although by no means a total cessation of such "operations," did not come about until Bürckel threatened those responsible with expulsion from the party:

> By instruction from Reichskommissar . . . Bürckel, the decree of April 19, 1938, has been extended so that even in case of the least offenses – disturbance of the peace, vilification of *Volksgenossen* (the ordinary citizens), or non-Aryans – not only the SA men involved in such activities but, first of all, the leaders in charge can expect immediate dismissal from their duties and expulsion from the SA and the party.[51]

Moreover, the Nazi leadership of the Ostmark found it necessary to separate its own concept of bureaucratic, pseudo-legal antisemitism from the Viennese robbery-and-pogrom antisemitism, and to do so in the *Völkische Beobachter,* the official party newspaper:

> Whereas National Socialism frequently had to direct the attention of the people of northern Germany to the private, in a sense apolitical dangers of the Jews, the task in Vienna is the opposite. Concerned to preserve the irreproachability and purity of the movement, it is the duty of responsible public education to contain the seething radicalism and to guide the understandable reaction to Jewish excesses throughout an entire century into orderly channels. For, as everyone needs to remember, Germany is a constitutionally governed state. That means

that in our Reich nothing happens without foundation in law. . . . No one here conducts pogroms, not even Mrs. Hinterhuber against Sara Kohn in the third courtyard on the mezzanine by the water tap.[52]

Beginning in late April the SS occasionally quelled "wild operations." Eventually even a "security patrol service for the prevention of individual operations" was established, although that by no means meant that "private" outrages not organized by the party really ceased. They continued on a reduced scale and especially in October were on the rise once again. Furthermore, the "energy" of the Viennese antisemites branched out into new areas of activity such as housing, where, either through brute force or threat of deportation to a concentration camp, Jewish tenants or owners were forced to leave their apartments. In the realm of economics, takeovers of Jewish business establishments led to bitter quarrels among party comrades.

The penchant for pogroms among Austrian antisemites did not entirely fit the technocratic antisemitism the Nazi leadership and its representatives wished to pursue in the Ostmark through pseudo-legal and political means. Accordingly, in the spring of 1938, the leading officials tried to curb and channel outbreaks of race hatred and greed for loot, or rather use them in an organized fashion in service of their own objectives. To accomplish this, they developed administrative and pseudo-legal directives and installed new government bodies and administrative machineries. As a result, in addition to the pogrom-like excesses of the Viennese Nazis during the initial stage, the gradual, step-by-step government-organized pillage and terror of the new rulers eventually took their place. Now police, SD, and Gestapo officers also conducted searches of residences, confiscations, and arrests. Almost half of the first 270 or so Austrians deported to Dachau were Jews.

An efficient, orderly Entjudung, or "de-Judaization," of the Austrian economy was to be guaranteed by the Vermögensverkehrsstelle, the Bureau of Property Administration, in charge of hiring, confirming, replacing, and supervising temporary trustees of Jewish-owned businesses and by reviewing already completed Aryanizations and overseeing new ones.[53] There was a real effort to accommodate the requests of old party comrades in the redistribution of such properties; however, there were many more Austrian National Socialists greedy for booty than there were spoils available to apportion, so even the pseudo-legal Aryanization constantly gave rise to conflicts among party comrades and quickly degenerated into cronyism. The Völkische Beobachter deftly summarized the one issue on which the Austrian pogrom-and-booty antisemites and the party technocrats saw eye to eye: "The Jew has to go; his dough stays."[54]

Confronted with the pressures of daily private and pseudo-legal government terror, the victims saw no remedy other than "emigration," the fastest
possible escape abroad, although to speak of emigration in its customary sense
would be misleading if for no other reason than that Jews fleeing Austria had
no legal recourse to take even part of their property with them.

> In that respect the situation in Austria differed fundamentally from that in the
> Altreich. There, until about mid-1938, the constant threat to life and freedom
> did not exist. Furthermore, there were official routes for transferring property,
> especially to Palestine through Ha'avara. Furniture, household equipment,
> valuable paintings, and *objets d'art* could be removed from Germany without
> undue difficulty. In Austria the conditions of emigration from [the rest of]
> Germany were considered amazingly favorable.[55]

In the Ostmark efforts to leave the country legally were hampered by a rapidly
growing number of bureaucratic hurdles. To assemble all necessary documents,
applicants had to run the gauntlet. Dozens of formalities at various government
agencies had to be taken care of and nonsensical regulations had to be observed.
Just to receive a single document, the Steuerunbedenklichkeitsbescheinigung,
the certification that the applicants had paid all taxes in full, required still
other certificates from the government office of the applicant's district of
residence, from the appropriate office in the municipal government at the court
house, from the central tax office, and from the district tax office. Everywhere
applicants had to stand in line for hours and days; they were subject to the
whims of generally ill-tempered civil servants and were made to understand
that they were second-class people. Another impediment through which one
had to make his way was the passport office on Wehrgasse, in Vienna's fifth
municipal district. Recollections of its victims can convey only limited insights
into the consequences of official caprice, venality, and cruelty toward Austrian
Jews.

> How horrible was the Wehrgasse! A far too small office in an old Viennese
> house in a narrow suburban street where thousands crowded together, shoved,
> sweated, and cursed. The average petitioner observing the regulations made
> no progress whatsoever. Submitting an application meant standing in line a
> whole night and half a day. But who would actually get his turn? Time and
> again groups jumped the queue, led by bloodsucking Aryan *Intervenienten*
> ("interveners") from the neighborhood coffee houses, these "protégées" went
> directly to apply or sign documents. To hire interveners required an outra-
> geous fee but eliminated the need to stand in line. Persons with that sort of
> "protection" did not have to show up with a stool and provisions at eleven

o'clock the previous night to spend the next seven hours roaming the neigh-borhood. After pre-queuing in some side street, they did not have to run breathlessly just a few minutes before six for the best place in the Wehrgasse. They did not have to traverse the Wehrgasse for the nth time while being mis-treated by malicious guards. After hours of waiting they did not risk having to obey the sadistic order "whole row, turn around" to replace those in the front who had waited the longest with the most recent arrivals.[56]

The civil servants, whose job it was to check all documents and finally stamp the passport, shamelessly exploited the new regulations and the predicaments of the petitioners. "Everybody knew that at Wehrgasse everything was for sale." A certain police officer who was authorized to sign the passports was infamous for his rapacity. "That man all but drowned in bribes. Within a few months he must have acquired a huge fortune, as did the Aryan interveners."

A large number of clever Aryans specialized in turning the misfortunes of the persecuted into a profitable business for themselves. In these schemes the Gallop law office occupied a position all its own. For extremely wealthy Jewish families the lawyer Dr. Heinrich Gallop and his partner Dr. Erich Rajakowitsch routinely handled all formalities attending emigration. As Charles J. Kapralik reports, Rajakowitsch had excellent connections to the Gestapo.[57] Their routine was to force clients to transfer

> their entire Austrian assets to their office. In return, Messrs. Gallop and Rajakowitsch promised them . . . new passports and safe departure. Needless to say, their fees, which were paid from these transfers were more than ample. . . . Clients who were not all that wealthy the Gallop law office did not bother to accept. They left the merely well-to-do to the many lesser Nazi lawyers.

Dr. Rajakowitsch was also involved in the Aktion Gildemeester, an emigration aid organization that allegedly also assisted impecunious Jews in their efforts to emigrate.[58]

The consequence of the (a)social logic that grew out of these "shady oper-ations," local antisemites' desire for self-enrichment, and the governmental channeling and "legislation" to legitimize expropriation was the "abolition" of the people robbed of their means to sustain life – in short, the "total solu-tion to the Jewish Question," as Reichskommissar Bürckel already had stated unmisunderstandably in an internal detailed report on "The Jewish Question in Austria" in the autumn of 1938: "The thing to remember at all times is that if Aryanization is the goal and the Jew is to be deprived of his livelihood, the Jewish Question has to be solved in its entirety, for to accept him as a permanent ward of the state will not do. Therefore, conditions have to be created for his leaving the country."[59] Consequently, Bürckel at that time still proposed building retraining camps, or rather work camps, for 30,000 Jews.

The Establishment of the Zentralstelle für jüdische Auswanderung in Vienna

In this tense atmosphere of anti-Jewish outrages and bureaucratic efforts to keep them within bounds, in a situation that had reduced Austrian Jews to fair game, the Sonderkommando of Referat II-112 took up its work in Vienna. In the days immediately following the Anschluß, in March and April of 1938, it consisted of only Hagen and Eichmann; moreover, Hagen remained active in Vienna only from March 12 to April 11. The oversight of Referat II-112 in the SS-Oberabschnitt Österreich, later Oberabschnitt Donau – Region Danube, was entrusted to Eichmann who arrived in Vienna on March 16.[60]

Contrary to Hannah Arendt's claim that, upon his arrival in Vienna, Eichmann first had to organize the release of Jewish community representatives "from jails and concentration camps"[61] to be able to negotiate with them, the Hagen–Eichmann Sonderkommando, with the help of lists prepared in Berlin, had persons arrested, most of them members or officials of Jewish organizations such as B'nai B'rith. One of the SD-Sonderkommando's tasks was to seize documents belonging to Jewish organizations and important private citizens.[62] In the subsequent months crates of confiscated materials were shipped to Berlin until in the summer of 1938 an Österreich Auswertungskommando, an Austria Evaluation Task Force, had to be formed in Referat II-112 to keep up with the information.[63]

Eichmann personally took part in the raid on the building of the Israelitische Kultusgemeinde, Vienna's Jewish Community Center at Seitenstettengasse on March 18, in the course of which documents such as a receipt for a contribution to Schuschnigg's plebiscite campaign were confiscated. At the end of the raid, the leaders of the Jewish Community, such as its director, Dr. Desider Friedmann, and its general manager, Dr. Josef Löwenherz, were arrested. The propagandistic exploitation of the receipt resulted in the Austrian Jewish community having to pay a "contribution" of 500,000 RM, supposedly an "equivalent" to the money Schuschnigg's campaign had received.

In March and April, chaos erupted in the governmental agencies charged with issuing regulations and directives for Austrian Jews; clear delineations of authority were not available in Berlin or in Vienna. Leo Lauterbach, then attached to Sir Wyndham Deedes' mission to conduct talks with leading authorities concerning the plight of Austrian Jews and possibilities of remediation, described the impossibility of pinpointing jurisdictions. In Vienna the commission learned that all decisions would be made in Berlin; the outcome of a meeting with legal assistant Kurt Lischka and Dr. Rudolf Lange in the Gestapa, Berlin, on the other hand, was that

> the problem of the Austrian Jews would not be handled in Berlin but solely in Vienna.... The agency in charge of these matters, as we were told emphatically, was the Gestapo in Vienna staffed by Dr. [Friedrich] Hasselbacher, [Otto] Kuchmann, and Eichmann, civil servants from Berlin, whom Dr. Lange would join shortly. Our question as to who was in charge of financial issues like emigrant money transfers, remained unanswered in spite of numerous telephone follow-up calls and the efforts of the Berlin Gestapo to pry clarifications from its Vienna branch office.[64]

To Lauterbach the situation seemed marked by confusion, uncertainty, and flux. Nevertheless, by April he had arrived at a remarkably penetrating analysis of emerging tendencies:

> A clear policy for dealing with "the Jewish problem in Austria" has neither been announced publicly, nor were we informed of it in the course of the few interviews we were able to obtain. But it is impossible to dismiss the impression that this policy will depart significantly from that followed in Germany and that its goal may very well be the total destruction of Austrian Jewry. To all appearances the plan is the elimination of Jews from economic activity and their deprivation of all financial resources to force them to starve to death or leave the country destitute at the expense of powerful Jewish organizations abroad and with assistance from those nations willing to grant them refuge.[65]

That more or less describes the strategy that was to emerge from the circle of National Socialist rulers in the Ostmark and the still rather inconspicuous Eichmann. During the initial confusion as to who was responsible for what, Eichmann had single-mindedly taken dictatorial control of reestablished Jewish organizations. For these forcibly reorganized bodies his orders were law. By mid-April, after conferring with Dr. Six, Eichmann had devised a plan concerning which Jewish organizations were to be reinstated in Austria – the Kultusgemeinde (the Jewish Community), the Zionistische Landesverband für Österreich (Zionist Association for Austria), and the Agudas Yisroel to represent Orthodox Jews.[66] For Jews who were neither Zionist nor Orthodox, an organization modeled on the Hilfsverein der Juden in Deutschland (Jewish Aid Society of Germany) was to be founded. The only Jews permitted to serve as officers were to be Zionists or those classified as "Jewish-neutral." Additionally, for the Zionistische Landesverband für Österreich, Eichmann planned to establish a newspaper entitled *Die Zionistische Rundschau*. He alone would determine its content.

By correspondence, Eichmann kept Herbert Hagen – his former superior had returned to his previous position at SD Referat II-112 – apprised of how the plans he had discussed with Dr. Six were progressing. At the end of April he already could tell "Dear Herbert" that the reorganization of a representative body of Austrian Jews under his control had been initiated. Within a week Dr. Löwenherz, just released from detainment, was to design "a detailed program of action concerning the Kultusgemeinde and the Zionistische Landesverband für Österreich, complete with a detailed roster of positions and a list of persons to fill them."[67] As to the collection of the extorted levy, Eichmann commented tersely, "they already have paid RM 200,000." Describing his activities in general terms, he remarked that "the preparations for starting Jewish political activity with emphasis on Jewish emigration" were complete; the Kultusgemeinde and "the whole Zionist outfit" would be in business soon. Given these accomplishments Eichmann apparently considered his task in Vienna finished: "More than likely I will not remain here as a specialist [the term is underlined], though the next man has to get here first to be trained on the job. I have heard that after that I'll be off to the UA [SS-Unterabschnitt] – Subregion]. I can live with that. Two or three years from now I'll probably be knocking on your door in Berlin."[68] But that was not to be.

Since May, Eichmann's job in Vienna consisted mainly of his dictatorial supervision of the Kultusgemeinde and the other Jewish organizations he had re-created. These, as he told Hagen, had to report to him weekly: "Tomorrow I will inspect the Kultusgemeinde and the Zionists again. I do that at least once a week. I'm in total control here. They don't dare take a step without checking with me first. That's how it should be since it guarantees better ways of keeping them on their toes."[69] Eichmann also censored the manuscripts of the *Zionistische Rundschau*[70] and made his first attempts at involving himself in accelerating the expulsion of Austrian Jews. "At least I lit a fire under those gentlemen, believe you me!.... I set an emigration quota of 20,000 destitute Jews for the period of May 1, 1938 to May 1, 1939 [the number is underlined twice], which the Kultusgemeinde and the Zionistischer Landesverband have promised to meet."[71] Obviously, Eichmann considered the "emigration" of 20,000 Jews annually a desirable goal. In reality, though, many more were to be driven from the Ostmark in a far shorter period of time.

Another of Eichmann's tasks was to interrogate incarcerated leaders of Jewish organizations. A memorandum in a Referat II-112 file reveals that the former president of the Kultusgemeinde, Dr. Desider Friedmann, "has already been interrogated several times by SS-Untersturmführer Eichmann at the Rossauerlände police prison" and that an "additional interrogation is planned on the subject of Jewish contacts with British political groups, which will be conducted by E. as well."[72]

When the Kultusgemeinde reopened in early May under the direction
of Dr. Josef Löwenherz, its newly created department for emigration was
confronted by a flood of people seeking advice and help for leaving Austria.
Tens of thousands of emigration forms were distributed; approximately 45,000
completed forms supposedly were returned shortly thereafter.[73] Thousands of
people had been robbed of their jobs, incomes, savings, and property: They
needed assistance for their very survival. On account of the soaring expenses
for "emigration aid" and charitable measures coupled with a simultaneous
reduction of income, the Kultusgemeinde soon found itself in dire financial
straits. The needed funds could be raised only with the help of international
Jewish aid organizations. For this reason Dr. Löwenherz, with Eichmann's
permission, contacted representatives of the Joint Distribution Committee.[74]

Eichmann, meanwhile, enjoyed his work. Only a few months earlier he had
sorted index cards and written reports about the activities of Zionist organizations. All that was behind him now. Now, here in Vienna, he had executive
powers. People could be jailed or sent to a concentration camp at his command.
His work consisted mainly of putting pressure on the intimidated officials of
the Kultusgemeinde. Now he could make others work for him and supervise the
officials he had appointed to draw up and execute proposals and plans. All he
had to do was to choose, accept, or reject. The thirty-two-year-old Eichmann,
who had accomplished nothing in his earlier profession, now was empowered
to order about people who only recently had been esteemed, honored members
of Austrian society, far superior to him in training and professional experience. Now he could, as he phrased it with obvious pride, "light fires under
them."

Even though he was in line for a position as department chief with the SS-
Unterabschnitt, he voiced his regret to Hagen about having to leave his present
sphere of activity: "You know, I'm truly sorry [both words are underlined in
the original] that I probably will have to give up this work that I enjoy doing
and with which I have become so familiar after all this time."[75]

In Berlin, Eichmann's superiors Hagen and Six lobbied for his position in
Vienna to be upgraded to the level of a department under his directorship.[76]
Although that turned out to be impossible, it was decided "to put him on
a fast track for promotion by one or two ranks" and "to provide him with
two additional specialists."[77] All this was justified with reference to "the constantly growing amount of work in Referat II-112" and the alleged danger that
"encroachments of other party and government agencies on this competitive
territory could otherwise not be prevented."[78]

Such arguments struck home. Eichmann, whom one of his supervisors in
an evaluation in the summer of 1938 described as an "energetic and impulsive

person" possessed of "great abilities for independent administration of his area of expertise; capable especially of discharging organizational and negotiating tasks independently and extremely well; and recognized as a specialist in his area of expertise,"[79] in September 1938 was promoted to SS-Obersturmführer, the equivalent of a first lieutenant in the army. In January 1939 he was promoted to SS-Hauptsturmführer. Furthermore, two specialists with officer's rank joined him between September and October 1938. They were the brothers Rolf and Hans Günther (Germans from the Altreich) on the staff of the Zentralstelle.

In the summer of 1938 the officials of the Kultusgemeinde proposed a simplification of the bureaucratic procedures for emigration. Dr. Löwenherz or his coworkers designed a plan for a Zentralstelle für die Auswanderung der Juden Österreichs, the Central Bureau for the Emigration of the Jews of Austria, and its responsibilities.[80] Most likely through Eichmann, these proposals reached Reichskommissar Bürckel, who on August 20, 1938, after conferring with Dr. Best,[81] established the Zentralstelle für jüdische Auswanderung (the Central Bureau for Jewish Emigration) under the direction of Dr. Stahlecker, the SD chief of SS-Oberabschnitt Donau. The Bureau was nominally administered by Stahlecker; however its de facto chief was Eichmann. The Zentralstelle was housed in a palace in the Prinz-Eugen-Straße near Belvedere Castle, owned until 1938 by the Rothschild family.

In a multipage memorandum Eichmann informed the SD-Hauptamt about the establishment of the Zentralstelle für jüdische Auswanderung by order of Reichskommissar Bürckel and of Stahlecker's appointment as its director. Eichmann justified this supposed initiative on the part of the SD-Oberabschnitt by referring to the time-consuming formalities attending the procurement of papers needed for emigration:

> Instances of Jews happily [sic] anticipating emigration only to find themselves standing in line for days and weeks at the various offices to complete their emigration papers were growing by leaps and bounds here in Vienna. Partly because of incompetence of the civil servants in charge, partly because of organizational shortcomings, problems [sic] appeared that counteracted [sic] our efforts in promoting the forcible exit of Jews from Austria.[82]

Eichmann listed the duties of the Zentralstelle as providing opportunities for emigration through negotiations for entrance permits and obtaining foreign currency; establishment and surveillance of retraining centers; supervision of Jewish political organizations; publication of guidelines; and effective, sustained cooperation with all institutions in Vienna involved in the political, police-related, and financial aspects of Jewish expulsion.

More than anything, this letter demonstrates to what extent Eichmann's methods of operation were designed to further his own career. There was no need to speed up the process of emigration. Tens of thousands of men and women justly fearing for their lives were eager to flee abroad, and the officials of the Kultusgemeinde had tried to support this mass exodus as much as possible and to remove stumbling blocks. Eichmann had not invented anything. He had merely adopted existing proposals and, perhaps somewhat modified, had passed them on to higher-ups. Within his organization, though, he passed them off as his own work and soon bragged about the numbers of those driven out.

At the SD-Hauptamt in Berlin, the establishment of the Zentralstelle aroused immediate attention. An August 26 telex to the SD-Führer of the SS-Oberabschnitt Österreich reported that, with Stahlecker's appointment as its director, the SD had taken on a task "in whose fulfillment the SD Head-quarters was keenly interested, since it was of national importance." In expec-tation of its heavy workload, the Hauptamt requested "support personnel for SS-Untersturmführer Eichmann who had been charged with conducting its functions."[83]

Needless to say, the "national importance" of this new institution did not lie in the removal of the bureaucratic harassments Eichmann described, although for Jews desperate to escape daily terror by fleeing the country they constituted an ever-present problem. The real intentions of the SS organizations in creating the Zentralstelle become readily apparent in one of Hagen's reports from early September 1938. At the end of August, Hagen, at Six's request, made a trip to Vienna to inspect this new institution. In his September 12–dated report to his superior, Hagen emphasized its advantages and significance in extending the influence of the SS-SD. He considered it an improvement over the previous methods in that the issue of all papers necessary for emigration could now be completed within eight days and that now there existed a mechanism for accu-rately tracking the "number of those wanting to emigrate – their professions, property, etc."[84] As a strategically important aspect of the future course of action on the part of the SS-SD, he stressed that because of the particular posi-tion the Zentralstelle occupied within various agencies, "the superiority of the Sicherheitsdienst in the resolution of the Jewish question in Austria was abso-lutely guaranteed, eliminating the possibility of any other agency participating in the decision-making process."[85]

Hagen had attended several discussions of Zentralstelle officials, members of the Kultusgemeinde, and appropriate government agencies and could certify a "strict application of policy in the treatment of the Jewish question." He was particularly pleased that the victims had to pay not only for the bureaucratic management of their expulsion, but additionally they financed part of the materiel and personnel costs of the Zentralstelle:

> In no way does the Zentralstelle constitute a burden for the Sicherheitsdienst, neither financially nor materially since it contains Referat II-112 and supports itself through the fee each Jew is obliged to pay. The Oberabschnitt Donau is responsible only for the salaries of the employees of Department II-112. Orderlies, guards, automobiles, materials, etc., are paid solely by the Zentralstelle.[86]

Hagen had only one complaint: The number of employees at the Zentralstelle was insufficient. He considered it necessary to provide Eichmann with seasoned experts in addition to the aides and secretaries already there. From the point of view of the SS, the advantages of this institution, established in Vienna just two weeks previously, were such that he planned to report separately on the possibilities of applying the expertise gathered in Austria throughout the Reichsgebiet, the entire German Reich.

So, shortly after its creation, Eichmann's Zentralstelle was to serve as a prototype for future establishments and methods throughout the Altreich. Hagen recognized the trend-setting significance of the Vienna model from the perspective of the SS-SD: compulsory expulsion of those robbed of their possessions, payment for the management of "emigration" either by the victims themselves or through foreign currency provided by Jewish organizations abroad, and extension of the power of the SD by assuming executive privileges.

At the Zentralstelle, applicants were processed in a sort of administrative conveyer belt system. Franz Novak began his career as an SS-Hauptscharführer (master sergeant) in Eichmann's retinue at the Zentralstelle; in a 1961 interrogation he described his work in the "Document Acceptance" section, where emigration application forms had to be submitted. The application

> was deposited into a pouch; the Jew first went from one agency involved in the process to the next – they were all gathered together in the Palais Rothschild – and then all other documents arrived from other agencies. They were all gathered in that pouch in proper sequence. When all necessary papers had arrived, I passed them all together in the pouch I mentioned earlier to the "Document Pickup" section.[87]

In the beginning Anton Burger and Karl Rahm worked in that section.

In Jerusalem Adolf Eichmann cited these supposedly objective and correct procedures of the Zentralstelle as evidence that he had never been an antisemite.

> I had no problems with the Jewish political officials. I also don't believe that any one of them would complain about me. Not even now ... for they know that I did not hate Jews. I have never been an antisemite and have never hidden

that fact. I am not trying to praise myself by saying so. All I want to say is that
our collaboration at the Zentralstelle was objective and correct. Even when I
was still in the *Volksschule* (basic nine grades) I had a Jewish friend. When we
met for the last time, we took a walk down a country road in Linz. At that time
I was already wearing the NSDAP emblem in my buttonhole.[88]

What Eichmann and all former SS men of the Zentralstelle for obvious reasons did not mention in their post-1945 testimonies was that in dealing with
defenseless Jews, they had acted out the part of members of the Aryan "master
race" in their black uniforms, doing so in the most primitive, brutal way. Jewish
applicants in the Zentralstelle, as the recollections of the victims reveal, were
systematically harassed and mistreated.

By the end of 1938 a routine had come into being according to which
persons "willing to emigrate" had to "prequeue" at Schwarzenberg Platz on
the preceding night to stand in line in the Prinz-Eugen-Straße the following
morning until the Zentralstelle opened its doors at 7:30 A.M. One of the persons
affected by this "custom" described it this way:

> On the right side ordinary Jews were lined up, on the left the "Dachauer," those
> who had returned from Dachau, in wrinkled clothes and easy to recognize
> because of their shorn heads. Their turn came first, not because they had
> suffered more than the others but because they had tight "deadlines" and were
> supposed to "disappear" as soon as possible. SS men drove them across the
> street at a run and led them inside.[89]

Inside, men and women had to queue up once more until the envelope with
all the preconfirmations had been checked at the counter operated by the
Kultusgemeinde.

> Then and only then was it possible to approach the sacred countenances of the
> Aryan controllers. At a row of counters these pre-confirmations were examined
> and collected. Other counters did not require pre-confirmations but also had
> to provide information about matters such as outstanding amounts of one's
> telephone bill and similar trifles.[90]

At the counters for payment of Reichsfluchtsteuer, the tax for escaping the
German Reich, and the Judenabgabe, an additional post-Kristallnacht tax
levied after November 12, only those who had nothing left at all had a fairly
easy time.

> But woe to those who still owned something! That money mill pressed it out
> of them as surely as a grain mill squashes the kernel. If no more labels could be
> invented, open blackmail was the next step to tax the Jew for what the traffic
> would bear in bribes. . . . Tears, begging, supplications, nothing helped. The tax

had to be paid. No one could predict who would have to pay and how much. It struck like lightning out of the clear blue sky.[91]

The goal of all these efforts was to secure the Unbedenklichkeitsbescheinigung, which certified that no restrictions existed about its owner leaving the country.

> How many people never received it! Those who had to deal with a vicious, blackmailing employee, those ensnared in a hopelessly complicated Reichs-fluchtsteuer or with a Judenabgabe so exorbitant that the money could not be raised, those dealing with a hostile tax clerk refusing to forgive even the smallest outstanding amount – they all were condemned to remain in that hell and wait for the merciless, inevitable end in want and horror.[92]

The employees of the Zentralstelle did not just apply bureaucratic harassment: Personal humiliation and attacks were the order of the day. Time and again, individuals among the waiting were singled out, led into special rooms, and subjected to interrogations in the course of which the members of the SS forced their victims to recite humiliating self-accusations. Cruel mistreatments were routine. One man who already had been subjected to similar torment reported that he answered the question "What are you?" not with a statement about his profession because physical violence would have been the response. He knew that already, so he rattled off, "I am a Jewish swindler, a scoundrel." The SS men expressed their satisfaction: "Very good, very good."[93]

On October 21, 1938, after working for two months as chief of the Zentral-stelle, Eichmann submitted a report of his activities to the SD-Hauptamt in Berlin. With subliminal pride he explained to his superiors that the number of Jews processed for emigration by the Zentralstelle had risen to 350 per day. He claimed that up to September 30, 1938, some 38,000 Glaubensjuden (religious Jews) had left Austria legally. Together with those who left the country illegally, Eichmann arrived at an estimate of 50,000 expelled Jews.[94] What Eichmann forgot to mention and what the readers of his report at the SD-Hauptamt obviously failed to notice was that, of the roughly 40,000 driven out between August and the end of September under government supervision, at most a quarter could have been handled by the Zentralstelle.[95] Yet the handy figure of 50,000 driven from their former homeland apparently was so impressive that Heydrich seized upon it as proof of the Zentralstelle's efficiency. These inflated figures were touted not only at the SD's internal meetings: Newspaper articles, likewise, used them to mislead. The *Völkische Beobachter* of May 13, 1939, for example, claimed that "after its ten-month existence" the Zentralstelle had been a major force in bringing about "the emigration of a total of 99,672 Jews of the Mosaic creed."

The Appropriation of the "Vienna Model"

How severe the pressure weighing down the Viennese Jews was and how brutal
the machinery of bureaucracy and expulsion worked in the Ostmark is evident
from the discussion of the Jewish Question on November 12, 1938, at the Reich
Air Ministry, which commended developments in Vienna as exemplary for the
entire Reich, where things were lagging behind.[96] Göring knew all about the
dismal state of the Reich's finances. Accordingly, under his chairmanship and
in the wake of the nationwide pogroms, the discussion of November 12 focused
almost entirely on the quickest way of excluding the Jews from the German
economy. Almost as an afterthought, a "contribution" of one billion RM was
imposed on them.[97]

Heydrich, on the other hand, focused on the issue of expulsion:

> Excluding the Jew from the economy is well and good. Still, the basic problem
> remains: The Jew has to leave Germany. May I make a few suggestions? In
> Vienna, at the order of the Reichskommissar, we instituted a *Judenauswan-*
> *derungszentrale*, a Center for Jewish Emigration, with whose help we expelled
> no fewer than 50,000 Jews, while in the Altreich during the same period we
> managed to expel a mere 19,000. . . . There we did it in such a way that through
> the Jewish Kultusgemeinde we demanded a certain fee from rich Jews wanting
> to emigrate. With these fees, augmented by foreign currency, a certain number
> of poor Jews too could be expelled. The problem, after all, was not getting rid
> of the rich Jews but getting rid of the Jewish mob.

Göring, taking a fatherly approach, voiced reservations about this course of
action: "Boys, boys, have you really thought this through? It's not just a question
of getting rid of hundreds of thousands of the Jewish mob. Have you considered
whether this method may not ultimately cost us so much foreign currency that
we can't sustain it?" But since in Vienna steps had been taken to keep Jewish
money from leaving the country, Heydrich countered that each Jew could take
only a small amount of cash, the Vorzeigegelder, token amounts, which met
with Göring's approval. He finally accepted Heydrich's proposal "to establish
a similar Zentrale in the Reich with participation of the appropriate agencies"
and, by avoiding errors he had pointed out, "find a solution for the Reich."[98]

Shortly afterward, in January 1939, the Ministry of the Interior under
Heydrich's leadership established the Reichszentrale für jüdische Auswanderung, the Reich Center for Jewish Emigration, which was to coordinate
the activities of all organizations involved in Jewish expulsion and to establish
and supervise a uniform, compulsory consolidation of Jewish organizations
throughout the Reich.[99] This organization was to support expulsions; raise

funds in Germany and abroad to ship especially poor Jews out of the country; and conduct a centralized management of applications, documents, and certificates.[100] In his interrogation Franz Novak recalled, "in Berlin following the sample of the Zentralstelle für jüdische Auswanderung in Vienna, the same kind of organization was set up," to which he and one of the Günther brothers were posted "to help the Berlin institution get organized."[101]

With Göring's appointment of Heydrich as director of the Reichszentralstelle and the subsequent founding of the Reichsvereinigung der Juden in Deutschland, The Reich Association of Jews in Germany, under the permanent control of the SS, Heydrich and his organization gained an important advantage over other Party and government agencies involved in the planning and execution of antisemitic policies. Based on their new authority, the SS and Heydrich were able to impose their concepts of solving the Jewish Question on government agencies and, based on the paramount importance of Jewish emigration, demand ultimate say in decision-making processes regarding all aspects of Jewish policy. In respect to Jewish policies, this development constituted a decisive shift from *Normenstaat* to *Maßnahmestaat*, from government by law to government by ad hoc decision.[102] This form of organization constituted just one of several means for an accelerated application of antisemitic policies in the procedures of the new Reichszentrale. Its establishment did not speed up the expulsion of Jews from Germany, as Heydrich's people had envisioned. In fact, in the eyes of the SS technocrats, its performance, when compared with the "exemplary" expulsion statistics of Eichmann's Zentralstelle in Vienna, made it a failure.

In a June 1939–dated draft entitled "Das Judentum in Deutschlund" ("Jewry in Germany") Hagen stated that since August 1938 the Zentralstelle in Vienna had succeeded in sending approximately 110,000 Jews "into emigration," whereas the expulsion figures of the Reichszentralstelle were considerably lower. "For example, the total number of applications for emigration submitted at the Zentralstelle in Berlin during April and May was a mere 6,187."[103] SS-Standartenführer Six put it even more bluntly: "The stagnation of Jewish emigration in the Altreich in spite of the opening of the Judenzentrale," he informed his superior Heydrich, "led me to examine conditions in Vienna during my last visit there. I found that in contrast to Berlin, Vienna is able to maintain its emigration quotas through the initiatives and pressures of the state police."[104] To discuss this matter, Six proposed a meeting of Heydrich, Müller, senior executive Lischka of Gestapa, Eichmann, Hagen, and himself; however, because of the outbreak of the war, this meeting didn't take place.

In regard to robbing, persecuting, and expelling Jews, the Nazis in the Ostmark obviously were far ahead of those in the Altreich. Tens of thousands of Austrians were eager to participate in the construction of a new social order based on race and so accelerated the process of destroying Jewish livelihoods in Austria and, in fact, the entire Reich. Because of stronger pressure from below, Austrian pogrom antisemites' forging ahead, and internal National Socialist squabbles about distribution of spoils, Nazi administrators and bureaucrats in Vienna felt pressured much earlier than their counterparts in the Altreich to devise pseudo-legal procedures and organizational innovations and to create new administrative machinery for handling these challenges. Moreover, these pressures would not lessen after 1938: They provided the impetus for earlier organization of mass deportations from Vienna than from other cities of the Greater German Reich, and for their speedy completion by Fall 1942.

Eichmann's Zentralstelle, the SD, and Heydrich took full credit for one of the effects of the widespread terrors visited on the Jews. They did so by claiming as their own accomplishment the high number of people who, in justified panic, wanted to flee abroad. The motive of these organizations and individuals was to secure and enhance their own positions in the National Socialist power structure. Since the beginning of 1939, Heydrich and the Reichssicherheits-hauptamt, which combined the SD and the Gestapo under one roof, occupied a central position in shaping the destinies first of the German, Austrian, and Czech Jews and later the destinies of almost all European Jews. Eichmann and his men built their subsequent careers on this foundation.

From Unemployment Line to Herrenmenschen Elite

Beginning in the early fall of 1938, the number of personnel of the Zentral-stelle für jüdische Auswanderung was constantly enlarged. Clerical workers, orderlies, and guards were in high demand. Moreover, in keeping with the Zentralstelle's status as a prototype, starting in the summer of 1939, entire groups of employees were transferred, first under Eichmann's direction to establish a Zentralstelle in Prague and shortly after that to set up Referat IV D 4 at the RSHA in Berlin. In Eichmann's shadow, the SS men who in Vienna had started in low-level positions rapidly scaled the hierarchical ladders of the Zentralstellen while new employees filled their now-vacant positions. In this fashion the Zentralstelle Vienna served as an apprenticeship program for training expulsion experts. The Austrians who were hired after the brothers Günther, in contrast to those two men from Erfurt, had neither administra-tive experience nor had they been members of the police or the SD before 1938. Only some of them had been members of the SS. They also had not distinguished themselves as particularly rabid antisemites.

After the Anschluß, thousands of Alte Kämpfer – Austrians who had joined the Nazi Party or one of its affiliates before 1933 – and "illegals," who had been members of the NSDAP between 1933 and 1938 when the party was outlawed in Austria, expected to be rewarded for their real or alleged "contributions to the movement," demanding restitution for their sacrifices. They either took part in the fight for the spoils during Arisierungen or demanded secure employment in the community, state, or party apparatus.[105] As was true in the Entjudung of the economy where, according to a report by Staatskommissar für die Privatwirtschaft (State Commissar for the "Private Sector") Walter Raffelberger, the applications for taking over Aryanized property outstripped available businesses three to one; a far greater number of applicants sought employment in the public service sector than there were positions.[106] To make matters worse, the ranks of both groups of old party comrades were swollen by people popularly referred to as Märzveilchen, "March violets," who had joined the NSDAP after the Anschluß or tried to join so that their party membership book would entitle them to enter the competition for material privileges.[107]

In light of these shortages, real or exaggerated merits in service of the movement, as well as nepotism and coterie membership played important roles in the distribution of jobs in community, state, and party offices. Demonstrated qualifications and expertise were of decidedly lesser importance. In an August 1938 secret report the director of the office responsible for the party's political organizations complained about party structure in the Ostmark and the Austrians recently hired by party organs. "These workers will have to be trained from the ground up . . . because most of these twenty- to twenty-five-year-olds have not performed any meaningful work since they left school." Above all, he complained about problems with the so-called Illegal Fighters because they demanded

> extremely high-paying positions whose requirements, because of their lack of qualifications, they are unable to meet. Yet, whenever these illegal fighters are placed in such positions, they start making even more demands even though their performance bears no relation to the advancement they have been given. Once they occupy such positions, many develop delusions of grandeur.[108]

It seems that also at the Zentralstelle, positions were handed out to secure the livelihoods of party comrades of greater or lesser merit. Except for Anton Brunner, who was not hired until Summer 1939, all the Eichmann men belonged to the same age group. In 1939 they ranged from twenty-five to thirty years of age, a little younger than Eichmann. Franz Novak was born in 1913 in Wolfsberg in the Austrian province of Carinthia; Alois Brunner in the town of Rohrbrunn in Burgenland in 1912; Anton Burger from Neunkirchen in Lower Austria was born in 1911; Karl Rahm, born in 1907, came from Klosterneuburg near Vienna; Franz Stuschka was born in 1910 in Liesing near Vienna; and Herbert Gerbing in 1914 in Mödling near Vienna. Anton Zita was born in 1909 in Göllersdorf; Josef Weiszl, born in 1912 in Felsöderna, grew up in Vienna after he and his parents moved there from Romania when he was an infant. Richard Hartenberger (1911), Ernst Girzick (1911), Ferdinand Daurach (1912), Ernst Brückler (1912), and Alfred Slawik (1913) were born in Vienna. Except for the Carinthian Franz Novak, all were Austrians from Burgenland, Vienna, or Lower Austria.

Like Eichmann, all Austrians at the Zentralstelle had experienced severe ruptures in their professional development during the 1930s. None had succeeded in building a secure life in Austria. For a number of reasons almost all had lost their jobs early in that decade, had remained unemployed except for brief periods of work now and then, or had joined the Austrian Legion in Germany. During and after the Anschluß not a single one of them worked in the trade he had learned during his apprenticeship or that he had pursued for any length of time. All looked for new employment, either in the public sector or with the party.

The example of Karl Rahm most clearly illustrates the desire of "old party comrades" to secure some position in the public service sector. He had completed an apprenticeship as an engine fitter and from 1927 to 1933 had been in the Austrian army. After leaving the military, he was unemployed for three years, only occasionally working at his trade. In 1934 he joined the NSDAP and the SS in Klosterneuburg and was "illegally" active. According to him, his illegal activities involved Böllerwerfen, tossing powerful explosives akin to firecrackers; Hakenkreuzfeuern, creating fiery displays in the shape of the swastika; and peddling outlawed newspapers. He also had been an NSBO (National Socialist Cell Leader).[109] Unemployed in April 1938, he filled out a questionnaire of the Betreuungsstelle für die alten Parteigenossen und Angehörigen der Opfer der nationalsozialistischen Bewegung im Bereich des Gaues Niederösterreich (Support Organization for Old Party Comrades and the Families of Those Sacrificed for the National Socialist Movement in the NSDAP Province Lower Austria), describing his desired position as that of a "civil servant in the municipal government of Vienna."[110]

At the same time, he applied at the personnel office of the city of Vienna for employment in one of the city's public works departments. The leader of Rahm's SS-Sturmbann (storm battalion) supported the application "because the applicant was an old illegal SS member."[111] In May, Rahm visited the Betreuungsstelle concerning his application, with questionnaire and hand-written resumé in hand. But instead of contacting the municipal office for "preferred employment of 'old fighters,'" the Betreuungsstelle got in touch with the employment office of the metal and metalwork industry.[112] Although Rahm was invited to an interview at the end of June 1938 at that employment office, he declined to appear, claiming that he was working in the administrative commando of the military engineer barracks in Klosterneuburg and, therefore, could not come. Yet, this activity that supposedly prevented his appearance at the employment office did not keep him from working from June to November at a Jewish-owned grain company in the process of liquidation, as he stated in a resumé written in 1940.[113] It is safe to assume that Rahm was not working there as an engine fitter but in his capacity of an SS-Oberscharführer to monitor that company's dissolution.

Late in the fall of 1938 he was out of work once more; nevertheless, he did not accept the referral from the metal industry's employment office, which, because of a shortage of skilled workers, would have had no difficulty placing a trained engine fitter in the Altreich. Instead, he applied to Vienna's central office of criminal investigation for a job in the department of corrections.[114] As it turned out, Rahm ended up neither as an employee nor a civil servant for the city of Vienna nor with the police. In January 1939 he got a job at the Zentralstelle as an office worker. Eventually his career would take him to Prague, where he became Hans Günther's deputy director of that city's Zentralstelle für jüdische Auswanderung. He ended his career as the last SS-commandant of the Theresienstadt (Terezin) concentration camp.[115]

Much like Rahm, Anton Zita, a trained carpenter who from 1930 to 1937 had worked periodically as a carpenter's helper in Vienna, in the spring of 1938 applied at the Betreuungstelle in Vienna. As a long-time "illegal" member of the NSDAP and the SS, he sought any public service job, which according to his own list, he defined as a position with the trolley system, the railroad, the fire department, the gas works; or as a handyman in a school; or as a concièrge.[116]

The first employees to be hired in Autumn 1938 for work in the Zentralstelle were the Alte Kämpfer, who until the Anschluß had been members of the SA and the Austrian Legion. During and after the dissolution of the Legion in the summer of 1938, they read the handwriting on the wall – the waning strength of the SA in the internal power struggles among various National Socialist organizations and factions – and shifted from the SA to the SS.[117]

Franz Novak was a professional typesetter who in his youth had joined the German Turnerbund, the gymnasts' association, the Hitler Youth in 1929, and shortly afterward the SA. In 1934 the twenty-one-year-old had participated in the National Socialist July coup in his hometown of Wolfsberg, a center of armed confrontations in Carinthia. In the Lavant Valley, as in Wolfsberg, approximately 1,500 armed National Socialists had overpowered the government and reigned supreme for several days.[118] When confronted by the army, a group of rebels, Novak among them, escaped across the border into Yugoslavia. Shortly afterward he fled to Germany and joined the Austrian Legion. He returned to Vienna with the Legion just after the Anschluß. When the Legion was dissolved, he joined the SS on July 1, 1938, applied for a job with the government printing office, and when none materialized, he applied with the SD. In the summer of 1938 he worked for the SD for two months as a civilian employee before being posted to the Zentralstelle, where he remained for about six months. In the succeeding years the locations of his SS career moved in step with Eichmann's. In 1939 Novak accompanied him to Prague to set up that city's Zentralstelle für jüdische Auswanderung, and after that to Berlin.[119]

Anton Burger had learned the trade of a commercial clerk in Neunkirchen, Lower Austria. In 1930 he volunteered for the Austrian army and came into contact with the Deutscher Soldatenbund, the German Soldiers' Association. He joined the NSDAP in 1932. He claimed to have been dismissed from the army in 1933 because of his political activities for the NSDAP. Soon after that he left Austria for Munich, where he reported to the Austrian Branch of the SA and became a member of the Austrian Legion. During the National Socialist coup of 1934, he and other armed members of the Legion entered Upper Austria near Kollerschlag. After a short engagement the group returned to Bavaria.[120] To save face politically, the SA confined those legionaires involved in this border violation at the fortress Landsberg on the river Lech but, as Burger wrote, released them "after seventeen days of honorable custody."[121] In 1937, while he was stationed at the SA camp Rheinhessen near Wackernim, he tried unsuccessfully to gain employment with the German police.

With the Legion, Burger arrived in Vienna after the Anschluß and was housed first at the SA barracks on Sterneck Platz in the second district and later in the same building as Franz Novak in Vienna's twelfth municipal district.[122] Like Novak, Burger joined the SS in the summer of 1938, was hired by the SD, and posted to the Zentralstelle that fall. In a questionnaire dated February 1939, he listed his address as Prinz-Eugen-Straße 22, the seat of the Zentralstelle. Under "occupation" and "rank" he listed "commercial assistant, SD." He too served in Vienna only for a short time and was transferred to the Zentralstelle in Prague in mid-1939.[123]

Alois Brunner, born in southern Burgenland, had been apprenticed to a businessman in Fürstenfeld, Styria. In May 1931, at the age of nineteen, he joined the NSDAP in Fürstenfeld and the SA about six months later. According to his resumé, he had to give up his job with the Fürstenfeld businessman in 1932 because of his active SA membership. That year he also attended a three-month private course in criminology in Graz. In early 1933 he worked for two months as a district representative for a Graz loan association in Hartberg, Styria, and between May and September of that year leased a café of the 'Café-Restaurant Wien' chain in Hartberg, an enterprise he claimed "gobbled up his entire paternal inheritance."[124] In September 1933 he went to Germany and contacted the Austrian Legion. Clearly he did not leave Austria for political reasons, for in a 1938 NSDAP questionnaire he answered the question "did you have to flee to the Altreich because of your illegal activities?" with "no, the Kreisleiter (district leader) ordered it because I wanted to take a job in Switzerland."[125] Why his alleged search for a job in Switzerland would have led him to Germany he did not say. From September 1933 to June 1938 he was a member of the Austrian Legion and within those five years achieved the rank of SA-Stabsobertruppenführer, Staff Sergeant, in the Nachrichtensturmbann (SA signal batallion). After his return to his home in Burgenland in the summer of 1938, the "businessman" was briefly employed as external branch representative of the Kreisbauernschaften (district farmers associations) Eisenstadt and Oberpullendorf, and at the Reichsnährstand (Reich Cooperative of Food Producers) in Eisenstadt, which apparently did not provide much satisfaction. So the SA-Stabsobergruppenführer volunteered, as he wrote in his resumé, for the SS and was posted to the Zentralstelle sometime in mid-November 1938.

In addition to these former members of the SA, the personnel of the Zentralstelle also included long-time SS members who had spent years in that organization's camps in Germany.

Ernst Brückler from Vienna was a trained cabinetmaker who lost his job in 1932 when he was twenty years old. He had been a member of the Hitler Youth before joining the SS in 1932. In the summer of 1933 he had registered with the SS assembly camp in Munich and was billeted in the SS camp Ranis. In 1937 he served as an SS guard at the airport in Bremerhaven but returned to Vienna in 1938.[126] At the beginning of 1939 he became a member of the security guard at the Zentralstelle.

After finishing his apprenticeship as an electrician, Ernst Adolf Girzick was unemployed. He joined the army in 1931 and from then on was a member of the Deutscher Soldatenbund and the NSDAP. When the army dismissed him in 1933, he was unemployed again. He was arrested in January 1934 for throwing lit firecrackers at people and sentenced to five and a half years of prison, of which he served just two at the detention center of Stein on the Danube. He was released through an amnesty in the summer of 1936, joined the Austrian Legion in the Altreich, and was stationed in the SS camp Ranis. Although he had worked as a streetcar conductor in Dresden since November 1937, he volunteered for service in the Ostmark in the summer of 1938 and

beginning in August of that year had at least a temporary position as an assistant at the Vermögensverkehrstelle, the Property Processing Office.[127] While
working there, he applied for a service job with the municipality of Vienna. The
Betreuungsstelle supported his application because he was a "highly accomplished party comrade" and "old illegal fighter," a candidate for the *Blutorden*,
the "Blood Order of the NSDAP."[128] Girzig was not hired by the municipal
government either, but was appointed to the Zentralstelle in 1939.

Franz Stuschka, who could boast neither a completed public school edu-
cation nor a completed job training program,[129] had been a member of the SS
during his service in the Legion in Germany before being employed in Vienna's
Liesing district employment office in 1938, dismissed in 1939, and then hired
by the Zentralstelle.

It is worthy of note that a great number of old party comrades had moved in
German-national or National Socialist environments since their childhood or
youth during Austria's First Republic and, accordingly, had been socialized in
a völkisch racist milieu. Many, such as Novak, Stuschka, Gerbing, Zita, and
Girzick, also had been involved in sports under the auspices of the German
Turnerbund and later quite naturally had linked up with the Hitler Youth or
the SA, which were way stations to the Nazi Party or the SS. This context
also explains why their resumés and personnel files contain little evidence of
antisemitism – the exception being that of Herbert Gerbing, who stated that
he lost his apprenticeship in a drugstore as a sixteen-year-old Hitler Youth
because his employer "was a Jew."[130] Obviously, hatred of Jews was such a
given for Austrian National Socialists that applications for party offices did not
even demand explicit proof.

In addition to old fighters, the personnel roster of the Zentralstelle included
a smaller group of "March violets." Richard Hartenberger was a trained lithog-
rapher and, according to his own statements, had been closely associated with
the Social Democratic Party. Until 1938, although frequently unemployed, he
worked as a printer and joined the SS in April of that year. Through the good
offices of his SS-Sturm (assault unit), he found employment in the Vienna
customs office where he worked as a customs officer in matters involving Jewish emigration.[131] On December 1, 1938, after several months in the customs
office, he entered the service of the SD, which sent him to the Zentralstelle.

Josef Weiszl, like Hartenberger, also had been a member of the Social
Democratic Party in the late 1920s. A sales clerk, he had been out of work for
an extended period of time in the 1930s and had joined the Vaterländische
Front, the Nationalist Fatherland Front. After the Anschluß, Weiszl applied
successfully for Nazi Party membership.[132] His brother-in-law Wilhelm Höttl,
who had been working for the SD in Austria even during the illegal period,

"eased" Weiszl's entry into the SD. Weiszl became a member of the Zentralstelle staff in November 1938.[133]

Anton Brunner, born in 1898 in Croatia, had come to Vienna with his parents and had been a soldier in World War I. In the 1920s he had been an employee in an industrial company and a member of a union and of the Social Democratic Party. Although out of work from 1934 to 1938, after the Anschluß he had become a senior clerk in the Reich Commissioner's office where he was involved in the liquidation of religious organizations and their assets.[134] Only in the summer of 1939 was Anton Brunner, who was not a member of the SS, transferred to the Zentralstelle.

The differences in the political lives of the individual members of the Zentralstelle in no way differentiated their conduct in performing their duties. Whether "Märzveilchen" or Alte Kämpfer, all insulted and mistreated the Jews at the Zentralstelle. At the 1950 trial of Richard Hartenberger one witness testified in court that not only the accused but almost all Zentralstelle SS men had beaten Jews.[135]

The careers of the Vienna Zentralstelle staff characterize them as rather typical representatives of Austrian National Socialists. They had succeeded in rising from unemployment or refugee status to become members of supposedly elite organizations. Eichmann's men enjoyed their power, just as did their chief. In their black uniforms, these former failures now could play the Herrenmenschen, now could order about "Jewish subhumans," scream at them, humiliate them, and mistreat them as they pleased. To do so they required no practical or ideological training: Antisemitism was not something they had to learn. As they rose in society, at least in their own estimation; as many of them moved into Aryanized apartments furnished with Jewish émigré property; as they lorded their power over others – the promised "new social order" postulated by National Socialism came true for them.

2   The Unsuccessful Beginning: The Deportations to Nisko on the River San

The first deportations of Jews from Nazi-ruled territory took place in the early fall of 1939. With the beginning of the war, the voices demanding the expulsion of Jews still living in the Großdeutsche Reich had by no means fallen silent. Quite the contrary: Many felt that, through the conquest of Poland, Germany was now in possession of territories to which Central European Jews could be moved by force. Such plans of expulsion found wide acceptance among the leadership of the Third Reich as well as among ordinary Nazis. These first deportations did not originate in Eichmann's proposed resettlement projects, as is sometimes claimed, although he and his men did play a key role in their organization because the aim of the Nisko project was merely expulsion, not the resettlement of Jews.[1]

Even though at the start of the war almost two thirds of the Austrian Jews already had been forced into emigration[2] and their businesses, houses and apartments, property, and savings had been appropriated by the state, the party, or Aryan Volksgenossen, this state of affairs satisfied neither the National Socialist leadership nor segments of their NSDAP base, the population of the Ostmark. The continuation of expulsions and the start of organized mass deportations were not based solely on the goals of National Socialist top functionaries and administrators to rid Austria of all Jews: In Vienna, lower-level party branches voiced the same demands. An October 3, 1939 letter from the leader of the Ortsgruppe Rossau, a section of Vienna's 9th municipal district, to the Kreisleiter and the Kreis headquarters, provides an example of the "mood" of party members and Volksgenossen, and justifications for requested expulsion measures.[3] Under the subject heading "Jewish Question," the writer complained that so many Jews were living within the area of his Ortsgruppe and, in fact, had been sent there from other districts. Especially revealing are his proposals for changing this situation.

Located at the Ringstraße between the university and the Donaukanal borders on the inner city, the Ortsgruppe Rossau comprised that part of the 9th district that then as now was a solidly bourgeois neighborhood where Siegmund Freud lived and worked until his escape from Vienna. By mid-September 1939 approximately 1,500 Jews supposedly still lived there, roughly 20 percent of the entire population of that area. Among other things, the Ortsgruppenleiter, the local section head of the Nazi Party, complained about the "shameless" behavior of some Jews who tried to buy foodstuffs without ration cards. Aryans having to rent rooms from Jews, he feared, gave the Jews the green light to commit Rassenschande, "defilement" of the "Aryan race" through marriage or sexual liaison with Jews. He also considered it his duty to cite numerous examples in pointing out that, on the average, "Aryan housing conditions are notably inferior to those for Jews." He closed his multipage missive with a probably exaggerated description of popular opinion:

> The mood of the population regarding the Jews is at the boiling point. It is thanks only to our wholehearted expenditure of effort that up to now not a single instance of violence has occurred. But I am fully aware that this situation cannot continue indefinitely, and that enforcing such restraint is a thankless task for a political leader surely is obvious to you, too. Time and again people point out that the Jews alone are responsible for the war and should be treated accordingly. They don't understand why Jews receive the same amounts of foodstuffs as Aryans. They don't understand why Jews are not being conscripted for any kind of labor whatsoever and are free to conduct their shady business as usual. Without exception they are convinced that even now the Jews have ways and means of receiving more goods than their fair share. But we cannot provide proof since that is the job of the police, which in our *verjudetem Gebiet* [Jewified district] they are powerless to perform. The population frequently considers it a weakness that party organizations are not authorized to remedy such grievances. The population feels severely discriminated against as long as Aryans are forced to dwell in damp cellars while Jews have license to turn gorgeous apartments into pigpens.[4]

The Ortsgruppenleiter advocated an additional tightening of segregation in the form of forced expulsions. He suggested "putting male Jews to work in the mines" and "confining the female riffraff in camps nearby" or the need to consider "an 'evacuation' to Poland east of the river Vistula, because it makes no difference whether 2.5 or 2.7 million Jews live in Poland." Should these suggestions not be workable, in the opinion of this low-level National Socialist functionary, the Jews should be moved to health-threatening flats – mainly in basements – or apartments "especially endangered during air raids – on the fourth or fifth floors."[5]

Independent of such helpful hints, some higher SS and administrative authorities developed similar intentions. The assault on Poland and the rapid military victory were attended by a general intensification of racist policies. Together with the Wehrmacht's march into Poland, special SS units were mobilized, the Einsatzgruppen, Special Operations groups of Himmler's Sicherheitspolizei (Security Police or Sipo). Their mission was "to combat all elements hostile to the Reich or to all things German in [conquered] enemy territory behind the fighting troops."[6] They arrested members of Polish-nationalist organizations, Communists, Socialists, and occasionally Catholic clergy[7] from prepared lists or arbitrarily, and shot people alleged to be guerillas or suspected of espionage or sabotage. Polish Jews were mistreated, and random "evacuations" of civilians and lootings became the order of the day.[8]

Beyond that, in accordance with Hitler's desire and that of the SS, there was to take place a völkisch-political Flurbereinigung, a large-scale program of ethnic cleansing to effect territorial consolidation and separation of racial groups. This particular program of expulsion and liquidation, as Heydrich described it concisely in a mid-September meeting with Oberst (Colonel) Wagner, the Assistant Quartermaster General of the Oberkommando des Heeres (OKH – Army High Command), would be directed against "Jews, the intelligentsia, the clergy, and the nobility."[9]

Despite partial cooperation of members of the Wehrmacht in this völkische Flurbereinigung and the discriminating treatment and partial expulsion of Polish Jews, in the fall of 1939, Wehrmacht authorities in occupied Poland attempted to limit the worst instances of arbitrary cruelty.[10] These efforts also affected members of the SS. For example, army soldiers and SS men who, in plain sight of officers of the Wehrmacht, had conducted mass shootings for "no reason whatsoever" – members of an SS artillery regiment and the Geheime Feldpolizei (GFP – Secret Field Police) – had to answer to a Feldkriegsgericht, a military court operating behind the front lines, for having murdered "about fifty Jews who had been conscripted for bridge repairs. In the evening, when the work was finished, they had driven them into a synagogue and had shot them all WITHOUT CAUSE."[11] Similar courts-martial attempts to punish mass shootings of Jews led Heydrich to complain to Hitler, who on October 4 issued an amnesty for "any deed caused by vexation over the abominations committed by the Poles."[12]

As part of the general Flurbereinigung, mass expulsions of Jews, in the form of resettlements, also were planned.[13] At a September 21, 1939, SD-Hauptamt meeting of senior administrative officers including Eichmann and Heydrich, in addition to other topics, announced Hitler's approval of the deportation of Jews into the part of Poland soon to be referred to as the "Generalgouvernement" and Abschiebung, the forcible evacuation, of Jews across the German–Soviet demarcation line. Within the coming weeks Polish Jews were to be gathered in the larger cities and towns "to ensure better means of control and later evacuation."[14] Heydrich's racist program had four aims: "a) Jews as soon as possible into cities and towns; b) Jews from the Reich to Poland; c) the remaining 30,000 Gypsies also to Poland; d) systematic transport of Jews from German territories in freight trains."[15] "Poland" more than likely referred to the area of the Generalgouvernement rather than those parts of Poland integrated into the German Reich. Here those areas are called "German territories."

Heydrich spelled out these plans concerning Poland more concisely in a Schnellbrief, express letter, on the subject of the "Jewish Question in the Occupied Areas" dispatched that same day to the heads of the Einsatzgruppen in occupied Poland. With reference to the preceding meeting, the letter reiterated the top-secret nature of "the planned course of action, that is, the Endziel, its final goal."[16] Heydrich's language differentiated emphatically between (1) the Endziel, which would require extended deadlines and thorough technical and economic preparations; and (2) the various stages in the process of realizing this final goal. The interim stages could be carried out in short periods. The specifics of the tasks involved were not to be determined by a central authority, and the purpose of the guidelines was "to encourage the heads of the Einsatzgruppen to work out the practical details." Clearly, these guidelines were meant to leave room for variations in their application in situ. Heydrich considered the rapid transfer of Jews from rural areas to the larger cities and towns basic to accomplishing the final goal. The "areas Gdansk (Danzig) and West Prussia, Poznań (Posen) and eastern Upper Silesia" – in short, those parts of Poland shortly afterward integrated into the German Reich – "if at all possible . . . were to be emptied of Jews" or at least contain only very few "cities of concentration." Externally, according to Heydrich, the justification was to be that "the Jews had been heavily involved in guerilla assaults and looting expeditions." Two years later this sort of language would be used again in the occupied areas of the Soviet Union to legitimize mass murder there.

What sorts of Endziel-associated plans required extended economic and technical preparations remained unspecified. Possibly at that time the term referred to a type of reservation for Jews in the area between the Vistula and San Rivers in Galicia. What remained vague in the Schnellbrief, Heydrich hinted at in a meeting with Army Commander-in-Chief Walther von Brauchitsch on September 22 in his musings about a "Jewish state under German administration near Kraków (Cracow)."[17]

The proposed speed of the evacuation measures caused conflicts between the leaders of the SS and the Wehrmacht. The OKH was intent on approving preparatory initiatives only, and they protested the acceleration of the concentrations ordered in Heydrich's letter. Accordingly, Heydrich modified his original order so that the timetable and intensity of the concentration of Jews "would in no way interfere with military movements."[18] Liaison with local military authorities had to be established and maintained. In this technical rather than substantive argument the OKH had maintained the upper hand to preserve at least a minimal say in the decision-making process. Heydrich considered this turn of events such a stumbling block in the execution of his plans that in a meeting with his senior administrative officers on October 3, 1939, he observed, "the old problem of SD/Police on one side and the Wehrmacht on the other . . . had reappeared in all its gravity."[19] On July 2, 1940, looking back to the conflicts between Wehrmacht and SS over the völkische Flurbereinigung in occupied Poland, he ascribed military leaders' "ignorance of the enemy's ideological position" as the reason for their opinions in matters of combating the enemy.[20]

In the midst of these tensions between the SS and Wehrmacht, in early October 1939 Eichmann received the order to organize the deportation of Jews into Polish territories east of the Vistula.

The Organization of the Deportations

Eichmann did not start with the establishment of a Zentralstelle für jüdische Auswanderung in Prague until July 1939 because after Germany's incorporation of Bohemia and Moravia as a German protectorate, the Protektorat Böhmen und Mähren, in the spring of that year, Heydrich had ordered "the cessation of emigration to the degree possible" because, given the limited opportunities for securing entry visa for other countries, a wave of Jewish emigration from Bohemia and Moravia "might paralyze Jewish emigration from the rest of the Reich."[21] Not until June 21 did Heydrich give permission to establish a Zentralstelle to promote Jewish emigration from the Protectorate, provided it did not interfere with the expulsion of Jews from the German Reich. So, in July 1939, Dr. Stahlecker, now commander-in-chief of the Sicherheitspolizei in Bohemia and Moravia, could report that after lengthy negotiations with various German authorities, based on the approval of Reichsprotektor (Reich Protector of Bohemia and Moravia) Heydrich, and in accordance with the Gruppenführer's order, a Zentralstelle für jüdische Auswanderung had been established.[22] Just as in Vienna, Stahlecker entrusted its direction to

Eichmann. With some of his staff from Vienna – Novak, Burger, Rahm, and Stuschka – Eichmann organized the Zentralstelle in Prague as a carbon copy of the one in Vienna.[23] Representatives of the Prague Jewish community were sent to Vienna for "schooling" and representatives of the Vienna Kultusgemeinde were shipped to Prague to instruct their fellow sufferers there.

SS-Oberführer Heinrich Müller was chief of Gestapa Department II, head of the Reichszentrale für jüdische Auswanderung and, since the establishment of the Reichssicherheitshauptamt, chief of its Office IV (Combatting Enemies). On October 6, 1939, Eichmann received instructions from him to initiate discussions with the office of Gauleiter Wagner, the provincial party chief in Katowice (Kattowitz), "concerning the 'evacuation' of the 70,000 to 80,000 Jews of the Katowice district to the east across the Vistula."[24] Simultaneously, Jews from the Moravian city of Ostrava (Mährisch-Ostrau) at the Polish-Czech border were to be pushed out as well.

The suggestion to push the Jews of Ostrava to Galicia almost certainly was due to the insistence of SS authorities in the Protectorate. On September 18, 1939, Stahlecker and Regierungsrat Dr. Hermann met in Ostrava and discussed the possibility "of evicting several thousand Jews to Galicia."[25] This was nearly three weeks before Eichmann received his instructions. Preparatory steps such as an Erfassungsaktion, an operation seizing 8,000 Jews, and a Sicherstellung, the seizure of their apartments, already were in progress. As early as September, Eichmann must have known about plans for deportations to Galicia; documents reveal that he had noticed the expansion of Einsatzgruppe I into the area east of Kraków and had tried to arrange a consultation with its commander.[26]

Upon receiving his orders, Eichmann went to work immediately. In the succeeding weeks he continuously traveled back and forth to Berlin, Vienna, Ostrova, Katowice, and Galicia. Frequently neither his superiors nor his subordinates knew where to reach him by telephone or telex. He involved his entire staff and initiated the deportations through targeted pressure on the Jewish communities in Ostrava and Vienna. On Friday, October 10, he received his instructions in Berlin. After recording preparatory activities there, he left for Vienna and the very next day was discussing the deportations of Jews from Vienna with upper-echelon employees of Reichskommissar Bürckel's office. He instructed his employees at the Zentralstelle to start organizing resettlement transports to Poland for the following week.[27]

An October 10, 1939–dated letter from Dr. Stahlecker to Reichskommissar Bürckel demonstrates what expectations the leading SS authorities actively engaged in "Operation Nisko" brought to their assignments. Stahlecker regretted not having had the opportunity to confer with Bürckel in person "about questions concerning the Jews, among other matters,"[28] during his visit in Vienna on October 7 and 8. Through Eichmann, Stahlecker knew that one of Bürckel's representatives had visited the Zentralstelle and "had pressed for a speedy solution to the Jewish Question." As would become apparent a few weeks later, Stahlecker had made hopelessly unrealistic promises by claiming, "very pleasing aspects for the total solution of the Jewish Question in Austria had presented themselves." He added, "there is hope that a large number of [Austrian Jews] can be deported. As soon as this matter is decided once and for all, you will receive a report from Vienna. At any rate, I am hoping that this question will be finally solved in brief period."[29]

Early in October, Stahlecker obviously hoped to "drive out the majority of Jews still living in Vienna in a very short time by means of" then in preparation "deportations to Poland and the Soviet border." His terminology is noteworthy: "The total solution of the Jewish Question in Austria" and the "finally solved Question" already approached the term Endlösung, Final Solution, later used by the SS. At that particular time, though, this concept still meant an expulsion of the Jews, as complete as possible, rather than their planned and organized mass murder.

Eichmann was working closely with Stahlecker. After having spent the weekend in Vienna, he hurried to Ostrava where on Monday, October 9, he conferred with Rolf Günther, Theo Dannecker, and Anton Brunner at the office of the head of the local Stapo. There he announced that on the orders of Müller of the Gestapa, "a Jewish transport from Ostrava and another from Katowice" were to be "organized as quickly as possible."[30] Those being deported were to serve as an advance party in the territory chosen for the first transports. The expanse was roughly the area of Rozwadow-Annopol-Krasinik southwest of Lublin. There the first arrivals were to build a transit camp of wooden barracks that would house the transports to follow. For this reason, in contrast to later deportations, this group was to consist entirely of "impecunious male Jews suitable for physical labor," mainly contractors, workmen, and engineers, "as well as no fewer than ten Jewish physicians provided with medical equipment necessary for ambulatory care." Dannecker and Anton Brunner were to approach the military transport command post in Opole (Oppeln) to arrange for suitable trains, and these two were to supervise the purchase and loading of building materials. The entire operation was to be announced to the Kultusgemeinde in Ostrava as a transport for the construction of a "retraining camp." The Ostrava Kultusgemeinde was to pay for all transport expenses and building materials.

Later that day Eichmann and Rolf Günther went on to Katowice for negotiations with Wehrmacht and administrative authorities and to meet with Gauleiter Wagner the following day, October 10.[31] Here Eichmann announced – different from his explanations the previous day – that Heydrich had ordered "two transports each from Ostrava and Katowice."[32] Jews capable of work were to be deported from Katowice as well; Ostrava, however, would furnish all construction materials and tools for building the barracks. He pointed out that the highest echelons would observe the preparations for these deportations attentively because after the completion of these four transports, "an evaluative report" would have to be "presented to the Reichsführer-SS (RFSS) and Chief of the German Police, Himmler, through Heydrich, the Chief of the Sicherheitspolizei. In all likelihood" it would ultimately "be sent to the Führer himself." Then they would have to await "the order for the 'regular' transport of Jews" because "the Führer," allegedly, "had ordered the Umschichtung, the deportation of 300,000 Jews from the Altreich and the Ostmark to come first."[33] Gauleiter Wagner's office received Eichmann deportation plans enthusiastically, for Wagner had already planned "to round up the Jews of his Gau without further delay and to have the Staatspolizei drive them beyond Kraków." He pledged Eichmann his full support in organizing the Katowice deportations.[34]

At that time the organizers still did not know where to direct the trains. Eichmann and Stahlecker flew from Ostrava to Kraków on October 12 to locate a suitable place for the planned camp. The plan was "to fly from there to Warsaw and then continue to the area under consideration by car, a Mercedes and a Lancia, which were to follow them to Warsaw."[35] In addition to locating a suitable area for the camp, Stahlecker and Eichmann's scouting expedition helped them explore the availability of housing and foodstuffs, railroad lines, and a station suitable to serve as the terminal point for the transports. Which authorities Stahlecker and Eichmann contacted in Galicia in the course of the next days remains unknown. On October 15, Eichmann's telex from Kraków to Ostrava announced: "Railway station for transports is Niesko [sic] on the river San. Will arrive in Ostrava today Sunday."[36]

Eichmann hastened from Ostrava to Vienna for a meeting on Monday, October 16, at the Zentralstelle with Dr. Karl Ebner of the Vienna Gestapo and Dr. Becker, a staff member of Reichskommissar Bürckel's office. He was assured that he would receive "all necessary authorizations from Bürckel personally."[37] Bürckel, he was told, had asked for an accelerated deportation schedule for Vienna and had been "more than pleased" that the deportations rendered superfluous the plans for erecting such a camp for Jews in the Ostmark; that was because construction costs would have amounted to 500 Reichsmark per person.

One of the main concerns of the assembled gentlemen in preparing these deportations was to keep the property that the Viennese Jews would leave behind from falling into the hands of greedy Aryans. Dr. Ebner emphasized "that especially the wild Aryanization of apartments and all other property had to be nipped in the bud to avoid a repetition of the situation in November,"[38] the savage lootings by Vienna's antisemites during the November pogroms of 1938, which a year later were obviously still haunting the memories of National Socialist administrators. They agreed that it might be possible to organize two deportation transports per week "with 1,000 Jews each." The first was to leave Vienna on Friday, October 20, 1939, at 10 PM from the Aspang Rail Station.

At that time the Kultusgemeinde was still saddled with the responsibility of setting up the lists of 1,000 to 1,200 "émigrés," as well as their notification and assembly for transport.[39] The Kultusgemeinde also had been directed to send out the following announcement:

> To the Jewish Population:
>
> The Zentralstelle für Jüdische Auswanderung in Vienna has instructed the Israelite Community to carry out the planned resettlement of Austrian Jews to Poland. According to information the Community has received from the best-informed sources, Jews emigrating to the designated area in Poland will be able to settle there wherever they wish, work, and build new lives for themselves without constraints. Temporary housing and food will be provided. Representatives of Jewish organizations will be on hand to provide assistance upon their arrival.[40]

The mass expulsion of Roma and Sinti that Heydrich had mentioned in the September 21, 1939, meeting in Berlin also was dealt with in connection to the Nisko project.

SS-Oberführer Artur Nebe, the head of the Reichskriminalpolizeiamt, the Reich Criminal Police, had called Eichmann to find out "when he could send the Berlin Gypsies."[41] Eichmann's October 16, 1939, telex to Nebe suggested attaching railcars filled with Gypsies to the trains transporting Jews. Additionally, he provided up-to-date information about deportations of Jews from the Ostmark, the Protectorate, and the Altreich – plans and dimensions soon to be contradicted by reality:

> Regarding transport Gypsies, this is to inform you that on Friday, October 20, the first transport [with Viennese Jews] departs from Vienna. To this transport, 3 to 4 cars of Gypsies can be attached. For the time being, transports are now leaving on a regular basis from Vienna for Austria, Ostrova for the Protectorate, and Katowice for the formerly Polish territories.

Because Eichmann was still convinced that the transports would take place as regularly as clockwork, he promised "flawless execution of this matter."[42] Deportations from the Altreich were to begin within three or four weeks.

The first transport of more than 900 men left Ostrava on October 18, 1939.[43] Two days later, as Eichmann had announced, a train from Vienna followed. Nine hundred and twelve men had gathered on October 20 at Aspang Station, guarded by a detachment of the Vienna Schutzpolizei, the Viennese Municipal Police (Schupos), and SS men. Unwieldy luggage was loaded into the baggage cars; two cars were filled with construction equipment furnished by the Kultusgemeinde. En route the SS men exchanged the deportees' Reichsmark for złotys but not at the official rate of 1–2 but of 1–1.5. During the journey the police apparently behaved fairly decently. Individual SS men, as one of the deportees reported in a letter written in January 1940, "were even friendly for a change."[44]

Upon arrival in Nisko this treatment changed instantly. Except for hand luggage and backpacks, the deportees received none of their luggage. Some had to surrender their pocket watches and chains to the SS; others were kicked and were slapped in the face. They were lined up four abreast and driven to the uncompleted camp in a five-hour foot march. Whenever elderly or sick men asked to rest or could not keep up, the "SS men kicked and beat them until they were lying helplessly in the filth of the road. What happened to them later I do not know. . . . The Viennese Schupos also changed their tune and turned vicious."[45] When they reached a soggy meadow near the village of Zarzecze where deportees from Ostrava, guarded by SS with loaded rifles, were constructing barracks, the deportees from Vienna were herded together. Workmen had to step forward and were marched into the camp. Most of the rest, the majority of the Viennese Jews, were chased off by the SS, the police, and military personnel, toward the River San near the Soviet border.

> Suddenly the front row of the group, guided by the SS whose number kept increasing along the way, turned into a huge meadow. . . . The rain came down harder and harder. I can't describe precisely what happened next because we endured hours of extreme panic and uncertainty. Suddenly the SS started shooting, screaming, "see to it that you get out of here. One hour from now anyone still within five kilometers of here in any direction will be shot. The same will happen to anyone daring to return to Nisko. Get over there to your Red brothers".[46]

Other transports from Katowice and the next one from Vienna were handled in similar fashion.[47] Only about 200 of the 1,600 men in the two Vienna transports were moved into the camp. The majority were driven away and left to their fate.[48]

The camp near Zarzecze was initially administered by Theo Dannecker. Among others, Vienna Zentralstelle members such as Alfred Slawik, Anton

Zita, and Ernst Brückler joined him to serve as SS guards. Dr. Rajakowitsch was there allegedly to censor the deportees' letters.[49] The roughly 600 men incarcerated there had to erect barracks, fences, and other installations and build roads and ditches. They were returned to Vienna and Ostrava only after this Gesamtaktion, collective action, was discontinued in April 1940.

The Discontinuation of the Deportations

On October 19 the SD-Hauptamt sent telegrams to Vienna and Ostrava announcing that by order of SS-Oberführer Müller the "resettlement and deportation of Poles and Jews into the territory of the future Polish rump state" needed "centralized direction," on account of which permission from that agency would have to be secured.[50] When Rolf Günther checked back with Regierungsrat Hermann on October 20, he learned that "based on the directive from the Reichssicherheitshauptamt . . . all transports of Jews would have to stop."[51] Even the planned second transport from Ostrava, supposedly already agreed upon by Eichmann and Müller, was cancelled; however, the organizers of expulsion did not give up that readily. On October 24, Eichmann instructed his employees in Ostrava to halt the "redeployment" of Jews from the Protectorate. Because preparations for the next transport were essentially complete and Jews who had tried to escape from Ostrava had been arrested, he authorized a partial transport of 400 men "to save the prestige of the local state police."[52]

After the second deportation transport of roughly 670 men on October 26, the Vienna Zentralstelle also tried to maintain the original plan of additional expulsions to Galicia and instructed the Kultusgemeinde accordingly. When Dr. Löwenherz mentioned resistance within the Jewish community, Eichmann lied without compunction: The Jews would enjoy complete freedom of movement within the Nisko area; they would be able to settle there and establish new livelihoods. The Nuremberg Laws would not apply there. Eichmann even pretended to permit journalists and representatives of foreign organizations to inspect this colony founded on and governed by humane principles.[53]

A Berlin Gestapa telex that reached the Zentralstelle on October 28, 1939, clarifies why the deportations were discontinued. SS-Oberführer Müller reported that the Oberkommando of the Wehrmacht had, in fact, not prohibited all transports into the area south of Lublin until mid-November. It would still be possible to accommodate deportation transports of Viennese Jews "to the extent that they did not interfere with prisoner transports." Because such a schedule could not be arranged from Berlin, Müller recommended contacting the army transport authority directly from Vienna. Alois Brunner's inquiries, however, made it clear that "the movement of several army divisions from the east to the west . . . precludes scheduling any transports of Jews from Vienna."[54] Even the partial transport from Ostrava that Eichmann had authorized did not reach Nisko but came to a stop shortly after crossing the Czech border near Katowice, where the deportees were interned.[55]

For the moment the ambitious deportation goals of the SS and civilian administrative organizations had failed. They had been making tremendous efforts to expel tens of thousands of people as quickly as possible into Poland or across the border into the Soviet Union. Eichmann and his men were acting in cooperation with the politically responsible agencies of the various countries involved. All of the participatory organizations had obviously been waiting to start the organized mass expulsion of Jews or, as in Nebe's case, the expulsion of the Roma and Sinti.

Eichmann's superiors had reason to be satisfied with his activities. He had gone into high gear; he and his apparatus had taken the initiative within the parameters of the assigned task. They had succeeded in tearing thousands of people from their moorings without attracting undue attention, fooling them with fraudulent tales of retraining camps and "free settlement," and maneuvering them into a transit camp in Galicia or, more accurately, driving them across the German–Soviet line of demarcation. By accomplishing all that, in the eyes of their SS superiors Eichmann and his men had gained status as skillful organizers and so had qualified themselves to carry out further, even more ambitious assignments. They were ready to climb the next rung of the career ladder. Just a few weeks after the failure of additional deportations to Nisko, Eichmann was appointed head of RSHA Referat IV D 4; Rolf Günther accompanied him to Berlin as his deputy.

The collapse of the far-reaching deportation plans was not the consequence of resistance on the part of the General Governor Hans Frank[56] or his deputy, Arthur Seyß-Inquart,[57] but of logistics. Not enough trains were available, and Wehrmacht transports had priority. Lack of cooperation among the SS, Wehrmacht, and Reichsbahn also inhibited the fledging deportation machinery. It faltered, then came to a standstill, because its cogs did not yet mesh.

Yet even after the failure of the rapid expulsion of Austrian Jews to Poland or the Soviet Union, the organizations involved in this scheme in Vienna did not abandon their calls for further measures. In a memorandum, Dr. Becker from Gauleiter Bürckel's staff informed Regierungspresident (Regional Commissioner) Barth about a meeting with Hauptsturmführer Eichmann of the Zentralstelle für jüdische Auswanderung, in the course of which Eichmann announced the interruption of the "emigration action to Poland" until

February of the following year. Until then, however, Eichmann would step up "the regular emigration of Jews, which presently involves about 2,500 persons monthly." He already had received the go-ahead from appropriate authorities in Berlin and also had dealt with the Vienna Kultusgemeinde. "Mr. Eichmann hopes that by referring to the February reactivation of the Poland-related actions he will be able to increase emigration once again to 4,000, even 5,000 persons per month."[58]

The deportations to Nisko had been terminated after the first few transports, and so the goal of the concerned authorities – the expulsion of all Jews from Vienna and the Protectorate – had not been reached. Still, the SD focused on "resettlements," a method of achieving the Endlösung. More, they inspired visions of a world solution. In mid-December "the Endlösung of the Jewish Question in Germany" was the subject of intense debate at Eichmann's former place of employment, the SD-Hauptamt Referat II-112, at that time on the verge of being reorganized.[59] One of the issues was where to settle the Jews, whether there was to be a *Reservat*, a reservation for Jews in Poland, or whether they were simply to be sent to the future Generalgouvernement in Poland. A reservation was to be administered by Jews in order to reduce the need for German civil servants. Only the top positions would be filled by Germans. It was also considered appropriate for such a reservation to "remain under the supervision of the Sicherheitspolizei until the resettlement of Jews from Reichsgebiet, Ostmark, and the Protectorate Bohemia and Moravia was completed." A final decision "whether 'regular' Jewish emigration should continue even with the establishment of a reservation" was considered imperative because its existence, in terms of foreign policy, might be "a means of putting pressure on the Western powers and at the end of the war provide opportunities for raising the question of a World Solution to the Jewish Problem."

These points of the December 1939 debate in Referat II-112 concerning the "final solution of the Jewish Problem in Germany" later constituted the core of the strategies that would dominate the internal discussions and plans of National Socialist and government authorities in charge of carrying out antisemitic policies. The plans of 1940 shifted the possible location of a Jewish reservation, with so-called self-government under supervision of the Sicherheitspolizei, from Poland to Madagascar; Dannecker and Eichmann were heavily involved in working out the details. In 1940–1941, deportations of Jews into the Generalgouvernement did take place, organized by the newly established RSHA Referat IV D 4, directed by Adolf Eichmann.

3   The Development and Initial Activities of Referat IV D 4

In the autumn of 1939 the expulsion of Jews by the SS was carried out as ethnic cleansing within the framework of National Socialist Volkstumspolitik (racial and national policies).[1] Himmler had been appointed Reichskommissar für die Festigung des deutschen Volktums (Reich Commissioner for the Strengthening of Germandom) in October 1939.[2] One of his first directives in that capacity concerned population resettlements in conquered Poland. On October 30 he ordered that between November 1939 and February 1940 the following mass transports were to take place:

1. All Jews from the former Polish, now Reich German, provinces and areas
2. All Congress Poles from the province of Gdansk (Danzig), West Prussia
3. A still-to-be-determined number of especially hostile Polish population from the provinces of Poznań (Posen), South and East Prussia, as well as Upper Silesia.

Together the leaders of the Higher SS and Police Vistula, Warthe, Northeast, Southeast, and East – the Generalgouvernement (German-occupied Poland) – were to design plans for resettlement and were to take responsibility for "emigration and transport" in their respective areas. "The Polish administration or, rather, the 'self-administration,'" was to take charge of housing those who had been expelled.[3] Such a monstrous program that would have affected hundreds of thousands of people – the Polish Jews themselves in these areas now annexed to Germany and referred to in category 1 numbered about half a million – could not be carried out, especially within four months and in the absence of a yet-to-be-established SS and police administration.[4]

Nevertheless, various SS leaders in the annexed Polish areas started to carry out Directive 1/II.[5] Wilhelm Koppe, the SS and Police leader in the Warthegau, devised a plan for the forceful evacuation of 200,000 Poles and 100,000 Jews into areas around Warsaw and Lublin between mid-November 1939 and the end of February 1940.[6] By the end of November, Heydrich reduced immediate expulsions by establishing a long-range plan (*Fernplan*) and a short-range plan (*Nahplan*). The latter applied exclusively to the Warthegau and called for "the transport of as many Poles and Jews as necessary to facilitate the settlement of incoming ethnic Germans from the Baltic region." Within the first half of December, 80,000 Jews and Poles were to be "transported to the General-gouvernement to free up the area."[7]

Even as late as November, before the arrival of the first transports, Hans Frank, the Governor General of the Generalgouvernement into whose realm these hundreds of thousands were to be moved, still considered resettlement of expelled Poles and Jews a manageable task. He was convinced that he could turn the Generalgouvernement into a huge area of concentration. From the very outset of his rule in the Generalgouvernement, he minced no words about the racist strategies he envisioned in the wake of such a concentration:

> 2.5 to 3 million Poles and Jews – they are not used to living cleanly and in an orderly fashion.... The winter will be rough. When there is no bread for the Poles, I don't want to hear any complaints.... Short shrift with the Jews. A pleasure to take physical measures against the Jewish race at last. The more who die, the better.... The Jews are to feel that we have arrived. We want to have between half to three-fourth of all Jews east of the Vistula. We will oppress them wherever we can. Everything is at stake here. The Jews from the Reich, Vienna, everywhere – Jews in the Reich – we have no more use for them.[8]

Clearly, Frank too advanced the idea of gathering Jews in areas east of the Vistula, the same area already under consideration in the vague plans about a Judenreservat.

As did Frank, other rulers in the newly founded Generalgouvernement also strove to produce an increased mortality rate for Jews, for the establishment of a reservation for Jews not only demanded plans for accommodations but also inspired deliberate efforts to create the worst possible living conditions for the deportees. For example, during a November 1939 inspection tour with Seyß-Inquart, the Deputy Governor of the Generalgouvernement, SS-Brigadeführer (Brigadier General) Friedrich Schmidt, argued that the area along the line of demarcation at the River San "because of its swamps, could serve as a reservation, a choice more than likely to produce a notable reduction of Jews."[9]

The first measures of expulsion simultaneously designed to create space for the resettlement of Volksdeutsche went into effect under such ominous portents. In December 1939 the SS in the Warthegau, in cooperation with local mayors and government administrators, carried out Heydrich's first Nahplan.

According to a report from an SS office in Posen, 87,883 "resettlers" were transported into the Generalgouvernement. The Reichsbahn's train schedules broke down, however, due to personnel and technical shortfalls within the Ostbahn, the eastern railroad, while administrative offices in the Generalgouvernement experienced disruptions in communication systems and other problems.[10] The persons being resettled suffered the consequences of such poorly improvised conditions, a fact even German government officials in charge of receiving these resettlers were quick to point out. Because men, women, children, and the old and frail had been confined to unheated cattle cars in the fierce cold for days on end without food and sometimes without water, frostbite and disease were rampant. People died en route; thousands more required medical care upon arrival.[11]

From the point of view of the organizers, large-scale resettlements required central coordination of the expulsions and joint transport scheduling with the Reichsbahn. To provide it, Heydrich established in the RSHA a separate Referat designated Räumungsangelegenheiten (Evacuation Affairs). On December 21, 1939, Heydrich wrote the commanders and inspectors of the Sicherheitspolizei and the SD and the Higher-SS and Police leaders Krakau, Posen (Posnań), Breslau, Danzig, and Königsberg. Under the heading "Evacuations in the Eastern Provinces," he informed them that during a meeting two days earlier, the centralized handling of the duties of the Sicherheitspolizei in carrying out the evacuations in the East had been decided. He had appointed SS-Hauptsturmführer Eichmann as his Special Section Chief in the RSHA Referat IV, and SS-Hauptsturmführer Rolf Günther as Eichmann's deputy.[12]

This Referat initiated its activities with an early January 1940 meeting chaired by Eichmann. Officials of Sicherheitsdienst Inspectorate in the integrated Polish territories and representatives of the Ministries of Economics, Transportation, Finance, and the Treuhandstelle Ost (Trusteeship East) were in attendance.[13] Between reports about the horrific conditions during "evacuations," they discussed Himmler's orders for the expulsion of all Jews from the annexed Polish territories. The officials of the Inspectorate supplied the numbers for "the immediate evacuation of Jews: from the Northeast 30,000, from the Southeast 120,000–125,000, from the Warthegau (Łódź/Litzmannstadt) 200,000." Additionally, 80,000 Poles were to be expelled from the Warthegau immediately "to make room for Volksdeutsche, ethnic Germans from Galicia and Volhynia." Other discussion concerned technical regulations regarding topics such as transport escorts, the range of persons to be expelled, provisions, and related matters. No starting date for the evacuations could be set because railroad loading stations for departure and receiving stations in the Generalgouvernement had not yet been determined. RSHA officials wanted to work up an evacuation plan (Räumungsplan). Eichmann's Referat staff, who inspected the locations affected by these evacuations, reported on recurring problems, as did SS-Hauptscharführer Seidl at a meeting with Eichmann, Rolf Günther, and Dr. Rajakowitsch on January 22 and 23, 1940, in Posen about the obstacles in devising a train schedule.[14]

Simultaneously, German government agencies in the Generalgouvernement protested the practice of mass deportations ever more vehemently. They no longer wanted to accept into the areas under their jurisdiction tens of thousands of people who owned nothing but what they could carry. Yet, in January 1940, Heydrich still thought he could ignore objections from the Generalgouvernement by ascribing them to negligible technical difficulties. He was convinced that, with the establishment of Referat IV D 4 for central regulation of matters related to evacuations, these misgivings would lose their justification.[15] He was still set on the idea that 40,000 Poles and Jews, for the benefit of Baltic Germans, and 120,000 Poles, for the benefit of the Volhynian Germans, soon would be deported to the Generalgouvernement. He also was determined that the expulsions of all Jews of the new eastern Gaue, and of 30,000 Gypsies from the entire Reich, were to follow. The planned expulsion of 1,000 German Jews from Stettin was mentioned in passing; their apartments supposedly were urgently needed due to wartime economic conditions.[16]

By the beginning of January, local offices in Stettin had ordered the Jews to relinquish their flats and to gather in an empty warehouse. Through the intervention of the Reichsvereinigung der Juden in Deutschland this measure had been prevented at literally the last moment.[17] In mid-February, however, the deportation of these 1,200 or so persons was initiated. The SS showed no mercy. In the middle of the night they drove men, women, old people and children from their apartments or retirement homes and escorted them to the freight depot. Each person could only take a small valise and 20 złoty. Cash, valuables, household equipment, and food had to be left behind. The deportees also had to sign a "Certificate of Relinquishment."[18] After being transported to Lublin by rail, they had to march in the freezing cold for more than twenty kilometers on snow-covered country roads to Piaski, Glusk, and Belcye. The exertion of the march claimed about seventy victims, mainly old people and small children. Because of their lack of resources, these deportees endured particularly poor shelter in barns and stables; lack of food and medicine raised the number of dead to 230 within a month.[19]

The expulsions provoked ever-increasing criticism from civilian administrative offices in the Generalgouvernement. For administrative reasons Governor General Frank now objected as well. In February 1940 the deportations into the Generalgouvernement led to conflicts among the top officials of the Third Reich. In a meeting on the topic of Ostfragen (Eastern matters) in mid-February 1940, attended by Himmler, Lutz Schwerin von Krosigk, Frank, and Warthegau Reichsstatthalter (Reich Provincial Governor) Arthur Greiser, Göring explained that the Generalgouvernement would have to accept the "orderly emigration of Jews from Germany and the new Eastern Gaue," provided the transport trains were registered with Frank in an orderly and timely fashion.[20] Frank objected, pointing out that the current method of resettlement had made reconstruction of orderly, comprehensible administration impossible. Even a reduced resettlement plan would demand a solution to the problem of provisions. Himmler, on the other hand, in his role of Reichskommissar für die Festigung des deutschen Volkstums, wanted to create space for 70,000 Baltic Germans and 130,000 Volhynian Germans. For the benefit of the latter, "Polish peasants in Posen, West Prussia, and southern East Prussia would have to be resettled in the course of the current year."[21] He claimed to have postponed the transfer of 40,000 Germans from Lithuania, 80,000–100,000 from Bukovina (northern Romania), and 100,000–130,000 from Bessarabia (southwestern Ukraine). In exchange, approximately 30,000 Germans from the Lublin area east of the Vistula designated for the Judenreservat would have to be transferred to the new eastern Gaue. He was confident he would have no trouble reaching an agreement with Frank on methods concerning future "evacuations."

Obviously, at that time Himmler still had not abandoned the plan of setting up a "Jewish reservation" in Galicia east of the Vistula. None of the top representatives of the occupation administrative organizations present at Göring's conference protested. Nevertheless, a month later the plans to create a reservation in Galicia and to direct mass deportations to the Generalgouvernement had turned into waste paper, at least for the time being. Himmler and Frank had not reached consensus. In a decree dated March 23, 1940, Göring, probably in response to urging from Frank, prohibited all evacuations until further notice.[22] For the moment his directive rendered most of Himmler's and Heydrich's originally wide-reaching expulsion orders as well as step-by-step reductions of the "evacuation orders" unrealizable. During the following months only limited resettlements benefiting Volksdeutsche could be carried out.

Warthegau Reichsstatthalter Greiser, pointing out the "temporary" status of the Łódź Ghetto, sought special permission to secure the evacuation of its Jews to the Generalgouvernement, but also failed. The establishment of that ghetto in December 1939 was to serve as a transitional step, primarily designed to "cleanse" the entire city of Jews, as Regierungspräsident Friedrich Uebelhör phrased it. The aim was to "cauterize the entire canker."[23] Through this development, however, the ghetto in Łódź/Litzmannstadt, "the transitional device for concentration to facilitate speedy expulsion," turned into a lasting establishment where hundreds of thousands were crammed together in steadily worsening conditions and pressed into forced labor.[24]

So before the newly established Referat IV D 4 could even design its extensive "evacuation" plans and translate them into action, its sphere of activities had been drastically curtailed. Rather than removing hundreds of thousands of people from the newly occupied eastern Gaue, Eichmann's section expelled just a limited number of "Aussiedler" who had to make room for Baltic and Volhynian Germans moving into the Generalgouvernement. In February 1940 a few deportations, labeled "transports of Jews and Poles," from the Warthegau to the Generalgouvernement had been carried out.[25] In early March administrative organizations in the Generalgouvernement had contacted Eichmann, asking that each "evacuee" bring food for at least eight days. Eichmann forwarded this request to the Aussiedlerdienststelle (resettlement office) in Posen, arguing, "in this instance those to be expelled were peasants able to supply their own foodstuffs from their farms."[26] Between the beginning of 1940 and mid-March approximately 40,000 people were deported from Gau Wartheland to the Generalgouvernement. Then the pace slowed even more.[27]

Beginning in April 1940 those field offices of Referat IV D 4 in charge of organizing resettlements in Posen and Łódź were referred to as Umwanderungszentralstellen. SS-Sturmbannführer Albert Rapp directed the Umwanderungszentralstelle in Posen until early summer of 1940; after that, SS-Untersturmführer Siegfried Seidl took over and soon after that, SS-Hauptsturmführer Rolf-Heinz Höppner. The field office in Łódź was directed by SS-Obersturmbannführer Hermann Krumey. Also tied to Eichmann's expulsion apparatus was another official in charge of evacuation of Poles and Jews, in the office of the Inspector of the Sicherheitspolizei and the SD-Danzig: he was SS-Hauptsturmführer Franz Abromeit.

In the course of 1940 this apparatus carried out several resettlement operations. Some 12,000 Poles from the administrative district of Zichenau in Danzig-West Prussia, for example, were to be expelled.[28] That summer, Eichmann sent Himmler's order to "free at least 1,000 'hearths' per week for Germans from Volhynia."[29] To settle German peasant families from Galicia, 20,000 Poles from the Saybusch district in eastern Silesia were to be evacuated in August.[30] All deportations were conducted by rail and routed via Łódź/Litzmannstadt to the Generalgouvernement. Telegrams from Łódź to the RSHA Referat IV D 4 served as confirmation and final report about each deportation train. A December 17 telex, for example, reported under the heading "Transport of Poles – Lithuanian Operation" that train 3145 carrying 957 Jews had arrived in Łódź/Litzmannstadt on December 17, 1940, at 5 AM and after inspection left for its final destination of Lukow [in the Generalgouvernement] at 6 AM. This transport would probably conclude this operation for the remainder of the year. The foodstuffs provided for this transport in Soldau [Danzig-West Prussia] amounted to: sausage 500 kilograms, bread 1,000 kilograms, legumes 200 kilograms.[31]

Altogether, about 17,000 people from Upper Silesia and 30,000 from Danzig-West Prussia were deported to the Generalgouvernement in 1940.[32]

In the Shadow of the "Madagascar Plan"

In addition to directing RSHA Referat IV D 4, Eichmann also supervised all Zentralstellen and Jewish organizations in the Altreich, the Ostmark, and the Protectorate. He frequently traveled to Vienna and Prague, where Alois Brunner and Hans Günther were responsible for the activities of the Zentralstellen. During the first six months of 1940, the Reichszentrale at Berlin Kurfürstenstraße was managed mainly by Theo Dannecker. Sometimes Eichmann ordered the representatives of the reorganized Jewish organizations in Vienna, Prague, and Berlin to appear in Berlin to receive their instructions, as he did, for example, in March 1940. On that occasion he pushed for increased emigration by threatening resettlement.[33]

The Wehrmacht's attack in the West in May 1940 in violation of the neutrality of the Netherlands, Belgium, and Luxembourg had resulted in the collapse of France, which led to the north of the country being ruled by a German military government while the southern part of France was governed by the collaborationist regime of Marshal Philippe Pétain. With the occupation of France the idea of deporting European Jews to the island of Madagascar – until then merely a notional prospect of the Nazi leadership – now attained relevance.[34]

In the summer of 1940 vague concepts of a Jewish reservation on that island became the subject of preparatory studies coordinated by Franz Rademacher, Secretary of the Auswärtige Amt (Foreign Office), and Eichmann or Dannecker at the RSHA.[35] By early June, Rademacher, the director of the AA-Referat D III (responsible for "The Jewish Question," race policies, and keeping German embassies abroad informed of important domestic political developments), had composed a paper delineating the "work and responsibilities" of his Referat, elaborating on the question "Where to put the Jews?"[36] He envisioned as one war aim the removal of all Jews from the continent of Europe or making use of the Ostjuden, the Jews of Eastern Europe, as pawns against the Jews of America and to remove only Westjuden, Western European Jews, "for instance to Madagascar." Reich Foreign Minister Joachim von Ribbentrop endorsed expulsions on principle. In talks with Italy's Duce, Benito Mussolini, Hitler intimated the nature of the plan[37] and by July, General Governor Frank and Reichsstatthalter Greiser were informed as well. Greiser, however, even then voiced doubts about its feasibility, pointing out that Jewish expulsions to designated areas overseas depended on the cessation of hostilities. He, on the other hand, "in the interest of the Warthegau, somehow" had "to solve the Jewish Problem before the onset of winter" and, therefore, proposed a temporary solution in the event of a protracted war – that is, expulsion into the Generalgouvernement.[38]

In June, Heydrich learned of the deliberations in the Auswärtige Amt and approached Ribbentrop with a letter to remind him that he was in charge of issues concerning Jewish emigration. He made it clear that to resolve the totality of the problem – about three and a quarter million Jews in territories now under German jurisdiction – emigration no longer provided a solution and, therefore, a "territorial final solution" was called for. He asked to be included to any future discussions on the topic of the "Final Solution of the Jewish Question."[39] The phrase "territorial final solution" evidences that in the summer of 1940 Heydrich understood "Final Solution of the Jewish Question" to mean the deportation of Jews and their internment in a Reservat. In response to Heydrich's request, Ribbentrop ordered the plans being developed in the Auswärtige Amt to be handled in cooperation with the appropriate departments of the RSHA, and Rademacher complied. He notified RSHA Referat IV D 4 of his preparatory work, which dealt mainly with issues of foreign policy as, for instance, proposals for the cession of Madagascar as part of a peace treaty with France, converting the island into a German mandate.[40]

At the RSHA, plans were also in the making. The leaders of the Jewish communities of Prague and Vienna as well as of the Reichsvereinigung der Juden in Deutschland had been summoned to Berlin for a meeting on July 3, 1940. There, Eichmann declared that at the end of the war "a total solution to the European Jewish Question probably" would have to be sought. About four million were to be "settled" in a country he did not describe in any detail. He charged the representatives of these Jewish organizations with compiling a report that was to gather all considerations necessary for the realization of such a plan.[41] Based on the experiences that the Zentralstellen had gained (including the Nisko operation) on the reservation plans that had been developed as early as December 1939 at Referat II-112, as well as on the information demanded from the officials of the Kultusgemeinden, Eichmann, Dannecker, and Rajakowitsch prepared a fourteen-page detailed report elaborating on the

Madagascar Project. Dannecker sent it to his "dear comrade" Rademacher in the Auswärtige Amt on August 15, 1940.[42]

While the Auswärtige Amt and the RSHA projected designs for a kind of "final solution," German authorities in the formerly French parts of Alsace and Lorraine that were now incorporated into the German Reich initiated expulsion programs reminiscent of earlier events in occupied Poland. Robert Wagner and Josef Bürckel, Gauleiters of neighboring Reich Gau of Baden and of the Palatinate (Pfalz), respectively, had been appointed to head the civilian administration in Alsace and Lorraine. One of their tasks was to "Germanize" these new territories.[43] Consequently, on July 16 all the Jews of Colmar had been assembled in front of the police station and transported across the line of demarcation into France. Approximately 3,000 Alsatian Jews were deported to unoccupied France.[44] Between mid-July and mid-September 1940 approximately 25,000 French citizens were expelled from Lorraine, all its Jews among them.[45] In August local NSDAP organizations in Kehl and Breisach, on their own initiative, loaded German Jews from both cities onto trucks and drove them across the border. Through the intervention of the Reichsvereinigung der Juden in Deutschland at least some of those expelled were able to return shortly afterward. These activities on the part of subordinate party organizations anticipated the broadly conceived mass deportations from Baden and Saarpfalz, preparations for which began in the early fall. Through the joint efforts of Gauleiters, regional Gestapo organizations, and RSHA Referat IV D 4, about 70,000 Jews from Baden and Saarpfalz were shipped in nine transport trains to the unoccupied part of France, where they were interned in camps such as Gurs, Rivesaltes, and Les Milles.[46] Similar to what had happened in Vienna in the autumn of 1939, these deportations into the unoccupied part of France apparently were based on the cooperation of local, regional, and central Nazi authorities. As in the Ostmark, some clever Volksgenossen in Baden were also keen on acquiring Jewish property, goods, and housing in accordance with the motto "They won't ever come back."[47] Whereas in the summer of 1940, Nazi experts had plotted to deport four million Jews in connection with the Madagascar Plan, by December 1940, Eichmann envisioned in a memo for Himmler the removal of 5.8 million Jews "from the European economic sphere of the German people to a territory yet to be determined."[48]

Deportations from Vienna in the Beginning of 1941

As did Greiser, other leading National Socialists also did not want to await the end of the war to remove the Jews from their sphere of power. One of the first who tried to restart deportations to the Generalgouvernement through a direct appeal to Hitler was Bürckel's successor in the Ostmark, the new Reichsstatthalter Baldur von Schirach. On October 2, 1940, the after-dinner conversation in Hitler's apartment turned to the situation in the General- gouvernement. Governor Frank reported that the "activity in the General- gouvernement can be described as successful. The Jews in Warsaw and other cities now are isolated in ghettos. Kraków soon will be 'clean' of Jews."[49] At that point Schirach joined the conversation, and a ghastly discussion ensued. Schirach remarked that in Vienna he still had 50,000 Jews whom Dr. Frank needed to take off his hands. According to Frank, this was impossible. Gauleiter Erich Koch then pointed out that he, too, had not yet expelled either Poles or Jews from the Ziechenau area. Certainly these Jews and Poles had to be absorbed by the Generalgouvernement now. Frank protested this demand as well. He emphasized the impossibility of accepting such numbers of Poles and Jews because no shelters whatsoever were available. No decisions were made on that occasion though Hitler elaborated on his thoughts concerning Poland. To him the population density in the Generalgouvernement was of no conse- quence whatsoever. Its function was to be that of a central labor procurement office. He did not go into detail about the fate of the Jews but had laid its foundation.

A letter dated December 3, 1940, from the Chief of the Reich Chancellery informed Schirach of Hitler's approval of deportations from Vienna. According to Schirach's report, Hitler had decided "that, to ease Vienna's severe housing shortage, the 60,000 Jews still living in the Reichsgau Vienna should be expelled into the Generalgouvernement with all due speed while the war still is in progress."[50]

In January 1941, the scheme to deport 60,000 Jews from Vienna became part of Heydrich's "short-range plan 3," which in addition to the deportations from Vienna stipulated the evacuations of, for the most part, gentile Poles. This was to make room for the settlement of ethnic Germans and for projected military training camps in preparation for launching the war against the Soviet Union. During the January 8 meeting Heydrich explained to leading occupa- tion functionaries that "Nahplan 3" during 1941 intended to evacuate in toto more than 800,000 persons to the Generalgouvernement – in the first stage, 240,000 persons from Poland, and 10,000 from Vienna before the end of April 1941.[51]

The renewed deportations from Vienna beginning in February 1941 were organized in such a way that the persons whom the Zentralstelle targeted for resettlement in the Generalgouvernement had to appear in a so-called

collection camp housed in a former school at Castellezgasse 35 and, beginning in the fall of 1941, at Sperlgasse 2a and Malzgasse 16. These were their
instructions:

> Any amount of cash may be brought along. An official of the Reichsbank
> will... exchange each person's Reichsmarks into złotys. Every Jew selected for
> emigration is to prepare and submit a complete list of his assets, property rights,
> and entitlements.... The proceeds from their sale are earmarked for defraying
> the expenses of emigration and resettlement and the definitive solution of the
> Jewish Problem.[52]

The Kultusgemeinde was responsible for furnishing the internees with rations
in the collection camps and during transport. Those selected for deportation
were notified in writing. Sometimes people were picked up by SS men accompanied by members of the Erhebungsdienst, an organization formed by the
Kultusgemeinde to gather the Jews into the collection camps.[53]

After approximately 5,000 Viennese had been deported to Polish small
towns, such as Opole and Kielce in February and March 1941, the organizers
halted the transports.[54] But why were the deportations discontinued?

Although the highest civil and military authorities had been present and
had raised no objections at Heydrich's January 8 conference, already in February 1941 the quartermaster staff officer of Army Group B in occupied Poland
had second thoughts about the "resettlement of Jews and Poles" to the
Generalgouvernement.[55] In a letter to the Army High Command, the staff
officer acknowledged having knowledge of Hitler's order to "resettle Jews and
Poles," which had been communicated at Heydrich's conference. Nevertheless, he wanted to report about problems that continually had arisen. In one
example, he mentioned 700 Jewish deportees who, because of lack of proper
accommodation in the village, had to be housed in a synagogue. Because several cases of typhus had occurred, the officer worried that the epidemic could
spread to the Wehrmacht soldiers in garrison. In principle he blamed the SS
resettlement functionaries for not informing the military authorities in advance
and demanded precise schedules for all resettlement trains. The Quartermaster
General of the Army High Command seized upon the suggestion and deemed
a change of the current status of uncoordinated resettlement transports "an
urgent military necessity."[56] If the further deployment of troops to the Generalgouvernement should proceed according to plans, a new decision of Hitler's
(Führerentscheid) "must be effectuated in a short time." It is unclear whether
Hitler was really confronted with the objections, but the pent-up concerns
had to be met at the medium level. As the pressure to prioritize the military

build-up was growing in March, a conference to bring together all agencies involved in processing resettlement issues in the Generalgouvernement – civilian and military administrators as well as SS officers – was scheduled.

At this conference, which took place in Posen on March 14, 1941, Eberhard Westerkamp (head of the department of interior of the civil administration of the Generalgouvernement), Colonel Goertz (army railway transport officer), and Major Gericke (quartermaster staff officer of Army Group B) declined with various arguments to accept further transports of Poles and Jews to the Generalgouvernement.[57] Adolf Eichmann, as representative of the SS resettlement branch, gave an overview concerning the status of the deportations. Although he conceded that new priorities had brought about the halt of all settlement transports in the German Reich, he tried to insist on implementing "transports of 5,000 Jews from Vienna and a further 4,000 Jews already concentrated in camps." Eichmann's proposals were dismissed immediately. Major Gericke insisted that he had "regrettably to take up an unconditionally negative position" ("unbedingt ablehnenden Standpunkt"); the transport officer seconded that refusal. Finally the conferees agreed upon accepting two transports already en route and a cessation of all deportations as of March 16 "for the time being." The results of the conference were communicated to main agencies by telex.[58]

On March 15, Eichmann's superior, Heinrich Müller of the RSHA, notified the Zentralstelle that from March 16 until further notice "it will be impossible to conduct additional evacuation transports from the annexed German eastern provinces or Vienna to the Generalgouvernement."[59] Not only deportations from Vienna but all "resettlement" transports by train to the Generalgouvernement were to be stopped. The Reich Minister of Transportation affirmed:

> For the time being no special trains for resettlement operations (evacuations of Poles and Jews for the settlement of Volksdeutsche or for Wehrmacht needs) can be made available in the East, not even for local traffic. . . . Because of the suspended evacuations of Poles and Jews to the Generalgouvernement, the settlement of Volksdeutsche must be reduced significantly since the special train transport of settlers from the Altreich to the annexed areas had to be interrupted due to technical transport-related problems.[60]

Even though Hitler himself had ordered the deportation of 60,000 Jews from Vienna, the transports had to be suspended due to the objections of the army. Wehrmacht officers and generals did not oppose the "resettlement of Jews" out of humanitarian motives but for utilitarian reasons. The logistics of the build-up of troops in occupied Poland were of paramount importance for the war against the Soviet Union.

The decision to suspend the expulsion program prematurely spelled the failure of Heydrich's entire Nahplan 3, which ground to a halt in mid-March; however, Eichmann and his men soon found new fields of activity in newly conquered territories in the Balkans. Beginning in May 1941, Eichmann's Referat, now called IV B 4 (Jewish Affairs and Evacuation Matters), organized expulsions of Slovenes from areas in Yugoslavia now de facto annexed to the German Reich, from Lower Styria (Steiermark), and Upper Carinthia (Kärnten).[61] From Maribor in Slovenia, SS-Sturmbannführer Höppner and SS-Obersturmführer Seidl directed the expulsions with the help of the Umsiedlungsstab Untersteiermark (resettlement staff of Lower Styria). From the beginning of June through mid-September, 300 persons per train were sent to Belgrade, among them Jews and "Gypsies."[62] In Veldez, Franz Novak, a native of Carinthia, served in the same capacity as did Seidl in the expulsion of Slovenes from Upper Krain in western Yugoslavia.[63]

4   From Expulsion to Mass Murder: 1941

With the start of the German war of annihilation against the Soviet Union in the summer of 1941, racist policies in the entire Greater German Reich and the German-occupied areas entered a new phase. What position did the decisions of the leaders of the Third Reich occupy in this process? How did the occupation authorities, civil administrative bodies, and armed forces in the areas annexed or dominated by the German Reich operate during this time? What function did Eichmann's Referat IV B 4 occupy in the step-by-step transition from the policies of segregation, despoilment, expulsion, and ghettoization to the organized annihilation of people whom the SS or German ghetto administrators classified as *arbeitsunfähig*, unfit for work? How were the first nationwide deportations of Jews and of Roma and Sinti to Łódź/Litzmannstadt organized?

Deportation Plans in the Spring and Summer of 1941

At the end of July 1941, Reich Marshal Göring commissioned Sicherheitspolizei and SD Chief Reinhard Heydrich to work out "all necessary preparations . . . for a total solution of the Jewish Question in the German sphere of influence in Europe" and to "present a comprehensive proposal concerning the organizational, substantive, and material preparatory issues for the implementation of the desired Final Solution to the Jewish Question as soon as possible."[1] If additional central authorities should be impacted by these preparations, they too were to be involved.

This document does not reveal clearly what concepts were associated with terms such as "Gesamtlösung" or "Endlösung der Judenfrage," but caution against hasty conclusions is called for because, at that time, leading National Socialists referred to other problems with precisely the same jargon. Heydrich, for example, in an early October 1941 speech at the Czernin Palace in Prague, divided one of Hitler's directives into a Nahaufgabe, an immediate task, and an Endlösung, a final solution: "And now, gentlemen, a few thoughts about the Endlösung, which I insist must be kept confidential at all cost, but which I want to share with you now because you need to know about it to avoid making mistakes in the execution of the Nahaufgabe, the immediate task at hand." In this instance "Endlösung" did not refer to the so-called "Jewish Question" but to the Czechs living in the Protectorate of Bohemia and Moravia, for which Heydrich had just been appointed Deputy Reich Protector. Specifically he meant that "this area has to become German and that the Czechs ultimately have no right to remain there," for history proves that from here "time and again dagger thrusts have been directed against the Reich."[2] During the war, however, Czech workers were to be "harnessed" for work in German armament production and would, therefore, receive what "slop" – Heydrich's term – they needed to maintain their strength. So this particular final solution would be deferred to the end of the war.

Yet, despite the ambiguity of these terms, the bulk of historiography concludes that, with Heydrich's empowerment, Göring simultaneously had ordered the physical destruction of European Jews. In support of this conclusion historians argue that, at that particular time, Hitler either had just issued a directive for the murder of European Jewry or that it already was in existence.[3] They cite Eichmann's and Auschwitz commandant Rudolf Höß's post-1945 testimonies as evidence for the existence of such a Führerbefehl (Führer's Order) in the summer of 1941, but historians do so without giving due consideration to the connection between the defense strategies of the accused and the defendants' claims and the questionable date of the "evidence."[4] Could a reconstruction of internal connections of coeval documents produce a different picture of the decision-making processes?

Between the fall of 1939 and 1941 several deportations of Jews from the Ostmark, the Protectorate, the Warthegau, Stettin, Baden, and Saarpfalz had been carried out. In addition to those, leading National Socialist functionaries considered deporting a far greater number of Jews and "Asocials" from their domains or spheres of influence. But they always were confronted by the as-yet unsolved problem of locating areas to receive such deportees because the Madagascar Project developed in 1940 could not be put into effect immediately. This became obvious when in the spring of 1941 Propaganda Minister Goebbels, who also was Gauleiter of Berlin, considered "evacuations" of Berlin Jews. A conversation during one of Hitler's luncheons had made him aware of the 60,000–70,000 Jews still living in Berlin. It was made clear to him that allowing such a large number of Jews to remain in the capital of the Reich had become intolerable. No decisions were made then, but Goebbels came away convinced "that a suitable evacuation proposal was sure to gain the Führer's approval."[5]

On March 20, 1941, during a Propaganda Ministry meeting called for the purpose of hammering out such a proposal, Adolf Eichmann, the RHSA specialist of evacuations of Jews, reported to Goebbels' representatives and the representatives of the Reichsicherheitshauptamt that the Führer had charged his superior, Heydrich, "with the final evacuation of Jews" and that Heydrich "had submitted a proposal eight or ten weeks earlier." Heydrich's plan, however, had not been initiated "because at this time the Generalgouvernement was unable to accommodate even a single Jew or Pole from the Altreich." Eichmann also reminded the group that, in light of the tight labor market, Jews were needed as workers, pointing out that "on account of the aging Jewish population the number of Jews suitable for labor already was low, and that they were almost impossible to find." There were even plans to import 42,000 male and 30,000 female Jewish workers from the Warthegau to the Altreich. Still, Eichmann insisted on the need to continue the deportations. The potential victims were not to come exclusively from Vienna, as had been the case in February and March 1941: "Though the Führer has issued a written order for the evacuation of 60,000 Viennese Jews whom the Generalgouvernement would have to accept, at the moment no more than 45,000 are at hand. Therefore, the remaining 15,000 can perhaps be removed from Berlin." Eichmann was instructed to "work out a proposal for the evacuation of Berlin Jews"[6] for Gauleiter Goebbels.

The protocol of the March 20, 1941, meeting explains how leading National Socialists prepared the way for decisions of far-reaching consequences and planned to develop proposals for deportations of Jews. During lunch the leaders of the Third Reich chatted about the reduction of Jews in Berlin. One of the participants called together "experts" to have them work out plans, which were to be presented to Hitler for approval. Eichmann was fully informed about current policy developments concerning the Jews. The problem of engaging Jewish labor, a problem that he had described, had been the subject of a secret directive Göring had issued to the Reich Statthalters on February 18, 1941, ordering them to remove obstructions that impeded the employment of Jewish labor.[7] A March 14, 1941, directive from the Reichsarbeitsministerium, the Reich Ministry of Labor, instructed the public employment offices to create conditions conducive to employing Jews: because of the prevailing employment situation their labor was essential. Eichmann mentioned that Arthur Greiser, the Reich Statthalter of the Warthegau, offered to provide 73,000 men and women to work in the Altreich but that offer was not accepted. Early in April 1941 Hitler decided that "Jews from the Generalgouvernement and the Warthegau could not work in the Reich."[8]

In the summer of 1941, requests for the expulsion of Jews to Poland or even farther east multiplied. Eichmann was one of the first to be confronted with them. In July 1941 he received a memorandum from his coworker SS-Sturmbannführer Höppner, who shortly before, on June 7, had traveled on the first deportation train from Maribor, Yugoslavia, to Belgrade during the resettlements of Slovenes from Lower Styria. He had since then returned to his place of operation in the Umwandererzentrale, the Resettlement Center, in Posen. From there Höppner informed his "dear comrade Eichmann" on July 16 about discussions in the Warthegau Reich Statthalter's Office. Höppner considered some of the proposals recorded in the attached minutes bizarre but nevertheless workable and requested Eichmann's opinion. The memorandum concerned the solution of the Jewish Question in the Reichgau Wartheland, suggesting the establishment of a barrack camp for "all Jews of the Warthegau"; the facility was to be adjacent to a coal transport line. Such a camp would require fewer police for guard duty; furthermore, the danger of epidemics, which "always existed in Łódź and other ghettos," would be much reduced. The second part of Höppner's memorandum referred to the murderous considerations raised by the question of food supplies for the Jews in the Wartheland: "The danger exists that this coming winter there will not be enough food for all the Jews. Whether the most humane solution would be to do away with those who are unable to work through some speedy means deserves serious consideration. That, in any case, would be preferable to letting them starve to death."[9]

In closing, Höppner mentioned that Reich Statthalter Greiser had not yet commented on these topics and that Regierungspräsident Uebelhör was unwilling to let the Łódź ghetto disappear. That was because it seemed quite profitable for him. Nothing is known about Eichmann's reaction or his assessment, although he probably did not lose sight of these deliberations. We know that because, in ways that have been little explored so far, he contributed to the soon-to-begin realization of these seemingly fanciful suggestions.

Since the start of "Operation Barbarossa," the war of annihilation against the Soviet Union, the plan to expel large numbers of West and Central European Jews to the conquered Soviet territories – to "the East," in Nazi jargon – was rampant in the various organizations involved in anti-Jewish policies throughout the National Socialist occupation apparatus covering most of Europe. In the summer of 1941 all National Socialist functionaries and the Wehrmacht still operated on the assumption that, as a Blitzkrieg, this campaign would also speedily come to a successful end. Accordingly, the imagination of functionaries in search of areas to accommodate the deportees already focused on the vast, supposedly uninhabited regions of northern and eastern Russia. This pushed into the background the island of Madagascar as the destination for expelled European Jews. It was replaced by the still nebulous project of establishing a National Socialist–dominated Ostraum (eastern territory).

Dr. Karl-Theodor Zeitschel, SS-Sturmbannführer and councilor at the German embassy in Paris, formulated this change in the expulsion plans most concisely. At the end of August 1941 he presented plans to his superior, Ambassador Otto Abetz, pointing out that the "continuing conquest and occupation of the far-flung Eastern territories" could "provide the final, satisfactory solution to the entire European Jewish problem."[10] Zeitschel assumed that six million Jews lived in the newly conquered areas of the Soviet Union, and that these, "in the course of the reorganization of the Ostraum, would somehow have to be gathered" and transported to a special, confined territory. "At that time," as far as he could see, "it should not be too much of a problem" to bring "western European Jews and those jammed into the ghettos in Warsaw, Litzmannstadt, Lublin, etc." to those areas as well.

Clearly, Zeitschel's proposals did not just focus on the ultimate fate of Jews living in France, but they developed his personal perspective on how "to rid Europe of Jews in record time," a type of final solution. He also saw his suggestions as an alternative to the Madagascar Plan. Sending Jews to this African island, in his opinion, was not feasible because, even after Germany's successful conclusion of the war, insoluble transportation problems would prevail and other, more pressing problems would demand solutions rather than "sending huge numbers of Jews on cruises on the seven seas."[11] Zeitschel suggested that Abetz present his plans to the Reichsaußenminister, the German Foreign Minister, who in turn would contact Reichsleiter Rosenberg, the recently appointed Minister für die besetzten Ostgebiete, Minister for the Occupied Eastern Territories, and the Reichsführer-SS. It would also be a good idea to acquaint "Reich Marshal Göring, who is presently very open to solutions to the Jewish problem, with this plan."[12]

In early September 1941, independent of Zeitschel's ideas, Rosenberg, the new minister for the Occupied Eastern Territories, was thinking along similar lines. After learning that Germans from the Volga region were to be re-settled by the Soviet authorities elsewhere within the Soviet Union, he suggested as a countermeasure the "deportation of all Central European Jews to the eastern areas under our administration." It was the task of Rosenberg's employee Otto Bräutigam "to secure the Führer's approval for this project." So Bräutigam "saddled" his Mercedes and drove to the Führerhauptquartier, the Führer's headquarters, where he found an interested listener in Colonel Rudolf Schmund, who accepted the proposal and assured him that this was "a very important matter" in which the Führer was "vitally interested."[13]

At the center of the National Socialist government machinery where such "projects" already had been considered, these suggestions found enthusiastic reception. In mid-July, Hitler already had made it clear to Croatian Marshal Slavko Kvaternik that there were to be no more Jews in Europe. Where these Jews would be sent, to Siberia or Madagascar, was of no importance.[14] During the summer the initiation of deportations to the East still was tied to the victorious conclusion of the recently unleashed Operation Barbarossa. In mid-August 1941, a conference was held at the Ministry of Propaganda. It was attended not only by Goebbels' representatives who had been present in March, but also by representatives of the RSHA and Albert Speer, as well as a senior civil servant of the Interior Ministry.[15] There Eichmann announced that in regard to the question of Jewish evacuations from the Altreich, "the Führer had rejected Obergruppenführer Heydrich's proposal for such action for the duration of the war." In response Heydrich had commissioned "a plan for partial evacuations from larger cities."[16] So by August, Hitler had not yet issued a final order. Goebbels' diaries also reveal that everything was in abeyance until the successful conclusion of Operation Barbarossa, although his entries leave no doubt about his determination to expel people to the East.[17] His representative at the August conference phrased it crudely by insisting that Berlin Jews unfit for work were to be "carted off to Russia."[18]

As did Hitler, Reich Minister of the Occupied Eastern Territories Rosenberg at that time believed that the desired overall solution to the Jewish Question should be pursued in earnest only after the end of the war with the Soviet Union.[19] At the beginning of September 1941 he produced a "Brown Folder" for official use, which contained directives for the civil administration of the Ostland. The first sentence of the section designated for establishing anti-Jewish policies in the occupied Ostland stresses that all measures pertaining to the Jewish Question in the occupied areas had to be based on the assumption that the Jewish Question of the entire European continent would be solved after the war.[20]

Hitler also had promised Generalgouverneur Frank that he would be able to "expel the Jews from the Generalgouvernement." In a paean on the "progressive victory of our glorious Wehrmacht in the East" on July 22, 1941, Frank especially stressed the need to "remove the Jews from the Generalgouvernement as quickly as possible," for Hitler himself had proclaimed that "in the future the

Generalgouvernement would no longer be a final destination but exclusively a transit camp."[21] Frank was the Nazi occupation functionary under whose power most Jews had been congregated. When pressed for the concrete application of these plans, however, insurmountable hurdles appeared. In an October 1941 meeting with Rosenberg, the minister, in answer to Frank's question about the possibility of "removing the Jewish population of the General-gouvernement to the occupied Eastern territories," stated that he had received similar requests from Paris but "at the moment could not" see "any possibility for carrying out such resettlement plans." He did, however, assure Frank of his willingness to support "Jewish emigration east at a later time, all the more so since all asocial elements within the Reich" were to be sent "to the thinly populated Eastern territories anyway."[22]

According to the documents, in the summer of 1941 the ideas and plans of leading National Socialists concerning the "Solution of the Jewish Question" focused on the expulsion of European Jews and "asocial elements" to the East,[23] incorporating already existing strategies and practices. Following the military subjugation of Poland and France, plans for deporting German, Austrian, and Czech Jews, as well as Roma and Sinti, to the territories of recently defeated opponents had been devised and partly carried out. In contrast to earlier military operations, in the summer of 1941 the anticipated victory did not materialize. Consequently, the supposedly "thinly inhabited Eastern territories" would serve the National Socialists only to a limited degree, if at all, in the deportation of Jews and "any and all asocial elements."[24] This caused delays. The expulsion experts had to develop new strategies. Even though Heydrich, the RSHA, Goebbels, and other government representatives pushed for a rapid start of large-scale deportations, Hitler did not give them the green light until August.

In all available documents from the summer of 1941 the single indication about plans for murdering Jews in a large-scale, organized fashion outside the areas affected by Operation Barbarossa are the "partly seemingly fanciful" proposals that Eichmann received from the Warthegau. At the time, National Socialist administrators busied themselves with murderous considerations of "taking care of" people classified as unable to work – doing so with "some kind of quick device." Organized by Eichmann and his men, shortly thereafter deportation transports of German, Austrian, and Czech Jews, or of Roma and Sinti, would roll. Starting in December 1941, large numbers of people were murdered with poison gas for the first time outside the so-called Euthanasia Program. The Austrian Roma and Sinti were the first group of people expelled from Central Europe to be murdered, without exception, near Chełmno (Kulmhof) in the Warthegau.

The Wehrmacht, RSHA Referat IV B 4, and the Destruction
of the Serbian Jews and "Gypsies"

The beginning of the genocide of the Jews and "Gypsies" in Serbia provides an illustration of how far the transition from expulsion to murder had progressed by the summer and early fall of 1941; how administration and occupation authorities operated even without specific orders; and what part the Wehrmacht played in these activities. By September 1941 the organizations in charge of accepting, coordinating, and organizing proposals for deportations from German-occupied areas throughout Europe were swamped. A telephone conversation between the Auswärtige Amt (AA) and the RSHA demonstrates this clearly. On September 13, Eichmann, probably busy with the preparations for deportations to Łódź and perhaps elsewhere, was confronted with another demand to transport Jews to the East: he received a call from Foreign Office Legation Councilor Franz Rademacher, who informed him of urgent requests for the expulsion of Jews from Serbia, now under German military administration. The Auswärtige Amt had received a telegram from the German ambassador in Belgrade, who insisted on the speedy "arrest and removal of at least all male Jews" because of their alleged participation in "acts of sabotage and rebellion." The ambassador had contacted the AA to find out whether 8,000 Jews could be shipped down the Danube from Belgrade to an island in the Danube delta in Romania, provided Romania agreed. The ambassador reacted to the negative reply by immediately sending a second telegram reiterating his plea. "Should it be refused again, the only recourse" he could see "would be immediate expulsion to the Generalgouvernement or Russia."[25] This telex was the reason for Rademacher's call. Rademacher penciled Eichmann's response in the margin of Ambassador Felix Benzler's telegram: "According to Sturmbannführer Eichmann at RSHA IV D VI [should be IV B 4], accommodation in Russia or the Generalgouvernement impossible. Not even Jews from Germany can be sent there. Eichmann suggests shooting."[26]

In diplomatically less blunt language, the Auswärtige Amt informed the ambassador of the impossibility of deporting Serbian Jews to the occupied parts of the Soviet Union. Benzler, however, did not give up but wrote directly to Foreign Minister Ribbentrop. At the same time the AA had prepared a memorandum for Ribbentrop, insisting that should they interfere with the reestablishment of public order, the 8,000 Jews would have to be "liquidated" by the military commander in Serbia. The memorandum made reference to the then-widespread practice in the occupied areas of the Soviet Union: "In other areas other military commanders handled far greater numbers of Jews without even talking about it."[27] Ribbentrop decided to confer with the Reichsführer-SS about whether he could take charge of these Jews and "send them to eastern Poland or some other place."[28] During the meeting of representatives of the AA and the RSHA it was decided to send a joint delegation made up of Rademacher and Eichmann to Belgrade. Because Eichmann was detained by more important tasks, Sturmbannführer Friedrich Suhr and Untersturmführer Franz Stuschka, who began his career in the Zentralstelle für jüdische Auswanderung in Vienna as a member of Eichmann's entourage, accompanied Rademacher on his fact-finding tour to Belgrade.[29]

To their surprise, the three gentlemen from Berlin learned that "the problem Benzler had raised had been taken care of," as Rademacher noted in his report, because Wehrmacht units had shot the male Jews.

> The remainder of about 20,000 Jews – women, children, and old people – and about 1,500 Gypsies, whose men also were to be shot, were to be gathered into a ghetto in the so-called Gypsy section of Belgrade. . . . Ultimately, as soon as the technical details have been worked out within the framework of the total solution of the Jewish Question, these Jews will be shipped by water to the reception camps in the East.[30]

Franz Böhme, formerly a member of the army of Austria's first republic, and now the commanding general in charge of Serbia, had issued an order to army units to execute, as a "reprisal measure," all male Jews already confined in concentration camps. In early October 1941, during a battle between a section of an army signal corps regiment and a unit of Serb partisans, twenty-one Wehrmacht soldiers had been killed. Soon rumors ran rampant among occupation troops in Serbia that the dead soldiers had been mutilated. Although an immediate autopsy of the corpses conducted by Wehrmacht physicians proved that this was not the case and despite their findings immediately being reported to higher staff authorities, Böhme insisted on retaliation:

> On October 2 during an attack on units of the army signal regiment between Belgrade and Obrenovac, Communist gangs bestially tortured and killed twenty-one soldiers. In retaliation and as atonement, 100 Serbian prisoners for each murdered German soldier will be shot immediately. The head of the military administration will choose 2,100 inmates of the concentration camps Šabac and Belgrade (mainly Jews and Communists) and determine location, time, and burial places. The execution squads are to be furnished by the 342nd Division (for KZ Šabac) and the 449th Corps Signal Batallion (for KZ Belgrade). The head of the military administration will request these through the commanding general in Serbia. The head of the military administration will instruct the camp administration to inform the inmates of the reason for their execution.[31]

Without doing so intentionally, General Böhme's order de facto introduced the genocide of Serbian Jews and "Gypsies" through mass executions by the Wehrmacht. Obviously, neither he nor the Wehrmacht units conducting these mass murders had needed direct orders from the highest levels of the military leadership, much less a "Führerbefehl"[32] for killing thousands of male civilians who had no connection whatsoever to partisan activities. The procedure Eichmann had proposed per telephone and which the German Foreign Office had endorsed in its memorandum was carried out locally without the input of either. The members of the delegation could return to Berlin to report to their superiors. Eichmann's Referat did not, however, forget about the remaining Jews and "Gypsies" in Serbia – the women, children, and old people who survived the winter of 1941–1942 in the concentration camps. In the spring of 1942 they were murdered by members of the SS. In the summer of 1942 Dr. Harold Turner, the head of the military administration in Serbia, could report to General Alexander Löhr, the new chief of Wehrmacht Southeast, that in Serbia the Jewish Question, like the "Gypsy problem," had been "liquidated" in its entirety.[33]

The Logistic Preparations for the Deportations to Łódź/Litzmannstadt

On September 18, 1941, Himmler wrote to Warthegau Gauleiter and Reich Statthalter Greiser that the Führer would "like to see the Altreich and the Protectorate emptied and freed of Jews from west to east as soon as possible." For this reason he, Himmler, was determined "even before the end of the year, if at all possible, to transport the Jews of the Altreich and the Protectorate to the eastern areas newly incorporated into the Reich during the past two years. After this first phase, they will be expelled even farther east during the following spring." He planned for "about 60,000 Jews from the Altreich and the Protectorate to spend the winter" in the Łódź ghetto and announced that Heydrich, "who would conduct this Jewish emigration," would contact Greiser.[34]

Because the expected rapid victory over the Red Army did not take place, the organizations in charge of the expulsions opted for proceeding step-by-step. Plans for mass expulsions of all Jews living within German domains were temporarily limited to plans for Jews still living in Germany, Austria, and the Protectorate of Bohemia and Moravia. Accordingly, as Goebbels recorded in his diary at the end of September, the Führer was of the opinion that "the Jews had to be removed from all of Germany gradually" and listed Berlin, Vienna, and Prague as the cities to be "freed of Jews" first. He hoped to see "a considerable number of the Berlin Jews being transported East in the course of 1941."[35]

Obviously the proposed "partial evacuations of larger cities," to which Eichmann had referred earlier, had been approved. So temporary solutions had to be found because at that time not even Jews from Germany could be placed in the Generalgouvernement or in the occupied areas of the Soviet Union, as Eichmann had informed Rademacher. Expulsions were no longer to be deferred until the victory over the Red Army; instead, thousands of Central European Jews were to be moved into a type of intermediate camp.[36] In Himmler's letter to Greiser the reference to 60,000 Jews to be sent to Łódź is interesting because that same number already had appeared in connection with the deportations from Vienna in the winter of 1940–1941, and Eichmann had mentioned it at the March conference in the Propaganda Ministry; there he drew attention to an "order by the Führer for the evacuation of 60,000 Jews."

Why the expulsion experts focused their attention on the Łódź ghetto in the Reichsgau Wartheland, the part of Poland then annexed to the German Reich, cannot be determined.[37] No documents explaining the reasons for this decision have surfaced, although one reason probably is the fact that the easternmost base of Eichmann's deportation apparatus was located in the Warthegau. His coworkers Dr. Seidl, Krumey, and Höppner had been active in the Umwandererzentrale in Posen or its branch in Łódź/Litzmannstadt and knew how to apply tried and true methods in the technical management of mass deportations. Furthermore, Eichmann was aware of plans in the Warthegau to murder people considered unfit for work. As a result, the organizers may very well have decided to place deportees into the space made available in the ghetto in this fashion. That Eichmann took part in choosing Łódź also can be deduced from the fact that he led subsequent negotiations with appropriate authorities of the German administration in the Warthegau. These authorities, however, objected to Himmler's deportation order of 60,000 Jews to Łódź, provoking busy, often agitated correspondence. No protocols of the negotiations between Eichmann and regional or local authorities are available; therefore, the controversies, methods, and even the authorities involved in these negotiations can be reconstructed only from later reactions recorded in this correspondence.

In a September 24, 1941, letter the mayor of Litzmannstadt complained to Regierungspresident Uebelhör about recent deportations to the Łódź ghetto and about others deportations still to come. Just a short time earlier he had voiced strong objections "to having to accept 2,900 Jews from Leszno (Leslau), a city and provincial government district of the Warthegau," despite which they had been settled here. Now he saw himself "confronted with an apparent fait accompli of soon having to take not only an additional 20,000 Jews but also 5,000 Gypsies into the ghetto."[38] More than anything, the ghetto administrators objected to the transfer of Roma and Sinti because of the danger they were alleged to represent to "law and order" and the "flawless execution of Wehrmacht contracts." Confronted with such complaints, Uebelhör raised these concerns in a letter to the Reichsführer-SS. He claimed to have been informed of Arthur Greiser's intended allocations to the Łódź ghetto and insisted that the danger of epidemics as well as matters of security, military economic concerns, and availability of foodstuffs argued against them. "If Łódź were a ghetto of attrition pure and simple, packing the Jews in even more tightly might be something to think about," although even here the danger of epidemics to the 120,000 or so Germans living in Łódź would merit consideration too.[39]

Uebelhör voiced even more strident protests to Himmler in a telex of October 9, 1941, which he signed as Regierungspräsident and SS-Brigadeführer. He claimed to have discovered – apparently by studying written documents – that the "officials in charge in this matter, SS-Sturmbannführer Eichmann of the Reichssicherheitshauptamt and the official in charge of Jewish affairs at the Litzmannstadt Staatspolizei office, by making false statements had gained the approval of the representatives of the Reich Ministry of the Interior at the conference of September 29, 1941."[40] He corrected these supposedly false claims from his own point of view and in closing leveled grave reproaches: He could only describe the tactics Eichmann and the official in charge of Jewish affairs in the Litzmannstadt Gestapo office had employed "as horse dealer tricks adopted from the Gypsies" and asked that both men be disciplined.

Himmler dismissed Uebelhör's arguments out of hand,[41] but Heydrich thought it necessary to shield his deportation specialists. In a letter of October 19, 1941, he informed the Reichsführer-SS of the start of the deportations on October 15, 1941, "in spite of the difficulties SS-Brigadeführer Ueberhör has created" and spelled out his own opinion about these controversies. Heydrich had reprimanded Uebelhör in a telex: Through his opposition to the settlement of Jews and Gypsies from the Altreich as ordered by the Reichsführer-SS, he had hindered the current preparations "for the implementation of these measures." He expressed his vexation with Uebelhör's "attacks based on petty, insignificant matters" on SS leaders under Heydrich's command. "SS-Sturmbannführer Eichmann (RSHA) and Dr. [Robert] Schefe (Stapo office Litzmannstadt) acted in compliance with their orders."[42]

The conflict did not end there. Higher Wehrmacht authorities approached Himmler with arguments similar to Uebelhör's. General Thomas, Chief of the OKW Office of War Economy and Armament, in a letter to the Reichsführer-SS expressed his worry that housing 20,000 Jews and 5,000 "Gypsies" in the Litzmannstadt ghetto would cause "disruptions in important war production." The head of the ghetto administration had informed him that factory buildings and workshops would have to be cleared to accommodate the

25,000 expected arrivals and hence interrupt the production of "war-related goods manufactured there." He asked "for relocation of Jews and Gypsies from western areas threatened by air attacks to other ghettos, such as Warsaw."[43] Himmler's response to the Office of War Economics and Armaments rejected these worries as groundless, with the comment that local authorities were concerned only about their own "comfort levels." Both Gauleiter Greiser and Regierungspräsident Uebelhör, the intended recipient of this rebuff, received copies of this letter.[44]

The correspondence further reveals that in mid-September Eichmann traveled to Łódź to oversee on the spot the organization of the deportations. There he also conferred with Schefe and Hans Biebow, the director of the ghetto administration. As far as can be ascertained, the subject was the number of Jews to be deported to Łódź.[45] The figure of 60,000 in Himmler's letter apparently served as a guideline open to negotiation rather than as a set figure to be met under any circumstances. Which authorities determined the deportation of Roma and Sinti from Austria cannot be determined. Himmler's letter does not mention them. The September 24, 1941 letter from the Litzmannstadt mayor to Uebelhör mentions them for the first time, so Eichmann must have included the demand for their deportation in his negotiations with local German authorities. Bargaining about the number of Jews to be placed in the ghetto finally produced agreement on 20,000 deportees.[46] This agreement, for the head of the ghetto administration, probably was akin to a direct order. It was reported to Greiser; presented by Eichmann and the cooperating Gestapo officials in Łódź/Litzmannstadt to the Reich Interior Ministry in a meeting on September 29, 1941; and pushed through over the objections of the German ghetto administration, the mayor, Regierungspräsident Uebelhör, and the Wehrwirtschaft- und Rüstungsamt. Eichmann, with Himmler's, Heydrich's, and Greiser's support, could afford to ignore the objections of local administrative bodies grounded in their interest in the uninterrupted exploitation of Jewish forced labor.[47]

The Deportations to the Warthegau and the Start of Mass Murders of Persons "Unable to Work"

Early in October 1941 the chief of the Ordnungspolizei (Order Police) by express mail informed subordinate organizations that they were to furnish escorts for deportation transports to Łódź/Litzmannstadt. Starting on October 15, "the Sicherheitspolizei would expel a total of 20,000 Jews to the Litzmannstadt ghetto from the Ostmark, the Protectorate of Bohemia and Moravia, Luxembourg, and the cities of Berlin, Frankfurt/Main, Hamburg, Cologne, and

Düsseldorf." Additionally, there would be "5,000 Gypsies from the Austrian Burgenland." These evacuations would be handled by trains furnished by the Reichsbahn, and carrying 1,000 persons each. According to an agreement with the Chief of the Sicherheitspolizei and the SD, the Ordnungspolizei would take charge of guarding the transports "by furnishing escorts at a ratio of 1:12; the detachments for the Gypsy transports are to be increased slightly."[48] Some historians consider this directive of the chief of the Ordnungspolizei as the source of the wave of deportations to Łódź; this, however, was probably caused by a no longer extant order from RSHA Referat IV B 4; the document is reference number IV B 4/2963/41 g 799 to Stapo offices and Zentralstellen für jüdische Auswanderung.[49]

Arguments arose during internal RSHA deliberations about the size of the quotas from the various cities. Because of the stubborn insistence of SS-Unterscharführer Richard Hartenberger, a low-level representative of the Vienna Zentralstelle für jüdische Auswanderung, 5,000 Jews were to be deported from that city to Łódź. His superior, Alois Brunner, praised him in a letter: "During his assignment in Berlin, Hartenberger exerted himself in an exemplary manner for the apportionment of Viennese Jews in the evacuations to the Litzmannstadt ghetto. He also helped Vienna maintain its apportionment of 5,000, even though Vienna is not considered an area threatened by air strikes."[50]

That RSHA decisions about and preparations for the deportations to Łódź date back to September is obvious because Vienna's Israelitische Kultusgemeinde was informed about them that month. On September 30, 1941, Alois Brunner told Dr. Löwenherz that "in view of air attacks that necessitate the relocation of the Aryan population, segments of Jews from the Altreich, the Protectorate, and Vienna will be taken to Litzmannstadt." There, those able to work would be "employed in armament plants and paid for their labor." Families would be resettled as complete units. The selection, rounding up, housing, and plundering of the victims was to follow the manner that already had been practiced in the spring of that year. The first transport was to depart for Łódź on October 15, the last on November 3, 1941. Each person was allowed to carry luggage up to 50 kilos, "as well as bedlinens, pads, a warm blanket" and cash up to 100 Reichsmark. The Kultusgemeinde was granted the right to "petition for the deferment of individuals from transport in case of weighty circumstances," which, according to a file entry, applied mainly to employees of the Kultusgemeinde.[51]

"Aryans" despoiled those about to be deported of their last possessions, "purchasing" the deportees' furnishings and utensils at the lowest possible price. Vienna's Deputy Gauleiter Scharizer saw himself forced to speak out against such practices at least verbally. In a October 25, 1941 memorandum to the Kreisleiters, he attempted to explain that "under no circumstances was the general public to gain the impression that ultimately our anti-Semitism would end up enriching some at the expense of the Jews."[52] In that context he cited reports he had received about "even some party members now buying furniture and utensils directly from Jews about to be resettled. They always try to do so at the lowest possible price." According to Scharizer, this common Viennese practice was "strictly prohibited and causes damage to the Reich. The property of expelled Jews is the property of the Reich. Only through designated organizations such as the Verwaltungsstelle für jüdisches Umzugsgut (Vugesta), the Gestapo's administrative organization in charge of Jewish property in Vienna, may individuals lawfully participate in the process." In closing he threatened to refer cases coming to his attention to legal punishment by the Party.

By early October, the deportation transports from Vienna were being prepared according to Brunner's instructions. The Zentralstelle compiled the lists of those to be deported. At that time, employees of the Kultusgemeinde and their families, persons in possession of emigration papers, the blind, the totally disabled, the seriously ill, disabled and decorated war veterans, and persons living in retirement homes and work camps still were exempted.[53] If the Kultusgemeinde did not petition for exemption, individuals were notified in writing to report with their luggage at the indicated time to Vienna School No. 2, Kleine Sperlgasse 2a, the assembly camp for Jews. Failure to appear, they were threatened, would result in a visit by the police. According to a statistic on the "Resettlement-Emigration Transports" assembled by the Kultusgemeinde in February 1942, on October 15, 19, 23, 28, and on November 2, 1941, a total of 5,002 men, women, and children had been deported from Vienna to Łódź.[54]

Upon completion of the deportations of Austrian Jews to the Warthegau, 5,000 Roma and Sinti from Styria and the Burgenland, some of whom had been held prisoner in the so-called Gypsy camp of Lackenbach, also were removed to Łódź.[55] In compliance with a directive from the Schutzpolizei detachment, they were "expelled to the ghetto in Litzmannstadt" in five transports. One transport each was to leave Mattersburg in the Eisenstadt (district of Lower Austria) on November 4 and 6; one was to leave from Fürstenfeld (district of Feldbach in Styria) on November 5; and two from Pinkafeld (district of Oberwarth, Styria) on November 7 and 8, 1941, respectively.[56]

The basic details of the subsequent fate of the deportees in this ghetto are known and have been described in relatively detailed fashion.[57] A centrally issued order for the immediate murder of all those deported to Łódź did not exist. Probably only those whom National Socialist administrators classified as "unable to work" were to be killed. Yet those responsible for deporting and housing the deportees in the ghetto set into motion a deadly mechanism to accomplish that goal: Through hunger, disease, and epidemics the victims became "unable to work" within a short time, and so, according to administrative logic, because they were "unable to work" had lost the right to exist.

The deported Roma and Sinti were the first to fall victim to this murderous logic. Through their confinement in the "Gypsy camp," they arrived in Łódź already physically weak and prone to falling victim to disease. They had hardly any warm clothing and lived crammed into a separate section of the ghetto under catastrophic conditions. In no time an epidemic of spotted typhoid broke out, carrying off these already severely weakened people. In fact, those in charge of the ghetto did not fight the epidemic; instead, they waged combat against those already infected by the disease and those threatened by it: In early January they ordered all Roma and Sinti still alive to be killed in the gas vans of Chełmno/Kulmhof.[58]

The fate of the Austrian Roma and Sinti, the first group of people deported to Łódź, demonstrates that in the Warthegau the operators of the recently installed machinery of murder did not need any government order for the destruction of a particular segment of the population. By mid-January 1942 these victims had been totally annihilated. Self-induced predicaments served to legitimize radical measures supposedly necessary for eradicating epidemics. Although the mass murder of Roma and Sinti already was in progress in Chełmno, the process of racial classification and segregation of this group had not yet been completed, and Himmler did not issue his order for the confinement of "Gypsy-like persons" in concentration camps until December 1942.[59]

As a June 9, 1942–dated situation report (Lagebericht) of the Litzmannstadt Staatspolizei office reveals, of the persons deported from Central Europe to Łódź, more than half had been murdered in Chełmno:

> In the course of the development of the Gau ghetto, it became necessary to create space for the Jews to be settled there. For this purpose a fairly large number of Jews "unable to work" was evacuated from the ghetto and handed over to the Sonderkommando. Since January 16, 1942, a total of 44,152 of the Polish Jews have been expelled. Of the 19,848 Jews who were sent to this ghetto from the Altreich, Austria, and the Protectorate of Bohemia and Moravia in October 1941, 10,993 have been evacuated, which has made room for about 55,000 Jews.[60]

The specific nature of these mass murders in the Warthegau is reflected euphemistically in this document from police superintendent Günter Fuchs, the Sachbearbeiter für Judenfragen (specialist on Jewish affairs) of the

Litzmannstadt Gestapo. He refers to "the necessity" to "create space for the Jews to be settled" there. In a May 1, 1942, letter to Himmler, Greiser reports to his Reichsführer, "the operation of Sonderbehandlung [Special Treatment] of about 100,000 Jews, approved for my Gau by you in agreement with the Chief of the Reichssicherheits-Hauptamt, SS-Obergruppenführer Heydrich," can be completed "within the next 2–3 months."[61]

This letter suggests that in the fall of 1941 a kind of agreement between Himmler and the RSHA on the one hand, and Greiser or local authorities on the other, had been forged. Perhaps authorities in the Warthegau had agreed to take deportees from the Altreich if Himmler and the RSHA promised to support the Sonderbehandlungen.[62] This agreement between Himmler/Heydrich and Greiser probably had been worked out by mid-level officials, and in Eichmann's meetings with Gestapo personnel in Łódź and/or other authorities in the Warthegau, the "fast-acting methods" for murdering "work-incapable" people mentioned in Höppner's letter were the topic of discussion. Höppner's hints were not mere fabrication but probably a reference to a murder unit that in 1940 had been placed under the Chief of the Higher SS and Police in the Wartheland. In East Prussia, this "Sonderkommando Lange," among other duties, had "evacuated sick people"; that is, it had murdered patients of psychiatric institutions as part of the so-called Euthanasia Action. Some employees of the Stapo office in Posen knew about this Sonderkommando, which conducted killings with carbon monoxide in mobile gas chambers.[63]

The organization of the annihilation process in Chełmno was marked by close cooperation of the various organizations of the RSHA and the Warthegau. The members of the Sonderkommando whom the Stapo office had posted to Posen in October and November 1941 to prepare the killing facilities in Chełmno initially had served under the command of Deputy Police Chief and SS-Hauptsturmführer Lange. Members of the Sicherheitspolizei, the Łódź Staatspolizei office, or the Schutzpolizei also were posted to Chełmno.[64] The guards and killing personnel for Chełmno were essentially recruited from SS and police forces already stationed in the Warthegau. The RSHA Referat II D 3 in Berlin further developed the gas vans and tried them out on Soviet prisoners of war in Sachsenhausen in October and November. Complete with drivers, they were sent from Berlin to Chełmno at the end of November or the beginning of December 1941.[65] The Litzmannstadt Stapo office Sachbearbeiter für Judenfragen, who had cooperated with Eichmann in September 1941, now was responsible for the "resettlements" from Łódź to Chełmno that were "to create the needed space" in the ghetto.[66]

This evidence suggests that Eichmann played an important part in turning Höppner's "fanciful" suggestions of Summer 1941 into reality, and that he occupied a key position in the preparations for the murder of people who, because of age or reasons of health, could not be exploited as slave labor. He probably functioned as an intermediary who accepted and examined proposals from subordinate organizations, discussed them with members of other sections of the RSHA, and passed them along to his superiors. If his superiors approved them, he participated in planning sessions and took charge of their implementation, disregarding any and all resistance. Nevertheless, from the point of view of the deportation technocrats, the result of the negotiations with the authorities in the Wartheland was disappointing. The objections of the authorities in Łódź had caused a reduction from 60,000 to 25,000 deportees. A much greater number of German, Austrian, and Czech Jews were to be expelled, so new destinations for deportations had to be located. Among these, new destinations presented themselves in Dr. Stahlecker's new area of operation. One of Eichmann's longest-term acquaintances, Stahlecker now was the head of "Einsatzgruppe A of the Commander of the Sicherheitspolizei and the Sicherheitsdienst" in the Reichskommissariat Ostland.

At a conference in Prague on October 10, 1941, Heydrich and his coworkers specifically addressed this development. The main agenda item of this meeting, which both Eichmann and Günther attended, was the "solution to the Jewish Question in the Protectorate." Heydrich described his problems with the planned deportations of the approximately 88,000 Jews still living in the Protectorate:

> The evacuations have caused difficulties. The plan was to start them about October 15 in order to let them proceed one after another until November 15, involving up to 5,000 Jews from Prague only. But at this time we must still be considerate of the authorities in Litzmannstadt. Only the most burdensome Jews are to be sorted out. Minsk and Riga will receive 50,000.[67]

"Minsk" and "Riga" referred to the areas of activities of Einsatzgruppe A under the command of SS-Brigadeführer Stahlecker in Riga and Einsatzgruppe B led by the chief of the Reichskriminalamt (Reich Criminal Police Headquarters) SS-Brigadeführer Artur Nebe, located in Minsk until mid-September 1941. The Einsatzgruppen leaders in these areas of operation might "accommodate Jews in the camps set up for Communist detainees. According to SS-Sturmbannführer Eichmann, this is being negotiated already."[68] Clearly, at the beginning of October, shortly after the preparations for the deportations to Łódź, Eichmann already had paved the way with Stahlecker for the next wave of deportations.

Heydrich's plans also did not omit the second group of victims to be part of the deportations to Łódź/Litzmannstadt. "The Gypsies to be evacuated can be sent to Stahlecker in Riga; his camp is designed on the model of Sachsenhausen."[69] At that time, however, no camp akin to a concentration camp existed in or near Riga, and Stahlecker had only just started conducting preliminary negotiations in Latvia.

5   Controversies over the Deportations to the Occupied Areas of the Soviet Union: 1941

The day after Heydrich's consultation in Prague, Stahlecker began exploring the possibilities for housing in occupied Latvia people to be deported from Central Europe. For this purpose he contacted Generalkommissar Dr. Otto Heinrich Drechsler, the local head of the German civil administration in Riga. Visiting Drechsler in his apartment, he explained, "according to the Führer's wish, a large concentration camp for Jews expelled from the Protectorate and the Reich was to be established in the Riga, Jelgava (Mitau), and Tukums (Tukkum) area."[1] Drechsler was to assist him in acquiring the necessary materials. Stahlecker's reference to "the Führer's wish," which he did not describe in any detail,[2] met with reserve. Drechsler was not pleased to hear about this plan to erect a concentration camp for German and Czech Jews – he did not want more Jews in his territory – but declared, "certainly everything had to be done in response to the Führer's wish."[3] In the weeks and months to come, however, this initial reserve escalated into controversies among SS, civil administrative bodies, and army departments in the occupied territories of the Soviet Union with dire consequences to the way the deportations were carried out and, hence, the fate of those being expelled.

Most of the voluminous historical literature about the Holocaust deals only in passing with the fate of the more than 65,000 people who in 1941–1942 were deported from Germany, Austria, and the so-called Protektorat Böhmen und Mähren to the occupied parts of the Soviet Union. The opinion prevails that the deportations of people to the area its German occupiers referred to as Reichskommissariat Ostland were the first from Central Europe to deliver their human cargo to immediate annihilation at their destination.[4] In the fall and winter of 1941–1942, however, the systematic killing mechanism, which necessitated cooperation between SS units and civilian and/or military organizations, did not yet function as smoothly as this

conclusion infers. With few exceptions little is known about the exact format
of these deportations and the events that took place after the trains arrived
at their destinations. That dearth of detail contrasts with the importance of
this wave of deportations, especially because of their volume.[5] Almost half
of the people Eichmann's apparatus had deported by the end of 1942 from
Germany, Austria, and the Protectorate to areas east of the former border
of the German Reich were expelled to the Reichskommissariat Ostland. So
many decades later, neither all data of the transports destined for Minsk,
Kaunas (Kovno), and Riga, nor reasonably accurate numbers of victims have
surfaced.[6]

Even less reliable information exists about the institutional prerequisites
for this wave of deportations. Several general and specific studies on the
Holocaust, the SS, and Operation Barbarossa address some of these aspects. But
the structures and motives underlying the decision-making processes, jurisdictions, and competences concerning accommodations and the deportees'
labor; and those related to the selections and killing Aktionen of the various,
often competing, German administrative organizations of the SS, individual
Wehrmacht units, and civil administrations in the "Wild East" of the Third
Reich still are shrouded in darkness.[7]

Research on the fate of these expelled Central European Jews is rather more
difficult in that it has, in a sense, been overshadowed by the mass murder of
Soviet Jews.[8] The occupied areas of the Soviet Union under German administration became a gigantic abattoir where the Herrenmenschen in German
uniform murdered, starved, or condemned to death by disease or epidemics
not only Soviet Jews but also hundreds of thousands of men and women
representing many different groups – Soviet prisoners of war, Communists,
"Gypsies," civilians suspected of being or aiding partisans, and inmates of
psychiatric institutions. A great deal went on behind and parallel to the
fronts of Operation Barbarossa. The Einsatzgruppen mobile killing units of the
Sicherheitspolizei and the SD, their local accomplices, and SS formations and
police contingents, as well as individual army units, went on a rampage.[9]
What follows is an examination of the relation of SS and Wehrmacht in
respect to the Mordaktionen, the killing sprees, whose victims were Soviet
prisoners of war, Fremdrassige (people of "alien" races), and "asocials" in the
occupied territories of the Soviet Union in the second half of 1941. Those
events set the stage for the fate of the Central European Jews deported to
Riga and Minsk beginning in November 1941. The second purpose of this
sub-chapter is to outline the basic patterns of handling the expelled people
at the points of destination and to trace the decision-making processes in

the various hierarchies, in addition to the conflicts among the participating authorities.

The Barbarization of the Conduct of War and the Relations between the SS and Wehrmacht

Shortly after the start of Operation Barbarossa the first massacres of the Jewish population took place in the German-occupied city of Kaunas in Lithuania. Lithuanian civilians, encouraged by Einsatzgruppe A commander Dr. Stahlecker, had begun killing Jewish inhabitants in the streets by bludgeoning them to death. About three weeks later, Stahlecker, in cynical SS jargon, reported:

> in Kaunas a total of 7,800 Jews were done in, partly through pogroms, partly through shootings by Lithuanian commandos. All corpses have been removed. Additional mass shootings are no longer possible. So I summoned a Jewish committee and explained to them that until now we have had no reason to interfere in internal squabbles between Lithuanians and Jews.

He reported a supposedly spontaneous popular uprising in Kaunas following the retreat of the Red Army, in the course of which "about 2,500 Jews had been slain."[10]

In a report written three months later, Stahlecker described his *modus operandi* more clearly: His mission had been to set in motion and effectively channel "self-cleansing efforts to reach the objective of 'cleansing' as quickly as possible."[11] At least initially, however, Einsatzgruppe A did not want to commit murders in public because, after all, "these uncommonly harsh measures" against Lithuanian Jews "were bound to draw attention in German circles, too."[12] For future need, Stahlecker considered it equally necessary "to create a factual record of the liberated population applying the toughest measures against Bolshevik and Jewish opponents on its own account, without discernible encouragement from German authorities."[13] In addition to exploiting local antisemites as his instruments, Stahlecker made it a point to praise the "overall good" relations with the Wehrmacht, which in particular cases "as, for instance, with Panzergruppe 4, under Generaloberst [Erich] Höppner [correct spelling is 'Hoepner'], had been very close, if not to say cordial."[14]

Although one might consider as an exaggeration Stahlecker's claim of such close cooperation between the SS and Wehrmacht, other sources suggest that his statement was quite realistic. During the butcheries that Lithuanian antisemites committed in Kaunas during the first days of occupation, the leaders of the German army took no steps to protect the civilian population. According to the traditional law of occupation such protection would have been their duty. But evidence proves that they were fully informed about these mass murders. Furthermore, one of the Kaunas massacres took place in the immediate vicinity of an Armee-Führungsabteilung, an army leadership center, in plain sight of a crowd including German soldiers.[15] The attitude of top-level Wehrmacht representatives was marked by passive compliance and deep-seated antisemitism.[16]

The Wehrmacht reactions to the mass murders of segments of the Soviet civilian population within the framework of Operation Barbarossa differed profoundly from their reactions in the war against Poland. When, in the fall of 1939, members of the SS and the Wehrmacht killed Polish civilians in occupied Poland, some of the culprits had to answer for their deeds to Feldgerichte, mobile military courts.[17] The disagreements between SS and Volksdeutsche Selbstschutzverbände, "self-defense" units of ethnic Germans in Poland, on the one side, and the Wehrmacht as the executive power in the occupied zone on the other, had at least inhibited the escalation of racial persecution. But in the summer and fall of 1941, under the direct sponsorship of the SS or through the Einsatzgruppen, far more extensive murder campaigns against Jews took place in the conquered parts of the Soviet Union. Then, Wehrmacht organizations failed to react and no firm stance materialized against the mass murder of civilians.[18] How did this change in attitude come about?

In early 1941 there had been discussions and agreements between Wehrmacht and the SS leaders about the question of ultimate authority in the "pacification" of the territory to be conquered. That issue had been settled in favor of the Einsatzgruppen. We see then that months before the start of Operation Barbarossa the SS leaders already were determined to avoid open conflicts with the Wehrmacht of the sort that had occurred in Poland and to gain as free a hand as possible in implementing their tasks.[19] The army had duly granted the SS these desired rights, as the OKW declared on March 26, 1941, after reaching agreement with the RSHA: "Vis-à-vis the civilian population, the Sonderkommandos are entitled to initiate executive measures within the framework of their mission and on their own recognizance."[20]

All along it had been the intention of the military leadership to conduct Operation Barbarossa as a war of annihilation without concern for prevailing martial and civilian norms of conduct. This was reflected in directives such as the Kommissarsbefehl, the commissar decree; in the Gerichtsbarkeitserlaß, the official jurisdiction directive; and various other decrees for the treatment of Soviet prisoners of war.[21] Beyond that, the specific concept that the enemy was

"Jewish-Bolshevism" had spread within the Wehrmacht as well. The "Directives for Troop Comportment in Russia," disseminated by the OKW before the start of the campaign, already branded the Jews as enemies:

1. Bolshevism is the deadly enemy of the National Socialist German people.
2. This struggle demands ruthless, energetic action against Bolshevik agitators, guerillas, saboteurs, and Jews, and total obliteration of all active and passive resistance.

On September 12, 1941, the alleged connection between Bolshevism and Jewry was emphasized even more when OKW chief Field Marshal Wilhelm Keitel ordered "concerning the Jews in the newly-occupied territories," the "fight against Bolshevism . . . requires ruthless, energetic action especially against the Jews, the main carriers of Bolshevism."[22]

Wehrmacht generals at the eastern front transformed such instructions from above into appeals to their units to develop "respect" for the familiar practices of the Einsatzgruppen. In this vein a directive of Sixth Army Commander-in-Chief Field Marshal Walther von Reichenau prescribed "the soldier is to show full 'appreciation' for the necessity of wreaking harsh but fair vengeance on Jewish subhumanism." Other generals issued similar orders.[23] Such directives did not result in mere "appreciation" for the massacres perpetrated by the Einsatzgruppen: In some instances they led army units directly to support SS formations at mass murders of designated groups of prisoners of war and segments of civilian populations. For example, prior to the murder of more than 33,000 Jewish men, women, and children by members of Einsatzgruppe C in the ravine of Babi Yar near Kiev on September 29 and 30, 1941, legitimized in an Einsatzgruppen situation report as a "retaliation measure for arsonist activities," the military commandant of Kiev, Generalmajor Kurt Eberhard, had complied with agreements concerning the capture of the victims. Furthermore, after the mass murder, an army engineer unit dynamited the edges of the ravine to obliterate all visible traces of the massacre.[24] In the days immediately following their taking command of the various conquered territories, army commanders routinely ordered the registration and marking of Jews, employed them in forced labor, and sometimes ordered their evacuation or ghettoization. In so doing, they significantly advanced conditions conducive to subsequent SS murder Aktionen. Since the autumn of 1941, some Wehrmacht units even conducted shootings of Jews and "Gypsies" without SS assistance – generally under the guise of combating "partisan activity."[25]

Moreover, various Wehrmacht authorities, although fully informed about the frightful extent of these massacres, could find positive aspects in these activities, as for example, the elimination of "useless mouths," as a

December 2, 1941, report from the Armament Inspector for Ukraine to General Thomas reveals:

> The solution to the Jewish Question in Ukraine was difficult, first of all because in the cities the Jews constituted the majority of the population.... The comportment of the Jews was fearful from the start – they were eager to please. They sought to avoid anything displeasing to the German administration. That deep down they hated the German administration and the army goes without saying and is hardly surprising. But there is no proof whatsoever that the Jews *en masse* or even in larger groups were involved in any acts of sabotage.... That the Jews *per se*... represented any sort of danger whatsoever for the German army cannot be claimed. The army and the German administration were satisfied with Jewish labor, efforts which certainly were fueled by no feeling other than fear. Immediately following the cessation of combat activities, the Jewish population remained unmolested. Only weeks, often months, later did the planned shootings of Jews by formations of specially designated units of the Ordnungspolizei take place.... They occurred quite publicly with the participation of Ukrainian militia, and, unfortunately, the participation of members of the Wehrmacht. The manner of executions involving men, old people, women, and children was gruesome.... Until now probably 150,000 to 200,000 Jews have been executed in the part of the Ukraine belonging to the RK [Reichskommissariat Ukraine]. Until now economic considerations have not affected these activities, but in toto one could claim that this sort of solution to the Jewish Question, pursued in Ukraine, ... has produced the following results:
>
> a) elimination of a portion of sometimes useless eaters in the cities
> b) elimination of a segment of the population doubtlessly hostile to us
>   ....
> e) negative effects at least on troops in immediate contact with these executions
> f) increasing brutalization of the formations carrying out the executions (Ordungspolizei).[26]

This report reveals the extent of the convergence of the ideological goals of the SS Weltanschauungstruppe, the force committed to a specific worldview, and the seemingly objective goals of the top representatives of the Wehrmacht in the occupied Soviet Union. From the point of view of a Wehrmacht officer, these murderous activities were ghastly and their real or imagined brutalization of the direct and indirect perpetrators necessitated criticism. Simultaneously, however, in terms of military and material objectives, they incurred approbation because their purpose was the preventive elimination of latently hostile segments of the civilian population and the acquisition of foodstuffs for the Heimatfront, the home front, and one's own military forces.[27] Additionally, this report demonstrates partial divergences that for the most part concentrate on the problem of procuring workers. Among the results of the mass murder of Jews listed above, item c) stresses "the elimination of badly needed artisans frequently of utmost importance to Wehrmacht interests" as a serious disadvantage, followed by the grave observation, "if we shoot the Jews, let the prisoners of war die, commit the majority of the inhabitants of large cities to starvation and next year also lose a part of the agrarian population to hunger, the question remains unanswered just who is supposed to produce economic values here."[28] This purely practical limitation to the annihilation of segments of the civilian population led to pointed differences of opinion between the SS and several Wehrmacht commanders in the occupied areas of the Soviet Union.

The practical considerations the Wehrmacht leadership described here probably did not cause the mass murders behind and within the front lines beginning in June. They did, however, serve as a precondition for its own brutalization in waging war and in carrying out its occupation policies, for its own Auskämmungaktionen (clearing an area of Jews) and the willful, planned starvation of hundreds of thousands of Soviet prisoners of war. The Wehrmacht's internal enemy image of "Jewish Bolshevism" explains the readiness of its members to cooperate in the mass murder of Soviet Jews[29] and so aided and abetted the genocides perpetrated by the SS.[30]

Killing Aktionen in Riga and Minsk

German troops occupied the Latvian capital on July 1, 1941. Soon afterward some of the approximately 40,000 Riga Jews who did not flee or were not evacuated during the retreat of the Red Army fell victim to pogroms instigated by antisemitic Latvians. Stahlecker and other members of Einsatzgruppe A had sponsored these persecutions, although formations of the local Fascist organization Pērkonkrusts, the so-called Donnerkreuzler or Thunder Cross, these under Victor Arajs, also acted on their own authority.[31] The SS units accepted some Latvian "volunteers" into their own units or organized them into a sort of auxiliary police. In a summary report of January 1942, SS-Sturmbannführer Dr. Lange of Einsatzkommando 2 estimated that until October 1941 approximately 30,000 persons had perished in these organized murders conducted throughout Latvia "with the aid of selected members of the Latvian auxiliary police." He added that "another few thousand Jews have been eliminated in Selbstschutz Formation initiatives after" these self-defense groups "had received appropriate encouragement."[32] In early November, according to this report, approximately 30,000 people were confined in the Riga ghetto.

Immediately after taking over Minsk, the German Fourth Army erected a huge prisoner camp that housed not only Soviet prisoners of war but also all male inhabitants of Minsk between eighteen and forty-five years of age. A senior official of the Organisation Todt, the Third Reich's vast public works and slave labor agency, reports that in this camp 140,000 people were crowded into the smallest possible space. The prisoners could scarcely move and "were forced to relieve themselves where they stood." The availability of food for prisoners was by no means certain: "Many of the prisoners of war, whose lack of food rations is virtually impossible to alleviate, have gone without food for six to eight days and in their hunger-induced animalistic apathy demonstrate only one single aim: to find something edible."[33] Instead of providing the prisoners with food, the security guards of the Wehrmacht enforced the "discipline" of starvation with pistols and rifles.

Very quickly the prisoners of war and civilian prisoners in Minsk faced a situation similar to that of people in the ghettos of occupied Poland. By July 1941 tens of thousands faced starvation while the German authorities did nothing to improve the situation. Rather, with their next moves the SS and Wehrmacht continued in line with their murderous logic. In July 1941 Fourth Army authorities approached Einsatzgruppe B. Together with the Geheime Feldpolizei, the Einsatzgruppe was to "clean up" the camp by executing "criminals," "functionaries," "Asians," and Jews on a daily basis.[34] The civilians were released. There can be no doubt: The SS did not need to impose itself on the Wehrmacht. Obviously, Wehrmacht authorities were pleased to receive the support of other German units during its "combing actions."

The SS units also continued their mass murder of segments of the civilian population. Units of Einsatzgruppe B in Minsk first slaughtered "the entire Jewish intelligentsia (teachers, professors, lawyers, etc., with medical personnel excepted)." A ghetto was established for the remainder.[35] In August the Minsk ghetto was raided constantly. The log of Police Battalion 322 from Vienna-Kagran, since June 1941 a part of the Polizei Regiment Mitte (Police Regiment Center), records one of these raids. According to the entry of August 31, 1941, a so-called Judenaktion started at 3 PM. One company was in charge of cordoning off the ghetto; another, together with an NSKK (National Socialist Motor Corps) company and the SD, conducted "the search." They arrested all male Jews between fifteen and sixty years of age and "Jewesses not wearing the compulsory yellow tag on their clothing." A total of 916 people were transferred to the police prison. The next morning they were murdered ten kilometers east of Minsk. The execution squad furnished by the police battalion shot "330 Jews (40 of them Jewesses)."[36] In August, Himmler attended one of the countless mass executions near Minsk. Allegedly, he became nauseated and ordered that "more humane" means of killing be devised.[37] Accordingly, in September, Nebe, the head of Einsatzgruppe B and who had been the chief of Amt IV (Crime Fighting) in the RSHA, ordered to Minsk a chemist from the Institute of Criminal Technology; he was to bring explosives and gas hoses in order to conduct "experiments" on inmates of psychiatric institutions.[38]

In addition to these experiments, which continued with gas vans in Sachsenhausen on Soviet prisoners of war,[39] the Minsk ghetto experienced more waves of murder, in which, according to Einsatzgruppe B activity reports, units of the Wehrmacht and the Ordnungspolizei cooperated in a "supportive" manner during a September mass murder labeled as a Großaktion, a large-scale action.[40] In September or October 1941, Eichmann also briefly visited Minsk. As he stated during his interrogation in Israel, he too attended an execution and had not been able to tolerate the sight of these killings. He had gone to Minsk at the order of his superior and had arrived at the execution site only toward the end of the mass shootings. "When I arrived, I saw only how young marksmen, I believe their uniforms had the Death's Head insignia on the lapels, shot into a pit . . . shot into it, and I still see a woman, arms flung backwards. My knees buckled and I took off."[41]

That Eichmann was sent to Minsk for no reason other than to observe an execution is highly unlikely. Because Heydrich, in the October 10, 1941 document cited earlier, mentioned that Eichmann already had begun taking deported Jews into the camps of the Einsatzgruppen, it is safe to assume that he went to Minsk in his capacity of deportation specialist to discuss and fine-tune the arrival of deportees from the Reich. Furthermore, Dr. Ehrlinger, Eichmann's former superior at the SD Hauptamt, Abt. II, who had been instrumental in the build-up of the SD in Vienna in 1938 and in Prague in 1939, just happened to have his seat of operations in Minsk in October/November 1941. The highest SS functionary in occupied White Russia, Eichmann's old acquaintance now was the chief of Sonderkommando Ib of Einsatzgruppe A.[42]

Conflicts in the Reichskommissariat Ostland

In the meantime a civil administration in Ostland gradually had been established. Since September 1, 1941, the Reichskommissariat Ostland, under Hinrich Lohse and with its headquarters in Riga, consisted of the General Kommissariat Latvia, Lithuania, and "White Ruthenia" (Belorussia), soon to be joined by the General Kommissariat Estonia. The Reichskommissariat Ostland was subordinate to Rosenberg's Reich Ministry of the Occupied Eastern Territories. In August 1941 Lohse already had established "interim directives for the treatment of Jews in the area of the Reichskommissariat Ostland." The purpose of this initiative was to "secure [at least] the minimal measures [that have been] set up by regional and area commissars wherever and for however long further measures in the spirit of the final solution to the Jewish Question were not possible." In addition to this vague reference to a "final solution," whatever form it might ultimately take, compulsory registration and wearing the yellow star helped in assembling lists of all Jewish inhabitants. With a view to regional conditions, the effort was to "cleanse the countryside of Jews," to concentrate them in the large cities, to establish ghettos, and to employ able-bodied Jews as forced labor.[43]

In keeping with these efforts, the German Commissar General in Riga established a ghetto for 30,000 Latvian Jews in a part of town referred to as the "Moscow Suburb." The Jewish "Council of Elders" already appointed earlier by the military administration, was retained, and an Ordnungsdienst, a Jewish ghetto police, established. The employment of the Riga Jews worked out "favorably," as the Commissar General described it.[44] Wehrmacht organizations, the forest service, and other institutions all availed themselves of the services of Jewish forced laborers. Through Stahlecker, reports of impending deportations of Central European Jews to the Reichskommissariat Ostland reached Riga in October. This news met with resistance within several branches of affected civil administrators. Following these notices, Generalkommissar Drechsler learned specifics from SS-Sturmbannführer Dr. Lange: The concentration camp was to be built twenty kilometers upstream and was to house 25,000 people. The first arrivals could be expected about November 10, 1941, and Lange had orders to continue his work at accelerated speed. Allegedly, Drechsler passed Reichskommissar Lohse's rejection of this measure to Lange who, although he acknowledged it, merely reiterated his own orders. Drechsler also informed the Reichskommissariat of the plan to establish a second camp "for 25,000 within the framework of the Minsk ghetto."[45]

When Lohse, Drechsler, and SS-Sturmbannführer Lange met in Riga on October 24, they once more reiterated their positions. Lange claimed to have acted "entirely on the order of Obergruppenführer Heydrich. According to Heydrich's order, speed is of the essence because the first transport is to arrive on November 10."[46] Lohse complained mainly about not having been notified in due time of "planned directives of such extraordinary political importance" and announced his intention "to get to the bottom of this matter next morning, October 25, in Berlin."[47] How he fared in Berlin is not known. He probably was told more or less what Dr. Wetzel, the official in charge of racial policy in the Reichsministerium für die besetzten Ostgebiete, had stated in a draft of a letter to Lohse on October 25, 1941, concerning the "Solution of the Jewish Question." In the letter Wetzel reported, "Oberdienstleiter (Senior Service Director) [Viktor] Brack at the Führer's Chancery has volunteered to assist with the procurement of the necessary shelters as well as the gassing apparatuses."[48] This equipment, however, did not yet exist in sufficient quantity, which is why Brack had suggested sending the chemist Dr. Helmut Kallmeyer, one of his own men, directly to Riga to take care of "all further actions" locally. Lohse was advised to contact the Führer's Chancellery directly to ask for the chemist and any additional personnel.

Wetzel also pointed out that "Sturmbannführer Eichmann, the specialist of Jewish questions at the Reichssicherheitshauptamt, had approved this course of action" and had briefed him on the establishment of camps for Jews in Riga and Minsk, "which, perhaps, also would take in Jews from the Altreich. At this time Jews from the Altreich were evacuated to be sent to Litzmannstadt and other camps, and from there to be routed later still farther east for labor service, provided they were fit for work."[49] Dr. Wetzel, a municipal court judge, had no objections to employing gassing apparatuses to murder people deemed unfit for work.

> In view of the situation, there are no reservations to employing Brack's technical aids in order to eliminate Jews who are unable to work. In this way events such as reportedly took place during the shootings of Jews in Vilnius will no longer be possible. Publicly conducted shootings cannot be tolerated.[50]

The comment about Kallmeyer's mission suggests that, in Berlin, plans existed for establishing near Riga an extermination camp with permanent gas chambers, the planning for which did involve Eichmann. These plans, however, were not to achieve realization.[51] Instead, beginning in January or February 1942, gas vans developed and tested by the technical department of the RSHA Referat II D E, without the participation of the Führer's Chancellery, were dispatched to Ostland. In the early months of 1942, Dr. Kallmeyer was sent to Bełżec, then under construction as the first extermination camp of the future Aktion (Operation) Reinhard.

How Lohse reacted to all these plans for murder remains unknown. Possibly he objected to the erection of an extermination camp for Soviet and Central European Jews within his realm of authority and insisted on the relocation of the planned camps farther east. Apparently, neither did Berlin dispel his original concerns about the deportation of Central European Jews to the Reichskommissariat. Because Lohse remained in the Altreich until early November, no one in his office in Riga knew anything about further plans while

administrators there confronted a series of problems demanding immediate
decisions of far-reaching consequence for the lives or deaths of tens of thousands of people.

On November 8, 1941, Dr. Lange announced, "according to a notice from
the Reichsicherheitshauptamt Berlin, . . . 50,000 Jews are to be transported to
the Ostland," of whom 25,000 from the Reich and 25,000 from the Protectorate
would be sent to Weiβruthenien (Belorussia) and to Riga.[52] The first transport
from the Reich was to arrive in Minsk on November 10, followed by additional
trains every other day until December 16. The remaining transports would be
arriving between January 10 and January 20, 1942. The first transport to Riga
was to arrive on November 19; the remaining ones would follow every other
day until December 17, and again between January 11 and 29, 1942. Lange
mentioned the possibility of "directing five of the transports bound for Riga to
the ghetto in Kaunas." Lange's push for completion of the Salaspils camp near
Riga had been unsuccessful; so, instead of the barracks under construction
there, former troop accommodations near Jumpramuize (Jungfernhof) would
have to serve as accommodations for the first transports.

Regierungsrat Friedrich Trampedach, the head of Department IIa (Politics) in Lohse's Reichskommissariat, who was in charge of handling Lange's
announcements in Riga, forwarded Lange's report to Reich Kommissar Lohse
in Germany, pleading with him "to stop these transports since Jew camps [sic]
had to be moved considerably farther east."[53] Clearly, regional authorities in
Riga, as in Łódź/Litzmannstadt, opposed having to accept deported Jews; here
as there, they advocated sending them to reception stations farther east. This
news, however, did not reach Lohse in Berlin; by then he probably was already
on his way back to Riga. Instead, Dr. Georg Leibbrandt, who two months later
would represent the Ostministerium at the Wannsee Conference, answered
Trampedach's telex: "Concerning Jewish transports to Ostland – detailed report
on the way. Jews will be sent farther east. Camps in Riga and Minsk only temporary stations. Therefore, no objections here." The recipient's handwritten
notes state that Obergruppenführer Friedrich Jeckeln, the Higher SS- and Police
Leader (HSSPF), was to be contacted to move the transit camp farther east if
possible.[54]

During Lohse's absence in early November, Wehrmacht authorities in
Lithuania protested to the Reich Kommissar's headquarters the killings of
Lithuanian Jews. Trampedach received the complaint from the Wehrmacht
Chefintendant Ostland, the army's chief procurement officer, that "in Vil-
nius expert Jewish craftsmen were being liquidated; their skill in the army
repair shops and other armament factories cannot be equaled by locals."[55]
Trampedach's November 7, 1941, telegram instructed the office of the Area

Commissar of Vilnius to prohibit these killing sprees. "With all means at my disposal I am trying to prevent the Wehrmacht being deprived of Jewish workers whose contributions to war production are irreplaceable." In a note for internal use only, Trampedach went on to say that in view of such events, "a generally binding instruction to that effect" seemed necessary.[56]

Another letter from the Ministry for the Occupied Eastern Territories arrived in Riga in early November; it asked Lohse for a statement. Probably in October 1941, Lohse, in response to reports by administrative units answerable to him, had prohibited further of the more or less public massacres of Latvian Jews in Liepāja (Liebau) that had been perpetrated by Latvian "Self-Defense" units. During his absence the Reichskommissariat in Riga was ordered to respond to RSHA complaints that "the Reichskommissar Ostland has prohibited the execution of Jews in Liepāja."[57] A letter from Generalkommissar Wilhelm Kube to Lohse, dated November 1, 1942, arrived at the same time. In it, Kube complained about the methods some SS units had employed in the killing action in Belorussia. "To bury the mortally wounded alive is an obscenity of the first order. Such an incident must be reported to the Führer and the Reich Marshal."[58]

Trampedach had handled all these communications and presented them to Lohse on the latter's return to Riga. On November 8, during Lohse's absence, Trampedach already had drafted a response to the letter from the Ostministerium. Lohse, adding two lines, signed and sent it to the Ostministerium on November 15. Under the heading "Executions of Jews," his letter explained that the "'wild' executions of Jews in Liebau" had been forbidden because their methods were "utterly irresponsible." The letter also asked for instructions whether the inquiry from the Ostministerium "is to be interpreted as an order for the liquidation of all Jews in Ostland" and was to be carried out "without regard to age, sex, or economic expediencies (as, for example, Wehrmacht requirements of highly skilled workers in armament factories)." Up to that point Lohse simply used the draft that his assistant had prepared. He then added: "Certainly cleansing the Ostland of Jews is our primary mission. Its accomplishment, however, must be balanced with the demands of a war economy."[59] The final sentence is again that of his assistant, arguing that "neither Rosenberg's 'Brown Folder' directives concerning the Jewish question nor any other instructions" unequivocally demand the undifferentiated murder of all Jews.[60]

This document proves that at that point neither Reichskommissar Lohse nor his assistant had received precise orders concerning the extent of extermination measures directed toward the local Jewish populace. In a few isolated cases the Reichskommissariat had even interfered in massacres: Only a few days earlier, further executions of Jews in Vilnius had been prohibited in response to Wehrmacht protests, and clear-cut directives had been demanded. Both Lohse and Trampedach were familiar with Leibbrandt's previous day's telegraph message that the Jews would be moved farther east. Neither interpreted that to mean the undifferentiated murder of all Jews. Lohse, who had formulated his August 1941 guidelines cited earlier as temporary measures toward the eventual "final solution to the Jewish Question," had just conducted negotiations in the Ostministerium in Berlin. In the course of these discussions he more than likely learned about the planned use of "the Brack Remedy," the means to murder persons "unfit for work." Although he stressed that for him "cleansing the Ostland of Jews" was a given, he, like his assistant, obviously had no idea just what this "cleansing" or "final solution to the Jewish Question" meant in concrete terms and who was to be affected by the SS murder apparatus. The Reichskommissariat's basic questions received no clear answers. Two letters from the Ostministerium to the Reich Kommissar did address Lohse's inquiries, but their content was either outdated or in practice applied in a variety of ways.

Confusion also reigned among administrative offices as to the location of the camp. At a December 12, 1941 meeting, Leibbrandt informed Lohse that Heydrich had announced that the camp planned for the Riga area would be erected "in the area of Pleskau (Pskov)."[61] When in early December the Wehrmacht offensive near Moscow ground to a permanent standstill and the Red Army prepared its counter-offensive, hopes for a speedy military victory over the Soviet Union turned into a chimera and with it the relocation of the camps in the East. As to a camp near Pskov, there was no further mention of it. The second letter from the Ostministerium arrived in Riga on December 22 and under the heading "Jewish Question, Response to Letter of November 15, 1941" referred the recipient to the clarification achieved "in the meantime through verbal discussions," elaborating that "economic concerns are at no time to influence the solution of the problem. Furthermore, all issues arising locally are to be solved in cooperation with the leader of the Higher SS and Police."[62]

In reality, neither the treatment of local Jews nor of those deported from Central Europe to the Reichskommissariat Ostland was as unequivocal as the formulation to ignore the economic realities prescribed. Likewise, the activities of the SS in various areas of the occupied territories were by no means uniform. Whereas in White Ruthenia and Latvia massacres of Russian and Latvian Jews took place in November and December, in Lithuania mass murders of local Jews came to an end in mid-November, and the people crammed into the ghettos of Vilnius and Schaulen (Šiauliai) were obliged to perform forced labor.

Deportees from Central Europe were not handled in identical fashion either. On November 20, 1941, Dr. Lange of Einsatzgruppe A informed the Reich Kommissar that the Jewish transports were arriving in Minsk consecutively in the manner planned but that the first five of the twenty-five transports originally designated to go to Riga had been diverted to Kaunas. On November 28, Lohse approved the proceedings as ready for discussion with Jeckeln, the Higher SS and Police Leader South. Lohse's objections did not prevail; rather, he agreed to the measures Jeckeln and the SS units would see fit to establish. That very day he even ordered that from then on, "no protests" were to be raised "against transports from the Reich."[63]

The Establishment of the "German Ghettos" and the Temporary Halt of Deportations to Minsk

In the letter cited above, Lange did not tell the Reich Kommissar of the killings of the Belorussian Jews who had "prepared" the arrival of deportees in Minsk. On November 7, 1941, approximately 12,000 ghetto inhabitants had been murdered in a large-scale massacre so that the freed-up space now was available for the Jews expelled from Central Europe. A "German Ghetto" was established as part of the Minsk ghetto.[64]

Local administrative authorities immediately protested the installation of this sub-ghetto. In a letter of November 20, 1941, the Wehrmachtsbefehlshaber Ostland (Army Commander Ostland) opposed transporting Jews from Germany to White Ruthenia. Through a report of the 707th Division, he had found out that 25,000 German Jews were to be shipped to that destination and that, in fact, 1,500 Jews from Hamburg already had arrived there: "The influx of German Jews, far superior in intelligence to the bulk of the Belorussian population constitutes a severe danger for the pacification of White Ruthenia, the Jewish population of which is made up of Bolsheviks capable of any hostile, anti-German stance."[65] As proof of this allegedly dangerous anti-German stance, the officer referred to Geheime Feldpolizei reports that accused Jews of having attempted "through threats" to force farmers either not to harvest at all or to destroy their crops.

> As was the case wherever reports about sabotage, agitation of the populace, resistance, etc. necessitated action, the Jews were revealed as the source, as the instigators, and most of the time as the perpetrators as well. Like them, the

newly-arriving Jews will attempt with all means at their disposal to contact Communist organizations, etc. and agitate.[66]

In addition to these ideologically tainted descriptions of the "enemy," the Wehrmachtsbefehlshaber also cited real problems by commenting on the difficult transport situation:

> Army Group Center has asked me to halt the transports of Jews as the railroads are needed for increased supply shipments. I have forwarded this request to the Chief of Transportation. For the erection of winter quarters, transport of construction materials, glass, coal, etc. in addition to regular supplies is so acute that Jewish transports have to be deferred for these reasons alone.[67]

These objections of Wehrmacht organizations to the deportation of German, Austrian, and Czech Jews to Minsk were successful in that after the arrival of the first seven deportation trains of November 1941, the remaining ones planned for that year were temporarily suspended.

In Minsk, civil administrative units also protested additional deportations. Kube, the Reich Kommissar of White Ruthenia, expressed his problems in determining the ultimate fate of the Central European Jews deported to Minsk. On November 29, 1941, he had undertaken an inspection of the German Ghetto in Minsk, during which the German-Jewish chairman of the "Jewish Council" informed him that some people had been unlawfully deported. Kube asked for a list of names of these individuals and, because he was unsure what rules to establish concerning these German Jews, asked Lohse "personally for official guidelines."[68] He reported that of the announced 25,000 deportees, only 6,000–7,000 had arrived so far, among them "World War I veterans decorated with The Iron Cross first- and second-class, war-wounded veterans, half Aryans and even three-quarter Aryans." Also in this group were skilled workers "capable of achieving a daily production quota five times that of Russian Jews." He also commented on the dismal food supply and housing, and the alleged danger of epidemics.

Kube refused to issue an order for the murder of these Jews: "I will not give the SD the order for the treatment [he probably meant "Sonderbehandlung, "Special" Treatment] of these people on my own authority, even though certain groups of the Wehrmacht and the police already are keen to pocket the belongings of the Jews from the Reich." He claimed that the SD already had "confiscated" items belonging to the deportees.[69] Kube protested his willingness to help solve the Jewish Question but differentiated between German and Russian Jews: "People from our cultural environment differ from the local animalistic hordes." How the Baltic "volunteers" deal with Jews is obvious from the question whether "to put the Lithuanians and Latvians whom the local population abhors in charge of this butchery. I couldn't do that." So, to preserve the honor of the Reich and the Party, he asked Lohse for clear instructions "in arranging the necessary in the most humane way possible."[70]

In early January 1942, sidestepping official channels, the Minsk Stadtkommissar (City Commissar) contacted the Ostministerium directly. He had learned that "in Berlin the decision had been reached... to ship approximately 50,000 additional German Jews to Minsk within the next weeks and months."[71] In his opinion this was not feasible because Minsk had suffered severe destruction and, in addition to 100,000 civilians, already housed 7,000 Jews from Germany and 15,000–18,000 Russian Jews. The Ostministerium overrode his objections: "According to a report from the Reichssicherheitshauptamt, 25,000 Jews from the Reich had been apportioned for Minsk, to be housed temporarily in the local ghetto." So far, as a result of transportation problems, only 7,000–8,000 had been transferred to Minsk, "but as soon as these problems have been solved, the rest too will arrive in Minsk."[72] Obviously, both the RSHA and the Ostministerium were intent on leaving the door open for continuing deportations to Belorussia. Independent of all this, Trampedach of Abteilung IIa at the Reichskommissariat in Riga already had decided that Lohse's November 28, 1941, directive that "no more objections were to be raised against any transports from the Reich" was to be observed.[73] Kube, on the other hand, in a letter to Lohse, supported the City Commissar's argument against suddenly quartering 25,000 additional people in a destroyed city, but closed his letter stating, "nevertheless, it goes without saying that the Reich Minister's order will be followed."[74]

Mass Killings in Kaunas and Riga's "Bloody Sunday"

Since the July 1941 massacre in Kaunas, the murder apparatus of the SS and its local helpers in occupied Lithuania had achieved terrifying dimensions. Within four months, between July and early November 1941, approximately 80 percent of Lithuania's Jewish population had been killed – more than 150,000 men, women, and children. According to the infamous Jäger Report of December 1, 1941, except for the Arbeitsjuden, the "work Jews" and their families, there were no more Jews in Lithuania. SS-Standartenführer Karl Jäger originally had planned to murder the remaining 40,000 people in the ghettos of Vilnius, Kaunas, and Schaulen (Šiauliai) as well: "These Arbeitsjuden, including their families, I wanted to do in as well, which, however, resulted in a sharp reproach from the civilian administration (the Reich Kommissar) and the Wehrmacht and triggered the prohibition, 'these Jews and their families will not be shot!'"[75] The final large-scale Aktion killing Lithuanian Jews had taken place on November 6 in Vilnius, claiming more than 1,000 victims. Following that, the SS more or less complied with the instructions of the Reich Kommissar or the Wehrmacht.

In mid-November 5,000 people had been shipped in five transports from Berlin, Frankfurt/Main, Munich, Vienna, and Breslau (Wrocław), but they had ended up in Kaunas instead of Riga. Obviously they were not classified as Jewish workers "indispensable for performing war-economic tasks." Jäger's henchmen murdered them in Fort IX in Kaunas, as Jäger, carefully differentiating between men, women, and children, painstakingly recorded in his ledger of mass murder: "November 25, 41, 1,159 (male) Jews, 1,600 Jewesses, 175 J.-childr. (resettlers from Berlin, Munich, and Frankfurt a. M.); November 29, 41, 693 Jews, 1,155 Jewesses, 152 J.-childr. (resettlers from Vienna and Breslau)."[76]

At the end of November and in early December, housing the deportees in camps in the Riga area still was not possible because Jungfernhof consisted of only a few barracks, and the camp at Salaspils had yet to be built. So HSSPF Jeckeln, who was mainly responsible for the November 30, 1941, shootings near Riga, proceeded in the same way as the SS had done shortly before in Minsk. The Operations Report USSR of January 5, 1942, mentions the delays in the construction of the Riga camp (Salaspils) and the matter of responsibility for the massacres of Riga's "Bloody Sunday," suggesting a direct connection between housing problems and the murders:

> The first five transports destined for Riga were rerouted to Kaunas. The Riga camp designed to house 25,000 Jews is under construction and will be finished presently. For now, HSSPF in Riga, SS-Obergruppenführer Jeckeln, has launched a shooting Aktion and on Sunday, November 11, 1941, eliminated approximately 4,000 Jews from the Riga ghetto and one evacuation transport from the Reich.[77]

But Jeckeln's execution detachments could not handle the mass murders by themselves, so, after several hours, members of Dr. Lange's Einsatzkommando also took part: "Originally this Aktion was to be handled by HSSPF personnel; however, after several hours, the twenty-man security guard from the EK2 had to be deployed as well."[78]

In another massacre a week later, on December 8, thousands of Latvian Jews from the Riga ghetto were murdered as well. Overall, more than 25,000 people from this ghetto had been killed.[79] Only after Riga's Bloody Sunday did the

SS admit arriving deportees from Central Europe to the camps of Jungfernhof and Salaspils, and, beginning on December 10, into the now empty parts of the Riga ghetto.[80] From then on, the murder squads no longer shot deportees immediately upon arrival. The transport with deportees from Berlin, arriving in Riga on November 30, was the only exception. These variations in the fate of the deportees suggest that in the fall of 1941 no uniform orders existed mandating the immediate and undifferentiated murder of all deported Central European Jews. Clearly, then, decisions over life and death of the deportees lay not entirely with regional organizations of civilian administrators, the Wehrmacht, and the SS, but these matters certainly constituted part of their responsibilities.

After initial conflicts among various organizations, a modus operandi had developed in Ostland during the period under discussion. It consisted of murdering Latvian or Belorussian Jews without consideration of possible "war-economic complications," doing so to make room for deported Central European Jews whose stay in these camps or ghettos was to be merely temporary. The murder of deportees "unfit for work" probably already had been planned but depended on the availability of poison-gas devices. That the people who were deported to the Baltic region with the first six transports in November 1941 were murdered, virtually without exception, by the SS and its local helpers is almost certainly not the result of a centrally issued order. Presumably these murder Aktionen were in part due to the inability of SS authorities in Latvia to prepare shelters in a timely fashion and in part the result of the civilian administration's wishes to relocate these camps farther east. The squabbles among various local authorities over the importance of economic considerations probably impacted the extent of these murderous activities in regard to Latvian and Lithuanian Jews. Yet in the murderous logic of the SS offices the temporary reprieve of Lithuanian Jews, beginning in November 1941, probably sealed the fate of the 5,000 people deported from Central Europe to Kaunas. The deported Jews who were sent to Minsk at the same time were not killed immediately; as soon as makeshift housing was available in Riga, through construction or because of the mass murder of Latvian Jews, the deportees no longer faced execution squads the moment they arrived.

The case of Soviet Jews also raises questions about the existence of a uniform order for murder. In November serious confrontations between the SS on the one hand and the Wehrmacht and civilian authorities on the other arose in Lithuania as to whether Jews confined in ghettos and employed as forced laborers should be shot by SS units. In Vilnius the call for a stop to the murders carried the day; the SS did not insist on their continuation. Either a change of the SS plans for murder occurred in November or the instructions had been flexible from their inception, depending on the reactions of the Wehrmacht. The Israeli historian Yitzhak Arad considers the cessation of the mass murders in Lithuania the result of Wehrmacht and civilian administrative intervention.[81]

The conflicts of November and December 1941 in the Reichskommissariat Ostland did demonstrate the impact of Wehrmacht protests. For example, Wehrmacht objections to the extermination of Lithuanian Jews at least temporarily saved the lives of tens of thousands. Likewise, the demands of Wehrmacht organizations in Minsk to halt deportations of Central European Jews to White Russia were honored, if only for six months. Obviously, the SS was incapable of maintaining its agenda in the face of determined opposition of Wehrmacht commanders.

What needs to be pointed out is that the problems faced by the organizers of the expulsion of Central European Jews during the deportations to Ostland were similar to those that they encountered during the deportations to Łódź. A few local civilian and military organizations involved in receiving the transports and accommodating the deportees protested. The reactions of the SS expulsion specialists also resemble those already in evidence in the Warthegau: In December 1941, the SS Kommandos near Łódź started killing "selected" persons in gas vans. The functionaries in Ostland also were advised to use poison gas for killing people "unfit for work," and early in 1942 gas vans actually were made available to them. Even though, in contrast to Łódź, there were active SS units who by then were "used to" the mass murder of men, women, and children, the overwhelming majority of deportees in Riga and Minsk, as in Łódź, were housed in prepared ghettos and at least temporarily pressed into forced labor.

Łódź, Riga, and Minsk were the locations selected in the fall of 1941 to serve as the receiving stations for deported Jews or Roma and Sinti from Germany, Austria, and the Protectorate. These sites received gas vans in late 1941/early 1942 and, for the most part, persons deemed "unfit for work" were murdered there. All of this suggests the centrally steered nature of this process coordinated by the RSHA and Eichmann's Referat. In fact, the only two 1941 documents containing deliberations over the killings of "work-incapable" Jews with poison gas do relate directly to Eichmann. He personally managed the negotiations with the responsible institutions at the target locations. All clues suggest his having proposed or supported this killing method in his discussions with Gestapo and ghetto administrative personnel in Łódź, with SS organizations in Minsk, with the officials of the Ostministerium, and having advanced its adoption in cooperation with central SS offices in Berlin.

The poison-gas murder of those people categorized as unfit for work began in Chełmno/Kulmhof in December 1941 and horrifically continued in the succeeding months. Beginning in the spring of 1942, in addition to the gas-van victims in the Warthegau and the Reichskommissariat Ostland, hundreds of thousands of people met death in the extermination camps of Aktion Reinhard in the Generalgouvernement.

6   The Development of the Genocide
       Program: 1942

At the end of November 1941, the RSHA under the letterhead "Referat IV
B 4" sent out invitations for a conference scheduled for December 9, 1941,
at the Headquarters of the International Criminal Police Commission, at Am
Großen Wannsee 56–58 in Berlin. The invitation was signed by Heydrich
and addressed to the state secretaries of various ministries and representatives
of specific occupation organizations; it announced the topic of discussion as
the "organizational, functional and material preparation for a Final Solution
of the Jewish Question in Europe" and to bring about consensus "on this
concept at the appropriate central authorities."[1] Apparently, the conference was
rescheduled only at the very last minute for, as late as December 8, Rademacher
from the Foreign Office presented State Undersecretary Luther, one of its
participants, with a draft entitled "Foreign Office: Wishes and Ideas for the
Planned Total Solution of the Jewish Question in Europe" in preparation "for
tomorrow's session with SS-Obergruppenführer Heydrich."[2]

The postponement of the Wannsee Conference is most frequently explained
as a consequence of the Japanese attack on Pearl Harbor and the United States'
entry into the war. Only occasionally do historians point to the decisive reason:
the ultimate failure of Operation Barbarossa.[3] The end of the German advance
on Moscow and the Red Army's counteroffensive beginning on December 5
buried all hopes for a rapid victory and all plans based on the speedy conquest
of the Soviet Union.[4] Among them, the expulsions of hundreds of thousands
of people to areas of the Soviet Union that leading NS functionaries had
envisioned for that purpose during the summer could not be realized in the
immediate future. In Autumn 1941, SS authorities had placated Warthegau
and Ostland regional administrative authorities by promising that deportees
would be placed there on only a short-term basis before being permanently
deported farther east. Now those promises were moot. Furthermore, because of
constantly increasing transportation and supply problems that the Wehrmacht

experienced at the eastern front, the SS had to accept various Wehrmacht organizations' objections to further transports of deportees.

From the point of view of those responsible for expulsions, this situation must have represented a serious setback. Although deportations to Riga continued in December, not even the previously arranged deportations of Central European Jews to Minsk could be conducted as planned. If and when they could be continued remained uncertain. New target locations for deportations had to be found, and this time they were located in the territory ruled by Hans Frank, to which Eichmann and his men already had directed deportations from Vienna in the spring of 1941.[5] Now the authorities in the Generalgouvernement no longer could hope to be able to deport Jews from their own administrative area "to the East." At an administrative conference in Kraków in mid-December, Hans Frank revealed the status of official thinking when he commented on the result of his negotiations on that subject at a Berlin conference where he had been told: "Why cause us all these headaches? We don't know what to do with them in Ostland or in the Reichskommissariat Ukraine, for that matter. Liquidate them yourselves."[6]

From this, Frank drew the following conclusion:

> Gentlemen, I must ask you to steel yourselves against all intimations of pity. We have to destroy the Jews wherever we encounter them. . . . For us the Jews are an extremely dangerous plague of locusts. . . . We can't shoot these 3.5 million Jews [presumably those in the Generalgouvernement]; we can't poison them, yet we should be able to find some means that somehow will lead to extermination successes through portentous measures about to be proposed in the Reich.[7]

This was Frank's anticipatory reference to the discussion to be held with Heydrich in Berlin in January, and to which Frank was planning to send his state secretary. Although Frank's goal was for the Generalgouvernement to be as free of Jews as the Reich, he only hinted how this genocide was to be carried out: "Where and how this will happen is the responsibility of the authorities we will create and put in place here and whose competences I will announce to you in due time."[8] The Generalgouvernement's preparations for "annihilation successes" lay in the construction of the extermination camp Bełżec, although by December it had not yet progressed significantly. The Führer's Chancellery had sent the killing personnel, who had staffed the recently reduced euthanasia program, to direct the construction of the camp and its permanent gas chambers. In Chełmno, on the other hand, the mass murders were carried out with SS-developed mobile gas vans.

Eichmann knew by mid-October 1941 that, for the construction of a concentration camp in the environs of Riga, Oberdienstleiter Brack at the Führer's

Chancellery was willing to furnish personnel and cooperate in the production of gassing devices. It remains unclear whether Eichmann was involved in establishing the contacts among Brack, civilian authorities in the General-gouvernement, and Odilo Globocnik. Globocnik was the former Gauleiter of Vienna, then the SS- und Polizeiführer of the Lublin district, and later chief of Aktion Reinhard, so named in Heydrich's honor.[9]

In any case, Eichmann visited Bełżec while it still was under construction, as he stated during his interrogation in Jerusalem. After allegedly informing him about the Führerbefehl, Hitler's order concerning the Final Solution, Heydrich sent him to Globocnik in Lublin to find out how the preparations for the construction of extermination camps were progressing. Accordingly, Eichmann went to Poland where one of Globocnik's coworkers showed him a camp under construction. A police captain speaking a southwestern dialect – obviously Christian Wirth, a native of Stuttgart and the future commandant of Bełżec – had explained that the barracks had been made air-tight so that the exhaust gases of a submarine motor could be channeled into them to murder people.[10] Construction of the Bełżec extermination camp began in November 1941 and was completed in late February 1942; so Eichmann probably did not inspect the camp any earlier than December 1941, or perhaps even as late as January or February 1942.[11] As usual, this inspection tour probably did not serve the sole purpose of inspecting camp construction, but also to conduct preparatory meetings with Globocnik and his staff about the deportations of Central European Jews to the Lublin district.

In the fall of 1941 Eichmann had been confronted with complaints from firms in the Reich protesting the deportation of allocated Jewish forced laborers. In a meeting at the end of October with representatives of the Wehrwirtschaftsrüstungsamt (the armed forces' armament procurement office) at the Oberkommando der Wehrmacht, Eichmann and Lösener had assured them that permanently employed Jews would not be deported without approval of the state employment offices and armament inspectors.[12] This subject also was to be discussed at the Wannsee Conference.

At the Wannsee Conference on January 20, 1942, Heydrich reminded the representatives of ministries and occupation authorities that he had been appointed by Göring as the Reich Marshal's deputy in charge of the "Preparation for the *Endlösung*, the Final Solution of the European Jewish Question."[13] He provided "a brief review of the fight against this adversary," including statistics on the "emigration" of 537,000 Jews from the Altreich, the Ostmark, and the Protectorate. Because of the war and the "possibilities opening up in the East," Himmler had prohibited emigration, for, "with Hitler's permission, evacuation of the Jews to the East provided new solutions." These evacuations, however, were to be considered "nothing more than alternative possibilities (Ausweichmöglichkeiten)," in the course of which practical, hands-on experience "with an eye on the approaching Final Solution of the Jewish Question" was to be gathered.[14] The Final Solution would involve "about eleven million Jews" from all of Europe, including England, Italy, Portugal, Sweden, Switzerland, Spain, and the European part of Turkey. They would be "employed as workers in the East," as a result of which "the majority doubtlessly would perish through natural reduction; "finally any remaining residual stock" were to be "treated appropriately," that is, murdered.

Because the inclusion of Jews from the countries he enumerated in this killing program would be possible only after the subjugation of the entire continent, the ultimate realization of what Heydrich termed the "Final Solution" could occur only after the victorious conclusion of the war. This statement reveals that Heydrich's vision of the Final Solution also involved a long-range goal he already had formulated on other occasions: an SS racist postwar ideal. This long-range goal, however, did not preclude initial steps: "In the course of the practical implementation of the Final Solution, Europe will be cleared from west to east. The Reich, including the Protectorate of Bohemia and Moravia, if for no other reason than to relieve housing problems and other sociopolitical issues, will be dealt with first."[15]

Following his two-fold legitimization of the "evacuations" of Jews from the German Reich as a safety valve and precursor of the Final Solution throughout Europe, Heydrich discussed the planned deportations. The types of people to be evacuated were to be defined concisely. Jews above the age of sixty-five would be transported to an "old people's ghetto" – Theresienstadt was slated to serve in that capacity – rather than being deported to the East. Also to go to Theresienstadt would be "Jewish war veterans who had been severely wounded and Jewish veterans decorated with the EK I (the Iron Cross, First Class)."[16]

After discussing details such as the classification of so-called Mischlinge, the offspring of "mixed marriages" between German Jews and Aryans, and exceptions for Jews employed in companies and organizations vital to the war effort, the participants considered "various sorts of solutions."[17] The representatives of occupation administrations from the Generalgouvernement and of the Ministry for the Occupied Eastern Territories asked that "certain preparations for the Final Solution be made locally, though it would be vitally important to avoid unrest among the local populace."[18] Frank's representative phrased most concisely what they had in mind: he proposed to initiate the Final Solution in the Generalgouvernement because there "transportation problems did not play a primary role and considerations of work deployment would not impede the course of action." Furthermore, he argued, in the Generalgouvernement

the majority of Jews to be affected by the Final Solution were unfit for work
in any case. Because persons unable to work scarcely could have been eligi-
ble to work in the East, the phrase "certain preparations" cannot be anything
but a euphemism for mass murder of those classified as unfit for work in
"the affected areas themselves." Following the group's considerations of the
methods of murder, Heydrich closed the session with the request to provide
him with "support during the implementation of the labors involved in the
appropriate solutions."[19]

As the participants of the Wannsee Conference were negotiating, in coded
terms, the deportation and murder of people unfit for work, Himmler issued
written orders to the chief of the SS concentration camp administration
to employ Jews capable of work as forced laborers. "Since we can't expect
Russian prisoners of war in the foreseeable future, I will send to the
camps large contingents of Jews and Jewesses who are being emigrated from
Germany." The administration was to prepare itself to take in "100,000 male
and up to 50,000 female Jews" because "large economic contracts" soon would
be awarded to the concentration camps.[20]

Heydrich's "territorial Final Solution" of 1940 initially had envisioned the
expulsion of all Jews from German-ruled areas and their transportation to
Madagascar, with the destination later shifted to Siberia. Such plans were to
be realized only after the victorious end of the war. By January 1942, however,
they had evolved into anticipatory activities and "certain preparatory works,"
that is, into much more concrete measures. This meant that before and during
the Wannsee Conference decisive steps had been taken to change the "Final
Solution of the Jewish Question" from a strategy focusing primarily on total
expulsion into a systematic policy of genocide employing industrial methods. Simultaneously, at the turn of 1941–1942 the differences between civil
administrations in Ostland and the Generalgouvernement and the SS organizations responsible for the deportations were eliminated and future activities
coordinated. At the Wannsee Conference both groups agreed on a program of
selections, which for persons still able to work, resulted in a regimen of brutal
exploitation through slave labor and hence their "natural reduction," and the
immediate murder by poison gas of those deemed unfit for work.

The same methods already practiced in the Warthegau would be employed
as well in the Generalgouvernement and the Reichskommissariat Ostland. At
the end of January or in February 1942, Sturmbannführer Lange, who was the
Ostland SS representative at the Wannsee Conference, received gas vans for
murdering primarily persons, classified as unfit for work, who were confined
in camps in and around Riga. In the Generalgouvernement, where Hans Frank
was eager to boast success quotas in eliminating people to whom he referred

as "useless eaters" hundreds of thousands of men, women, and children were murdered in the extermination camps of Aktion Reinhard – beginning in Bełżec in March, in Sobibór in May, and in Treblinka in July 1942. In the spring and summer of 1942, Eichmann and his men were to deport tens of thousands of Central European Jews to these two regions; simultaneously they organized the deportations of "fit-for-work" people from Slovakia and France. These went to the concentration camps Auschwitz and Lublin. It is telling that Heydrich now applied the same asocial logic that Reichskommissar Bürckel had formulated in 1938 in Vienna when he coined the phrase "If Aryanization is to be conducted and the Jews deprived of their livelihood, the Jewish Question must be solved in its totality." Heydrich did so by citing "housing problems" and other "sociopolitical necessities" in anticipation of the Final Solution in the German Reich.

Eichmann referred to the "Final Solution of the Jewish Question" in specific terms only after the Wannsee Conference. At the end of January 1942 he sent a memorandum to all state police offices in the Altreich and to the Zentralstellen to announce that the recently conducted deportations represented "the start of the Final Solution of the Jewish Question in the Altreich, the Ostmark, and the Protectorate of Bohemia and Moravia." So far the deportations had been related to "especially pressing projects" because limited possibilities of placements in the east and difficulties with large-scale transportation had to be considered. Now because "new possibilities for placement" were being worked out and precise planning of the evacuations would be of prime importance, he ordered these offices to conduct a "precise determination of all Jews still living in the Reich."[21]

A short time later Eichmann published "Directives for the Technical Conduct of the Evacuation of Jews to the Generalgouvernement"; it was to cover all Jews in the Reich and the Protectorate except for those who lived in Mischehen (mixed marriages with Aryans), were conscripted for labor vital to the war effort, or were more than sixty-five years old.[22] At an organizational meeting in early March 1942 in the RSHA, Eichmann and Gestapo employees once more reviewed technical details of the planned deportations from the Altreich: persons to be selected, seizure of their property, and actual management of the transports.[23] The rules established at this meeting imposed uniform procedures on the machinery of capture throughout the German Reich. Organized in this fashion, the mass deportations from Germany, Austria, and the Protectorate were to be continued uninterruptedly until all persons fitting these categories had been expelled. At the end of May 1942 Eichmann summoned the representatives of the Vienna and the Prague Jewish communities, and the leaders of the Reichsvereinigung der Juden in Deutschland, to his Berlin office

to inform them of the planned "total evacuation of the Jews from the Altreich, Ostmark, and the Protectorate." Men and women younger than sixty-five
years of age would "emigrate to the East;" older people and wounded or decorated World War I veterans would be taken to Theresienstadt, "their future
permanent residence."[24]

Vienna 1942: Manhunts and Conclusion of the Mass Deportations

Between February 1941 and October 1942, the Zentralstelle transported the
majority of Jews still living in Vienna; these individuals were consigned for
"resettlement" or "emigration to the East," as the SS bureaucrats officially
termed these activities. Alois Brunner and his subordinates employed increasingly brutal means in the seizure and internment of their victims. Their preparations for deportations were based on practices Eichmann had introduced:
namely, employing Jewish organizations under direct SS supervision in performing specific tasks.[25] The people slated for "resettlement" in the Generalgouvernement or "the East" had to report to the collection sites at Sperlgasse
2a and Malzgasse 16. The Jewish Kultusgemeinde was responsible for their care
during their stay at these "assembly camps" and during transports. Those about
to be deported were notified by SS men accompanied by members of the so-
called Erhebungsdienst (locating service) organized by the Kultusgemeinde.[26]
Originally, assembly in these camps was supposed to be voluntary. However,
"should any Jews not obey the order of the Zentralstelle, their appearance
will be enforced by the police. Furthermore, such Jews can expect harsher
treatment. The Kultusgemeinde will receive the lists of the deportees three or
four days before each transport to inform them of their orders."[27] To prevent
escapes from the assembly camps, the Jewish guards were threatened with their
own deportation.

Later Alois Brunner tightened the collection process. Unwilling to rely on
voluntary compliance, he substituted raids and arrests. Additionally, Jewish
Ordner, keepers of order also called Ausheber (raiders) and often referred to
as "researchers" or Judenpolizei (JUPO), became an increasingly prominent
presence in the process. The SS employed them in the assembly camps and in
the Abholdienst, the collection service, to assist the people being "transferred"
with packing their belongings. The SS-Scharführers were accompanied by
Jewish "group leaders" whose duty it was to instruct the packers and to make
sure that none of those to be taken to the assembly centers escaped.

Other employees of the Kultusgemeinde had to remove the furnishings
the deportees had left behind. The Vugesta, a Gestapo organization expressly

founded for this purpose, sold most of the furniture and household equipment to "Aryan" race and party comrades at low prices.[28] The employees of the Kultusgemeinde were also coerced to carry out private orders from the SS members of the Zentralstelle. Such tasks included furniture transport, carpentry work, and installation of fixtures.

During the seizures of people designated for deportation, some SS men were especially brutal. Oberscharführer Herbert Gerbing, for example, enjoyed mistreating people during these raids. As one witness recalls, he grievously injured some of his victims: "When we left the house, I saw Gerbing battering a certain Dr. Gross with brass knuckles until the man's eye dangled from its socket and his nose was broken."[29] Occasionally not only previously notified persons were arrested during such raids but whole city blocks were cordoned off and searched. To increase the size of transports, SS men also hunted and arrested Jews in the streets:

> For each transport 1,000 people had to be selected in the collection camps. If the number of inmates fell below this figure, the standing order was to increase it. Trucks then roamed the streets and passers-by wearing the star were ordered to climb in. They then were taken to the camp and slated for deportation with the next transport.[30]

Josef Weiszl is credited with extraordinary zeal in hunting Jews. "He was the most horrible Ausheber and always performed 'merit tasks demonstrating his industriousness.' Not only did he drag designated Jews from their dwellings; he also grabbed anyone he encountered along the way or who lived in the same house where he was to perform a seizure."[31] During such raids Weiszl also sent to the collection camps people such as Jews living in so-called Mischehen who, according to the guidelines, were exempt from deportation.[32]

Eichmann's men in Vienna did more than their duty; the persecution of people continued after hours too. For example, in May 1942, as Weiszl and his wife were strolling through the gardens of Schönbrunn Palace, Mrs. Weiszl spotted a Jewish coworker classified as a Geltungsjüdin (an individual defined by the Nazis as a Jew) walking in this park off limits to Jews and without wearing the mandatory yellow star. Weiszl immediately confronted the young woman: "He cursed me and threatened me with immediate deportation."[33] The following day she had to report to the Zentralstelle and was detained for six weeks at the Rossauerlände prison. After that she was taken to the Sperlgasse assembly camp from which she eventually was released only through her mother's intervention; her mother was classified as "Aryan."

Occasionally Brückler, Zita, and Slawik were in charge of the Sperlgasse and Malzgasse camps. They treated the members of the Ordnungsdienst, the Jewish police, whose lives they held in their hands, like slaves.[34] The internees too fell victim to their whims. Slawik, for example, as one of his victims reported later, "always participated in the constant drubbing of Jews. During such activities – they were referred to as *Dampfmachen* (to put steam behind something or someone) – the inmates of the camps were chased about arbitrarily and for tiny or trumped-up infractions received slaps in the face or beatings, depending on the mood of the SS men."[35] In these camps the SS organized the transports. Anton Burger and other members of the Zentralstelle "commissioned" all internees: They had to surrender all personal documents, property inventories, and valuables, and their baggage was searched. These "commissionings" provided the SS with additional opportunities for violence.[36]

Alois Brunner, especially, was infamous among the victims.

> Brunner, the director of the Zentralstelle, we feared the most. He was unbelievably brutal. He was the one who despoiled the about-to-be-deported Jews of their few remaining pitiful belongings. The Jews had to stand for hours on end, trembling at the sight of him as he, with unbelievable harshness and curses, relieved them of their last possessions.[37]

In early 1941, some 53,600 Glaubensjuden (practicing "full" Jews) and about 10,000 Nichtglaubensjuden (assimilated Jews or "racially mixed persons") still were living in Vienna.[38] By the end of December 1942 only 8,000 persons classified as Jews according to the Nuremberg Laws remained, two-thirds of whom lived in "Mischehen" and so enjoyed precarious protection.[39] At the end of October 1942 the mass deportations from Vienna came to an end; the Zentralstelle had fulfilled its purpose. It moved from the Palais Rothschild to the Castellezgasse and was officially dissolved in March 1943. Brunner and his men had done a thorough job. By October 1942 they had deported approximately 50,000 people in the prescribed manner after robbing them first. They had more than met the expectations of their superiors.

The German historian Michael Zimmermann describes the deportation of Jews from the Ruhr area in 1941–1942 by police and other government agencies as an "administrative process" whose "realization . . . qualifies it as neither a cynical or sadistic action nor primarily as an activity characterized by an awareness of injustice or by sublimation" but as "more than anything an emanation of a routine marked by strictly formulated rules marred only occasionally by specific, concrete incidents."[40] This assessment may apply to the specific region under investigation but cannot be accepted as generally true, as the activities of Eichmann's men in Vienna demonstrate. Those who hunted men in Vienna by no means disregarded the "specific, concrete" nature of their work. Quite the contrary! They obviously enjoyed being the arbiters over life and death. They had no qualms about gaining personal advantages from their victims' personal and collective plight. They Aryanized dwellings for their own use and enjoyment and forced selected victims to perform slave labor. By fine-tuning the "Vienna Model" into merciless manhunts, they completed the mass deportations from the Ostmark at a time when even the expulsion bureaucrats in the capital of the Reich lagged far behind. Their superiors found their method so efficient that from then on they called in the Austrian man-hunters whenever and wherever deportations slowed or ground to a halt.

What happened to the deportees from Vienna? Five of the 1942 spring trans-ports were steered to Izbica in the Lublin district, and one went to Włodawa in the Generalgouvernement. There some of deportees were parceled out to small rural towns.[41] The transport of June 14, according to the transport police detachment's Erfahrungsbericht (activities report), did not go to Izbica as planned because the SS diverted it to Sobibór. At the Vienna railway station Alois Brunner and Ernst Girzik of the Zentralstelle had transferred the 1,000 people for this transport to the Schutzpolizei transport detachment. In Lublin an SS-Obersturmführer commandeered fifty-one of them, all able-bodied Jews ranging from fifteen to fifty years of age, and transferred them to a work camp. The transport detachment also handed over to him the list of the deportees' names and their money, altogether about 100,000 złoty. Franz Stangl, first lieu-tenant of the Schutzpolizei and commandant of Sobibór extermination camp, received the remaining deportees in a work camp adjacent to the Sobibór rail station. There the policeman from Upper Austria ordered these 950 Austrian Jews to be driven straight into the gas chambers.[42]

Eventually, most of the Jews deported from Vienna to Izbica also perished in the gas chambers of the Bełżec and Sobibór extermination camps. Additionally, about two thirds of the people sent to Theresienstadt in thirteen transports during the summer and fall of 1942 also were murdered after being sent on another transport. On July 17, one single deportation transport from Vienna went directly to Auschwitz.[43] Between early May and early October 1942 nine went to Minsk/Maly Trostinets.

The "German Ghettos" and Mass Murders in Riga and Minsk/Maly Trostinets

Between November 1941 and October 1942 Alois Brunner and his SS men from the Zentralstelle für jüdische Auswanderung in Vienna assembled several deportation transports. Each of these sent to the East 1,000 men, women, and children from the Aspang rail station in the third municipal district.

Dr. Siegfried Seidl, the commandant of Theresienstadt, which in the first six months of 1942 served mainly as a transit camp for Czech Jews, also sent transports to the East. What fate awaited these Austrian and Czech Jews upon their arrival at their destinations in the occupied Baltic areas or White Russia? In January 1942 Einsatzgruppe A reported that the first 10,000 Central European Jews deported to Riga had been housed in a "provisionally assembled reception camp in Jungfernhof, in a "newly constructed barracks camp near Riga" (Salaspils), and in a "detached section of the Riga ghetto." The plan still was to extend Salaspils so that all deportees "who survive the winter," as the report phrased it, could be confined there. Allegedly, only a small number of these deportees were fit for work; the vast majority consisted of women, children, and old people. Apparently, the mortality rate rose steeply "as the result of an unusually severe winter." Executions, according to the report, took place only sporadically and even then only because of alleged danger of epidemics: "In specific instances Jews with contagious diseases were separated from the rest and executed under the guise of being sent to a Jewish hospital or retirement home."[44]

The first transport of Jews from Hamburg arrived in Minsk on November 10, 1941. The victims were moved into the ghetto that same day. An SS reporter cynically mocked the expectations of these Jews as they attempted to make sense of their new reality: "That many Jews formed a totally incorrect picture of their future was obvious; they actually considered themselves pioneers about to be employed in the colonization of the East."[45] One way of feeding such illusions had been to furnish the 1941 deportation transports to the Reichskommissariat Ostland with construction equipment, tools, and machinery. One transport originating in Würzburg, for example, carried mattresses, sewing machines, stoves, cooking vats, tubs, crates of construction and agricultural equipment, and tools for artisans of many different trades.[46]

Conditions in the Minsk ghetto must have resembled those in Riga. Of the 7,000 persons in the "Reichsdeutsche Ghetto" of Minsk, 1,800 men were supposedly able to work, but half of them were ill with dysentery due to malnutrition and frostbite.[47] In Riga no mass shootings took place in December and January following the establishment of the "German" ghetto. At the beginning of February, however, a selection did take place in Riga's "German" ghetto, as a result of which about 1,100 mainly elderly persons from Berlin and 400 from Vienna were murdered in the Rumbula Forest. At the same time the SS killed about 1,000 inmates of Jungfernhof, but the death rate was highest in Salaspils, the camp still under construction.[48]

Alois Brunner is rumored to have accompanied the last deportation transport from Vienna; it arrived in Riga on February 10, 1942. During the journey he supposedly first tortured and then shot the seriously ill banker Siegmund Bosel.[49] The deportees on this transport went through their first selection upon arrival at the Skirotava rail station when Dr. Lange offered transport by truck to those for whom the march of several kilometers from the station to the camp seemed too strenuous. The trucks parked at the station were the gas vans discussed back in October; according to available testimonies, these were used for the first time in Riga in early February. The SS murdered about 700 of these deportees in these vans so that only 300 persons from this transport actually reached the ghetto.[50]

By early February a total of twenty deportation trains from Germany (Munich, Nuremberg, Stuttgart, Hamburg, Cologne, Kassel, Düsseldorf, Bielefeld, Hanover, Leipzig, Dortmund, and four from Berlin), Austria (four from Vienna), and the Protectorate (two from Theresienstadt) had gone to Riga. Including the deportees of the first five transports from Munich, Berlin, Frankfurt/Main, Vienna, and Breslau originally slated for Riga, and who were murdered in Kaunas' Fort IX upon arrival, the quota of 25,000 deportees the RSHA had announced the previous October was fulfilled in mid-February. At that time 11,000 of the 15,000 deportees who still were alive were confined in Riga's "German" ghetto, 2,000 in Jungfernhof, and the rest in Salaspils.[51] The fate of about 5,000 Berlin Jews sent to Riga or Raasiku (Estonia) between August and October 1942 in five transports remains unknown.[52]

The selection and subsequent murder of 1,800 people in March 1942 reduced the number of detainees in Jungfernhof to 450 men and women and, apart from minor fluctuations, that number remained stable until summer 1944. In March a selection also took place in Riga's "German" ghetto. Claiming that the victims were to be moved to a different camp to work in fish canneries, the SS murdered mainly elderly people and children. This massacre was the last large-scale "comb-out Aktion" there.[53] Including the inmates being returned from Salaspils, about 10,000 people now were confined in the "German" ghetto.

Despite the inhumane conditions, biting cold, hunger, forced labor, arbitrary camp rules, and frequent executions for the slightest infractions, most detainees tried to live as normal a life as possible.[54] A number of German organizations and private businesses – the SS, the army, the air force, the navy, and a branch of Mercedes-Benz – exploited the availability of Latvian and Central European Jews for forced labor.[55] Still, compared with a concentration camp, conditions in the Riga ghetto were less harsh. Here the SS did not probe even the most private aspects of life. Families were not torn apart; only parts of the detainees' luggage had been seized. With a mixture of self-delusion and determination to survive, the deportees who had escaped selections adjusted as best they could and until Fall 1943 were able to build a relatively stable community.

At their work places outside the ghetto they also established contacts with their Latvian associates; the deportees bartered goods, and smuggled foodstuffs into the ghetto to augment their starvation rations. They organized schools for the children and self-improvement courses for youths and adults, sponsored dances, and founded political groups. A modest cultural life developed. They organized regular recitals, concerts, and theater performances attended by the SS camp commandant, who sat in the first row. Two of the plays performed there were Lessing's *Nathan der Weise* and Goethe's *Faust*. When Anton Brunner visited the ghetto in May 1942, he and the camp commander attended a vocalist's recital. Most of the deportees from Vienna knew him and remembered him vividly for he was the one who had "commissioned" them.[56]

In the late summer of 1943, this precarious yet still relatively stable situation took a turn for the worse. By mid-1943 approximately 70,000 Jews were confined in ghettos throughout the Ostland and employed as forced laborers, 15,000 of them in Riga and 8,500 in Minsk.[57] In June 1943 a directive from Himmler ordered the transfer of all Jews living in Ostland ghettos to concentration camps. From then on their employment by Wehrmacht organizations was to be located solely within concentration camps. Male Jews were to be deployed mainly in extracting oil from shale, whereas those unable to work were to be "evacuated to the East," the euphemism for murder.[58]

Until November the inmates of the Riga ghetto gradually were transferred to various work camps, especially to the newly established Kaiserwald concentration camp on the grounds of the Meza municipal park in central Riga. There a large number of Central European deportees who had survived the ghetto fell victim to the arbitrary strong-arm tactics of SS camp supervisors and Kapos (foremen), and to hunger, cold, disease, and selections. As the front moved closer in July 1944, the camp was dissolved and its inmates removed across the Baltic Sea to Stutthof concentration camp in West Prussia. Of the 20,000 Central European Jews who had been deported to Riga in the winter of 1941–1942, about 800 survived the ghetto and various camps.[59]

The resumption of deportations to Minsk was slower, but differences in the treatment of deportees over the time span from 1941 into 1942 are clearly discernible there. Whereas in November 1941, Central European Jews still were being sent to the Minsk ghetto, beginning in May the SS murdered new deportees upon their arrival. Only a handful were selected to perform forced labor on the SS "estate" Maly Trostinets. Gas vans arrived in Minsk, too. In the early summer of 1942, as many as four reportedly were in use near Maly Trostinets.[60] According to an early-May train schedule from the regional office of the Reichsbahn in Königsberg, seventeen trains were scheduled for "transport of emigrants . . . carrying about 1,000 people each from

Vienna . . . destination Minsk." These were to run once a week from May 15 to early September 1942. The code "Da" preceding the train numbers 202–218 identified the "emigrants" as Jews. This schedule, however, could be maintained only partially.[61]

One of the first transports of Jews from the Reich to reach Minsk as part of the second wave of deportations was dispatched on May 6, 1942, and more than likely originated in Vienna. The report of the Schutzpolizei escort detachment records Alois Brunner's handing over the 1,000 persons of this transport at the Aspang station. They traveled through Lundenburg (Břeclav), Olmütz (Olomouc), Oppeln (Opole), and Warsaw to Wolkowitz (Volkovysk), where they were transferred from passenger cars to cattle wagons. At the order of the SD in Minsk the train stopped in Kojdanov from May 9 until May 11. The first casualties of this transport, three men and five women, reportedly were buried adjacent to the railway station. Then, after a ninety-minute trip, the transport finally reached Minsk on May 11 at 10:30 AM. The transfer, complete with the log and 50,000 Reichsmarks in "occupation money" bank certificates, took place at the offices of the Minsk SD. "On the return trip to Vienna the police escort detachment, on the order of the SIPO and SD commandant of White Ruthenia [sic] pursuant to the order of the RFSSuChdDtPol [Reichsführer-SS and Chief of the German Police Himmler]," returned Dr. Löwenherz from the ghetto to Vienna.[62]

The testimony of one survivor leaves no doubt that the circumstances of this transport and the behavior of the police escort produced an ordeal that cost some victims their lives. During the change of trains in Volkovysk the escort team beat the deportees so severely that old and frail people,

> unable to evade the clubs, lay sprawled helplessly on the platform. In the course of this night many lost their mind, became insane. The escort leader ordered their confinement in a separate rail car. What took [place] in that car defies description.

Upon arrival in Minsk some men were retained for luggage removal; all of the other deportees were sent on immediately. "Closed gray box-like trucks stood ready to transport the sick, the insane, and the old and frail. The victims were pitched into the vehicles, one on top of another: men, women, the old, the ill, the insane, the dead."[63]

An activity report from the SS-Unterscharführer (sergeant) of a special-duty battalion of the Waffen-SS describes the fate of the deportees of this transport who, unlike the survivor quoted above, did not belong to the small group of about eighty people whom the SS took to Maly-Trostinets as slave laborers. Shortly before the arrival of the deportees, a 2nd Platoon squad, consisting of an Unterführer (an NCO) and ten men, had made preparations near Maly Trostinets: "On May 5 we already started digging new pits near the commdr's estate. This work also took four days." As usual, the report employs typical SS jargon to describe the subsequent murderous activities: "On May 11 a transport of Jews (1,000 head) from Vienna arrived in Minsk and were moved immediately from the station to the trench. For this reason the platoon was deployed right by the pit."[64] This report, which describes in a similar vein the arrival of additional transports in Minsk or rather Maly Trostinets, does not clarify whether the victims were murdered in gas vans or were shot to death.

Nevertheless, it is safe to assume that for the most part these mass murders were carried out with gas vans because a mid-July 1942 telex from the head of the Sipo and SD leaves no doubt about the frequent deployment of the three vans stationed in Minsk:

> Every week the commandant of the Sipo and the SD White Ruthenia receives a transport of Jews slated for Sonderbehandlung. The three available gas vans cannot handle this volume. Please send an additional S-van (5 tons). I also request twenty exhaust hoses for the vans stationed here (2 Diamonds, 1 Saurer) because those now in use are leaking already.[65]

The deportation trains arriving weekly for "Sonderbehandlung" must have been those that left Vienna for Minsk on May 20 and 27 and on June 2 and 9, 1942, and which, according to the Waffen-SS-Unterführer's unfinished activity report, arrived in Minsk on May 26 and June 1 and 15 and, in his words, "were directed to the pit immediately."[66] One of the persons sent to her death in Minsk on June 2 was thirty-two-year-old Else Spiegel, who left her five-month-old infant Jona Jakob Spiegel in the care of acquaintances in Vienna. A short time later, with a different transport, the baby arrived in Theresienstadt; he survived and was liberated there in 1945 at age three.[67]

The activity report also lists three additional transports from the Reich during June and July 1942, one of which must have been a deportation train that left Theresienstadt on July 14, 1942, carrying 1,000 people.[68] At the Minsk rail station thirty-five men were selected as able to work, and they and their families were sent on to Maly Trostinets; the remaining deportees were murdered at once. The other two trains that the report mentions probably originated in Cologne and Theresienstadt. Yet another transport from Theresienstadt, number Da 221, which was to leave Volkovysk for Minsk at the end of July, was diverted at the last moment to Baranovici by Dr. Heuser, the Commandant of the Sipo and SD White Ruthenia, probably because a large-scale murder Aktion in the Minsk ghetto already was scheduled for that time.[69]

The victims of that late-July two-day murder spree that claimed the lives of about 9,000 persons affected people from both the Russian and the German sections of the Minsk ghetto: "Between July 25 and 27 new trenches were dug. During the Großaktion on July 28 in the Russian section, 6,000 Jews are taken to the pit. On July 29, 3,000 German Jews are brought to the pit. The following days were once more filled with cleaning weapons and equipment repair [sic]."[70]

In his report to Reichskommissar Lohse, Kube cited slightly higher numbers of victims. He informed Lohse that during the murder Aktion at the end of July "10,000 Jews had been liquidated," 6,500 of them Russian Jews, "mainly old people, women, and children – the rest consisted of Jews, no longer able to work, from Vienna, Brno, Bremen, and Berlin, who at the Führer's orders... had been sent to Minsk the previous November."[71] According to Kube, of the Jews who had been deported from Central Europe to the Minsk ghetto in November 1941, 2,600 still were alive. Kube's report stressed that "in the previous ten weeks about 55,000 Jews had been liquidated" in White Russia and raised cautious objections to additional transports of Central European Jews by drawing attention to alleged "psychological" difficulties among SD members. "Constantly having to lead new transports of Jews from the Reich to their final destiny taxes the physical and emotional strength of the men of the SD beyond reasonable limits." Kube requested Lohse "to halt additional transports of Jews to Minsk, at least until the threat of partisan activity had been eliminated for good."[72] He informed Lohse that "suddenly without directive from the Reichsführer-SS and without prior notification of the Commissar General a transport of 1,000 Warsaw Jews destined for the Luftwaffe command district here" had arrived, and he stated that he would liquidate every unannounced transport "to prevent further unrest in White Ruthenia."[73]

During the summer of 1942, Minsk and Maly Trostinets served as receiving stations for deportation transports from Central Europe, mainly from Theresienstadt and Vienna. From the beginning of August to the end of September 1942, more than 15,000 men, women, and children left Theresienstadt in ten transports; about 3,500 people arrived in four transports from Vienna from mid-August to early October.[74] The destinations of five additional deportation transports that left Theresienstadt in October 1942 remain unclear. As a Reichsbahn plan from the Generalbetriebsleitung Ost (National Railroad General Management Office East) in Berlin issued to subordinate branch offices in Minsk, Riga, and Kraków reveals, from August until October "special trains set aside for resettlers, harvest helpers, and Jews" were to be deployed for service between cities within the Reich and Theresienstadt, from Theresienstadt and Vienna to Volkovysk (to continue from there to Minsk), and from Berlin to Riga and Raasiku.[75] For the month of October the plan listed Izbica as the destination station for deportations from Theresienstadt; that suggests that those deportees were murdered in a death camp associated with Aktion Reinhard. On the other hand, there is evidence that in October 1942 five trains from Theresienstadt were sent to Minsk/Maly Trostinets.[76]

Of the more than 16,000 deportees from Theresienstadt (if those from the untraceable transports of October 1942 are included in the total the number would be higher than 24,000), only an estimated eight people survived the Maly Trostinets camp. One survivor of this group reported that the train carrying them to Minsk on September 12 came to a stop in an open field about fifteen kilometers on the other side of the city. Three SS men with machine guns at the ready stood at the front of each car. Upon leaving the cars, the deportees had to leave their baggage and coats, and to surrender their money, watches, and the like. A young woman found to have been in possession of a small amount of money was shot on the spot. Of these 1,000 people the SS commandeered forty-four men to load the baggage onto trucks and transported them to the camp. Everyone else was killed in the *dushegubkas* (soul killers), the Russian population's epithet for the gas vans deployed on the Eastern front. The victims' bodies were removed to mass graves in the Blahovshtina Forest.[77]

Isak Grünberg, another survivor of Maly Trostinets, had been deported with the last transport from Vienna at the beginning of October 1942. Because he was a mason, the SS men did not kill him immediately but took him, his wife, and three children (then eighteen, nineteen, and twenty years old) to the camp. There he worked as a mason and his wife as a seamstress. He remembered that about 1,200 prisoners, mainly Jews of whom some came from Poland, and Soviet prisoners of war were confined there. Other prisoners apparently came from Theresienstadt and Auschwitz. Czech survivors spoke of 400 Jewish deportees from Vienna and Theresienstadt and 200 Soviet prisoners of war.[78]

The prisoners had to take care of the 250-hectare agricultural estate, including horse and cattle stables, and to sort the luggage and clothing of the people who had been transported to Minsk and murdered there.

We had to work twelve to fifteen hours daily under the worst possible conditions. Soon barracks had to be erected...a pumping station was built and electricity brought in. The fields had to be farmed and cellars dug. There were unbelievable amounts of work in the workshops, the tailor shop, the laundry, the carpentry shop, the shoemaker's shop, the tannery...and everything on the double. Every job was timed, and heaven help those who couldn't meet their quota.[79]

Supposedly, most of the Soviet prisoners of war were employed in digging mass graves. Regular selections took place during roll call.

> The commanding officer, SS-Sturmführer [sic.?] Eiche, and, likewise, Scharführer Dosch, conducted these selections by simply pointing to a prisoner – "you left," "you right," followed by the command "march!" A short time later we heard the rifle salvos.[80]

These executions took place in a little forest nearby. Mrs. Grünberg was murdered as a result of one of these selections.

But in 1943 the SS started to destroy the traces of mass murder near Maly Trostinets. The Soviet prisoners of war had to open the mass graves and burn the partially decomposed corpses on grates made of railroad tracks. In the course of 1943 and 1944 most of the prisoners at Maly Trostinets were murdered: The number of inmates fell to eighty or ninety. When the Red Army approached Minsk in June 1944, the SS dissolved the estate and the camp and on June 30 set fire to the barracks with prisoners trapped inside.[81] Isak Grünberg and two of his children managed to escape shortly before the murder of all remaining prisoners. He estimated that perhaps twenty-five to thirty were able to save themselves.

In the course of 1942 and 1943, the inhabitants of the German and Russian ghettos in Minsk were also reduced gradually through various killing actions. In 1943, German organizations in Minsk also adopted the organized scavanging of corpses practiced in the extermination camps. Kube, obviously scandalized, relayed to Lohse a report from a German administrator of a penal institution in Minsk who pointed out that "gold bridges, crowns, and fillings had been pulled or broken out of the mouths" of German and Russian Jews even before they were murdered in an Aktion. "Since April 13, 1943, 516 German and Russian Jews had been done in.... About fifty percent of the Jews had gold teeth, bridges, or fillings. Hauptscharführer Rübe from the SD was personally present each time and always took the gold items with him."[82]

Lohse forwarded the report to Reichsminister Rosenberg and in an attached letter quite openly expressed his rejection of this kind of "combating the enemy." That "the Jews are to receive special treatment needs no further discussion. However, that in the course of such treatment actions such as Generalkommissar [Kube] reports on June 1, 1943, take place seems scarcely believable." Lohse then raised a painfully obvious question: "What is Katyn compared to that? What if such events were to become known among our opponents and they capitalized on them? Such propaganda probably would be ineffective only because readers and listeners would refuse to believe it."[83]

Even more directly than letters cited earlier, these pieces of correspondence clarify from what angle both of these leading administrators of the German civilian government between 1941 and 1943 criticized the murderous activities of the SS and their helpers. They had no quarrel with "correctly" organized executions; they had no quarrel with what they apparently considered humanely executed murder in gas vans: they approved and supported the mass murder of Soviet and Central European Jews. Their criticism focused on what they considered excesses, proceedings that in their view could damage German prestige.[84]

The last killing actions employing gas vans in White Russia, during which inmates of the Minsk ghetto were murdered, occurred in October 1943. During a ten-day operation involving three gas vans, once again thousands of Jews were murdered.[85] The place of origin and date of departure of twenty-one of the transports to Minsk/Maly Trostinets in 1942 can be traced. More than 25,000 men, women, and children from Theresienstadt, Vienna, and Cologne were sent there to die. Furthermore, in all likelihood additional trains with Jews from Germany also departed to Minsk/Maly Trostinets in the summer and fall of 1942. The systematic murder of deported Central Europeans in the occupied areas of the Soviet Union did not start in November 1941 but half a year later in White Russia and depended on the deployment of gas vans. Like Chełmno (Kulmhof), Maly Trostinets was a killing center where members of the SS killed at least 30,000 Jews deported from Central Europe and tens of thousands from White Russia.

A Mini-Deployment with Consequences: The Vienna Deportation Specialists in Berlin

After the close of the mass deportations from Vienna in October 1942, Alois Brunner and some of his Zentralstelle coworkers were transferred to Berlin. Allegedly Brunner himself characterized his mission in the capital of the Reich as "teaching the Saupreußen, those 'Prussian pigs' how to deal with those Schweinehunde, the Jews."[86] One reason for employing the Viennese "specialists" in Berlin was that, shortly before, Gerhard Stübs and Franz Prüfer, the directors of the Judenreferat at the State Police headquarters, along with other Berlin Gestapo members, had been arrested for suspicion of embezzlement and personal enrichment by stealing confiscated Jewish property.[87]

Brunner and his team busied themselves to speed up the roundup and deportation of Berlin's Jews with "Viennese methods." One of Brunner's first steps was to establish new assembly camps. For this purpose buildings in addition to the synagogue at Levetzow Street were to be reorganized. From the Jüdische Kultusvereinigung (JKV) retirement home at Große Hamburger Straße 26, all furniture was removed; only mattresses and straw-filled sacks were to remain so that 1,200–1,500 people could be squeezed into the building.[88] A retirement home at Gerlachstraße served as the assembly camp for deportation trains to Theresienstadt. On November 17, Brunner demanded that the JKV supply twenty Jewish "Ordner" ("stewards"/policemen to keep order), two nurses, and two "'perfect' typists who were to take turns working twenty-four-hour shifts."[89] A few days later Weiszl ordered the Jewish community to provide twenty additional stewards.[90]

The Gestapo method of using the mail to notify people of their "evacuation," a method practiced since 1941, had prompted some of those slated for deportation to go into hiding or try to escape, whereas others opted instead for suicide.[91] Increasingly, larger contingents of uniformed police were deployed in pairs to ferret out men and women who had not been notified. The police employed surprise raids on their apartments and delivered them to an assembly camp. Brunner changed all that. The people to be deported were not to have any chance whatsoever to evade arrest. He ordered a city map to be drawn up; on it, all buildings and city blocks inhabited by Jews were to be clearly marked.[92] With his efforts facilitated by this map, he organized large-scale arrests.

During these raids specific blocks were cordoned off; Greifkommandos (seizure detachments) entered the buildings and ordered whole families to pack their things. In the presence of SS and police they then were loaded onto trucks and transported to the assembly camp where Jewish stewards had to help them carry and stow their luggage. These sorts of raids were especially feared among the victims.

> In the evenings the SS in cars and rented moving vans drove through the city, nabbing every Jew wearing a star. They also conducted brutal house-to-house searches in the areas inhabited by Jews. Whoever saw these infamous cars escaped as quickly and inconspicuously as possible, or, if it was too late for that, covered the star as well as possible or tore it off.... Even more terrifying were the raids on the buildings. As soon as the car came to a stop, SS men surrounded the entire city block, which made escape impossible. As long as the raid was in progress not even Aryans could enter or leave the buildings. Two SS men always worked in tandem. In full gear and with handguns ready they entered the apartments clearly marked with the star at the door and with rude threats took what they found: persons, foodstuffs, money, and valuables. What they could not carry they destroyed.... Then they sealed the apartments, loaded their prisoners into the furniture van, and were off to the next Jewish

city block. When the van was so crowded that not even an SS man could stuff another Jew into it, the people were unloaded at the assembly camp and the raid continued. Sometimes up to thirty vans traversed Berlin in this fashion, and we, who had to work in the camp, experienced a feverish hustle and bustle, not knowing whom among these poor people we should help first or how to comfort them when they cried for their husbands and sons who, still at work in the factories, would return to a sealed apartment.[93]

In the assembly camp the personal data of the arrested persons were recorded and their luggage searched. Before being deported they had to provide declarations listing their assets. Day and night the employees of the Reichsvereinigung der Juden in Deutschland had to set up and raise fees and set up lists and card files under the watchful eyes of the SS. The brutal pressure on the Jewish employees fueled the entire bureaucratic management of these formalities. Simultaneously, the stewards and the employees and functionaries of Jewish organizations served the SS as hostages. At Brunner's orders, Dr. Paul Eppstein, a member of the board of directors of the Reichsvereinigung, had to inform the employees that Jewish stewards had to accompany the SS Greifkommandos and help the victims pack. Should any of them not obey this order, warn others, or help them escape, the SS would hold that person responsible and he and his entire family would be threatened with deportation to the East.[94] In the case of successful escapes, the stewards had to fill the escapees' slots on the deportation transports.

Simultaneously Brunner reduced the personnel of the organizations of the Jewish community. In mid-November 1942 all employees of the Jüdische Kultusvereinigung had to assemble in the large meeting room at Oranienburgerstraße, where Eichmann, Rolf Günther, and Alois Brunner appeared for the distribution of tasks. Brunner had Moritz Henschel, Philipp Kozower, and Leo Kreindler, the leaders of the JKV, submit lists of all persons working in JKV establishments. He ordered the reduction in the numbers and deportation of employees working at hospitals, kindergartens, and other places. They had to report three days later at the assembly camp. On November 19, 1942, Brunner ordered the workers of the Fürsorge, the welfare department, to appear for a meeting. After their names had been called in alphabetical order and Brunner had inspected them, regaling them with "sarcastic, demeaning comments," half of the 130 men and women were selected to continue their work while the other half was slated for deportation.[95] During this selection, Leo Kreindler, the director of the welfare department, suffered a heart attack and died.[96] Brunner cynically commented: "Carry that Jew over there out of here. He'll be less cold someplace else."[97]

Although Brunner and his crew officiated in Berlin only until January 1943, they permanently impacted the organization of arrests and deportations: "Brunner's interim régime was short-lived but left indelible traces."[98] The employees and functionaries were not used to such openly displayed Herren-menschen airs, and all survivors comment on the brutalization in the treatment of the victims and the style and tone that the SS men from Vienna introduced in Berlin. In terms of National Socialist plans, however, specialists such as these had proven their worth and now could be employed in other parts of German-occupied Europe for hunting down people and organizing deportations. So Eichmann sent Alois Brunner and a number of other practitioners from the now idle Vienna Zentralstelle to northern Greece.

7   Collaboration and Deportations: 1942

While the mass deportations of Jews from Germany, Austria, and the Protectorate of Bohemia and Moravia were in progress and the annihilation camps were being constructed in the Generalgouvernement, Eichmann and his men became active even in states that were not under the rule of German civil authorities. During the Wannsee Conference, Heydrich had voiced the opinion that with the start of "various sizeable evacuations" within the framework of "the Final Solution in European areas we either occupy or influence," the matter would not present much of a problem. He was referring to Slovakia and Croatia because "for the most part, the major issues there already" had been "resolved." He also assumed that in "occupied and in unoccupied France . . . the capture of Jews for evacuation most likely" would proceed "without major difficulties."[1]

Since 1939 and 1941, respectively, Slovakia and Croatia were ruled by clerical-fascist régimes. The supposedly independent Slovak state was tied to the German Reich through a friendship treaty; the Croat Ustasha state had been established by the Axis powers of Germany and Italy. No Wehrmacht units were stationed in Slovakia, but the Croat state, including Bosnia and Herzegovina, contained a German area of occupation in the northeast and an Italian one in the southwest. The northern part of France was governed by a German military administration, but the civil administration and the executive power in both the occupied and the unoccupied zones were vested in Marshal Pétain's collaborationist Vichy government.

In 1942 more than 56,000 people from Slovakia, about 5,000 from Croatia, and 42,000 from France were deported to German concentration and annihilation camps. Did these collaborationist governments practice their own anti-Jewish policies to serve their own interests, or did they institute antisemitic measures solely in response to pressures from the German Reich? What organizations and institutions cooperated with Eichmann and his men in preparing and executing the expulsion programs? How sizeable was the part of the collaborationist governments in the persecution, internment, and deportation of Jews from the countries they helped administer?

The Cooperation of SS, Wehrmacht, and Vichy Authorities in the Arrests and Deportations of Jews in France in 1942–1943

Shortly after the beginning of the occupation of France in the summer of 1940, the office of the chief of the military administration in Paris began considering "the treatment of Jews in the occupied area." Dr. Best, since 1935 one of Heydrich's top employees in the SD-Hauptamt and now posted to the military administrative staff in Paris, advanced a proposal from Ambassador Otto Abetz suggesting the "removal" of all Jews from the occupied part of France and the expropriation of all Jewish property. The military administration urged caution because in administrative matters French government authorities had to be involved at all times. This was so that a targeted general order to French authorities and "raising the race issue" would not be "interpreted as intents of annexation."[2] The administrative staff advised against universally applicable measures against Jews. Individual directives, on the other hand, "over time could be concentrated in such a way as to be the equivalent of across-the-board measures." As a result of these deliberations, at the end of September 1940 only a requirement for Jewish registration was established in the occupied zone, and Jews were prohibited from returning from the unoccupied zone to the occupied part of France. The attention of the military administration focused almost entirely on the property of French Jews: Large companies, industrial complexes, and banks were to be placed under Treuhand control (trusteeship).[3]

On a legislative plane, the first discriminatory steps against Jews originated with the Vichy government in early October in the form of a Statut des juifs, a Law for Jews, which excluded Jews from public office and free professions. A second law enabled the prefects of regional governments to intern non-French Jews in "special camps." With this authority, French regional administrators imprisoned in camps in the south of France the German Jews who had been deported from Baden and Saarpfalz. The Vichy government had initiated the first directives without direct order from German authorities.[4]

In late summer 1940 the RSHA had dispatched Eichmann's long-time associate Theo Dannecker to Paris as Judenberater, Adviser for Jewish Affairs. His task was to develop anti-Jewish policies. At the beginning of 1941 he proposed the establishment of a Zentrales Judenamt, a Central Jewish Office, which was to be based on the model of the Zentralstellen. It was to set up files about Jews

and oversee a yet-to-be-established Jewish Zwangsvereinigung, an organization that all Jews would have to join; it also would supervise Aryanizations.[5] To
leading officers of the military administration and diplomats of the German
embassy, Dannecker and SS-Sturmbannführer Kurt Lischka presented these
proposals and the plan to establish concentration camps in the occupied zone
for non-French Jews.[6] To support the establishment of concentration camps in
the occupied part of France, Dannecker repeatedly referred to the camps that
French authorities already had erected for non-French Jews in the unoccupied
territory.

Dannecker's recommendations were accepted. The Office of the Military
Governor of France considered interning in concentration camps "Jews of
German and formerly Austrian, Czechoslovak, and Polish citizenship." French
authorities were to handle internments based on the Vichy government's law of
October 1940, "if for no other reason than to avoid foreign policy difficulties
from the start." The military administration and other German authorities
were to limit their involvement to overseeing "complete implementation."[7]

In the course of 1941 this strategy spawned three waves of large-scale arrests
in occupied France. During summons and raids in May, August, and December, French police, assisted by the Feldgendarmerie of the Wehrmacht, at the
order of the German military administration, arrested 8,700 male Jews and
interned them in the Beaune-la-Rolande, Pithiviers, and Drancy camps, all of
them administered by French authorities.[8] The December arrests were justified as reprisals for assassination attempts. The Feldgendarmerie and French
police arrested mainly French Jews of the bourgeoisie and detained them at
the Compiègne camp. Simultaneously the military administration ordered the
execution of "100 Jews, Communists, and anarchists," allegedly closely associated with those responsible for the assassinations of several German officers in
Paris.[9] Other proposals from Dannecker had also been carried out. In March
1941, after discussions with the military administration, the Vichy government
established the Commissariat Général aux Questions Juives, the Commissariat
General for Jewish Questions, first directed by Xavier Vallat, then, beginning
in the spring of 1942, by Louis Darquier de Pellepoix.[10] At the end of November 1941, the called-for compulsory consolidation of French Jews led to the
official establishment of the Union Générale des Israélites de France (UGIF),
the General Union of the Israelites of France, by French authorities.[11]

Beginning in mid-1941 thousands of men were interned in camps in the
occupied zone; the military administration explained the wave of December
apprehensions by claiming that 1,000 Jews were to be transported to the East
as workers. Yet, until Spring 1942, German authorities in France did not
conduct a single deportation. Only at the end of March, when authorities in

Berlin succeeded in having trains set aside for deportations, were the Jewish men already interned in French camps in the occupied zone put aboard to transports to Auschwitz.[12] At a conference of the RSHA Department IV B 4 in early March in Berlin, Dannecker had secured permission to conduct negotiations with French government agencies "about the expulsion of about 5,000 Jews to the East, subject to Heydrich's approval." The deportees were to be "male Jews able to work and no older than fifty-five."[13] During these talks Dannecker also learned about the imminent "expulsion of larger groups of Jews" from Slovakia and that the Slovak government "would pay RM 500 for each Jew taken off its hands." Proposals were made for establishing a similar fee for "the Jews of whom the French state was about to be relieved" and to conduct a "Vermögensfestellung, an appraisal of assets, of the Jewish community in both zones."[14]

During the preparations for the first deportation transport, Dannecker transmitted the technical details by telex to Department IV B 4 in Berlin. A total of 1,115 male Jews were to be sent to the "reception camp" Auschwitz. In contrast to later terminology, Dannecker's label for these transports still was "deportation."[15] The Oberkommando der Wehrmacht would pay the transportation expenses because the "retaliations" of December 1941 had been conducted at OKW orders. The military commander of France would provide the guard units. Provisions and "serviceable clothing (shoes)" for the deportees also would be furnished.

Before the first train left France for Auschwitz, Eichmann informed the German Foreign Office about the plan to expel "to the concentration camp Auschwitz in Upper Silesia, 1,000 Jews who had been arrested during the reprisal measures conducted in Paris on December 13, 1941, for assassination attempts on members of the Wehrmacht."[16] Eichmann wanted to make sure that the Foreign Office would "not object to these measures." Yet, even before receiving a reply, Eichmann asked for permission to expel an additional "5,000 Jews who had caught the attention of the state police."[17] The written reply from the Foreign Office with Staatssekretär Ernst von Weizsäcker's handwritten corrections stated: "On the part of the Auswärtige Amt, no objection will be raised to the expulsion to the Konzentrationslager Auschwitz, Upper Silesia of a total of 6,000 French or stateless Jews of whom the police have taken notice."[18]

As was true elsewhere, the example of France also demonstrates the specific contributions of occupation authorities and other agencies to the persecution and deportation of Jews. In 1941 the commander of the Wehrmacht in France, partially under the guise of reprisals, ordered the arrest and internment of thousands of Jewish men and the shooting of some of them as hostages. Although in occupied France Wehrmacht authorities did not go to the lengths they did, for example, in occupied Serbia, they were moving in essentially the same direction. Months later Eichmann's department organized the deportation to Auschwitz of the arrested men. At first the Wehrmacht took charge of financing and guarding the transports while the appropriate departments of the Foreign Office voiced no objections to the deportations. Between the end of March and the end of June 1942, roughly 5,000 people were deported from Compiègne, Drancy, Pithiviers, and Beaune-la-Rolande with the SS and army cooperating closely. All of the deportees, among them about 100 women, were registered at Auschwitz upon arrival. In the spring of 1942 the infamous selections at the ramp, where the SS chose those to be killed immediately in the gas chambers of Birkenau, did not yet take place at Auschwitz.

During the first six months of 1942 the structure of the German occupation apparatus changed. At Hitler's order, a Higher SS and Police leader was installed to take on the executive powers of the Sicherheitspolizei and the military commander. Originally, Dr. Stahlecker, Eichmann's former patron, was slated for this position. Stahlecker, however, had been killed by Soviet partisans when he was chief of Einsatzruppe A in the northern part of the occupied Soviet Union, and so Himmler appointed Karl Oberg, the former SS and Police chief of the governor of Galicia, as the HSSPF.[19] Dr. Knochen, one of Eichmann's superiors in the SD headquarters in 1936–1937, was chief of the Sicherheitspolizei and SD for the military commander in France. In May 1942 Herbert Hagen, Eichmann's former department chief at the SD headquarters, was sent to Paris as Oberg's personal consultant. By then an SS-Sturmbannführer, Hagen, after the incorporation of the SD-Hauptamt into Amt VI (External Affairs) of the RSHA, had worked under Gruppenleiter Knochen (Gruppe VI H – Identification of philosophical and political opponents abroad) as Referatsleiter (VI H 2 – Jewry and Antisemitism) and in 1940 had been posted to France with the Sonderkommando of the Sicherheitspolizei and the SD under Knochen. From Bordeaux he had built up the apparatus of the Sicherheitspolizei and the SD along the French Atlantic coast. Although Knochen and Hagen served under the HSSPF, they, not Oberg who had no experience with French internal politics and occupation policies in France and did not even speak French, determined SS policy in France.

In the late spring of 1941, German authorities in Paris increased pressure on the French administration to initiate large-scale raids on Jews in the Occupied Zone. The French suggested that interned Jews from the Unoccupied Zone should be surrendered as well.[20] During a follow-up meeting at Eichmann's Referat at the RSHA on June 11, 1942, the Judenreferenten from Paris, Brussels, and The Hague learned that Himmler had ordered the transfer of "larger groups of Jews to the concentration camp Auschwitz" for work, "with the proviso that the Jews of both sexes be between sixteen and forty years old," although "ten percent of Jews not capable of work" could be included. Dannecker worked out an agreement that 100,000 Jews were to be expelled from France, including from the Unoccupied Zone. France was to pay transportation expenses and a "head price of approximately 700 RM per Jew." The French also were to provide food for two weeks, and equipment.[21] The Judenreferenten did not, however, determine the time frame for these expulsions. After his return to Paris, Dannecker prepared the deportations while Eichmann's associate Novak intervened at the Reich Ministry of Transport to eliminate transportation problems. Some 40,000 Jews from France were to be deported first.[22]

Dannecker tried to persuade the French police executive Jean Leguay to arrest French as well as foreign Jews in the Occupied Zone. Leguay refused because such an intent exceeded the scope of French anti-Jewish laws; Dannecker then tried to overturn the refusal by insisting that French police had to obey German directives even in the absence of any directives from the Vichy government. A few days later Leguay informed Dannecker of the French government's refusal to order French police to arrest the requested number of Jews in Paris. Dannecker countered by announcing that he himself would take charge of this Aktion and for two weeks "would require at least 2,500 French uniformed police daily as well as additional plainclothes detectives."[23] The leaders of the Vichy government were informed immediately of Dannecker's demands. Pierre Laval, the head of the government, responded by making it clear that French police would not take part in this wave of arrests. Dannecker's SS superiors in Paris also reacted negatively to his highhandedness because they did not want to risk losing the collaboration of the French government.[24] Senior embassy official Karl Zeitschel, to whom Dannecker had explained his concerns, reported to Ambassador Abetz that not only French organizations but "even the Sicherheitspolizei is making every effort to sabotage a decisive handling of the Jews, waylay it with endless intrigues, or stall it altogether."[25]

At the end of June 1942 Eichmann rushed from Berlin to Paris to assist Dannecker.[26] According to a file entry bearing his and Dannecker's signatures, they "negotiated" the fastest possible expulsion of all Jews from France. They had dealt with their former superior at the SD-Hauptamt, Knochen, the commander of the Sicherheitspolizei. According to Dannecker and Eichmann, this meant "unavoidable exertion of pressure on the French government for continued, if involuntary cooperation." Eichmann and Dannecker mistakenly expected that after these preparations "implementation in the occupied part now would be clear and proceed without a hitch." They also assumed the need for a significant increase in the current speed of "three weekly deportations of

1,000 Jews each" to guarantee the smooth execution of the Final Solution of the Jewish Question.[27]

The pressure on French government executives, however, did not proceed as smoothly as Eichmann and Dannecker had imagined. During a conference attended by Oberg, Knochen, Lischka, Hagen, and a representative of the army on one side and René Bousquet, the French Secretary General of Police, on the other, the SS did not risk failure, although they did make it known that French government opposition during the arrests "certainly would not find favor with the Führer."[28] They did not insist on the arrest of French Jews, as Eichmann and Dannecker demanded. Bousquet and the SS officers agreed that French police in the Occupied and the Unoccupied Zones were to arrest only Jews of foreign nationalities.

A short time later thousands of non-French Jews fell victim to this compromise that the SS and Vichy government representatives had negotiated in early July. In mid-July Darquier de Pellepoix, the French Commissar General for Jewish Affairs, and Bousquet instructed French police posts to arrest stateless, German, Austrian, Czech, Polish, and Russian Jews in the Occupied Zone and to confine them in camps.[29] During the large Paris raid of July 16 and 17, 1942, in the course of which 22,000 Jews were to be arrested, the police apprehended about 3,000 men, 6,000 women, and 4,000 children. Some of them were interned at Drancy; the rest, among them thousands of children, were temporarily confined at the Vélodrome d'Hiver, the Paris stadium for bicycle races.[30] In August 1942 French government organizations also conducted large-scale raids on non-French Jews in the Unoccupied Zone. By the end of August the directors of the National Police and the regional police prefectures had ordered the arrest of 6,500 people. Together with the Jews held at Gurs, Vernet, Rivesaltes, and Les Milles, those arrested were sent from the Unoccupied to the Occupied Zone in several transports and there turned over to the German deportation specialists.

On July 20, during a telephone conversation with Eichmann and Novak in Berlin, Dannecker had asked whether children from France were supposed to be deported too. Eichmann decided "child transports can roll." Novak promised that transports of "all sorts of Jews" were possible, "including old people and those unable to work."[31] Obviously, Eichmann and Novak knew that since mid-July the technical installations for immediate mass murder of people the SS labeled incapable of work stood ready in Auschwitz-Birkenau.

In mid-July several so-called RSHA transports from Slovakia and the Netherlands had been sent to Birkenau. As the trains arrived, SS officers and physicians conducted selections at the ramp. On July 17, 1942, when 2,000 men and women from the Netherlands were "selected" in Auschwitz, Himmler personally inspected the selection and the immediate murder of about 450 of them with poison gas. It is reasonable to assume that at that particular moment the KZ Auschwitz took on its double function as a camp for slaves performing forced labor for such companies as IG Farben and later Krupp, Siemens, and others, and as an extermination camp for persons judged unable to work.[32] The deportation of the persons seized during the big raids in Paris began on July 19. One of the first selections the SS conducted at the ramp of the Auschwitz railway station occurred at the arrival of the first of these trains on July 21. Three hundred and seventy-five men were not deployed as forced labor but murdered immediately in the gas chambers.[33]

From mid-July to mid-November thirty-eight transports, each carrying 1,000 men, women, and children, left Paris. Holding Dutch, Belgian, Romanian, and Greek citizenship, these included persons categorized as "Jews appropriate for deportation," and who had been arrested by French police in the summer and fall of 1942.[34] Meanwhile, differing from Eichmann and Dannecker, the SS leadership in France had established its strategy of flexible cooperation with French government agencies and, consequently, had given up including in the deportations Jews who were French citizens. Himmler approved this agreement in September 1942. Theo Dannecker was removed from his post in Paris and, after he had served short stints in the French provinces, Eichmann transferred him as Judenreferent to the German embassy in Sofia.[35] SS-Obersturmführer Heinz Röthke took over the duties of Dienststelle IV J under the head of the Sicherheitspolizei in Paris.

By October 1942 no more transports were rolling from France to Auschwitz, and after four deportation transports in early November, another disruption of the expulsion program occurred. According to Röthke's notes, difficulties with the "availability of transport materials" were not to blame; rather, the issue was "how to capture Jews for transport."[36] When in November 1942 the Unoccupied Zone of France was placed under German and Italian occupation administration, the refusal of Italian government agencies in southeastern France to initiate anti-Jewish procedures similar to those employed by the German occupation administration created additional complications for the SS organizations.[37] In early February 1943 Eichmann asked Knochen to push for the "evacuation of all Jews with French citizenship," but Knochen in a letter to Eichmann's superior, Müller, reiterated the position of the French government and the Italian occupation authorities and advised caution to avoid "political reversals."[38]

Although no large-scale arrests of Jews holding French citizenship took place, French police did arrest individual Jews who supposedly had broken one or the other of the welter of discriminating regulations, and sent them to internment camps under French administration. When the deportations started up again in February and March 1943, Röthke focused his attention on these Jews classified as "non-expellable." French police executives reacted by threatening not to deploy the gendarmerie in the transport of French citizens from Drancy. At a meeting at the end of March, the French representative conveyed Laval's decision to the SS leadership, whereupon, Oberg decided that "the transports would be handled exclusively with the help of German police forces."[39] The deployment of these police forces, who were supposed to organize the victims into transports at Drancy without the aid of the French executive, was delayed by months because Alois Brunner and his subordinates from Vienna did not arrive in Paris until summer 1943.

1942: Religious-Materialistic Antisemitism in Slovakia and Cooperation in the Deportation of Slovak Jews

In the spring of 1942 the organization of deportations from Vienna had become such a matter of routine for the expulsion apparatus that four SS officials from the Zentralstelle could be spared to assist in the deportation of Jews from Slovakia. In the spring of 1942, according to Alfred Slawik, he, Ernst Brückler, Herbert Gerbing, and Robert Walcher were added to a detachment under the leadership of Dieter Wisliceny.[40] In August 1940 Wisliceny, Eichmann's former superior in Referat II 112, at the instigation of his former employee, had been made Adviser for Jewish Affairs at the German embassy in Bratislava.[41] The deportation of a total of 57,000 Jewish men, women, and children in 1942 from the Republic of Slovakia, a state not administered by Germany, was possible only through the cooperation of German government agencies and antisemitic forces in Slovakia.[42]

There had been pogroms in Bratislava and Trnava in November and December 1939, conducted mainly by members of the paramilitary SS-like Hlinka Guard and Slovakia's German minority. Wealthy Jews had been blackmailed or arrested. In November 1938 the Catholic priest Dr. Jozef Tiso, then the head of Slovakia's provincial government and later the president of independent Slovakia, ordered the expulsion of all Jews of German, Hungarian, Romanian, and Polish nationality from Slovakia to Hungary.[43] After the ultimate destruction of Czechoslovakia in March 1939 and Slovakia's official declaration of independence, the country was chained to the German Reich by a "protective treaty," and its government issued its first discriminating measures against Slovak Jews: It established an official definition of "Jew" and imposed employment limitations in the civil service and specific academic positions.[44]

Slovak authorities focused specifically on Aryanization, but the Jews' dispossession of property ended in distribution fights between Slovak government civil servants and friends and acquaintances of persons in positions of power on the one hand and the masses associated with the Hlinka Guard and members of the German Volksgruppe (ethnic Germans) in Slovakia on the other.[45] Based on the model of the Vermögensverkehrsstelle in Vienna, which Movarek, the chief of a similar organization in Slovakia, visited with Wisliceny in the fall of 1940, a Zentralwirtschaftsamt was established whose purpose it was "to do whatever is necessary to accomplish the removal of the Jew from Slovak economic and social life and to transfer Jewish property to Christian ownership."[46] The term "Christian" signaled corruption, elitism, and the appointment of dubious "Arisatoren" who often did not even possess a modicum of professional know-how to administer the business establishments they took over."[47] The methodology of "the elimination of the Jews from Slovak economy" strikingly recalls the process in the Ostmark beginning in 1938. The definition of who is a Jew in the so-called Judenkodex (Jewish Code), promulgated in September 1941, recalls the Nuremberg race laws but contained exceptions, which the president of the republic could invoke. The model for this clause probably was turn-of-the-century Vienna mayor Dr. Karl Lueger's motto "I decide who is a Jew," adopted by the Slovak clerical-Fascist régime.[48]

The next move of the Slovak Zentralwirtschaftsamt deprived the Bratislava Jews of their dwellings. Because living space in the city was scarce, Slovak government offices in the fall and winter of 1941 organized so-called dislocations of Jews from the capital.[49] More than 6,000 people, almost half of Bratislava's Jewish citizens, were affected by this measure. The displaced were resettled in rural areas or sent to newly established work camps in Nováky, Sered', and Vyhne.[50]

No pressure from German authorities had been necessary to produce the first discriminatory measures against the Jews in Slovakia, robbing and dislocating thousands of people and relocating them in camps. The process of disenfranchisement and marginalization had been set in motion by Slovakia's overwhelmingly religiously, economically motivated antisemitism. The alliance of Slovak and German interests remained intact even as the final phase of persecution, the deportations, was ushered in. The response of the Slovak government to the November 1941 Foreign Office inquiry as to whether Bratislava would agree to the expulsion from the Reich of Jews holding Slovak citizenship is enlightening. The Slovak government had no objections to the expulsion of its Jewish citizens living in Germany to the ghettos in the East alongside German Jews, provided "its legal claims to the moveable and fixed assets of these Jews would not be endangered by such expulsions."[51]

Whether the suggestion to deport 20,000 Jews from Slovakia at the beginning of 1942 originated in Berlin or Bratislava cannot be determined.[52] At any rate, because the number of Jews expelled to the East was "insufficient to supply the need for workers there," the RSHA approached the Auswärtige Amt with the request to ask the Slovak government for "20,000 young, healthy Slovak Jews for expulsion to the East." According to Foreign Office documents, the Slovak government "eagerly took up this suggestion," initiated the necessary preparations, and, as Eichmann informed the Foreign Office, even volunteered to pay 500 RM per deportee to cover housing, food, clothing, and retraining."[53]

Slovak authorities quickly initiated the registration of all male Jews between the ages of sixteen and forty-five and set up a special list of able-bodied men. At the same time they ordered the registration of unmarried Jewish women between sixteen and forty-five years of age and who had no children below the age of sixteen. The concentration of these registered men and women started shortly thereafter. Within a few weeks the examination, the concentration, and the completion of all formalities were achieved with a precision and speed uncommon in Slovakia.[54] After these preparations, technical issues such as ordering the trains had to be settled. In mid-March 1942 the German embassy in Slovakia received notice that SS-Obersturmbannführer Eichmann would come to Bratislawa for planning sessions concerning the "evacuation of 20,000 Jews from Slovakia."[55]

With the help of the four deportation specialists from Vienna, members of the Hlinka Guard and the Volksdeutsche Freiwillige Schutzstaffel (volunteer SS units for ethnic Germans in Slovakia) collected the Jewish men and women and moved some of them on foot, others in trucks to the collection camps in Nováky, Sered', Zilina, Poprad, and Bratislava.[56] Wisliceny had requested that Brunner send four SS non-commissioned officers from Vienna to train their Slovak commandants in camp management because mistreatment and robbery by Hlinka guards were commonplace in all of them.[57] According to Wisliceny, who had inspected them, the Hlinka Guard ransacked the prisoners' luggage at Zilina, and a brutal, permanently drunk commandant ruled the Bratislava collection camp: "The treatment of the girls and women concentrated there was exceedingly bad." Whenever he visited the camp, the commandant and his staff, including the NCOs from Vienna, were drunk: "Empty schnapps bottles were strewn everywhere." He was under the impression that the internees at Bratislava were "robbed even more thoroughly than those in Zelina."[58]

Late in March 1942 the deportation trains from Slovakia started to roll. The first transports consisted almost entirely of young people. Trains, each with 1,000 young women, arrived in Auschwitz at the end of March; transports with young men went to the concentration camp Lublin, later called

Majdanek.[59] These first transports to Auschwitz that Eichmann and his men had organized did not go through a selection on arrival. The SS moved all the young women into the camp, where they had to surrender their last possessions, their clothes and shoes, and where their hair was cut. They received torn, lice-infested uniforms of dead Soviet prisoners of war and wooden clogs. In rain and cold and without appropriate tools these women had to construct barracks, roads, and drainage systems.[60] Totally inadequate food rations, lack of sanitary facilities, mistreatment at the hands of the SS, and inhumane working conditions spawned a variety of diseases and a rapidly rising number of deaths.

Before their deportation these young Slovak Jews had been told that they were being taken to Poland to build shelters for their families who would follow soon. At the end of March the Slovak minister of the interior had made similar statements to journalists. In early April, Slovak government agencies announced that entire Jewish families were to be gathered in collection camps for deportation. People were collected and grouped into transports in district towns such as Trnava, Nitra, and Topol'čany.[61] There, too, excesses by members of the Hlinka Guard took place. As an exercise in humiliation they shaved the old men's beards. As photographs testify, the Viennese deportation specialists supervised the collection and transport of these victims. Within a single month, between the end of March and the end of April, twenty deportation trains, each with 1,000 men, women, and children, left Slovakia for Auschwitz and Lublin.[62] During the succeeding months the tempo slowed somewhat until it came to a stop in the fall. Some Slovak Jews had fled to Hungary. Thousands had taken advantage of the rules of exception set down in the Jewish Code and had obtained letters of protection from ministries and the president; these kept them and their relatives safe from deportation. Until mid-October, when the last transport left Slovakia, Slovak authorities, with the assistance of the Vienna experts, deported a total of 19,000 people to Auschwitz and a total of 39,000 to the Lublin region. In 1945 only 348 of them returned to Czechoslovakia.[63]

In 1942, without undue pressure from German authorities, the Slovakian government had surrendered two-thirds of that country's Jews to be murdered in Nazi camps. The isolation and persecution of the Jews apparently coincided with the Catholicism of the Slovak political leadership. President Dr. Tiso's position is clear from an August speech in which he posed the question whether the steps toward solving the Jewish Question were compatible with Christian principles: "No one, I believe, needs convincing that the Jewish element has threatened the life of Slovakia.... We have acted in accordance with God's command: 'Slovak, rid yourself of your enemy!' In this spirit we are creating order and will continue to do so."[64]

1942: Ustasha Genocides in the "Independent State of Croatia" and Deportations to Auschwitz

After the military invasion of Yugoslavia in April 1941, the country was dismembered. Germany and Italy annexed most of Slovenia (with small parts going to Hungary and "independent" Croatia), and Italy also occupied parts of the Dalmatian coast and some of the islands in the Adriatic Sea. Hungary annexed the upper and central Mur area, the Baranya, and Bačka. Bulgaria annexed Macedonia. The area of the former kingdom of Serbia and parts of the Banat came under German military administration; Italy occupied most of Montenegro and Kossovo.

Italy and Germany installed Ante Pavelić, the leader of the Ustasha,[65] as head of the so-called Independent State of Croatia, which included not only the previous territory of Croatia, but also part of Dalmatia, as well as Bosnia, Herzegovina, and Syrmia. Only about half of the inhabitants of this newly created puppet state actually were Croats – two million Serbs constituted almost one third of its population. Roughly 40,000 Jews, among them refugees from Greater Germany, lived in Croatia, Bosnia, and Herzegovina in 1941. Immediately following the installation of the régime, the Ustasha seized the property of the Serbian and Jewish populations. Serbian peasants were expelled. On April 21 the Pavelić government promulgated a decree that stipulated the appointment of Betriebskommissare, "factory commissioners," to control and administer enterprises of Serbian and Jewish proprietors. On April 30 the official definition of "Jew" was published, and additional steps toward expropriation followed.[66]

Although members of the Ustasha were the main culprits in the theft of Serbian and Jewish property, Volksdeutsche (ethnic Germans) were involved as well, and this resulted in conflicts between the representatives of these two groups.[67] The contest for booty in the Independent State of Croatia displayed obvious parallels to events in Slovakia. Here, as there, cliques close to the régime enriched themselves at the expense of the persecuted. In both countries representatives of the Volksdeutsche complained that their group was being shortchanged in the redistribution of the loot.

The Ustasha rank and file considered these property transfers their just rewards for their supposed political merits, as a German report of early 1942 makes clear.

> Up to now the Aryanization has been understood as distribution of rich sinecures because until the seizure of power Ustasha activists had to contend with severe problems. Many had to emigrate; they spent years abroad. . . . When these émigrés returned, they were rewarded with Serbian and Jewish businesses, unless they were recruited for government service. In economic terms, this

was certainly harmful because in spite of real or supposed political merits, these people are economic newcomers who cannot manage these businesses effectively.[68]

Despoiling Serbs and Jews was merely the first step of the persecutions: The Ustasha escalated its religious-racial strategies to genocide. Members of the Serbian population became victims of the whims of Croatian government agencies as well as of thieving and murdering Ustasha units. They fell victim to forced baptism, mass expulsions, incarcerations in concentration camps, and massacres. Ustasha squads slaughtered the Serbian inhabitants of entire villages in Bosnia and Herzegovina.[69]

The exact number of Serbian victims of expulsions and massacres cannot be determined with certainty. According to an early September 1941 report by Dr. Harold Turner, the head of the administrative staff under the military commander in Serbia, more than 100,000 Serbs already had been expelled from the Independent State of Croatia into the part of Serbia under German military administration. Moreover,

> According to reports, in Croatia alone about 200,000 Serbs have been murdered. These killings are common knowledge here. Because Croatia received its independence under the protection of the German Reich and because the German forces stationed in Croatia did not prevent these atrocities, Germany ultimately will be held responsible.[70]

In succeeding years the Ustasha continued its expulsion and annihilation policies against the Serbs. Edmund Glaise-Horstenau, the Austrian-born German general in Agram, in a February 1942 report, characterized the functionaries of the Ustasha as arrogant, arbitrary, rapacious, and corrupt. "Furthermore, the atrocities, pillages, and murders do not stop. Not a week goes by without new Säuberungsaktionen ("cleansing actions") in which the inhabitants of entire villages, including women and children, get wiped out."[71] Colonel General Alexander Löhr, Wehrmacht Commander Southeast, in a memorandum of February 1943 estimated that the Ustasha had murdered 400,000 Serbs.[72]

Jews and Roma (Gypsies) also became victims of arrests and mass murder. The Ustasha arrested and interned them in camps but, in contrast to Slovakia where dislocated persons were sent to work camps, in the Independent State of Croatia many waves of arrests immediately were followed by mass murders. Especially in the Jasenovac and Stara Gradiska concentration camps, Ustasha members murdered uncounted numbers of Serbs, Jews, and Roma.[73] Just how brutally the Ustasha camp personnel ruled in Jasenovac emerges from the report of a Jewish survivor from Zagreb who gave it to Franz Theodor Csokor, an Austrian writer, while the war still was in progress.[74] In January 1942, together with hundreds of other men, women, and children who had been driven from their homes, he was incarcerated in a Zagreb prison. Deriving from all social and age groups, the detainees had not been informed of the reason for their arrests but realized that all of them were Jews. Women and children were transferred to Djakovo camp and the men were taken by train to Jasenovac. At roll call the Ustasha, in full sight of all the prisoners, stabbed the old men who had collapsed during the march from the railway station to the camp and had been dragged along by their suffering comrades.

The next morning the 500 or so new arrivals were divided into two groups. Three hundred men older than fifty years of age were murdered by the guards with clubs and hammer blows; then the gold teeth and fillings were broken out of their mouths. The younger prisoners had to perform heavy labor under catastrophic conditions. Whoever fell ill or collapsed was killed.[75] Minute infractions resulted in cruel mistreatment: confinement in single bunkers in which the prisoners had to crouch, or instant death. The number of prisoners dwindled rapidly. Csokor's witness survived because his wife contacted the mayor of Zagreb, a family acquaintance, whose intervention secured his release from this death camp.[76]

The extent of the arrests and murders of Jewish men, women, and children in the Ustasha state is difficult to quantify. One point of reference is President Pavelić's comment to Italian Foreign Minister Galeazzo Ciano during a state visit to Venice: "Since the outbreak of the war, the Jewish population of Croatia had been reduced by two-thirds."[77] Dragutin Rosenberg, the deputy leader of the Zagreb Jewish community, estimated that of the 15,000 Jewish men arrested by the summer of 1942 only 1,200–1,500 still were alive in the various Croatian camps.[78]

Against this background, in the spring of 1942 the RSHA began preparations to include Croatia in the deportation program and sent SS-Hauptsturmführer Abromeit of Eichmann's RSHA Referat to Zagreb to work with Stürmbahnführer Hans Helm, the police attaché at the German embassy. The implementation of these plans was not slow in coming. In July 1942 the Croat government issued an order for all Jews to register and, in August, Abromeit organized deportations to Auschwitz.

In organizing the first transport of about 1,200 Jews on August 14, official guidelines had been ignored, which caused bureaucratic complications. In a letter to Auschwitz, Rolf Günther from Eichmann's Referat in Berlin ordered the return of several persons.

According to a report of the police attaché at the German embassy in Agram, the rush to organize this transport caused the inclusion of several Jews holding

Italian or Hungarian citizenship and whose names are not known. I ask that you identify the Italian and Hungarian Jews even before accepting the transport into the camp and hand them back to the leader of the Croatian transport immediately, as agreed per telephone with the police attaché. The transport leader will be responsible for their correct return to Croatia.[79]

Reacting to this mistake, the Zagreb office instructed Günther "to avoid problems by apportioning only those Jews for transport who can be seized in accordance with the directives."

On August 18, 22, 26, and 30, 1942, four additional deportation transports from Croatia reached Auschwitz. According to the Korherr statistic report, in 1942 a total of 4,927 Croatian Jews were deported to this concentration and extermination camp. The majority of the Croatian and Bosnian Jews, who did not manage to escape into the Italian zone of occupation, to the partisans, or abroad, fell victim to the rampages of the Ustasha or the inhumane conditions in the Croatian camps.[80]

8 The Destruction of the Jewish Community of Salonika: The Cooperation of the SS and the Wehrmacht

In modern times Salonika has been referred to as "Little Jerusalem" and "Jerusalem of the Balkans" on account of the strong presence of its Jewish community. The history of Jewish settlement in Salonika antedates Christ's birth.[1] Until 1943 its characteristic nature was the result of its settlement by the tens of thousands of Sephardim, the Spanish Jews whom los Reyes Católicos, the "Catholic Monarchs" Ferdinand and Isabella, had expelled from Spain at the end of the Reconquista, the reconquest of Spain, in 1492.[2] Well into the twentieth century most of them continued to speak Ladino, a language based on a Jewish dialect of Old Castilian enriched by Hebrew, Portuguese, Greek, Turkish, Italian, and French words and figures of speech that reflected the origin and successive waves of immigrants and the impact of their surroundings.

At the beginning of the twentieth century the 80,000 Sephardim constituted almost half of the entire population of Salonika. Sephardic Jews were employed in every kind of enterprise, in commerce, textile production, printing, and handicrafts. The number of them working in the harbor and as cargo carriers was such that ships could not be unloaded on the Jewish Sabbath. Clothing styles, social customs, food preparation, language, and even lullabies from Toledo and Seville, dating back to the times of Ferdinand and Isabella, passed from one generation to the next.[3]

In the 1920s and 1930s the number of Sephardim diminished due to emigration to Palestine and Western Europe, as, for example, to Paris, from where in November 1942 Jews of Greek origin were deported to Auschwitz,[4] and through the exodus to Turkey by a group of converts to Islam. According to the 1940 census, 67,000 people of Mosaic faith lived in Greece and about 2,000 more in the Dodecanese Islands, then under Italian administration. About 50,000 Jews were thought to live in Salonika and, on the eve of the war, Salonika with its synagogues and academies, rabbis and teachers, newspapers and printing shops still constituted the largest concentration of Sephardic Jewry.[5]

The destruction of this community commenced when Wehrmacht units occupied Greece. On April 9, 1941, the first army columns entered Salonika. All newspapers ceased publication, among them the Spanish-Jewish *El messagero* (*The Messenger*). Starting on April 15, the Jewish Community Council and the leaders of other Jewish organizations were arrested. The offices of the Salonika Jewish Community were searched and its archives and safe seized to put an end to its activities. Before the end of the month the German-controlled Greek newspaper *Nea Evropi* (*New Europe*) launched an antisemitic campaign and published the order that all Jews were to surrender their radios to German authorities. In early May all bookstores under Jewish ownership were closed down and expropriated. Zvi Koretz, the chief rabbi of the Salonika community, was arrested in Athens and taken to Vienna, where he had been a student in the 1920s, and in 1925 had written his dissertation "The Depiction of Hell in the Koran and its Models in Jewish Literature."

Until Italy's capitulation, the German occupation administration consisted of the Wehrmachtsbefehlshaber im Südosten/Armeeoberkommando 12 (AOK 12). After the beginning of 1943 it was Heeresgruppe E (Army Group E) and its subordinate Befehlshaber Saloniki-Ägäis (in the spring of 1941 the Kommandant rückwärtiges Armeegebiet 560); the Befehlshaber Südgriechenland, the Commander Southern Greece, and the Bevollmächtigte of the Reich, the Reich plenipotentiery in Greece, who until fall 1943 was Dr. Günther Altenburg. Furthermore, a field office for the Sicherheitspolizei and the SD was established in Salonika under the direction of the Luxembourgian Dr. Albert Calmes. This organization had its own prison camp, Pavlou Mela.

In May 1941 the military offices working with the Sonderkommando of the Sicherheitspolizei and the SD ordered the deployment of the Sonderkommando Rosenberg in Greece.[6]

Pursuant to an order of the AOK of April 19, 1941 (Abt. Ic/AO No. 1031/41 geh.), a Sonderkommando of Reichsleiter Rosenberg is working in the area of the 12th Army with the order to search state libraries, archives, the offices of high-level church authorities, the lodges of freemasons, and Jewish organizations for evidence of political activities directed against the Reich and to seize any pertinent materials. The Sonderkommando Rosenberg . . . is attached to the Kommandant rückwärtiges Armeegebiet. In view of the special extent and influence of the local Jewry in Salonika, a permanent work group will be established there within a few days. . . . To implement these confiscations, the Sonderkommando, upon request, is to be furnished additional personnel from the GFP.[7]

Several items in this document are noteworthy.

- April 19, the date of the order. Even before the conclusion of the military operations and the official armistice with the Greek army, the Twelfth Army high command already was considering the fate of the Greek Jews.
- The order for the deployment of the Sonderkommando in this district originated with the section of the General Staff responsible for collecting and evaluating enemy intelligence and counterintelligence (Abwehr, department Ic/AO).
- The Sonderkommando was attached to the Kommandant rückwärtiges Armeegebiet (later Befehlshaber Saloniki-Ägäis), and members of the Wehrmacht and officials in the GFP were attached to the Sonderkommando for possible Aktionen.

In mid-June a department of the Sonderkommando Rosenberg started its activities in Salonika by seizing thousands of books, manuscripts, and art works; by searching thousands of private dwellings and conducting interrogations of important representatives of the Jewish community; and by gaining access to bank safes. Furthermore, a list of members of Salonika's Jewish community fell into its hands, probably providing the basis for later persecution measures. In November 1941 the Sonderkommando Rosenberg already had written a final report about its activities in Greece. Until mid-1942, apart from isolated hostilities, life for the majority of Jews in Salonika followed much the same pattern as that of non-Jewish Greeks.[8] Severe inflation and increasing food shortages affected all of Salonika's citizens and in the winter of 1941–1942 led to famine.

Even though after a situation briefing in October 1941 Hitler reportedly instructed Himmler to remove "Jewish elements" from Salonika, for some time the RSHA took no action at all.[9] The position of Italian occupation authorities in Greece probably presented a major obstacle, as can be gleaned from a letter the Eichmann Referat of the RSHA Department IV B 4 sent to the Foreign Office in July 1942 under the heading "Treatment of the Jewish Question Abroad."

According to the situation reports of the Sicherheitspolizei and SD offices in Greece, marking Jews and Jewish businesses in Greece, which if for no other reason than coordinating anti-Jewish measures in all European countries in preparation of the Final Solution of the Jewish Question would be highly desirable, is absolutely necessary for political and police reasons. The same is true for Jews who emigrated from Germany and who because of their Communist and Axis-hostile activities constitute a particular danger.

Beyond that, Jews were blamed for the dismal food situation in Greece through their control of "usurious clandestine dealings and the black market."[10] To remedy the situation, the letter proposed the internment of "especially dangerous Jews."

In the opinion of the RSHA, this description characterized the situation throughout Greece; therefore,

> both Axis powers should be equally interested in improving it. For this reason the office of the Sicherheitspolizei and the SD in Athens asked Minister Altenburg, the official representative of the German Reich in Athens, to investigate at the appropriate Italian government office whether Italy would agree to marking the Jews in Greece. The Italian representative, Minister Ghigi, after consulting with the Italian Foreign Ministry in Rome, replied that Italy, "in view of the significant economic power of Italian Jews in the Mediterranean region, . . . would like to postpone the marking of the Jews in Greece."[11]

Additionally, because discriminating marking had not been adopted in Italy,

> Jews in Greece holding Italian citizenship would have to be exempted from being marked if Germany planned to introduce any such markings in its administrative sphere in Salonika. In view of the intolerable state of affairs in this area, the Italian objections don't strike me as justified, at least as far as the German-controlled area of Salonika is concerned.

The RSHA then approached the Foreign Office for a decision "whether the marking of Jews and internment of those Jews from Germany considered especially dangerous could be adopted at least in Salonika."[12] Yet preparations for marking and deporting Greek Jews, at first limited to northern Greece, still would take another six months.

At the same time that the RSHA contacted the Foreign Office about marking the Jews, local Aktionen against the Jewish community of Salonika occurred. These measures originated neither from Berlin nor from the Eichmann Referat but within the military administration of the Befehlshaber Saloniki-Ägäis. When the Greek Inspectorate General for Macedonia complained about Greeks being pressed into work details while the Jewish inhabitants of Salonika were exempt, the Befehlshaber Saloniki-Ägäis ordered all male Jews from Salonika between the ages of eighteen and forty-five to report on July 11, 1942, to be registered for work details. Some 9,000 men obeyed this order. For hours they waited in the searing heat of the Freedom Plaza. Whoever tried to sit down or shield himself from the sun was dragged off by the guards and had to perform punishment drills under their blows.[13] Ultimately, over the next several days 3,500 men were conscripted to perform forced labor in road and airport construction and in a chromium mine. Lack of sanitation facilities and inadequate food rations caused such inhumane living and working conditions that hundreds caught malaria, spotted fever, and typhoid: Within ten weeks 12 percent of the forced laborers were dead.[14]

In mid-October, after lengthy negotiations between Dr. Max Merten, the chief of the military administration of the Befehlshaber Saloniki-Ägäis, and the Jewish Community Council, a contract was signed stipulating the repeal of compulsory forced labor in exchange for a "ransom" of 2.5 billion drachmae and the surrender of Salonika's Jewish graveyard. Yet, this ransom notwithstanding, numerous Aryanizations took place in the fall and winter. Businesses were seized without compensation. In December 1942 Dr. Calmes, the head of the SD in Salonika, appointed Chief Rabbi Zvi Koretz, now back from his forced internment in Vienna, president of the Jewish community.

Preparation of the Cooperation among the SS, the Wehrmacht, and Political and Diplomatic Organizations

In January 1943 Eichmann introduced the final preparations for the destruction of the Jewish community of Salonika by sending his deputy Rolf Günther to Greece to clarify and coordinate the future plan of action with the leaders of the German occupation authorities.[15] The desired marking and deportation of 45,000 people from Salonika could not be carried out by a few SS members in a night-and-fog operation, so the approval and cooperation of the German military, political, and diplomatic organizations in Greece were crucial.

No detailed record of Günther's negotiations in Greece is available. Only the correspondence between Dr. Altenburg or the RSHA Referat IV B 4 with the Foreign Office allows a reconstruction revealing the dates of various meetings and their participants. Günther arrived in Athens in early January 1943 and discussed with the representatives of the Reich the plan of "evacuating" the Jews from Salonika. Altenburg's mid-January note to the Foreign Office about his discussion with the Italian representative confirms:

> I used my conversation with the Italian representative to inform him of SS-Sturmbannführer Günther's mandate concerning "the evacuations" of Jews within the German occupation zone of Saloniki-Ägäis. I assured him that Italian wishes concerning Italian Jews and those of neutral powers would be honored. Mr. Ghigi did not accept my news without regret, though he did state that in the German areas of occupation we certainly could do as we pleased. I informed Mr. Günther, who will fly to Salonika today, about the details of this meeting and have instructed him to discharge his mission in close contact with our Consulate General [in Salonika].[16]

In a telegram of January 15, Altenburg complained to the Auswärtige Amt that instructions to the Generalkonsulat in Salonika concerning Günther's mandate still had not arrived: "I ask that you take care of this matter with all due speed since Günther, in response to the Führer's order, has requested the assistance of the Consulate General and the local military authorities for the completion of his mission."[17] The Foreign Office responded with a telegram to Altenburg, reporting that the appropriate organization in Salonika had been notified.

> The Generalkonsulat has received these instructions: "SS-Sturmbannführer Günther, at the order of the Reichssicherheitshauptamt and with the approval of the Auswärtige Amt, has arrived in Salonika to conduct negotiations in Jewish affairs. Your support and instructions to military organizations to follow your lead are requested. It goes without saying that Günther can proceed only with Envoy Altenburg's approval."[18]

In a letter dated January 25 to the Auswärtige Amt, the subject of which was the "preparation and execution of the planned expulsion of Jews from the Salonika area within the framework of the Endlösung of the European Jewish Question," Günther himself named the organizations with which he conferred in Salonika.

> The necessary discussions about the execution of these evacuation measures, as embassy secretary Dr. Klingenfuß has been informed already, were conducted in early January in Athens with the Bevollmächtigte of the Reich in Greece, the German Generalkonsul in Salonika, Heeresgruppe [Heeresgruppe E under the command of Generaloberst Löhr], and the Befehlshaber Saloniki-Ägäis.[19]

Günther's letter did not reveal the names of any of the participants or the content of the talks in Salonika, and the activity report of the Befehlshaber Saloniki-Ägäis for the beginning of January through the end of June 1943 does not even mention these talks.[20] Yet, according to Dr. Merten's statements, there had been a conference in Salonika with a representative of the Reichssicherheitshauptamt

> attended not only by the Befehlshaber Saloniki-Ägäis in person but also all prominent members of the Heeresgruppe and the staff of the Befehlshaber from the Ics of both staffs as well as the Abwehr, the Geheime Feldpolizei, and the local SD down to the chief sanitation officers. In the course of this meeting all impending measures – marking Jews with stars and their ghettoization – were settled and the military organizations charged with their implementation.[21]

Whether all measures actually were settled at this conference is anyone's guess. What is certain is that the military organizations in charge, the general staff officers of the Heeresgruppe Löhr and of the Befehlshaber Saloniki-Ägäis, were informed before the start of the Aktionen against the Jews and had no objections to the Sturmbannführer's plans but, on the contrary, pledged their cooperation.

This course of action on the part of the military leadership is not exceptional because it reflects the position of the Oberbefehlshaber of the Wehrmacht in all of occupied southern Europe. Jews were considered enemies. Generaloberst Löhr knew about the measures for the solution of the Jewish Question and "the problem of the Gypsies" within his area of command and approved of them. At the end of August 1942, soon after Löhr took up his duties as Wehrmachtsbefehlshaber Südost, Dr. Turner, the chief of the military administration in Serbia, had informed him personally that in Serbia "the Jewish Question and the Gypsy Question had been totally liquidated" so that Serbia was the only country that had actually solved the problem of the Jews and the Gypsies.[22]

On October 1, Löhr and his fellow German and personal friend Glaise von Horstenau in their "notes for the Führer" recorded their complaints to the German commanding general in Agram about the protection that segments of the Italian occupation forces were providing for persecuted Jews in Croatia.

> The implementation of "Jewish laws" established by the state of Croatia is hindered to such a degree by Italian authorities that in the coastal areas, especially in Mostar, Dubrovnik, and Crkvice, numerous Jews are under Italian military protection while others are being ferried across the border to Italian Dalmatia and even to Italy. Such aid enables them to continue their subversive activities and in so doing undermine our common military objectives. According to an embassy report from Rome, the Duce had decided in early September 1942 that the Jews were to be treated according to Croatian law. Yet to this day both the Italian ambassador [Raffaello] Casertano and General [Mario] Roatta, the Supreme Commander of the Second Italian Army, claim not to have received any instructions to that effect.[23]

The top echelons of the Wehrmacht in Greece, Heeresgruppe E and its subordinate Befehlshaber Saloniki-Ägäis, voiced no reservations about the stigmatization and consequent deportation of a segment of the Greek civilian population. Because of the racial membership ascribed to these Jews, the Wehrmacht too considered them enemies and legitimized their deportation as a military necessity. As the former director of the military administration attached to the Wehrmachtsbefehlshaber Südost – Heeresgruppe E, Dr. Theodor P., explained during a witness interrogation in the 1960s,

> because of the explosive situation in Greece, the military leadership there constantly expected attacks from the south on the thinly-stretched German

front. The so-called Situation Viktoria was rehearsed constantly. We had to be prepared for enemy invasion troops from the south advancing on Salonika. In such a situation the presence of large numbers of hostile Jews would have been dangerous to the fighting German forces.[24]

In January 1943 there were no efforts on the part of political-diplomatic representatives of the German Reich or Wehrmacht organizations in Greece to prevent or delay deportations or the preparations for deportations, or to refuse being involved in such activities. Because military authorities ascribed enemy status to a part of the civilian population, it followed that they participated in their preventive elimination. So the final act in Salonika could proceed – and this needs to be highlighted – because of the diplomatic support of the Reich plenipotentiary in Greece and the consul general in Salonika, because of the approval of leading officers of Army Group E, and because of the active participation of the apparatus responsible for this section under the command of the Befehlshaber Saloniki-Ägäis. The cooperation of the various representatives of the SS, Wehrmacht, and the Foreign Office vital for the realization of the deportation plans had been secured. Now the hunters could cast their nets.

Registration and Confinement in Ghettos of the Jewish Community of Salonika

> On the Sabbath, February 6, 1943, a commission of the SD arrives in Salonika to apply the racial laws. It consists of six genuine monsters: Dieter Wisliceny, Alois Brunner, Gerbing, Takasch, Zita, and Brückler. Their leaders are the massive Wisliceny and the delicate Brunner, short of stature, thin, dark-skinned.... Brunner is chiefly in charge of applying the instructions. Zita is to serve as secretary.[25]

This list of the SD personnel is not quite complete. According to Alfred Slawik,

> in addition to Hauptsturmführer Wislizeny [sic], the SD commando was made up of Hauptsturmführer Brunner, I as Aktion leader, six men, and one Greek interpreter. The six men were Herbert Gerbing, Anton Zita, Ernst Brückler, Gesar Dagatsch [also spelled Takacs or Takasch in other documents], and Mathias Schefczig, as well as I and the Greek translator Jakob Bodurian.[26]

In 1936, SS-Hauptsturmführer Wisliceny, then an SS-Untersturmführer, had been Eichmann's superior in the Department II-112 at the SD Hauptamt. In the meantime not only Eichmann but some of his men had caught up with him or even passed him in the SS hierarchy through their zeal in the persecution of Jews. In 1943 Eichmann, as an SS-Obersturmbannführer, was two ranks above Wisliceny and director of the RSHA Referat IV B 4, and responsible for "Jewish Affairs and Evacuation Actions." Alois Brunner, who did not join the SS until November 1938, held the same rank as Wisliceny, who previously had been posted as "Adviser in Jewish Affairs" to the police attaché at the German embassy in Bratislava. In terms of expertise he had been a member of the Eichmann Referat; officially he had been a member of the Auswärtige Amt, which is why Rolf Günther, representing the RSHA, had to inform the Foreign Office of Wisliceny's posting to Greece. Dr. Altenburg had been notified as well.

> Obersturmbannführer Günther reports that the temporary reassignment of SS-Hauptsturmführer Wisliceny, who at this time is working at the German embassy in Pressburg (Bratislava), will be necessary for about six to eight weeks to prepare and complete the expulsion of Jews from the Salonika area. I request a statement concerning this expulsion and Wisliceny's posting.[27]

By the following day Altenburg had pointed out that, in a telegram on January 13, he already had responded to the issue of expulsion and had no objection to Wisliceny's reassignment. He added that he also had discussed "this matter" with the prime minister of the Greek puppet regime, "from whom no difficulty need be expected after that conversation as regards completion of this Aktion."[28]

According to Wisliceny's witness testimony at the International Military Tribunal in Nuremberg, Eichmann had ordered him to come to Berlin in January 1943 and had informed him of his posting to Salonika to solve the Jewish Question there in cooperation with the German military administration in Macedonia. February 1943 had been set for his leaving Bratislava. At the end of January, Eichmann had informed him that he had dispatched Hauptsturmführer Brunner to Greece to take charge of the technical management of all Aktionen. Organizationally, Brunner did not answer to Wisliceny but operated independently. "Then, in February 1943, we went to Salonika and contacted the military administration there."[29] Slawik, in his interrogation, also referred to a division of labor between Wisliceny and Brunner. "His [Wisliceny's] responsibility was limited to handling the paperwork and the negotiations with the various organizations whereas Hauptsturmführer Brunner and his men handled the actual roundups of Jews and the organization of the transports."[30]

Of the other six SS members who travelled to Salonika with Wisliceny and Brunner, four came from Vienna and surroundings – Herbert Gerbing,

Anton Zita, Ernst Brückler, and Alfred Slawik; Takasch and Schefczig had been Wisliceny's coworkers in Slovakia. No sooner had they arrived in Salonika, this group under the title of "Außenstelle (Field Office) of the Sipo and the SD in Saloniki IV B4" (later "Sonderkommando der Sicherheitspolizei für Judenangelegenheiten Saloniki-Ägäis"), in concert with the military administration of the Befehlshaber Saloniki-Ägäis, launched the persecution of the Jewish population. On Monday, February 8, Dr. Koretz had to appear at the Außenstelle. "Koretz's interview with the SD lasts a full two hours, and when he returns, he is deathly pale."[31] He informed the immediately assembled Council that the Gestapo had surrendered its authority in Jewish affairs to the SD and that from now on the Jews would have to wear the star and would be concentrated in ghettos.

The written version of these measures came from the Befehlshaber Saloniki-Ägäis's department of Military Administration addressed to the Jüdische Kultusgemeinde [Jewish Community Council] of Salonika:

> Based on the legislative authority invested in the Befehlshaber Saloniki-Ägäis, the following regulations are now in force:
>
> 1. All Jews living in Salonika, except for those foreign citizens who through possession of a valid passport can prove such status – are to be marked as such immediately, as are all Jewish business establishments, offices, etc. These identifications are to be made public through clearly visible signs in German and Greek.
> 2. All Jewish citizens of Salonika with the exceptions stated above – will immediately move to a specially designated section of the city.
> 3. Each affected Jew is responsible for covering all expenses accruing from directives 1 and 2. The entire Jewish community is responsible for defraying the expenses of those unable to pay.
> 4. The implementation of measures 1 and 2 will be the responsibility of the SD, which also will determine the details involved in the discharge of these measures, such as type of identification and determination of the city boroughs referred to in directive 2. By February 25, 1943, the Jüdische Kultusgemeinde will report completion of these directives to the signatory organization issuing this notification.[32]

The sequence of individual "measures of implementation" took place in rapid succession. On February 12 a directive signed by Wisliceny and addressed to the Jüdische Kultusgemeinde by the Außenstelle der Sipo und des SD in Saloniki IV B4 specified identification with the Star of David and simultaneous registration and issue of personal identification cards, and ordered all

Jews of Greek nationality to be so identified. To be categorized as Jews were
those

a) who were descendants of at least three racially Jewish grandparents
b) who were of mixed blood (Jewish Mischling) descended from two
   racially Jewish grandparents and who on June 1, 1941, belonged to
   the Mosaic faith or had been born illegitimately after that date and were
   descendents of a Jew.[33]

This directive also ordered the Kultusgemeinde to compile a list of the names,
dates of birth, and total number of persons who had received identification
cards. No petitions for exemption would be accepted. In Salonika, Kriegsverwaltungsrat (War Administrative Councilor) Merten took that same position vis-à-vis the Italian consul, Zamboni, who attempted to intervene on
behalf of Greek relatives of Jews holding Italian citizenship.[34] On February 17,
Wisliceny, in a second directive, issued more precise instructions for identify-
ing "Jewish businesses and dwellings" with posters and signs,[35] which resulted
in businesses so identified being set up for looting. As one victim reported,
"each Jewish store had to be identified by a sign in plain view saying 'Jewish
business' in Greek and German. Any soldier could enter and take whatever he
wanted without paying and without anyone being able to object."[36]

Merten's directive of February 13 prohibited the Jews of Salonika from
leaving their homes, using public transportation, entering streets and public
squares after dark and using public and private telephones. That very day,
Merten also extended Dr. Koretz' authority over all Jews living within the area
under the control of the Befehlshaber Saloniki-Ägäis, which subjugated several
smaller Jewish communities in the parts of eastern Thrace and Macedonia not
occupied by Bulgaria to the impending deportation measures.[37]

During this period the ghettoization of Salonika's Jewish population started
as well. Two areas inhabited by a large number of Jews were designated for
their concentration. Employees of the Kultusgemeinde speedily organized the
relocation of Jews living outside these precincts. Non-Jewish Greeks, members of the Wehrmacht, and Wehrmacht offices then occupied their spacious
apartments and houses.[38] The SD-Sonderkommando had deceived the representatives of the Jewish community into believing that these ghetto areas
would enjoy social and economic autonomy and would be subject to Jewish
self-government. "Preliminary plans for autonomous government already had
been established. Albert Arditti was already mentioned as a candidate for the
office of mayor. . . . Dr. Koretz was to serve as the chief of this little republic."[39]
Work groups of the Jewish community also produced the Stars of David, numbered 1–45,000. Each person received two and a personal identification card

bearing the same number as the star. After a certain date, all Jews five years and older had to wear the yellow star on their jackets and coats.

As in Vienna and Berlin, Brunner mercilessly drove the employees of the Jewish community into discharging these various directives. Under the pressure of the SD-Sonderkommando, the organizations of the Jewish community processed the prescribed tasks with feverish haste:

> The work proceeded day and night without interruption or rest. Every task had to be finished correctly by the deadline, the distribution of stars – the move into the ghetto. The most capable people – all bank or civil service employees have been commandeered. It's a humming beehive. They don't stop even for a minute. Often they work sixteen hours a day without break. One shift followed another. . . . Nobody could have worked more effectively, and certainly not at greater speed. Yet, the SD commission with its constant demands for statistics, lists, registers, and reports requires still more effort. This war of nerves never ends. Their goal is to push people into a state of constant fear.[40]

Whenever any directive from the SD-Sonderkommando was not carried out assiduously, the SS men responded with brutality. For example, Chief Rabbi Dr. Koretz had to be reachable in his office at all times. Once when one of his representatives answered the telephone while he was eating lunch,

> Brunner is at the other end of the line. He did not hear the familiar trembling voice. So he leaves his office at the SD headquarters at Velisarious Street and heads for the community center. There, with a whip, he lashes an employee and community council member Salomon Ousiel, who had answered the telephone, inflicting grievous injuries to his head. Trembling with rage, he [Brunner] yells that the community organizations can't be idle at any time, having to be in a state of high alert day and night.[41]

From Vienna and Berlin, Brunner also imported his tried-and-true method of providing the SS hunters with an auxiliary police force made up of potential victims. "Furthermore, at Brunner's command, a so-called Jewish Ordnertruppe was established, whose appointed chief was a certain Jacques Albala."[42] This troop consisted of 250 men whose core personnel was recruited from among members of Salonika's Jewish community, who had served as officers or noncommissioned officers in the Greek army, and of Jewish refugees from Central Europe.[43] Such forced participation of victims assured the rapid and efficient accomplishment of all steps ordered by the SD-Sonderkommando.

> It was a satanic stratagem that the Nazis employed to assure discipline and compliance of Jews as well as their subsequent deportation and annihilation.

Ironically, the Jews initially believed that the formation of this police force was tied to the elevation of the ghetto to an autonomous entity.[44]

The SD-Sonderkommando had achieved its first goal: The necessary preparations for the rapid deportation of about 45,000 people – their marking, registration, and ghettoization, and the establishment of an Ordnertruppe as ordered – had been completed by February 25. Consul Fritz Schönberg of the German Consulate General in Salonika had been keeping tabs on the progress of these preparations. On February 26 he reported to the Foreign Office in Berlin that "the initial measures against local Jews, marking them with the yellow Star of David and their ghettoization, ordered by the SD commission," had been "performed by the Jewish community representatives with remarkable speed." After describing these measures in detail, he laconically announced "a tightening of the measures against local Jews is to be expected."[45] The SD special commission also had reason to be pleased with its accomplishment. Clearly, Brunner's boast in the letter, cited in the introduction of this book, to one of his comrades back home – "our work here is progressing without a hitch" – was by no means exaggerated.

The Spoliation and Deportation of Salonika's Jews

After stigmatizing and confining them in ghettos, the military administration and the SD-Sonderkommando immediately initiated the next phase against the Jews of Salonika: Their isolation and the theft of their property set the stage for their deportation.[46] At the end of February, Kriegsverwaltungsrat Merten denied Jews membership in all manner of organizations and clubs, a measure that automatically prohibited trade unions and professional associations from taking steps to safeguard Jewish interests.[47] In early March the Jewish community was ordered to instruct all Jewish heads of families to submit declarations of assets for the entire family. Real estate, savings accounts, inventories of goods, machinery, and workshop equipment and materials had to be listed. Additionally, the family's entire private property had to be disclosed: gold, precious metals, coins, foreign currency, metal and ceremonial objects, carpets, paintings, stamp collections, draft and domestic animals, china, glass, and cooking utensils. The content of every closet was to be inventoried separately.

Fear spread among the Jews. Many sensed "the approach of the storm. They furtively discuss mass exile. This, they whisper, is the purpose of the registration and their concentration in the ghetto."[48] Some managed to flee, for despite the emphatic prohibition, people escaped the ghetto disguised as railroad officials, peasants, or freight haulers. Hidden in casks and crates, some reached Athens

by rail. Some of these escape routes became known; sanctions from the SD-
Sonderkommando were likely to follow. So, in early March, Chief Rabbi Koretz
had placards posted that urged everyone to remain calm and composed and
asked people "not to give credence to totally unfounded rumors. Everybody
was to continue discharging his responsibilities and trust those in charge at
the Kultusgemeinde."[49] The SD-Sonderkommando, however, was not satisfied
with a mere call for law and order but demanded hostages. The Council of
the Jewish community had to provide a list of 104 prominent Jewish citizens.
Brunner and Koretz informed those individuals that they would guarantee with
their lives the compliance of their fellow Jews. Not surprisingly, rumors about
the impending fate of the Salonika Jews increased. On March 8, Lucillo Merci,
a translator and liaison officer at the Italian Consulate at Salonika, recorded in
his diary that the city was rife with rumors that all Greek Jews were about to be
sent to Poland and those who were citizens of other countries would be forced
to return to their homeland.[50]

Meanwhile the SD-Sonderkommando, now expanded to a staff of twelve
and billeted in the appropriated villa of a Jewish resident at 42 Velissariou
Street and an adjoining building, was busy seizing Jewish property. Because the
members of the SD-Sonderkommando sought to combine the most effective
expropriation of the Jews of Salonika with the most satisfactory increase in
their own fortunes, they constantly arrested specific victims for interrogation.

> Seasoned hunting dogs roamed the city sniffing out prey. Any Jew thought to
> be wealthy was arrested and brought before the commission. After an excruci-
> atingly long wait, they subjected these persons to a preliminary examination,
> in the course of which they would be pelted with questions to force them to
> reveal their liquid assets – the jewels, gold coins, currency, objects d'art, carpets,
> antique furniture. The most brutal of the twelve 'executioners' was Brunner,
> the personification of Teutonic sadism in all its horror. He thrashed his victims
> with a whip made of the finest leather strips and metal threads and terrified
> them by holding a revolver against their neck, forehead or temple.[51]

Walter St., an expelled Austrian Jew, was one of those whom Brunner questioned and mistreated. He was arrested in 1938 in Vienna and incarcerated
in Buchenwald, from where he had been released in 1940, and had fled
first to Yugoslavia and from there, after the invasion of the Wehrmacht, to
Salonika. There soldiers of the Feldgendarmerie arrested him once again. One
day Hauptsturmführer Brunner interrogated him: "I remember this man very
well because he slapped me in the face. That was my first encounter with
Brunner."[52]

The villa at Velissariou Street served as both torture chamber and treasure
vault. Stolen valuables were stored there.

Through the contributions of all these victims the treasure chamber at Velissariou Street is crammed full with Ali Baba's magic treasures: Well-sorted and
heaped in separate piles, diamond rings and rings with other precious stones
of all colors and sizes; tie clasps, medallions, bracelets, gold chains, wedding
bands, watches of all types; coins sorted according to origin and date, US and
Canadian dollars, pounds Sterling, Swiss francs, etc. are heaped on the tables.
The floor was covered with containers of various sorts, rare objects, and large
rolled-up carpets.[53]

Before this loot was sent to Germany, the SS men helped themselves: "It goes
without saying that the gentlemen of the Sonderkommando first selected from
each shipment those coins, jewels, and other valuables that appealed to their
taste." The Sonderkommando's cook, a conscripted Greek, reported that, at
Wisliceny's departure from Salonika, he had to transport to the airport a
suitcase stuffed with valuables and paper money.[54]

The Sonderkommando was reputed to live in luxury in other respects as
well. Brunner's invitation to his comrade was not an empty promise.

The Sonderkommando's menus were exquisite.... There was no limit to the
beverages being served; they emptied one crystal goblet after another.... The
ground floor of the neighboring house was a temple of secrets and debauch-
ery. Through the soft carpets no floor could be felt. Richly draped velvet and
brocade hangings cascaded from the ceilings.... Low tables, easy chairs of all
kinds, shelves and glass cabinets, countless ornaments decorated the entrance
hall that led to fabulously furnished rooms resembling draped nests, discreet
boudoirs, and bridal suites recalling the palaces of Sardanapalus.... From
sundown to sunup, these rooms witnessed scenes of monstrous sensual
pleasures.[55]

A March 13, 1943, decree from the military administration of the Befehlshaber
Saloniki-Ägäis lent pseudo-legality to this systematic robbery of Jewish property. It did so by designating the Kultusgemeinde, which had been subordinated
directly to the control of the SD-Sonderkommando, as "manager of Jewish cash
property and Jewish-owned items of value." The decree did not apply to real
estate and a person's "entire movable and immovable property," which was
handled through a different directive.[56] In this case too a more precise order
signed by Wisliceny followed a short time later, on March 15, from the Security
Police Sonderkommando for Jewish Affairs, Salonika-Agean.[57]

These measures guaranteed the rapid, total spoliation of a formerly relatively prosperous Jewish community.

The Jews have lost their entire property.... Now there are no more social
differences, no social classes, no rich people, no one who owns anything. Now
only destitute Jews robbed of everything live in Salonika. Not a single one of

them can count anything his own but the rags covering his nakedness and a little valise he can carry by hand or on his shoulder.[58]

While this piracy was in progress, the technical preparations for deportation were accelerated. In early March the ghetto in the "Baron Hirsch" area adjoining the freight yard of a railway station had been refashioned into a deportation camp surrounded by high fence posts and wooden and wire fences. Beside the three gates, one of which led directly to the rail station, authorities installed signs in three languages, prohibiting entry to non-Jews.[59] On March 5 the inhabitants of this ghetto no longer were allowed to leave the area. Outside the fences the SS installed machine guns and floodlights to prevent escapes. The school now served as a food dispensary for the internees. SS-Oberscharführer Herbert Gerbing assumed the administration of the deportation camp; Vital Chasson, a collaborator, served as his interpreter and second-in-command.

According to Wisliceny's testimony, the SD-Sonderkommission requisitioned the deportation trains directly from the Wehrmacht transport command post. "All Brunner had to do was to state how many cars he needed and when," and the engines and railway cars stood at the station ready to go. Brunner also provided guards for the deportation trains by requesting a Schutzpolizei unit from Belgrade to accompany the transports.[60] Slawik, however, stated that the train security team consisted of Viennese Schutzpolizisten (uniformed "protection" police): "The Jewish transports guarded by Schutzpolizei from Vienna were taken to Poland or Theresienstadt, as it was then called. Schutzpolizisten specifically requested from Vienna were posted to Salonika."[61] The final preparations for mass deportations of Salonika's Jews to the death camps were now complete.

To deport the victims interned at the Baron Hirsch camp to Auschwitz with as little resistance as possible, Brunner and his men employed the same ruse they had used in Vienna. The SD Kommando pretended that all transports to Poland served the purpose of resettlement and that the deportees could start a new life there. Brunner forced Koretz to feed these lies to the victims:

> The SD orders the Chief Rabbi to assemble all internees in the Hirsch synagogue on Sunday, March 14, at 11:00 AM to inform them of their departure to Kraków. Everyone is present, and they despondently listen to the announcement. Koretz, however, remains confident, effusively reiterating these promises: "The large Kraków community will help us get established. Everybody will have employment appropriate to his wishes, abilities, expertise, and experience."[62]

The very next day this deception continued with another tried-and-true method dating back to Vienna as the head of each family to be deported received a "check" for 600 złoty, which supposedly could be cashed in Poland.

After these preparations the first deportation transport to Auschwitz was assembled. Rounding up the victims and loading them into the cattle cars proceeded without resistance. The internees of the Baron Hirsch camp were escorted to the freight yard and crammed into the cars; then the doors were sealed.[63] At Auschwitz-Birkenau, the destination of this train carrying 2,400 deportees, a selection took place immediately upon its arrival on March 20, 1943. About 1,700 of them were driven straight from the railroad ramp into the gas chambers; 417 men and 192 women were sent to the Stammlager, the main camp.[64] In mid-March the German Consulate General in Salonika reported to the Foreign Office in Berlin that the "resettlement" of the Jews from Salonika had "started today with the transport . . . to the Generalgouvernement." In the same jargon that had been used for legitimizing the expropriations, Schönberg also informed his superiors of future plans. "There is prospect for sending four transports per week [which logistically was impossible], so the entire Aktion will be completed in about six weeks. The fixed and liquid assets of the resettled Jews will be seized and deposited into a special account to cover transportation costs and debts."[65]

At the same time Schönberg pointed out that all authorities involved in the persecution of the Jews of Salonika were planning to deport not just Greek Jews but also citizens of other countries.

> In the discussions local German officials insisted that the purpose of these expulsions, the security of northern Greece occupied by German troops, could not be accomplished if non-Greek Jews were to be allowed to remain in residence there. I share this opinion. There are no differences whatsoever in the bloodlines of local Greek and foreign Jews. Apart from a tiny group, all are descendents of those Sephardic Jews who were expelled from Spain in 1496 and subsequently settled in the Levant.

Like the Greek Jews, the non-Greek Jews of Salonika were "hostile to National Socialist Germany." For this reason Schönberg endorsed "the proposal of the Befehlshaber Saloniki-Ägäis that negotiations be initiated with the appropriate governments concerning the return of local non-Greek Jews to their home countries."[66]

After the first transport of March 15, the deportation machinery did not miss a beat. That same day parts of the ghetto in the Aya Paraskevi section of the city were sealed hermetically and their inhabitants driven with kicks and lashes to the recently emptied deportation camp in the Baron Hirsch section. On March 17, a total of 2,635 people from the newly refilled camp were crammed into the waiting train and deported. In this fashion the SD-Sonderkommando cleared all the Salonika ghettos from March through May, 1943. Generally, each train carried 2,800 men, women, and children to their deaths. For a while, 3,000 men who in the spring of 1943 were employed as slave laborers by the Organisation Todt in military construction projects were exempt from this treatment. Their living and working conditions were as poor as those of the previous year's work details. Diseases and executions reduced the number of those able to work; few managed to escape.[67] The 1,800 survivors were sent back to Salonika on August 7 and deported to Auschwitz soon after.

One deportation train after another left Salonika. Altogether, eighteen trains carrying 45,324 deportees went to Auschwitz; one, the transport of August 2, with about 360 Spanish Jews living in Salonika and a group of "privileged" Jews, Koretz among them, went to Bergen-Belsen. After selections in Auschwitz, 11,147 of Salonika's Jews were assigned to the camp. Far greater numbers were murdered immediately upon arrival in Birkenau.[68]

Victims sent to the camp were forced to work in various Kommandos in the main camp or its satellites. Some, such as the girls from Salonika, after serving the SS doctors as research subjects, were killed in the gas chambers.[69] Because of the catastrophic conditions, the survival chances for Greek camp internees were especially low. As a former typist of the camp reports,

> I considered the fate of the Greek Jews in Auschwitz especially severe. Only very young and obviously strong people survived the initial selection on the rail siding, for they alone actually were taken into the camp. Nevertheless, within a very short time at Auschwitz-Birkenau they, because of the inadequate food and clothing and the harsh climate, declined more rapidly than inmates from Western and Eastern Europe. They were the least resilient and soon turned into *Muselmänner* (living corpses). Those who did not die of physical exhaustion or illness – typhoid, dysentery, etc. – eventually were gassed.[70]

Few victims from Salonika survived. One of them was Albert Menasche, who had been deported to Auschwitz in June 1943 and was employed first as a musician in the camp orchestra and later as a physician. Until January 1945 the number of male Greek Jews in Auschwitz, among them deportees from Athens, Corfu, and Rhodes, and who arrived between February and August 1944, fell, reportedly to 358.[71]

Diplomatic Controversies

In Salonika the SD-Sonderkommando kept the machinery of deportation in full motion and beyond that attempted to include even individuals who had not yet become entirely helpless victims of their persecutors. For example, because of his position in the International Red Cross, Dr. Leon Cuenca, a physician, had been exempted from having to live in the ghetto and from wearing the star of David. On the night of March 18–19, members of the SD-Sonderkommando forced their way into his house, kidnapped him and his wife, confined them in an isolated house in the Baron Hirsch camp, and from there sent them to Auschwitz on the next train. When Dr. René Burckhardt, the Red Cross representative in Salonika, queried Dr. Merten about the whereabouts of his colleague, Merten feigned surprise and called the SD office. Accompanied by SS-Hauptsturmführer Brunner, Burckhardt then went to Cuenca's house "where Brunner ordered the locked door to be opened." The SD then accused Burckhardt of aiding and abetting Cuencas's escape. This "escape story" served the military administration as justification for additional reprisal measures such as the arrest of twenty-five "hostages."[72]

In 1941, Alex Blumenfeld, who had left the German Reich, fled with his non-Jewish wife from Belgrade to Salonika. There Dr. Calmes, the director of the SD, had provided the couple with a certificate of their Mischehe, mixed marriage, and Blumenfeld's service as a German front line soldier in World War I. According to regulations observed within Germany, this certificate should have exempted Blumenfeld from deportation as long as the couple remained married. Nevertheless, in April he was arrested and taken to the Baron Hirsch camp. Mrs. Blumenfeld's intercessions with Calmes and Merten were unsuccessful. In mid-May she learned that Brunner had refused to release her husband and that he had, in fact, been murdered. Shortly afterward, Brunner summoned her, demanding that she divorce her husband. When she refused, Brunner, tried to cow her into compliance by applying physical abuse. In June, Lisa Blumenfeld was arrested and deported, although as an Aryan she was not sent to Auschwitz but to the Ravensbrück concentration camp via Bergen-Belsen.[73]

Supposedly, non-Greek Jews living in Salonika who were citizens of Axis powers, of countries sympathetic to the Axis cause, or of neutral countries also were exempt from deportation. According to Consul Schönberg's previously cited March 15 report to the Foreign Office, 281 Jews in Salonika held Italian citizenship, 511 were Spanish citizens, and about 60 more were citizens of Turkey, Portugal, Argentina, Switzerland, Egypt, Hungary, and Bulgaria. The Italian Consulate in Salonika persistently pursued the interests of Jews with Italian citizenship and of Jews applying for (re)instatement of citizenship. This official escape route – Italian citizenship for persecuted Jews – caused severe arguments between Italian and German officials and government organizations. As early as February the Reichssicherheitshauptamt in Berlin already was studying ways of preventing potential victims of the Final Solution from escaping deportation through the escape hatch of the Italian Consulate. In an early February 1943 letter to the Foreign Office, Eichmann proposed a tough approach: "Through the efforts of the Befehlshaber Saloniki-Ägäis to conscript the Jews in Greece for labor, it soon became obvious that especially wealthy Jews holding citizenship in various countries attempted and indeed succeeded in their bid for Italian citizenship at the Italian Consulate in Salonika."[74] With the start of the deportations, Eichmann expected the persecuted Jews to contact Italian government representatives in increasing numbers. "To stop this undesirable development, I ask you to negotiate with the Italian government that Jews who became citizens after an agreed-upon deadline will not be considered full-fledged Italian citizens and, therefore, will not enjoy the customary protection of the Italian government." He asked the Auswärtige Amt "to take care of this matter" because the "expulsions" were to start soon.[75]

Italian officials in Rome either rejected German diplomatic efforts outright or procrastinated: No official agreement resulted.[76] In Salonika, meanwhile, both Italian and German organizations doggedly followed their strategies. As Lucillo Merci observes in his diary, in March and April 1943 many people applied for (re)instatement of Italian citizenship.[77] The consulate complied generously with the full support of the Italian embassy in Athens and the Foreign Ministry in Rome because Italian government agencies were amazingly well informed about the fate awaiting the Jews at their final destination.[78]

On March 21, not even a week after the start of the deportations, Merci, after a meeting with Merten, recorded in his diary that Consul Guelfo Zamboni and he shared the same fears: "After all, it is known that the Salonika Jews are being sent to Poland. There the physically fit among them are put to work whereas the rest are liquidated. In the end, the physically fit also will be liquidated."[79] At the Italian Consulate it was also common knowledge that each week thousands of people from Salonika fell victim to this fate; so speed was essential. On April 21, Zamboni presented German officials with a list of persons who had been granted Italian citizenship. The Italian Consulate and Merten agreed that Italian-born Jews holding Greek citizenship would not be deported as long as negotiations between Rome and Berlin had not been concluded. For the moment, persons whose status remained uncertain were to be exempted too.[80]

A few days later, in the midst of this tense situation, Brunner caused an incident when on April 26 an Italian military train that also harbored twenty Jews with Italian documents was prevented from leaving for Athens. Merten, in a memorandum to the German Consulate General, reported that SS-Hauptsturmführer Brunner had informed him by telephone about "an Italian vacation train at the Salonika railway station with about twenty Jews aboard who obviously were trying to evade German authority." Zamboni intervened, complaining to Merten that "even though they were in possession of all required papers, Italian citizens were being kept from leaving Salonika. Furthermore, the indisputable rule was that Italian citizens needed only an Italian transit paper, not a special German permit."[81] During Merten's subsequent inspection of these papers in the presence of employees of the Italian consulate, the papers of thirteen of the eighteen persons in question could not be challenged, and they did go on to Athens. One of the travelers whose papers were also in order was detained because the GFP was investigating his alleged trafficking in gold. "A Jew by the name of Sam Navarro with his wife and mother also were prevented from leaving Salonika because, though ostensibly an Italian, he obviously has been made an Italian citizen only in view of the 'Jewish measures'."[82]

At the end of April, Merten notified Zamboni of the decision at the Foreign Office in Berlin, according to which confirmation and bestowal of Italian citizenship were to be solely the purview of Italian authorities. Just two days later, however, this decision, although it seemingly complied with the Italian position, obviously was not worth the paper on which it was written. Lucillo Merci's diary describes Merten's visit at the Italian Consulate on April 30. The German brought a list of names of Jews whose deportations were to be deferred, but announced that most of them already were in Poland. The Consul protested immediately, shouting: "Your conduct will have diplomatic consequences. . . . We were promised that natives of Italy would not be deported as long as no decision about their fate has been reached between Rome and Berlin."[83] Merten merely replied that he already had passed this list to the SD-Sonderkommando. Clearly, Brunner and his men had simply ignored the agreement.

Italian consulate and Foreign Ministry efforts, such as preparing a list of persons who had been deported in violation of the agreements, brought no results. For weeks the Auswärtige Amt did not even acknowledge receipt of a note the Italian embassy submitted in mid-May concerning "German measures against Jews of Italian nationality in Greece." In early June Italian diplomat Corrado Baldoni of the embassy in Berlin once more emphatically addressed some contested cases during a meeting with Under-statesecretary Hencke. Among other instances, he protested the treatment of the lawyer Moises Saul, a Greek citizen, who for a long time had been a legal advisor of the Italian Consulate General in Salonika. The SD had arrested Saul and his family for deportation. Following the intervention of the Italian consulate, the appropriate Wehrmacht office in Salonika (more than likely Merten's office) had stated that no deportation would take place provided that Saul and his family received an entrance permit for Italy from the Italian government. The permit had been issued, but the "military commander in charge" regretfully informed the Italian Consulate General "that in spite of formal assurances, Saul and family had been deported on the last train to Poland. The military authorities had not been informed, and the deportation had been ordered by SS-leader Wisliceny."[84] Baldoni demanded that the Saul family be permitted to travel from Poland to Italy, but Hencke responded evasively, promising merely to refer the matter to the appropriate authorities. Upon an inquiry by the Auswärtige Amt at the Consulate General in Salonika concerning the truth of Baldoni's statements, Schönberg replied that they were correct, except that Haupsturmführer Brunner, not Wisliceny, had initiated the deportation.[85]

Another point Baldoni raised with Hencke concerned a report that the Italian consulate in Salonika had received, "according to which the leader of the police unit responsible for Jewish affairs in Greece was preparing to enter the Italian zone with three Jews (apparently informers) to root out Jews who had fled from the German to the Italian zone of occupation, warning Hencke that German police were not to become active in the Italian-occupied areas.[86] He stated emphatically "that according to the Italian government, it was absolutely necessary for Germany to stop any actions concerning Jews in the Italian zone."[87] Upon request for clarification from the AA office in Salonika, Wisliceny justified himself in a memo headed "Travel to Athens for the purpose of locating escaped Jews," arguing that the SD had conducted no Aktionen in the Italian sphere of jurisdiction. Hauptstumführer Brunner with "members of the Sonderkommando and a gendarmerie contingent had been in Piraeus, in the German sphere of government, to take charge of the local Jews but had been unsuccessful because all the Jews from Piraeus had fled to Athens – the Italian sphere of jurisdiction."[88] Which version is the correct one and whether Brunner's mission really was a total failure is impossible to determine.

What is clear is that Brunner and his men, with the assistance of competent military and diplomatic authorities, were not satisfied with disenfranchising and robbing a centuries-old community and, in sixteen transports within the eight weeks between March 15 and May 9, 1943, sending more than 40,000 people to death in Auschwitz. Without paying the least attention to their own regulations or diplomatic agreements, Brunner and his subordinates hunted with merciless zeal those who had not yet been caught in their nets or who tried to escape. The "journey to Athens" probably was one of Brunner's last Aktionen in Greece. When at the end of May the Jewish community of Salonika had been all but annihilated and no further sizeable deportations were planned, Brunner and part of his Viennese SS team were transferred to France. According to Wisliceny, "Brunner left Salonika at the end of May 1943."[89]

9 Manhunts in France and Greece: 1943–1944

In 1943 the military defeats of the Third Reich and its Axis partners, from Stalingrad to the Allied landings on Sicily, demonstrated that Germany and her allies would not be able to win this war. In addition to immense personnel and material losses, the lost battles also had political consequences because not all of the Third Reich's treaty partners were willing to accompany Germany on the road to defeat. Italy capitulated in September 1943. Consequently, Wehrmacht and SS units were dispatched not only to Italy but also to parts of southern and southeastern Europe – southeastern France, Albania, sections of Yugoslavia and Greece – until then occupied by Italian troops. As a result of an acute shortage of personnel, the SS became increasingly dependent on the help of other executive or occupation authorities in its implementation of arrests and deportations. In 1943–1944 the continuation of deportations from Greece depended almost entirely on Wehrmacht support of SS plans or on execution of SS measures by Wehrmacht units in the absence of even a single SS representative.

The question arises as to the effects that changes in Europe's military situation exerted on the attitude of the collaborating regimes and how that attitude affected the conditions under which the "deportation specialists" carried out their task. In 1943 the willingness of the Vichy regime to support the SS in its pursuit of Jews holding French citizenship waned notably. In 1944, on the other hand, the cooperation of the SS-Sondereinsatzkommando Eichmann (Special Action Unit Eichmann) and the executive branch of the Hungarian government in rounding up, robbing, and finally deporting Hungarian Jews functioned so smoothly that, even shortly before the Axis military collapse, half a million people fell victim to disaster.

The Men from Vienna in France

In June 1943 Alois Brunner came to Paris with SS men Brückler, Gerbing, and Zita, who had assisted him in conducting deportations from Vienna and Salonika; he also brought along Josef Weiszl, Anton Söllner, Josef Ullmann, Josef Csany, and Max Koppel.[1] Until March 1943 about 50,000 men, women, and children had been deported from France to Auschwitz and Sobibór, but between March and June of that year not a single transport had left France for Auschwitz.[2] The German authorities in Paris had pressured the Vichy government to pass a law for the denaturalization of persons who had been awarded French citizenship after 1927. Two distinct drafts for a law on the "denaturalization" of Jews awaited Prime Minister Pierre Laval's signature.[3] The SS counted on the French police to conduct extensive raids upon adoption of this law.

The disruption of the transports in the spring and the expectation of mass arrests in the summer were the reasons for sending the Viennese deportation specialists to France. Right away, in early June 1943, Brunner, accompanied by Röthke, conducted preliminary discussions with representatives of the Union Générale des Israélites de France (UGIF) and forbade them to correspond with the Red Cross about the deportations.[4] A short time later he attended an internal SS meeting about the pending French law that would deprive many Jews of their French citizenship, and which all present expected to go into effect almost immediately. The publication of this law was to be followed by an immediate Erfassungsaktion, in the course of which 20,000 families and single French citizens of the Jewish "race" were to be arrested in Paris, and 6,000 in the "old occupation area" and 25,000–30,000 in the "newly occupied areas," excluding those under Italian administration. All arrested persons were to be collected at designated places in the various municipal districts or regional centers and then transferred to Drancy by bus. The SS officers envisioned June 24–25 as the target date for this Aktion. By mid-July all detainees "were to have been expelled to the East."[5] Contrary to SS expectations, however, the passage of this bill was delayed.

Just how heavily the SS in Paris depended on the cooperation of the French police in carrying out these arrests is obvious from efforts to requisition police reinforcements from the Reich. At the end of June, Knochen contacted the RSHA in Berlin to ask for 250 additional members of the Sicherheitspolizei who "speak French or at least have some knowledge of the language" to be sent to Paris to supervise French police during the expected large-scale raid and "help arrest as many Jews as possible with our own forces."[6] Gestapo chief Müller, however, sent his regrets for not being able to comply because of the "present extraordinarily tight personnel situation," and reminding him that he had, "after all, just recently sent him an SS-Führer with three SS-Unterführers [Brunner, Brückler, Gerbing, and Zita] for these purposes."[7]

In the meantime Brunner had accelerated the reorganization of the deportation camps. In the course of a late June discussion among Brunner, Brückler, and UGIF representatives André Baur and Léo Israelowicz, Brunner announced that the supervision of the Drancy camp would be removed from the French gendarmerie. With the cooperation of the UGIF its internal organization would also be changed.[8] At the beginning of July, Brunner and his team took command of Drancy, replacing the French police and gendarmes who had administered and guarded the camp. One of their first new measures was to sever the internees' contacts with the outside world: No longer were they allowed to receive letters and packages. Brunner also initiated the "categorization" of prisoners: Jewish marriage partners in "mixed marriages" and "Mischlinge" belonged to Category A, exempt from deportation. Persons to be deported fell into Category B. Jewish members of the camp's service team, consisting of seventy orderlies, thirty kitchen workers and workmen, ten physicians, ten nurses, and persons holding citizenship in countries from which deportations could not yet be conducted comprised Category C. The camp office also established a multicolored file for all detainees at Drancy.[9] Initially Brunner conducted the categorization in person and pressured individual internees to locate family members still at large. In most instances these "missionaries" did not obey this order.

After categorizing the victims at Drancy, Brunner immediately organized a deportation transport of 1,000 Jews whose departure from Paris-Bobigny he reported by telex in mid-July to the RSHA Referat IV B 4 in Berlin, to the inspector of the Oranienburg concentration camp, and to Auschwitz camp commandant SS-Obersturmbannführer Höß. The provisions that the UGIF delivered for the deportees filled a freight car. Brunner listed 6,500 kilos of potatoes; large quantities of flour, dried vegetables, baked goods, fat, sugar, salt, ersatz coffee, canned vegetables, meats, and fish; pastries, two casks of red wine, and 12 kilos of chocolate, and asked that such "high-quality foods not" be wasted "as KZ rations."[10]

For the prisoners at Drancy the new regime and its harassment came as a shock. At the slightest occasion Brunner and his SS men meted out brutal punishments. For example, early in July, Brunner sentenced two internees, supposedly guilty of passing mail, to deliver twenty-five cane strokes to one another in the presence of the entire camp population assembled in the prison yard.[11] This turning point in living conditions and the actions and character traits of those responsible for these changes made a lasting impression. French victims describe Brunner as a short, slight man with malevolent eyes and a vacant expression; he spoke in a monotone and acted coldly and deliberately. Reportedly he seldom hit prisoners himself, demonstrating a pronounced physical abhorrence of Jews. Georges Wellers, a former internee, describes that once, after having beaten a prisoner, Brunner paced back and forth for several minutes, holding his hands, "soiled" through the contact with his victim, away from his body before cleaning them carefully.[12] Prisoners remember Brückler as stocky and robust. Apparently, he had a well-developed need to spill blood and truly earned his nicknames "Boxer" and "Bestie" (brute/beast). Incapable of even the slightest mental exertion, he did not take part in the classification of inmates.[13]

In Drancy, Brunner also applied his old trick of exchanging the internees' money for złotys. They had to surrender their francs in exchange for a piece of paper made to look like a receipt: "In the Drancy emigration camp the Jew . . . and the members of his family deposited . . . French francs. It is the duty of the Council of Elders at his place of settlement to repay him their value in złotys."[14] Some people accepted this deception as real because they assumed that in the area of colonization in Poland they would own some personal property and would be able to purchase the necessities of life by redeeming these "receipts."[15]

In mid-July the representatives of the French Jewish community sent a note of complaint to Prime Minister Laval about the SS regime at Drancy, especially about the brutal physical maltreatment of internees and the cutoff of mail.[16] The petition had no direct impact on conditions in Drancy, but it did help stiffen Laval's growing resistance to depriving French Jews of their citizenship.[17] As a result, the long-debated denaturalization decrees never did become law. On August 7 Laval informed Knochen of his refusal to drive the game to the hunters if the Germans were immediately to deport those who would lose their citizenship.[18] Laval's decision also put an end to plans for large-scale raids involving thousands of French policemen or other security forces. Essentially the SS now had to be content with deporting persons they could capture with the help of spies and informers.

According to Marrus and Paxton, the most brutal manhunts of the war took place in the fall of 1943 on the Côte d'Azur.[19] SS posts in Paris and Berlin had planned mass arrests of Jews in southeastern France, where many non-French victims of persecution had sought refuge much earlier, but the SS efforts there had been stymied by the evasive behavior of the Italian occupation authorities.[20] After studying the SD reports about Jewish aid organizations in southern France, Brunner and Brückler went to Lyon and Marseille as a sort of "preparatory Kommando" before establishing their headquarters at the Excelsior Hotel in Nice. At that time their superior Adolf Eichmann also spent a few days at the coast of southern France.[21] Then, in mid-September, the SS and their local helpers initiated their manhunts in Nice. In streets, hotels, furnished rooms, and railway stations – everywhere the bloodhounds were on the trail. So-called *physionomistes* drove around in small trucks and arrested people they thought were Jews. Frequently these roving Kommandos did not even accept papers and identity cards as proof of identity. If men were circumcised, they were taken prisoner. Informers tried to blackmail wealthy Jews, only to surrender them to the SS.[22]

Also in mid-September 1943, Dr. Abraham Drucker, who had been employed as a physician at Drancy, and two of his colleagues were escorted to Nice via Marseille by a group of SD members. He was to take charge of the medical care of those who had been arrested during the raids and been tortured in the Hotel Excelsior, where the SS confined and questioned prisoners. The SS often interrogated and tortured its prisoners for hours to make them reveal the addresses and hiding places of parents, spouses, children, and other relatives. Day and night the detainees needed medical care for a variety of injuries – broken teeth and cut lips, broken bones, open wounds, bruises spread all over their bodies. According to Dr. Drucker's testimony, a number of them died of the torture to which they were subjected in the Hotel Excelsior.[23] As his report states, in addition to Brunner, SS men Vogel, Brückler, Ullmann, Bilartz, Zita, and Gerbing also were deployed in Nice. When Brunner and Brückler returned to Paris, subordinate SS members continued the manhunts, and the interrogations and tortures in the Hotel Excelsior. A young woman testified to having been arrested during a November 1943 house search by an Austrian SS man named Gerbing, and to having been interrogated by the Gestapo officers Zita and Ullmann at the Hotel Excelsior.[24]

Yet, despite all its efforts at the Côte d'Azur, Brunner's Sonderkommando caught only about 2,000 of the more than 20,000 persecuted people in that area. Brunner and his men's failure to apprehend large numbers resulted from the French executive's lack of participation in these raids, the refusal of most of the tortured arrestees to reveal the hiding places of their relatives and acquaintances, and the considerable segment of the French population providing hiding places for the persecuted.[25]

In the final months of these manhunts in France, mainly children, especially orphans who had lost one or both parents, fell victim to these persecutions. The arrest, deportation, and murder of the children of Izieu near Lyon provide a typical example. In the spring of 1944 more than forty French, Belgian, German, Austrian, and Polish orphans whose parents had been deported from France had found shelter in the Izieu children's home. At the order of

Klaus Barbie, whose duties at the office of the Kommandant of the Sicherheitspolizei and the SD in Lyon included "Jewish Affairs," the children's home was
"cleaned out" in early April 1944. The Rollkommando (raiding squad) arrested
forty-four children, almost all of them ranging in age from four to fourteen,
and the staff. In his telex announcing their arrest, Barbie also reported their
imminent transfer to Drancy.[26]

At the Referat IV B in Paris the subsequent fate of these children spawned
arguments. A handwritten note on Barbie's telegram reveals that "this matter
was discussed in the presence of Dr. v. B. [Kurt von Behr, an employee of
Rosenberg's staff in Paris] and Hstuf. Brunner." Rosenberg's employee pointed
out that for such situations Röthke had worked out "special provisions for
housing these children." Brunner objected stridently to such an arrangement:
He "knew nothing about such orders or plans" and on principle would not
brook any exceptions to sending Jewish prisoners to Drancy. He made it
abundantly clear that in this case, too, he would proceed according to his
established practices in matters of expulsion.[27] So the forty-four children and
their seven attendants were taken to Drancy and apportioned to the deportation
transports to Auschwitz. Thirty-four children and three attendants, together
with about 1,500 other internees (among the latter the then-sixteen-year-old
Simone Veil) were deported on transport 71 of April 13, 1944. The other
children and their teachers followed on a later transport. During the night of
April 15, immediately upon their arrival in Auschwitz, all thirty-four children
and the three adults were murdered in the gas chambers of Birkenau. The
remaining children and all but one of the attendants were murdered a few
days later. The SS selected only twenty-seven-year-old Léa Feldblum, one of
the children's teachers, for slave labor. She was the only survivor from the Izieu
children's home.

Brunner's strategy was to deport all Jews the SS apprehended, without
regard to possible objections from French authorities. As the brief dispute over
the fate of the children demonstrates, German authorities did not necessarily
accept Brunner's procedures without question, although they prevailed ever
more frequently. Brunner's success in pushing his agenda concluded with a
secret memorandum from the Referat IV B 4 in Paris under the ominous
heading "Concerning the Increase of Arrests of Jews in the sphere of the BdS
in France."[28]

The memorandum was contrived by Brunner and was signed by Dr.
Knochen, the commander of the Sicherheitspolizei; it stipulated the arrest
of Jews "regardless of citizenship or other circumstances" and the arrest of
entire families, including all relatives. Knochen and Brunner insisted on the
arrest of children: "Infants in children's homes are to be included in the Aktion.

During their removal, it is advisable to take along one of the Jewish parents, if available." To save gasoline and to improve the efficiency of the manhunts, entire city blocks or even sections of cities or towns, or, "in the country side, entire villages" were "to be cleaned out." The SS also wanted to pick up all Jews in French correctional facilities and work camps. The Judensachbearbeiter (officials in charge of Jewish affairs) were to appear at these facilities unannounced because a written request for the surrender of prisoners would be counterproductive: "In such instances the French would either simply release the Jews beforehand or transfer them to a different jail." The last directive of the memorandum regulated "payment of fees for information on hidden or disguised Jews." The amount of these bounties was not fixed: They were not to be too high "yet inspire zeal."[29] The plan was to pay the headhunters from the funds stolen from their victims at the time of their arrest.

The SS in Paris tried to increase arrests and deportations at any price. In 1943–1944 the SS had succeeded in having the French police Department of Jewish Affairs (the office of Commissioner Charles Permilleux) in Paris arrest some French Jews and transfer them to Drancy. They also managed to have French police continue to conduct raids in search of non-French Jews, and to have some provincial prefectures send out their gendarmes on raids on Jews who were French citizens, as for example, in Bordeaux in early 1944.[30] The real cause of dissatisfaction among the SS men, however, was their inability to lay their hands on the large number of Jews holding French citizenship. They knew that in early 1944 approximately 40,000 French Jews whose names and addresses were known to the police prefecture lived in Paris.[31]

During the last months of German occupation, most arrests were conducted by various branches of the Sicherheitspolizei. French fascists, such as the adherents of Jacques Doriot's Parti Populaire Français, the French Popular Party, and greedy informers also lent a helping hand to the SS. People were arrested on the street, in hospitals, and in children's and old people's homes. In May 1944 the SS tore bedridden patients, women, and children from their hospital beds, took them to Drancy, and from there transported them to the extermination camps. From the orphanage attached to the Rothschild hospital, children were abducted as well. On the day of the failed assassination attempt on Adolf Hitler, Brunner ordered the arrest of the children in the UGIF homes. Those 230 children left Drancy at the end of July 1944 on the last major transport to Auschwitz. Not until mid-August, when the Allied forces stood at the gates of Paris, did Brunner and his subordinates flee Drancy.[32]

According to a statistic the administration of Drancy assembled in mid-August 1944, a total of 26,419 persons had been confined there since July 2, 1943, the date when the Brunner Kommando took over the control of the camp. On August 17, only 1,464 were still there. Sixty-one had died during their confinement, sixty-four had escaped, and 579 had been turned over to Organisation Todt in France. Some 22,427 men, women, and children had been deported east, mainly to Auschwitz.[33] Between March 1942 and April 1944, the SS took a total of 75,000 people from France to the concentration and extermination camps in Poland. Of those, 2,500 survived. Two-thirds of the deportees were not French citizens, and about three-fourths of all Jews living in France in 1940 were not enmeshed by the deportations.

Georges Wellers, a former internee at Drancy, after examining the periods until and after June 1943, notes that the average number of deportees in one month of the first period was three times that of the period following June 1943. He considers the decline of arrests and consequent slowdown of deportations essentially the result of the Vichy authorities' increasing refusal to deploy French police in the hunt for Jews during the second half of 1943:

> In this manner Brunner saw himself reduced to his own team and that of the so-called "missionaries" at Drancy; the help of the Gestapo, the Feldgendarmerie, the "specialists" of ex-policemen in Jewish matters, the Doriotists, the Francists, the Milice, and all sorts of volunteers and paid informers.[34]

In France, Brunner and his men resorted to all the methods they already had employed in Vienna, Berlin, and Salonika, but they also applied new ones such as paying bounties. Intimidation, use of force, hostage-taking, and targeted disinformation yielded only limited results. Even with militia men and rapacious informers eager to cooperate, Brunner and his men could not offset one factor: though it occured too late for many of the victims, the partial diminishment of French authorities' participation at mass arrests and their extensive refusal to cooperate in the hunt for Jews with French citizenship. Although the SS men were able to conduct horrible raids with Kommandos such as those in Nice, a considerable number of their intended victims eluded them. Many were able to flee in time, stay in hiding, or find refuge with French helpers.

The development of deportations from France demonstrates clearly that the power of the SS and the fearful efficiency of the Eichmann men did have limits. As a result of the arrest Aktionen carried out by the French police and the handover of internees during the five-month period July–November 1942, almost 40,000 victims were deported to Poland. During the fourteen-month June 1943–August 1944 period, however, Brunner and his aides sent about 24,000 men, women, and children from Drancy to Auschwitz. Obviously, the SS depended on the vigorous support of other branches of the occupation and executive apparatus in the various European countries in order to capture, as they did in Slovakia, 60,000 people within a few months, or as they did in northern Greece, to capture 40,000 within three months and remove them to concentration and annihilation camps.

Greece 1943–1944

Because of the extension of German occupation throughout Greece after Italy's capitulation in September 1943, the Jews, who until then had found relative safety in the Italian-occupied areas of Greece, lost what protection Italian occupying authorities had provided.[35] All German troops on the Greek mainland and the islands were under the command of Army Group E and its commander Alexander Löhr. In Athens a Military Commander for Greece was installed as chief of the military administration, assisted by a member of the Higher SS and Police, the first of whom, Jürgen Stroop, was later succeeded by the Austrian Walter Schimana.[36] In the headquarters of the commander of the Sicherheitspolizei and SD (BdS) in Athens, a Department IV B was established, which in the fall and winter of 1943 consisted of Dieter Wisliceny, Alfred Slawik, Takasch, and Schefczig. After their departure in early 1944, Anton Burger, Siegfried Seidl's successor as commandant of Theresienstadt, led the department.[37]

The situation of the Jewish community of Athens differed in important ways from that of Salonika. In the capital of Greece, the Jews constituted a rather small group at the beginning of the war, only about 4,000 people. During the war years thousands more of those persecuted, mainly from northern Greece, sought refuge there. The Jewish community of Athens was for the most part fully integrated into Greek society, mainly, perhaps, because its members, unlike the Jews of Salonika, did not speak Ladino but Greek. "In the realm of the new Greek kingdom, people were not inclined to accept racist mass persecutions passively – the systematic evacuation and carefully planned destruction of an entire group of fellow citizens. People were hostile to . . . religious discrimination" as well.[38] This attitude found expression in concrete assistance. Many Greeks were well inclined toward Jews, and even some institutions helped them. Greek police, protected by their commander, reportedly produced large numbers of false identity papers, Greek-Orthodox priests baptized Jews because they knew that this provided a degree of protection and, without much questioning, blessed so-called "mixed marriages."[39]

As early as September 1943 Wisliceny tried in vain to force the leaders of the Jewish community of Athens to work with the SS. Rabbi Elias Barsilai, whom Wisliceny had summoned, evaded the order to make a list of all Jews living in Athens and of those having fled to Athens from northern Greece, to appoint a "Council of Elders," and to deliver a list of the total assets of the Jewish community.[40] He pretended not to be able to meet the deadlines for these tasks because of missing records and a shortage of personnel. When Wisliceny delivered an ultimatum, Barsilai conferred with other members of the Jewish community and leading members of the leftist resistance organization EAM-ELAS (National Liberation Front-National People's Liberation Army) to find a way to circumvent the ultimatum.[41] The Jewish community and the partisans struck a bargain: Barsilai transferred the assets of the Jewish community, roughly eight million drachmas, to the EAM-ELAS partisans who pledged to furnish forged documents and to shelter and protect all persecuted persons seeking refuge in areas under their control. At the end of September the rabbi and his family, with the help of such forged documents, went to Eleusis. Until the liberation they hid in a village near Trikkala. "Hidden with his family now in monasteries, now in the houses of the villagers, the rabbi experiences nothing but respect and care from the partisans and from those who took him in."[42]

After Barsilai's escape and that of other leaders of the Athens community, Wisliceny could not find a single experienced representative whom he could blackmail into compiling lists of the future victims. Without the names and addresses of the members of Athens' Jewish community, the SS was forced to publish a registration order for Jews; Stroop issued it on October 3, 1943. The majority of the persecuted ignored it. According to a situation report from the military commander in Greece, "of about 8,000 Jews only 1,200" had registered by November.[43] Most lived with false papers or went underground in Athens; they fled to friends or acquaintances in the countryside, sought protection with the partisans, or crossed the sea to Turkey's Asia Minor coast and from there continued their flight to Egypt or Palestine.

Wisliceny and other functionaries of the occupation apparatus in Greece had to acknowledge that an immediate arrest Aktion would be ineffective. The Eichmann Referat in the RSHA also argued for a postponement of any grand-scale raids in Athens. As Eberhard von Thadden, a senior officer at the Foreign Office, noted at the end of January 1944,

> Hauptsturmführer Novak, RSHA, states that RSHA has seconded special envoy [Hermann] Neubacher's opinion that the deportation of the few captured Greek Jews is not advisable as long as no larger-scale arrests have taken place. Only when the impression prevails that there will be no deportations will there be possibilities for additional successful Aktionen.[44]

As it happens, Neubacher, too, was an Austrian. Even so, between December 1943 and March 1944 no appreciable increases occurred in the number of persons appearing at the weekly report days, although life in hiding had become increasingly difficult as a consequence of food shortages and inflation. So in March 1944 the occupation authorities prepared a large-scale two-day Aktion, in the course of which members of the SS, German and Greek police, and the Wehrmacht were to arrest all Jews on the mainland. The raid took place on Friday, March 24, and Saturday, March 25, 1944. In Athens it was led by Anton Burger, Wisliceny's successor in Greece. On March 24, all Jews who reported for the weekly roll call at the synagogue were prevented from leaving the building. Because everyone appearing to report that day had to provide the number of relatives and their addresses, the SS and police units could arrest the family members of those prisoners that very day and confine them at the synagogue as well. "By early evening about 800 prisoners are in the synagogue, closely guarded and without any contact to the outside world," among them Jews of Italian, Spanish, Portuguese, and Turkish nationality.[45] Despite a protest by the Spanish ambassador, even they were not released.

On Saturday police and SS continued their raid in Athens by going to the addresses known to them and arresting all Jewish families they encountered there. That very day the prisoners were trucked from the synagogue to the Chaidari concentration camp near Athens, where shortly afterward the 600 or so Jews arrested in Préveza, Árta, Agrinio, and Pátra on the west coast of Greece also were incarcerated. On Sunday, April 2, 1944, a train with about 1,900 men, women, and children left the Greek capital.[46] In addition to the 1,300 people arrested in Athens, this transport also included Jews arrested on March 25 in various places on the west coast and then transported to Chaidari. In Lárissa additional railway cars carrying 2,400 prisoners who had been captured in Volos, Trikkala, and Ioánnina were attached to this transport.

The 1,800 Jewish inhabitants of Ioánnina lived in ghettolike sections of town. In contrast to Athens, Wehrmacht units stationed in this town in the Epirus were directly involved in preparing for and carrying out their arrests and deportation. In the summer of 1943 the 1st Mountain Division, deployed in northwestern Greece to combat partisans, already had branded the Jews of Ioánnina as particularly dangerous enemies: "[Greek] civilians maintain 'wait and see' attitude. No doubt about absolute hostile attitude. Ioánnina and local Jewish Committee to be considered center of a movement preparing revolt."[47]

Following the disarming of the Italian units in September 1943, the XXII (Mountain) Army Corps, including the 1st Mountain Division, assumed territorial control of the Epirus. In a meeting of the XXII Corps's Ic officer, representatives of the Feldgendarmerie, the Geheime Feldpolizei, and the Greek prefect of Epirus, assurances were given that the Jews of Ioánnina would remain unmolested "as long as they obeyed directives." Who could molest the Jews was

implied *ex negative*: "Jewish quarters will be off-limits to German soldiers." Yet,
during a raid at the end of February 1944, directed by the XXII Corps' Ic officer
and supposedly aimed at "Communist elements" in Ioánnina, the president
of the Jewish community and three other Jews were arrested. The report to
the Ic officer requested the "total neutralization or Sonderbehandlung of these
four men."[48] In Ioánnina all measures such as marking the Jewish quarter,
monitoring the Jewish community, and arresting its leading members originated entirely with members of the Wehrmacht. Wehrmacht authorities also
contributed decisively to the deportation of all Ioánnina Jews, scheduled for
the end of March 1944. The BdS in Athens approached Army Group E about
providing trucks and escort personnel, and the Heeresgruppe staff responded
positively to the request for "transporting the remaining Jews."

> In principal in agreement with the provision of trucks and escort teams by
> the 4th SS-Po[lizei] P[an]z[er] Gren[adier] Div[ision] for local needs. Please
> inform about scope and duration so all necessary materials can be ordered
> here.[49]

As if carrying out a military assault, Wehrmacht and police forces arrested
almost the entire Jewish community of Ioánnina. According to a Geheime
Feldpolizei report, this raid took place "under the direction of Major Hafranek
[or Havranek] of the Ordnungspolizei, including the Wehrmacht, the Feldgendarmerie, Ordnungspolizei, and Geheime Feldpolizei [Group] 621 (Ioánnina
branch office).... Greek police also were drawn in to participate."[50] At 3 AM
on March 25, Wehrmacht units encircled the ghettos; a short time later, a representative of the Jewish community was informed that within three hours "all
Jews and their entire families" had to appear at one of two collection points.
"Any Jewish relative not present at the collection point by 8 AM would be
shot."[51] The Wehrmacht and police units needed only a few hours to collect
and load more than 1,700 people.

> By 7:45 AM all sections were emptied and the Jews were at the collection
> points. Strong patrols of German Ordnungspolizei supervised the clearing
> of the ghettos.... The Aktion ran its course without incident. At 8:00 the
> removal process could begin. The trucks had been parked beforehand in the
> access roads to the collection areas. They were loaded under the supervision
> of the Feldgendarmerie and the German Ordnungspolizei. Additionally, each
> driver's assistant was responsible for accepting and counting the Jews assigned
> to his vehicle. At 10:00 all "Hebrews" had been loaded, and the column of
> about eighty trucks took off for Trikkala.[52]

The reporting Wehrmacht officer voiced the utmost satisfaction with these
mass arrests: "This Aktion must be considered an unqualified success since

95% of the apprehended Jews could be removed. The cooperation of the participating organizations, including the Greek police was exemplary."[53] German authorities appropriated part of the deportees' property. As a former soldier of the GFP in Ioánnina testified during a police interrogation in 1966, "every member of our unit received a special allotment from the assets of Jewish business 'estates' [sic!]."[54]

The report about the participation of Wehrmacht units in the deportations from the Greek mainland was passed on to superior military authorities in occupied Greece, and the special plenipotentiary forwarded it to the Foreign Office. In the daily report of March 26, 1944, Corps Group Ioánnina informed the Ia and Ic departments at the Army Group E supreme command that the "support of the measures the commandant of the Ordnungspolizei in Ioánnina, Préveza, and Árta had ordered had been carried out without disruptions." In early April 1944, another Ic situation report Army Group E staff received from Corps Group Ioánnina informed, among other items, that as a result of "the 'Jewish raids' in Ioánnina, Árta, and Préveza on March 25, . . . 1,725 Jews had been expelled." The report expressed official agreement that the majority of the Greek population "had welcomed this measure."[55] In mid-April Dr. Kurt von Graevenitz, Dr. Altenburg's successor as the Foreign Office representative in Athens, notified his superiors in Berlin, "almost simultaneously with the arrests and deportation of the Athenian Jews, Jews in the provinces, holding Greek citizenship, also had been apprehended and removed, which, for the most part, meant the Jewish colonies in Kastoriá, Ioánnina, Préveza, and Árta." Graevenitz was fully informed about the course and anticipated continuation of these deportations.

> Now – except for Jewish partners in "Mischehen" and escapees – there are no more Jews at large on the Greek mainland. The arrest and removal of Jews on Crete (600) or Corfu (1,000–1,500), on the other hand, has not yet been carried out. The total of Jews involved in the Aktion of a few weeks ago stands at roughly 4,700, including foreigners.[56]

As is clear from Graevenitz's report, in April German authorities contemplated the continuation of deportations. The Jewish inhabitants of the Greek isles were to be captured next and taken to Auschwitz. In the deportations from the Greek mainland mainly police and SD forces answerable to the BdS had been deployed, assisted by Wehrmacht units during mass arrests as, for example, in Ioánnina. This "division of labor" would be impossible on the islands. No branch offices of the BdS existed on Corfu, Crete, or Rhodes. Only Wehrmacht units of Army Group E were stationed there under the command of so-called Insel or Festungskommandanten, island or fortress commandants.

Anton Burger, a second SS man, and a translator were dispatched to both Corfu and Rhodes for a few days; however, the preparations depended on the activities of local Wehrmacht units and the instructions of the staffs of the echelons above them.

As early as April 1944, Wehrmacht authorities on Corfu deliberated on the possibility of expelling the Jews living on the island, which caused controversies among the officers in charge. The Geheime Feldpolizei branch office on Corfu reported that, according to information from the Jewish community, about 1,700 Jews lived on the island; their personal freedom, except for the requirement to report weekly, had not been curtailed. "We do not share the island commandant's opinion that the expulsion of the Jews would unsettle the Greek population." In the opinion of the official rendering the report, "the only problems with the expulsion . . . would be related to the shortage of shipping."[57]

The Ic branch on Corfu also could find no compelling reasons impeding the removal of the Jews. As was the case with the preceding round-ups on the mainland, a Judenaktion, according to the Oberleutnant of the Ic branch, "would, in no way provoke hostile attitudes toward Germany."[58] Next higher in the reporting chain, Department Ic of the Corps Group Ioánnina, agreed with the point of view of the Geheime Feldpolizei and the Ic branch office, and in a report about the island of Corfu informed Department Ic/AO at Army Group E headquarters that "2,000 Jews are still present, most of them inhabiting the city's outskirts." The deportation of these people, in the opinion of this officer, "would provide a not insignificant relief of the shortage of food supplies. At this time the SD and the GFP are busy preparing the deportation of these Jews."[59] In closing, the corps staff officer asked the Ic/AO department of Army Group E to "press the SD for implementation measures for the settlement of the Jewish Question."[60]

Whether Department Ic/AO of Heeresgruppe E honored that request is not known. In mid-May, about two weeks after these announcements, an official BdS inquiry from Athens concerning the deportation of Jews reached the staff of Army Group E. As the war diary records, Heeresgruppe E responded immediately by sending a telex informing the BdS in Athens, the Wehrmacht commandant of "Fortress Crete," the general command of XXII Mountain Army Corps, and the Admiral, Aegean Sea of the BdS's request for

> naval cargo space for accelerated transport of 350 Jews from Crete and 1,600 Jews from Corfu. . . . The Okdo. Hrg. E. approves the request for shipping space, provided that supplying the Wehrmacht and tactical plans would not be compromised. . . . Kdt. of Fortress Crete and Gen. Komm. XXII. Geb. AK. will be responsible for furnishing escort personnel.[61]

On Corfu and Crete the orders of Army Group E were handled with very differing speed. On Corfu the island commandant's reticence about the deportation of the island's Jewish inhabitants, already apparent in April, became more pronounced. When on May 13 an SS-Hauptsturmführer "with orders from the Reichsführer-SS to expel the Jews from Corfu," reported to Insel Kommandant Colonel Jäger. Jäger, in a two-page memorandum to his superiors, listed his objections to the "deportation of Jews from Corfu." He began by calling attention to the dependence of deportations on the availability of transport facilities, an issue that had not been solved because in the meantime the SS officer had left. Jäger argued that what shipping was available "would in no way be sufficient." The "arrest of 2,000 Jews would meet with severe difficulties and could significantly weaken the defense of the islands."[62] If any transport facilities were available at all, the members of the former Italian armed forces should be the first to be removed from Corfu, "who as former soldiers are far more dangerous than the Jews, about whom nobody had ever complained anyway." Jäger also pointed out that a Red Cross ship anchored in the harbor would make it impossible to keep the deportation transport a secret so that "atrocity propaganda" might result. In closing, Jäger summed up:

> Corfu is a military outpost. It cannot be desirable to purchase the evacuation of Jews at the price of moral damage to the troops, effective strengthening of [the credibility of] enemy news instrumentalities, incitement of gang activity, and loss of ethical prestige in the eyes of the local population since unavoidable brutalities cannot but produce disgust.[63]

The aim of Jäger's proposal was to postpone "the Aktion for an indefinite period of time," which, of course, meant not to implement it at all.

Jäger's emphatic critique apparently disconcerted his immediate superiors at XXII Mountain Army Corps headquarters. They forwarded it to the next higher level of authority, Army Group E, seconding parts of his argument. The corps headquarters considered the "planned measures appropriate only if the evacuation can be conducted suddenly, like a thunderbolt, resulting in immediate, total deportation, for otherwise the negative results stressed in the enclosed report would be unavoidable."[64]

Even though Corfu's island commandant favored indefinite postponement, he nevertheless did initiate preparations for the deportation, as is made clear by "a memorandum about the Jewish Question" that he and the Navy's Captain Magnus had authored. In mid-May authorities in Corfu inquired of the Navy's Aegean command whether additional shipping was available. There is no evidence of a reply, but on May 24 the requested ships docked in Corfu harbor.

Island Commandant Jäger took action immediately. "That same day the arrival of the ships was reported to the Gen. Kdo. XXII (Geb.) AK. with the request to permit SS-Obersturmführer Burger to carry out the Aktion now." Jäger tried unsuccessfully to reach Burger: "SS-Ostuf. Burger who had left Corfu on May 15, 1944, was being tracked from here by telephone in Igoumenítsa and Ioánnina but could not be reached and did not arrive here either."[65] Still, Jäger ordered the printing of flyers and posters commanding the Jews to report to the collection places. On May 28, the Aegean command recalled the ships, "even if J . . . transports not completed," as Jäger's and Magnus's file note explained. Burger reappeared on Corfu at the end of May, "five days too late," as the complaint ran. He had reported neither to the area commander nor to the island commandant. Eight men and a noncommissioned officer of the Feldgendarmerie in Ioánnina arrived at the same time. After joint reconnaissance by Jäger, Burger, and a sergeant of the GFP, the island commandant determined that the people about to be arrested were to be housed in the rooms of a citadel. When Magnus, the Seekommandant Westgriechenland (Naval Commander of Western Greece), arrived in Corfu, he promised Burger "to ask once more for special deployment of the ships despite reservations concerning the heavy consumption of gasoline (ca. 10,000 liters)."[66]

Despite the initial protests of the island commandant, despite several weeks' delay in preparations because of the lack of coordination in the arrival and departure of ships, despite Burger's disappearance from Corfu, and despite the overall shortage of fuel, the realization of the planned deportations appeared on the horizon. Army Group E, in its late-May decision, did not address any of the obstacles Jäger had raised, but in a telex to the Aegean naval commander, XXII Army Corps, and the Higher SS and Police leader, approved the "transfer of the 2,000 Jews from Corfu to the mainland . . . if it does not interfere with troop transports and supplying the islands, and will take place speedily without disruptions." The army, according to the Heeresgruppe headquarters, could not provide guard teams for the transports but requested "information concerning plans."[67]

Now the deportation machinery shifted into gear. In early June, Burger and his men, the GFP, the Feldgendarmerie, and the Greek police organized the capture of all Jews on Corfu. Burger coerced the Greek mayor and the chief of police into signing and publishing the text of a proclamation he furnished; it claimed that the Jews, always having sucked the life blood of the Greeks, would now be deported and their property turned over to the Greek people.[68] On June 9 all members of the Jewish community of Corfu had to appear in a large plaza; the detainees were interned in the citadel and forced to surrender all their valuables.[69]

In the meantime the transportation problem had been solved when the Admiral, Aegean approved the use of Siebelfähren, landing craft. Burger and his subordinates escorted the transport. They chose the island of Lefkáda as a way station. There the deportees were allowed to leave the ships and stay on the pier under guard. When a Greek priest tried to give something to one of the Jewish men – one witness said cigarettes, another claimed it was a package – Burger drew his pistol and shot the deportee at close range. Burger's former translator testified that another SS man said, "Toni, you didn't handle that well," to which Burger replied that of all the deported Jews from Corfu the dead man was the most fortunate.[70] After their stop on Lefkáda, the landing craft continued on their way to Pátra, where they arrived on June 17 at 6 AM. During the long journey the deportees suffered from heat and thirst; when several older and sick people died, their bodies were tossed into the sea.[71] Finally the SS interned the men, women, and children for a short time in the Chaidari concentration camp near Athens. Four days later, on June 21, a deportation train with more than 2,000 people, among them additional Jews arrested in Athens, left the Greek capital for Auschwitz.

In this particular case the military authorities also received detailed information about the progress of the deportations. An employee of the BdS informed the Ic officer of XXII Army Corps in writing "in the course of the Judenaktion on Corfu . . . a total of 1,795 people" had been "arrested and deported," their assets "to be turned over to the governor of Corfu to be managed and used for administrative purposes as he sees fit."[72]

The mid-May Army Group E directives for the deportation of the Jews were executed far more rapidly on Crete than on Corfu. On Crete, the organization of arrests and transports was solely the responsibility of Wehrmacht units. As early as August 1941, shortly after the military occupation of the island, the field commanders had ordered the registration of its Jews.[73] In February 1943 the Greek mayor of Chania, the residence of the largest Jewish community on Crete, presented a "list of the 'Israelites' living in Chania" to the Geheime Feldpolizei.[74] GFP Group 611 and members of the Feldgendarmerie carried out the raid in Chania in mid-May 1944. As a former staff sergeant of the Feldgendarmerie explained during a witness interrogation, this Aktion directed exclusively against the Jews of Chania was announced two days in advance. On the morning of May 21, the Feldgendarmerie and Geheime Feldpolizei blocked off the streets where the Jews lived, forced them to leave their homes, and drove them into the waiting Wehrmacht trucks.[75] A few days after being taken to a prison, the arrested men, women, and children were transported to Iráklion. Together with a few Jewish families arrested there and a group of non-Jewish prisoners, they were to be transported to the mainland in early

June.[76] On June 8, 1944, the steamer *Tanais* left Iráklion for Piraeus, carrying 492 civilian prisoners and fourteen escorts. According to the war diary of the sea transport chief of the Aegean naval command, "a submarine torpedo sank the ship on June 9." Presumably all Jews from Crete drowned, although there were a few survivors, for on June 16 the war diary states that thirty-seven Germans and fourteen foreigners were rescued from the steamer *Tanais*.[77] Extant documents do not reveal whether the deportees also could have been rescued in lifeboats.

The staff of Army Group E had been notified about the fate of the Jews from Crete. On June 9 its war diary recorded the loss of the *Tanais* by a direct torpedo hit: "On board 492 civilian prisoners (300 Jews), 74 escort members and crew."[78] Once again Graevenitz could send a report to the Foreign Office:

> According to an announcement by the chief of the Sicherheitspolizei, the last transport in the program of expelling all Greek Jews from Greece took place on the 21st of this month. It carried more than 2,000 Jews, 1,900 of them from Corfu, to the Reich. The Jews who were recently apprehended on Crete, several hundred, fell victim to enemy attack on their way to the mainland.[79]

Graevenitz was mistaken. This was not the last deportation train from Greece. During their last months in Greece, Anton Burger and his subordinates, with the assistance of the Wehrmacht, destroyed two more Jewish communities at the extreme end of Europe – those of the Dodecanese islands.

> One day in 1944 . . . there appeared on the island a Kommando of SS men without previous announcement who were introduced to me as members of the SD on a special mission. . . . I received their leader, who informed me that he had come to handle the transfer of the Jews of Rhodes to the mainland at Himmler's personal command; that except for Rhodes, this roundup of Jews ordered by the highest levels had already been completed throughout the southeast. . . . In response to my objections to this measure, the SD leader replied that the evacuations of Jews were measures handed down from the highest levels and that he had been instructed to insist that local authorities not create any problems for him. At that point I ended the meeting with this arrogant SD leader in order to discuss with my staff this matter, so flagrantly contradictory to my own basic conceptions. Further inquiries to Army Group and a thorough consideration of our predicament proved that this issue could not be averted.[80]

Ulrich Kleemann, former commandant East Aegean, made this statement when at the end of the 1950s investigations about war crimes were conducted against him in the Federal Republic of Germany. Certainly Kleemann's claims of initially refusing to cooperate with the SS and essentially having shown the door to the SD leader – Anton Burger – during their first meeting could be read as a ploy to protect himself; however, the controversy between Kleemann and Burger was confirmed not only in witness depositions by Wehrmacht veterans who had been stationed on Rhodes, but also by Burger's former translator.[81] According to his statements, his meeting with the general had infuriated Burger.

> The general, Burger said, had banged on the desk, refusing to support him. The general reportedly had insisted that the British would find out immediately that Jews were being transported here and would certainly launch a severe bombing attack on Rhodes. At any rate, he told Burger in no uncertain terms that he was the boss on Rhodes and would not brook Burger's meddling.[82]

Supposedly Burger, from a ship in port, contacted his superior office in Athens to give an account of the problems he encountered.

Whether the Army Group's directive to Kleemann to satisfy the SS officer's demands resulted from the general's inquiry or from Burger's Athens office's intervention at the General Staff remains unknown. Existing documents prove only that Department Ic/AO, the responsible authority on the staff of Heeresgruppe E, did issue that order.[83] So, on July 13, Kleemann, "in accordance with his executive authority," promulgated a decree according to which "all Jews on Rhodes, male and female of all ages" were assigned to the towns of Rhodes, Triáda, Kremastí, or Villanova as their temporary place of residence. The relocation of all Jews not living in one of these towns was to be completed by July 17. Also on that day all Jews were to be registered in the mayors' offices.[84] Kleemann's directive initiated the registration and concentration of Jews so important for subsequent procedures on Rhodes.

Among Wehrmacht officers and soldiers, conduct toward the Jews on Rhodes was not merely a topic of discussion; by mid-July inflammatory statements forced General Kleemann, in his capacity as commander of the Sturmdivision Rhodos, to acknowledge these discussions about the "solution to the Jewish Question" and pay tribute to the "National Socialist worldview":

> On Rhodes the Jewish Question has given rise to doubts whether I, as the sole person responsible for political issues vis-à-vis the local population, am handling this matter in a manner reconcilable with the National Socialist worldview. . . . I request immediate action to dispel doubts about the treatment of the Jewish Question among the troops and provide these guidelines:
>
> 1. the SS worldview is the unassailable and self-evident prerequisite and basis for handling all political, economic, and other situations touching on the sphere of command

2. the Jewish Question in the Dodecanese can be handled only within the framework of the entire situation and can be brought to its radical conclusion only when a number of conditions, which are being created at this time, have been met. Therefore, any soldier unfamiliar with the political, economic, and other conditions within the sphere of command of southeastern Greece is incapable of judging matters he knows only from his own limited perspective

3. awkwardness and unauthorized acts on the part of subordinate authorities in handling the Jewish Question and individuals' irresponsible comments that have been reported to me are being investigated and will be dealt with

4. in the interest of measures now in progress it is inappropriate to make the Jewish Question on Rhodes the troops' topic of conversation before its solution.[85]

"The radical solution of the Jewish Question" in the Dodecanese Islands continued with the concentration of Jews in the town of Rhodes, with the help of the Geheime Feldpolizei and the Feldgendarmerie. First the men, then shortly afterward, the women and children were interned in a building complex referred to as "Aeronautica," which previously had been used by the Italian air force.[86] Through his translator, Burger announced to the Jews that Rhodes was a military frontier area and so, because of their pro-British political stance, they would be shipped to Germany to work there. Only Turkish citizens were exempt from these deportations.[87] After the victims had been ordered to bring along all their valuables to the Aeronautica, they had to surrender them to the SS officers. Burger sent eleven bags of paper currency to the governor of the island. He and his men carried off to Athens nine suitcases containing gold, jewels, and precious stones.[88]

On July 24, less than two weeks after Kleemann's first announcement, with brutal blows Wehrmacht guards drove 1,700 men, women, and children from the Aeronautica onto three ships in Rhodes harbor.[89] During a stop on the island of Cos, about one hundred Jewish inhabitants of that island, who had been arrested by members of the Feldgendarmerie, joined the transport. In August 1944, after a brief internment at Chaidari, the SS transported 1,800–1,900 victims on the last deportation train from Greece to Auschwitz.[90] Some of the civilian population of Rhodes objected to the deportation of their fellow citizens. A situation report of Department Ic at the headquarters of Kommandant Ost-Ägäis sent to Heeresgruppe E Department Ic/AO states, "because of the deportation of Jews from the command area," occasionally "the Germans were even referred to as barbarians."[91] Wehrmacht officers on Rhodes, however, were able to see the deportation of Jews in a favorable light. For example, while testifying as a witness in 1958, a former major on

Kleemann's staff recalled that, in the course of conversations within the division staff, the fact that now there were "roughly one thousand fewer eaters on the island" was cited as a positive result of the "evacuations of the Jews."[92]

Wehrmacht authorities aided and abetted in deporting about 9,000 people from Greece in 1944 even more effectively than during the destruction of the Jewish community of Salonika in 1943. Without Wehrmacht assistance Anton Burger and the few SS men stationed in Greece would have been able to apprehend only a fraction of their prey. Wehrmacht units helped the SS arrest, guard, and transport men, women, and children. On Crete and Cos, they even implemented these steps on their own authority. If individual officers such as Colonel Jäger or General Kleemann voiced reservations about the deportation of Jews from their area of command, their superior officers ordered them to enact the measures the SS demanded, and they complied promptly. No one objected by referring to the basic legal principles of martial law.

The complicity of segments of the Wehrmacht followed a logic of its own because Wehrmacht officers saw the Jews as enemies. Additionally, patterns of rationalization came into play in attempting to legitimize the deportations as appropriate given the tight supply situation. What Wehrmacht officers in the occupied areas of the Soviet Union in the winter of 1941–1942 had supported as "the elimination of useless eaters," the officers in Greece, less crudely, welcomed as relief from the supply crisis through the removal of part of the civilian population.

10 Manhunts in Hungary and Slovakia: 1944–1945

While Brunner's Kommando in France and Anton Burger in Greece conducted manhunts with the support of the Wehrmacht, in the spring of 1944 Eichmann led his first personal mission outside the Greater German Reich against the last sizeable Jewish community of Central Europe. According to the 1941 census, more than 700,000 people belonging to Jewish religious communities lived in Hungary. In addition, according to Hungarian laws adopted in 1938, 1939, and 1941, about 100,000 Christians also were categorized as Jews.[1]

Since the 1920s Admiral Miklós Horthy had been Hungary's regent and head of state. During the interwar era, the main goal of Hungarian politics had been the revision of the country's borders with its neighbors Czechoslovakia, Romania, and Yugoslavia, established by the Treaty of Trianon. The reincorporation of areas that before 1918 had been under Hungarian administration provided an important reason for Hungary's alignment of its foreign policy with those of Fascist Italy and the Greater German Reich. After 1938 Hungary profited from the National Socialist Neuordnung (New Order), the restructuring of Europe through several territorial acquisitions. In 1938 the southern strip of Slovakia and in the spring of 1939 the Carpathian Ukraine, Slovakia's easternmost province, had been incorporated; in the summer of 1940 Hungary took over northern Transylvania from Romania, followed by the upper and central Mur area and the Bačka and Baranya regions from Yugoslavia.

In Hungary, where a religious-materialistic antisemitism was dominant among the ruling class, laws discriminating against Jews were passed especially after 1938: for example, the quotas the government set to limit Jewish participation in specific occupations and branches of the economy.[2] Because the Hungarian rulers probably were justified in worrying that an immediate, total expropriation of Jewish property would impact the country's entire economy negatively – Horthy, for example, feared the replacement of Jewish entrepreneurs by inept boasters – the Jews were cut out of the country's economic life gradually.[3] The country's leadership reflected a rather traditional religious antisemitism. The Hungarian national socialist movement, which enjoyed a far from insignificant following especially in the executive branch of government, the military, and the administrative apparatus, favored a much harsher persecution of the country's Jews.[4]

Shortly after the start of Operation Barbarossa, in which Hungarian military units participated, the government ordered the arrest of more than 10,000 Jews who were not Hungarian citizens and their expulsion to the recently conquered areas in Galicia and Ukraine; there SS Einsatzgruppen and Ukrainian auxiliaries murdered most of the victims near Kolomyya and Kamenetz-Podolsk (Kam'yanets'-Podil's'kyy).[5] Since the fall of 1941, Jewish men had been drafted into Labor Service battalions in increasing numbers and placed at the Eastern Front to support the Hungarian army. These men were exposed to the whims of their officers and purposefully provided with bad food and clothing allotments. Some Hungarian officers decimated their number through shootings; others derived sadistic pleasure from beating these defenseless men, subjecting them to punishment drills, driving them into swamps or minefields, or dousing them with water in the winter until they turned into ice sculptures.[6]

In early 1942, Hungarian military units led by General Ferenc Feketehalmy-Czeydner and gendarmerie forces under Captain Márten Zöldi massacred civilians in the Bačka and Baranya areas (Délvidék in Hungarian), Yugoslav areas Hungary now occupied. They murdered more than 3,000 men, women, and children at the banks of the Danube and in the streets of Novi Sad and other towns in the Bačka, and legitimized these killings as reprisals. About 700 of the victims were Jews, the rest were Serbs.[7] These massacres did have consequences for the officers in charge. The first inquiry immediately following this incident was suppressed but was revived in the spring of 1942 after the change of government. At the end of 1943, charges were brought against those responsible, and they were sentenced in a Budapest court. Four of the accused, Ferenc Feketehalmy-Czeydner and Zöldi among them, avoided serving their jail sentences by escaping to Vienna where they enjoyed the official protection of the German Reich.[8]

In March 1944, when the leaders of the Third Reich had reason to fear that Miklós Kállay's government might pursue Hungary's withdrawal from the Axis and thus further weaken Germany's military situation, Hitler ordered "Operation Margarethe": Hungary's occupation by Wehrmacht and SS units.[9] On March 18, the day Hitler summoned Horthy to Castle Kleβheim near Salzburg to force him to agree to the occupation, Wehrmacht and SS units already were marching into Hungary.

Eichmann's Sonderkommando in Budapest

In addition to other SS formations, Otto Winkelmann, the Higher SS and Police leader in Hungary, also commanded an SS Sonderkommando led by Eichmann, which in March 1944 had been organized at Mauthausen. It consisted of Eichmann's long-time coworkers and subordinates from the RSHA-Referat IV B 4 (after the reorganization of Department IV in April/May 1944 referred to as IV A 4b) and the Zentralstellen für jüdische Auswanderung.[10] Among others, Hermann Krumey, Dieter Wisliceny, Franz Novak, Franz Abromeit, Otto Hunsche, Theo Dannecker, Siegfried Seidl, Ernst Girzick, Richard Hartenberger, and Alfred Slawik were members of this Sondereinsatzkommando.

Through the influence of the newly appointed Dr. Edmund Veesenmayer as Bevollmächtigter des Großdeutschen Reiches und Gesandter in Ungarn, the plenipotentiary and ambassador of the Greater German Reich in Hungary a new government was formed under Döme Sztójay, the former Hungarian ambassador in Berlin.[11] In the appointment of ministers, Veesenmayer's line "better with Horthy than against Horthy" carried the day and the appointment of politicians from the traditional leadership class avoided a cabinet made up primarily of Hungarian national socialists, which RSHA chief Kaltenbrunner had demanded, and prevented Ferenc Szálasi's Nyilaskeresztes, the Hungarian fascist Arrow Cross Party, from getting in on the action. Four ministers in Sztójay's cabinet, among them Minister of Justice István Antal, already had served in previous governments.[12] So, on the level of government offices the continuity of the right-wing national rulers was essentially maintained, although two appointments for state secretaries in the Ministry of the Interior went to László Endre and László Baky, two functionaries active in Hungary's national socialist movement and notorious antisemites.[13] Without wasting time, the Sztójay cabinet debated and enacted antisemitic directives such as the one of March 29, which called for marking Jews. All Jews six years and older now were obliged to display the yellow star on their clothing. Only Jewish soldiers and officers who had fought in the Hungarian army during World War I and had either been decorated for bravery or were veterans classified as 75 percent disabled were exempt.[14]

Independent of government decrees, the SS and the Sonderkommando Eichmann immediately went into action on March 20, the day after their arrival in Hungary. To gain control of the Jewish community, Krumey and Wisliceny summoned some of its representatives and demanded lists of all Jewish organizations, their functions and social services, their membership numbers, and the names of their presidents and other officers. Additionally they requested a list of candidates for the formation of a "Central Advisory Board of the Jews in Budapest" to provide German authorities with a negotiation partner. The Zentralrat of Hungarian Jews was established the very next day, consisting of a president, Hofrat (counselor) Samuel Stern and seven representatives of the Neolog movement (the mildly "liberal" Jewish community), the Orthodox Jewish community, and the Zionists.[15]

To succeed in the deliberate deception of the members of the Zentralrat, Eichmann gave an hour-long presentation that made no mention of his instructions and intentions. He pretended to work toward establishing Jewish labor cadres. To achieve an allegedly consistent, centralized organization of Jews, he demanded a map that was to mark the location and the type of every Jewish facility and institution. He also employed crude lies: All anti-Jewish measures would be in force for the duration of the war only. At the end of the war, "Germans could once again be their old jovial selves and permit everything to be as it was before."[16] He would not tolerate any mistreatments. "Even if German soldiers committed cruelties, he was to be notified at once. He would call the perpetrators to task." Those who "want to enrich themselves with Jewish property he would punish severely, too."[17] With such tricks Eichmann tried to deceive the representatives of the Jewish community.

While Krumey and Wisliceny were mainly occupied with subjugating Jewish organizations to the rule of their new masters, other members of the SS Sonderkommando took part in the arrests that units of Higher SS and Police Leader Winkelmann launched immediately upon their arrival. Partly with the help of prepared lists, partly in cooperation with Hungarian authorities, people whom the SS considered politically suspect were arrested throughout Hungary, as were Jewish intellectuals and entrepreneurs such as Ferenc Chorin, the co-owner of the Manfred Weiß Industries, one of Hungary's largest heavy industry complexes and armament manufacturers. During the first days of the occupation, Winkelmann ordered his subordinates to arrest 200 Jewish lawyers and physicians: Their names were randomly selected from the Budapest telephone directory.[18] Within a short time the SS arrested thousands of people. By the end of March, according to Winkelmann's report to Veesenmayer, "a total of 3,364 Jews had been seized" throughout the country.[19] Later, German authorities in their internal correspondence referred to the arrests of individuals as Einzelaktionen, individual raids, to differentiate them from the Sonderaktionen (special actions) – the concentration, ghettoization, and deportation of hundreds of thousands. The SS imprisoned victims of the Einzelaktionen in the Kistarcsa, Topolya, and Csepel internment camps, which before March 1944 had served mainly as jails for political prisoners, and in the Mauthausen concentration camp.[20]

Those the SS arrested also served as hostages for blackmail. In the case of the industrialist Ferenc Chorin and his family, the SS set up a large-scale ransom scam without informing Hungarian or German authorities. After secret negotiations between SS-Standartenführer Kurt Becher, one of Himmler's special envoys, and the owners of the Manfred Weiß Industries, the SS organized Chorin's release from the concentration camp, and, in June 1944, the departure of more than forty of the owners' families to Portugal by way of Vienna, Stuttgart, and Madrid, in return for the majority of the company's shares, which also included shares in other industrial, mining, and financial enterprises.[21]

In addition to conducting arrests, members of Eichmann's Sonderkommando also were employed in requisitioning Jewish-owned apartments and houses. Franz Novak, for example, was busy locating living quarters for the personnel of German authorities in Budapest. As he later testified, he seized "suitable Jewish properties, mainly villas." Accompanied by Hungarian and German police, he first inspected the premises. "If a place was suitable, the Jewish residents were ordered to vacate it within three to four hours. They were free to take valuables and personal items. Furniture, bed linens, and anything else necessary to make the place liveable had to stay." Novak stated that most of the time the evicted persons took only what they could carry. It is not difficult to imagine what happened with the rest. Novak, looking back, pointed out that "in such instances irregularities never can be avoided entirely. Still, to the degree possible I always made sure to prevent excesses or self-enrichment."[22] Eichmann himself was lodged in a roomy, exquisitely furnished villa on the Rosenhügel, formerly the property of a Jewish family of entrepreneurs.

In close cooperation with László Baky and László Endre from the Hungarian Ministry of the Interior, Eichmann's Sonderkommando enforced anti-Jewish persecution measures without heeding existing laws or government directives. Guidelines for concentrating all Hungarian Jews and their enclosure in ghettos were established at a conference at the Hungarian Interior Ministry on April 4, 1944. The conference was chaired by State Secretaries Baky and Endre and attended by high-ranking officers of the Wehrmacht and the Hungarian army; Eichmann and members of his staff; the liaison officer between the SD and the Hungarian gendarmerie, Lieutenent Colonel László Ferenczy; and commandants of Hungarian gendarmerie districts. With the participation of local and regional Hungarian authorities and members of the SS-Sonderkommando, the gendarmerie was to transport all Jews "regardless of sex and age" from the countryside to the larger towns of each district and send Jews living in the cities to these ghettos as well. Those who had been arrested were to take no more than fifty kilos of luggage and food for fourteen days. "Money, jewelry, gold, and other valuables cannot be taken along."[23] The schedule for this concentration was to be staggered among six areas: Zone I, northeastern Hungary (gendarmerie district Košice), consisted mainly of Carpatho-Ukraine; Zone II, northern Transylvania (gendarmerie districts Cluj and Tirgu-Mureş); Zone III, northern Hungary (gendarmerie districts Székesfehérvár and Miskolc); Zone IV, southeast Hungary (gendarmerie districts Szeged and Debrecen); Zone V, western Hungary (gendarmerie district Szombathely); and Zone VI, Budapest and environs.

During the subsequent weeks this master plan for concentration and ghettoization was conducted with ferocity. The Hungarian Entjudungskommando (Dejudaization Kommando) led by Ferenczy and located in the Peter-Semmelweiβ-Street under the cynical business logo "International Warehouse and Transport GmbH" immediately prepared the concentration in northeastern Hungary. After Endre, at an April 12th conference in Munkács (Mukacheve), had given instructions to the representatives of the gendarmerie, police, and administrators of this region, Hungarian authorities in mid-April carried out the planned mass arrests in Zone I. The gendarmerie generally entered the hamlets and villages in the morning and forced Jewish families, with their sparse luggage and few rations, to gather in the synagogue or other Jewish facilities. At these gathering places the Hungarian forces robbed them of their money and valuables. The abandoned houses and habitations, even if they had been sealed, generally were looted speedily. A few days later the gendarmerie transported the prisoners to the district centers and interned them in ghettos, brickyards, and empty factories that had to serve as camps, or even in the open air.

In addition to representatives of the Hungarian Entjudungskommandos, SS officers of Eichmann's Sonderkommando, too, had been dispatched to the centers of concentration in northeastern Hungary. Ernst Girzick, for example, was employed in Mátézalka and Košice,[24] and Siegfried Seidl in Nyiregyháza. Seidl, the first commandant of Theresienstadt, had arrived in Hungary in mid-March with the SS Sonderkommando, and, according to his testimony, at first had merely carried out "routine tasks for the Sicherheitspolizei" in Debrecen. Before Easter he had been assigned to Budapest, had attended the meeting at Munkács, and had been posted to the local authorities in the Komitat Szabolcs in the northeastern Hungarian town of Nyiregyháza as a liaison officer of the Sondereinsatzkommando. There, in concert with local administrative organs and the gendarmerie, he had organized the round-up of the Jews of the Komitat and their ghettoization in the town.[25]

In the Komitat Szabolcs the Hungarian authorities also began the concentrations of Jews in mid-April. After confining the detainees at local collection areas for a few days, the gendarmerie took those Jews to Nyiregyháza where they had to share the already crowded shelters and insufficient foodstuffs with the local Jews who had been imprisoned in a ghetto since April 24.[26] In early

May the Jewish Council of Budapest sent a petition to Eichmann to protest the deplorable conditions resulting from the ghettoization in northeastern Hungary and, among other issues, specifically addressed the severe crowding of the people in Nyíregyháza.

> 4,120 persons from that city and 6,600 from the surrounding area were brought to the local ghetto, so a total of 10,720 people are squeezed into 123 dwellings, with an area of 9,165 square meters, including kitchens and entryways. This does not even provide one square meter per person. Moreover, the area has neither piped water nor drains, a danger even in terms of public health. The instructions permitted concentrated persons to bring food for fourteen days, but the evacuations from the villages happened so quickly that it was impossible to procure such amounts. So the food supplies of the Jews in Nyíregyháza are exhausted, and the local Jewish Council is unable to supply the ghetto.[27]

These protests brought no relief; instead, more and more people from the collection places in the countryside were crammed into the overcrowded district centers. By May 10 the ghetto population in Nyíregyháza had swollen to more than 17,000. During these concentrations the Hungarian authorities also robbed the detainees of money and valuables. Gendarmerie officials conducted brutal interrogations to coerce confessions about hidden property. In Nyíregyháza several people died as the result of being tortured by a gendarmerie officer.[28]

Within a few weeks a total of approximately 200,000 men, women, and children were arrested, robbed, and forced into ghettos in northeastern Hungary. Yet, even before the end of the concentrations in Zone I, German and Hungarian authorities already were preparing the mass arrests in northern Transylvania and the deportation of all victims of ghettoization from Hungary.[29] Also, since March 1944 the Hungarian government had been pressured to provide 100,000 able-bodied Jewish workers for the Greater German Reich, and in mid-April Veesenmayer had received Sztójay's assurances that Hungary would deliver 50,000 Jews within the next two weeks and another 50,000 in the following month.[30] These plans changed at the end of April. On April 23 Veesenmayer brought the Foreign Office up to date on the progress of ghettoization in northeastern Hungary and the new deportation plans. "Transport negotiations have started and provide for the deportation of 3,000 Jews daily from the Carpathian region beginning on May 15. If technically possible, simultaneous transports from other ghettos at a later time. Destination: Auschwitz."[31]

Veesenmayer did not name the person who started the negotiations about deportations from northeastern Hungary to Auschwitz, but it is safe to assume that these proposals originated with Eichmann. Veesenmayer supported them even though they compromised his own agreements with the Hungarian government:

> In order not to endanger the completion of the Aktion [deportations from northeastern Hungary], it seems appropriate to postpone the transport of the 50,000 "labor Jews" from the Budapest area, [although] I had requested [them] and the government has already confirmed. In view of current transport problems this will be necessary anyway. . . . Since Jewish Aktion is a total whole [sic!], I consider the outlined plan the correct path of action but ask for directives per telegram in case of concerns or special requests.[32]

At the end of April, Eichmann, Wisliceny, State Secretary Endre, and functionaries of the "Dejewification Kommando" made an inspection tour through northeastern Hungary to check the progress of ghettoization in Košice, Uzhorod, Nyiregyháza, Kisvárda, and Mátészalka. On that occasion the leaders of the German and the Hungarian Entjudungskommandos agreed to deport all ghettoized people in northeastern Hungary to the German Reich and designated Košice as the railway junction where the deportation transports would be transferred from Hungarian to German authorities.[33]

State Secretary Endre and his entourage then traveled on to Transylvania, where during meetings on April 26 and 28 he provided the representatives of civil administrative offices and other authorities with directives for the concentration and ghettoization in the gendarmerie districts of Cluj and Tirgu-Mures. On May 3, Hungarian forces began the arrests in Transylvania, adopting tactics similar to those employed in northeastern Hungary. Here too officers of Eichmann's Sonderkommando were active: Franz Abromeit in Baia Mare, Dieter Wisliceny in Cluj, Theo Dannecker in Oradea, and Siegfried Seidl in Tirgu-Mures, where he had been transferred after the completion of the ghettoizations in Nyiregyháza.

The Hungarian government's discussions and decisions were totally out of step with developments that the Entjudungskommandos were enacting. On April 26, almost two weeks after the start of the concentrations in northeastern Hungary, the Hungarian Council of Ministers passed a resolution about the ghettoization of Jews and approved delivery of 50,000 Jewish workers.[34] At the end of April the Hungarian authorities in charge organized two deportation transports, "each made up of about 2,000 able-bodied men and women ranging from sixteen to fifty years of age" from the Kistarcsa and Topolya internment camps to Auschwitz.[35]

Despite the implementation of these transports, the collaboration régime had not yet approved the deportation of all Hungarian Jews. Only at the end of April, when Veesenmayer confronted Sztójay with alleged Wehrmacht demands for the removal of ghettoized Jews from northeastern to central Hungary did the government finally agree. Sztójay had delegated the issue to Minister of the Interior Andor Jarosz, who in turn passed it on to his undersecretary Endre. Endre explained to his superior that central Hungary could not accommodate such a large number of people and recommended accepting Germany's offer to take charge of the ghettoized people and transport them to German concentration camps. The minister then forwarded this proposal to the head of the government.[36]

The final technical details and train routes for the deportation program were worked out at a train-schedule conference in Vienna in early May; Novak attended as the representative of the Eichmann "Kommando," and a member of the Hungarian Entjudungskommando was present as well. The rail lines from Košice via Prešov in Slovakia and from Tarnów to Auschwitz were designated as the main route, whereas the route from Mukacheve by way of Stryy, L'viv (Lvov), Przemysl and Tarnów to Auschwitz could be used only with permission of the military, should the military "allow any such traffic on that line at all."[37] The deportations of 325,000 Jews from Carpathia and Transylvania were to begin on May 15. "As planned, four trains carrying 3,000 Jews each will [be] readied for departure to target destination [Auschwitz] daily so that completion of evacuation Aktion from so-called zones can be expected by mid-June," Veesenmayer informed the Foreign Office in telegram style.[38]

At a meeting in Munkács a few days before the start of the deportations, the leaders of the Hungarian Entjudungskommando instructed the administrators of the ghettos in the technical management of transports. The victims would be shipped in 110 transports to Košice, where German authorities would take charge of them. Each train consisting of forty-five cars carrying seventy persons each could transport approximately 3,000 people. Foreign Jews and physicians who were not "replacable" were to be exempt. The Hungarians responsible for the deportations knew perfectly well that people would die en route. One gendarmerie officer explained that, if necessary, the cars were to be loaded with 100 persons each; people could be packed like sardines. The Germans needed tough people, not dainty fashion models. Whoever could not take that might as well perish.[39]

Beginning in mid-May, the Hungarian authorities, with the help of members of the SS-Sonderkommando, deported the rounded-up men, women, and children in northeast Hungary and Transylvania. Under the supervision of SS officers of the Eichmann "Sonderkommando," they daily loaded several trains with people from the various ghettoization centers and sent them to Košice, where German authorities received them and routed them to Auschwitz. As intended, approximately 3,000 people were crammed into the railroad cars, sometimes even more. Many had no luggage at all because they had been robbed of everything except the clothes on their backs, as Seidl explained during questioning. Five deportation trains left the Nyiregyháza area for Auschwitz between May 17 and early June.

Foreign Office Legation Councilor von Thadden found out just how rapidly the deportation apparatus had shifted into gear and what size it had acquired when he visited German authorities in Budapest in the latter part of May to learn first-hand from Eichmann himself all about the status of these deportations and the problems attending them. Thadden did not exaggerate when he stressed in his report that "with the enthusiastic support of the Hungarian state secretaries László Endre and Baky, the Jewish question in Hungary is speeding toward its solution." The concentration measures in northeastern Hungary and northern Transylvania had resulted in the seizure of about 320,000 Jews, "12,000 to 14,000 of whom arrived daily in the Generalgouvernement for further shipping."[40] In their meeting Eichmann insisted on employing German legation personnel to verify the citizenship of those about to be deported because otherwise, in violation of official agreements, non-Hungarians might be apprehended as well. "Only in this way could he guarantee that, given the necessary harshness of the Hungarian gendarmerie and the undeniable pigheadedness of his own field Kommandos the roughest blunders in the treatment of [Jewish] foreign nationals could be kept to a minimum."[41]

By May 24, as Thadden learned from Eichmann, 116,000 men, women, and children already had been deported.[42] So, in less than ten days the SS-Sonderkommando and Hungarian authorities had delivered a substantially larger number of people to their death in Auschwitz than the SS and its helpers in France did in two and a half years. The arrests and deportations had roused almost no opposition among the Hungarian population.[43] There too certain groups tried to profit from the discrimination and expulsion of their fellow countrymen. A report to the Ministry of the Interior from Szekszárd pointed out that mainly members of the lower middle class, owners of small businesses and tradesmen, looked expectantly toward the implementation of the Jewish Regulations "because they hoped to improve their own future by purchase or acquisition of businesses and industries until now in Jewish hands."[44]

In the zones of northern, southeastern, and western Hungary, Eichmann's men and Hungarian authorities continued the concentration of their victims in ghettos, followed by their deportation, with undiminished speed. In the six weeks until the end of June they had transported nearly 400,000 people to the Reich, as Winkelmann informed Veesenmayer.[45] With the exception of approximately 15,000 men, women, and children mostly from Debrecen, Szeged, and Baja, who at the request of Vienna's mayor Blaschke the SS-Sonderkommando in June 1944 were shipped via the transit camp Straßhof to Vienna and Lower Austria (Wiener Neustadt, Neunkirchen, and Gmünd) as work slaves,[46] and the "Kasztner Transport" of 1,700 ransomed Jews who reached Switzerland via the Bergen-Belsen concentration "camp for the privileged," all victims of the Hungarian deportation program ended up in Auschwitz-Birkenau.[47]

During the entire process of concentration, ghettoization, and deportation the Hungarian gendarmerie treated its victims with the utmost brutality. Physical abuse, theft, and torture were the rule.[48] The SS could not have carried out this monstrous deportation program in the spring of 1944, shortly before the military defeat of the Third Reich, without the support of the Hungarian authorities. This support became obvious that summer when in early July Horthy prohibited additional mass transports and demanded the dismissal of State Secretaries Endre and Baky and the recall of the SS from Hungary. For the time being this stopped the prepared mass arrest of the Jews in Budapest (in Zone VI) and their deportation to Auschwitz.[49] Although the German and Hungarian Entjudungskommandos were able to complete the deportations from Zone V and apprehend Jews from the Budapest area within the framework of this Aktion even after Horthy's prohibition, the ultimate fate of the Budapest Jews was the subject of drawn-out negotiations between Veesenmayer and the Hungarian government.[50]

The doggedness with which Eichmann and his men pursued their goal of delivering even more Jews to their doom was obvious in July 1944. In mid-July, despite Horthy's prohibition, Eichmann ordered deported to Auschwitz 1,500 people, most of them internees at the Kistarcsa camp. When the Budapest Zentralrat learned about this transport, its leaders informed certain church prelates and diplomats of neutral countries. Upon their immediate intervention, Horthy ordered the minister of the interior to stop this train, even though it already had left Kistarcsa. Shortly before reaching the border it was intercepted and returned to Kistarcsa. Eichmann knew exactly how this deportation had been foiled. To succeed anyway, he used a satanic ruse. On July 19 he summoned all leading members of the Zentralrat to his office in the Hotel Majestic on the Schwabenberg. There, he forced them to spend the entire day discussing trifles with one of Eichmann's coworkers to keep them incommunicado. Meanwhile, Eichmann ordered the German and Hungarian Entjudungskommandos to load more than 1,200 persons at Kistarcsa on trucks to take them to Rákoscsaba, where, brutally mistreated by their guards, they were driven into freight cars. In the evening, when the members of the Zentralrat finally were allowed to go home, the train already was on its way to Auschwitz.[51] On July 24, in a similar manner, Eichmann, ignoring Horthy's decree, ordered the deportation of 1,500 internees from Sárván camp.[52]

Through close cooperation of German, Hungarian, and Austrian antisemites, the deportation machinery in Hungary had seized almost half a million people within three months before being brought to a stop in the summer of 1944, shortly before what would have been the total extermination of the Jewish community.[53] Only newly appointed Interior Minister Miklós Bonczo's explicit statement that the Budapest Jews were to collected in camps outside the Hungarian capital, and without any follow-up plans "for their transports from there to the Reich," finally persuaded Eichmann in late August to request that the RSHA recall him and his Kommando "as now superfluous here."[54] Shortly thereafter, Himmler, fearing that Hungary might follow Romania's example of withdrawing from the Axis, immediately forbade further deportations of Hungarian Jews. The recall of the Eichmann Sonderkommando, however, dragged on.[55] Not until the end of September did the Foreign Office receive notification that "the SEK [Sondereinsatzkommando] has been officially dissolved as of yesterday with a final roll call." Official dissolution, however, did not mean that Eichmann and his men actually left Hungary: "Eichmann and the men he brought with him from Berlin essentially have been recalled to the RSHA but have been instructed to remain in Budapest for another week or so in expectation of a rumored internal political change of direction."[56]

These rumors involving Veesenmayer actually were concrete preparations for the "internal political change of direction" that took place presently. When Horthy, in view of the hopeless military situation, tried to negotiate a truce with the Soviet Union in early October, the SS kidnapped his son and forced him to turn over all government business to Szálasi's Arrow Cross on October 15.[57] This once more drastically changed the situation of the remaining Jews of Hungary. On October 18 Veesenmayer alerted the Foreign Office that this altered political situation also ushered in a new phase in the Jewish Question. According to Veesenmayer, Eichmann, who arrived in Budapest immediately after Szálasi's appointment, had negotiated with Hungarian authorities "to march 50,000 able-bodied male Jews from Budapest to Germany." Eichmann saw these death marches as part and parcel of the total destruction of Hungary's Jewish community, which was no secret to Veesenmayer: "After the successful termination of this trek, Eichmann intends to request another 50,000 Jews to . . . reach the final goal of clearing out Hungary."[58]

Independent of all this, the Arrow Cross members, immediately following the change of power, had initiated pogrom-like excesses. During the night of October 15–16, young members of the Arrow Cross Party already were arresting Jews; they went on a pillage spree, and in some cases they massacred their victims, as an eyewitness described:

> Day and night Arrow Cross patrols now turned the streets of Budapest into death traps. Wealthy, respected Jews and those who for some reason had aroused the displeasure of their non-Jewish neighbors were chased from their residences or hiding places, were robbed and tortured by the greenshirts, and then, generally toward evening or at night, were shot and dumped into the Danube. But more and more frequently corpses of Jews shot right then and there piled up in the streets by morning.[59]

In Pusztvám, Arrow Cross men even murdered an entire company of male Jewish conscripts working for the Labor Service.[60]

On October 20 the Arrow Cross and Hungarian police in Budapest began arresting Jewish men on the street and in their apartments to bring them to the collection point at a race track and to organize them into labor companies that were to dig trenches and construct fortifications south and east of Budapest. A short time later the Szálasi government published a directive ordering all Jewish men between sixteen and sixty and all Jewish women between eighteen and forty years of age to report for trench work. Tens of thousands of men and women were forced to dig ditches and erect defenses with insufficient equipment and dismal, if any, food rations, and they were mistreated by their Arrow Cross guards. Many of these victims died or were murdered by Arrow Cross men.[61]

Beginning in early November, in response to Eichmann's and Veesenmayer's demands, columns of Jewish men and women from Budapest were driven west. They were to be employed as slave laborers in the Austro-Hungarian border areas, especially in Lower Austria and Burgenland. These "foot marches," as Veesenmayer called these death marches on the country roads between Budapest and Vienna, took the lives of thousands. People who, in Budapest, had been classified as able-bodied were crammed into a brickyard in Óbuda for several days; there their Arrow Cross guards robbed and abused them before driving them in larger groups through Komáron and Györ to Hegyeshalom. Hunger, cold, and abuse caused many to die from injuries, disease, or epidemics. The Arrow Cross men killed anyone who lagged behind or collapsed. The roads were lined with corpses.[62]

Until November 12, according to a note from Eichmann, "about 27,000 Jews of both sexes, and who are able to march and work, were sent on their way to the

Reich." How many of them actually were turned over to German authorities in Hegyeshalom is not known. Neutral states' embassies' protests against these death marches contributed to Szálasi's decision to halt them.[63] Despite Eichmann's efforts to organize additional transports, this ended the deportation program. Just a few days before Christmas 1944 and just before the Red Army encircled the Hungarian capital, Eichmann took to his heels and left Budapest.

Brunner in Bratislava

After 60,000 Jews had been deported from Slovakia in 1942, approximately 20,000 still remained in 1943–1944, about 10,000 of whom had been able to escape, especially to neighboring Hungary.[64] Some 3,000 Jewish men, women, and children had been interned in the Slovak work camps of Sered', Nováky, and Vyhne. Some smaller work camps for Jews were administered by the Slovak army.[65]

When the deportations of Jews from Hungary began in the spring of 1944, many of the Slovak Jews who had fled there returned to Slovakia to escape concentration and deportation. Slovak authorities arrested a number of these illegal returnees, but the secret aid committee founded by leaders of the official Judenzentrale in Bratislava was successful in freeing a few of them.[66] In April 1944 Walter Rosenberg and Alfred Wetzler, two Slovak escapees from Auschwitz, were the first to provide the aid committee with authentic, detailed information about the organization and function of the concentration and extermination camp Auschwitz-Birkenau, which the committee passed on to representatives of Jewish organizations in Hungary and Switzerland, the Jewish Agency's branch office in Istanbul, and the papal nuncio in Bratislava.[67]

About 1,500 Jewish men and women took part in the Slovak National Uprising in August and September of 1944, which all Slovak opposition forces supported. Among those were the partisan movement, which in April 1944 began spreading ever more rapidly throughout central and northeastern Slovakia. Even entire garrisons of the Slovak army took part in the rising. In particular, younger internees from Nováky, Vyhne, and Sered' joined the partisan units in the insurrectionist "Czechoslovak Forces of the Interior," also known as the "First Czechoslovak Army." Able to fight, they battled Wehrmacht and SS units approaching from the west.[68]

After the suppression of the Slovak rebellion by those German forces, the SS assumed power in Slovakia. SD posts were established in the provincial towns of western Slovakia and in Bratislava, and there organized the arrests of Jews still living there. Even at that time Slovak organizations still were assisting the SS

in this endeavor: "Even though in Slovakia the German security organizations
had taken the Final Solution of the Jewish Question into their own hands,
they could not have conducted this Aktion on such a scale without Slovak
assistance," the historian Ladislav Lipscher observes. "The armed units of the
HG [Hlinka Guard] and the newly-created Home Defense (Domobrana) were
especially zealous in this endeavor."[69] Until mid-September the aid committee
in Bratislava did not know whether those arrested would remain in Slovakia
or whether the deportations to concentration and extermination camps would
start up again. Off the record the committee learned from an SS man that
Hauptsturmführer Alois Brunner was to arrive in Bratislava to settle the Jewish
Question once and for all. The message was clear: "That meant Auschwitz."[70]

The "deportation expert" Alois Brunner was posted to Bratislava in mid-
September 1944. He immediately seized control of the Sered' work camp,
where about 5,000 people were interned, and he conducted "discussions" with
aid committee representatives such as Gisi Fleischmann and Tibor Kovac.
When they told him about the inhumane treatment of Jews in Sered', Brunner responded cynically and dismissively, belittling the anti-Jewish measures
enacted in Slovakia until then. He would "tackle the problem radically" through
the "total concentration of all Jews still at large, especially those of consequence
in the economic sector and those protected by presidential exemptions." He
also announced that he would "not discharge his duties at a desk but in the
field."[71]

Brunner now applied a combination of methods he had employed in Vienna
and Berlin, Salonika, and France. As he assured the representatives of the aid
committee that the Bratislava Jews would merely be evacuated to Sered' to
be settled in a large work camp, Sered' already was being transformed into a
deportation camp modeled on the Baron Hirsch section of Salonika, and on
Drancy. Its detainees now fell victim to a brutal reign of terror. At Sered' a
delegation of the aid committee learned that

> a horrible St Bartholomew's Night had taken place there. At 10 PM all inmates,
> including old people, women, and children, had been forced to run in a circle
> until 4 AM while the drunken Nazi beasts Knollmeyer, Kubik, Heckel, and the
> bloodhound Obersturmführer Zimmermann . . . ruthlessly lashed them with
> rawhide whips, seriously injuring many.[72]

That night SS men also shot four people because they had fallen during this
race and their fellows in suffering could not pick them up at once to drag them
along.

Through an Aktion disguised as a burglary at the main office of the aid
committee the SS came into possession of the committee's files about all
Jews still living in Slovakia. Brunner used it at once to conduct large-scale

manhunts in Bratislava. Shortly before midnight of September 27, 1944, armed members of the SS, the German-Slovak Freiwillige Schutzstaffel (Volunteer SS), the Slovak Hlinka Guard, and the Wehrmacht, all under Brunner's personal direction, cordoned off whole streets and sections of town and drove Jews from their beds and apartments to the headquarters of the aid committee at 6 Edlgasse.[73]

On the morning of September 29, about 1,800 of those arrested "had to run the gauntlet, a narrow corridor lined by heavily-armed SS, FS, and Hlinka Guard members to a remote railway station" where, after hours of waiting, they were loaded into cattle cars. Sered' was the immediate destination of this transport train. There,

> at 6 AM [on September 30] came the order to line up for luggage inspection, and once again these 1,800 people had to stand in the yard for hours. Suddenly Brunner appeared. With yells, lashes, and shots the Nazi beasts within a few minutes drove from the barracks into the yard those baggage-laden Jews who previously had been concentrated in these buildings. Simultaneously, at the same pace they drove the new arrivals into the barracks and locked them up. By 10 AM the SS, raving like madmen shooting and cracking their whips, had finished assembling the first deportation transport of 2,000 persons. This transport left Sered' for Auschwitz that same morning.[74]

To the question of one detainee as to the destination of this transport, Brunner answered with a lie, claiming that they would be employed as laborers near Vienna.

Throughout Slovakia the hunt for Jews was handled in this fashion. Often Brunner traveled to various locations to conduct these raids in person, making good, in the most horrible way, on his threat not to officiate at his desk but in the field.[75] The SS interned the arrested Bratislava Jews in the Edlgasse collection camp before transferring them to Sered'. Here too the most severe physical abuses were commonplace. Survivors referred to this place as a "hell" or a "torture chamber."[76] The SS and its helpers blackmailed the victims into providing information about relatives and acquaintances living in hiding or under assumed identities. In Sered', Brunner himself interrogated Gisi Fleischmann, one of the leaders of the aid committee. She did not succumb to his blackmail attempts, even though he threatened to spare her life only if she revealed hiding places of friends. She betrayed no one, so Brunner ordered her departure to Auschwitz. On October 17th she was included in the fourth transport from Sered', and murdered shortly after her arrival.[77]

In the midst of organizing manhunts and deportations, Alois Brunner did not neglect perfecting the system of robbing his victims. He punished any member of the Hlinka Guard who relieved the persecuted of anything during raids or during the organization of transports. The pillage of the deportees, the confiscation of valuables, jewels, and money were to take place exclusively in Sered' under his supervision. Additionally, to appropriate valuables the deportees had hidden or left at home, Brunner spread the word among new arrivals that they could buy themselves free and remain in Sered' through payment of substantial sums of money or delivery of goods.

> In response to this offer, he actually received many sizeable deliveries of goods such as cattle, pigs, sheep . . . textiles of all kinds, medical and dental office equipment, machines, and gold and jewelry of high value. After all, the people he was concentrating were the so-called economically prominent Jews and those exempt by presidential decree, the only ones who still possessed any assets at all.[78]

After relieving them of their valuables or receiving their goods, the SS in charge added them to the next deportation transport. Special groups of Jewish artisans at Sered' were responsible for processing the loot and packing it for further transport. Finally, they even had to dismantle and load the machines and fixtures of the camp's work shops. Then the members of this forced labor column were taken to Theresienstadt on the last transport to leave Sered', on March 30, 1945.[79]

Brunner and his German and Slovak assistants continued these transports of human beings until the very end of the war. In eleven transports they deported a total of about 8,000 men, women, and children to Auschwitz during the fall and winter of 1944–1945, and 4,000 more to Sachsenhausen and Theresienstadt.[80] Only the military overthrow of the Third Reich finally put a stop to the terrible activities of Eichmann and his men.

11　The Postwar Era

In 1960, David Ben-Gurion's brief announcement in the Knesset about Adolf Eichmann's capture by the Israeli secret service made headlines around the world. Leading politicians in Austria, Eichmann's home country, were not exactly elated at the prospect of their compatriot standing trial in Jerusalem. Leo M., a police officer from Upper Austria who already had searched unsuccessfully for Eichmann in Salzkammergut in the 1940s, was summoned to the Ministry of the Interior in Vienna. According to his report, Minister of the Interior Josef Afritsch, a Social Democrat, personally conveyed the demands of the Republic of Austria:

> What I need from you is a report that proves that Eichmann is a German citizen, for if he is pronounced guilty as an Austrian, we will end up paying through the nose with *Wiedergutmachung* (restitution payments). During this trial a huge number of victims' associations will approach us with demands, understand?[1]

The police officer did and started looking for documents such as school records in Linz, Eichmann's hometown, that might help establish German citizenship. He found nothing. All documents certified him as a citizen of Austria. Nevertheless, the police inspector ultimately did find a solution: Austrian law stipulated loss of Austrian citizenship for any citizen who joined a military organization of a foreign country. Because in the 1930s Eichmann had belonged to the Austrian Legion in the German Reich, the inspector suggested applying this rule. His recommendation found grateful acceptance. "You did that very well," Minister Afritsch reportedly praised Leo M. during a subsequent meeting, relaying that other politicians were gratified as well: "My fellow ministers are much relieved."[2] Because of the nationality of one of the main culprits, there had been apprehensions that Austrian-origin Jewish victims of National Socialism might be able to support their more-than-justified claims against the Republic of Austria. Now any such claims would seem to have been precluded.[3] The minister conveyed the fatherland's gratitude to its faithful civil servant who had turned a fellow Austrian into a German; the gratitude came in the form of a substantial financial reward. Additionally, Leo M. also spent several months in Jerusalem on an official mission as a "trial observer."[4]

At the time Eichmann was arrested in Argentina, not a single one of his former coworkers or subordinates was in custody. The Günther brothers and Theo Dannecker – like Eichmann's immediate supervisor, Gestapo chief Heinrich Müller – were assumed missing or dead. In the immediate postwar years, four Eichmann men had been tried, sentenced to death, and executed: Anton Brunner and Dr. Siegfried Seidl in Vienna, and Karl Rahm and Dieter Wisliceny in Czechoslovakia. Wisliceny had testified as a witness at the Nuremberg trial of the major war criminals. Eichmann's closest associates – Alois Brunner, Anton Burger, and Franz Novak, like their former chief, had used forged papers to assume new identities in order to avoid having to answer for their deeds. In the immediate postwar years a contingent of Eichmann's subordinates had been arrested, tried in Vienna, and sentenced to relatively short periods of imprisonment. And when their periods of pre-trial detention was deducted from their sentences or pardons, then soon were free men. Eventually, amnesties made them respectable Austrian citizens once again, some of them still occupying the apartments they had appropriated for themselves during the expulsion of Vienna's Jews.

Paths of Escape

When military defeat and with it the end of the Third Reich was at hand, Eichmann and the majority of his men were in Prague. Gradually, in several groups, they set off heading southwest. Eichmann, with several of his subordinates, arrived in Salzkammergut at the end of April 1945; his superior, Ernst Kaltenbrunner, also had found refuge there.[5] Thirteen years earlier, Kaltenbrunner, a native of Linz, had persuaded Eichmann to join the SS; now both Upper Austrians had returned home. Eichmann did not, however, go to Altaussee to engage in military resistance, as he stated during his interrogation in Jerusalem, but to salvage part of the loot the SS had gained from the mass murder of the Jews.[6] In early May, Eichmann and his group consisting of Anton Burger, Franz Novak, Richard Hartenberger, Alfred Slawik, and Otto Hunsche hid dozens of crates, the content of which is unknown. One assumption is that, among other things, they contained victims' dental gold. The perpetrators buried the crates or took them to nearby alpine pastures.[7]

Eventually, Eichmann and most of his SS men managed to go underground by using false names or to disappear from the Salzkammergut area. For several months Eichmann himself was interned in various American prisoner-of-war camps in Bavaria, first under the name of Adolf Barth, later as Otto Eckmann, without being recognized as the former SS-Obersturmbannführer. From 1946 to 1950 he lived in northern Germany. Then, with the help of his "old comrades" of the Organisation der ehemaligen SS-Angehörigen, the organization of former SS members (ODESSA), Eichmann fled to Italy. In Rome, under the name of Ricardo Klement and with the support of the German priest Anton Weber, he acquired an International Red Cross passport and traveled to South America.[8] His family soon followed.

By way of Bad Ischl, Novak, Hartenberger, and Slawik escaped to Braunau/Inn where they hired themselves out to a farmer near Burgkirchen. Hartenberger is rumored to have crossed the border to Bavaria a short time later whereas Novak and Slawik kept working as farm laborers near the place of Hitler's birth. Through a former member of the RSHA Department VI, Novak got a fake identity card with the name of Dolak; however, he did not feel safe with this badly forged document, so he asked a helper in his native Wolfsberg, an individual whom he refused to name during his interrogation, to send him the birth certificate of a missing acquaintance named Tragbauer. With this birth certificate he went to Altaussee, registered with the police, and in Gmunden received an identity card with the name of Tragbauer. Shortly thereafter, Tragbauer/Novak and his family moved to Vienna where he started to work as a typesetter.

Because all this time he lived as the companion to his wife whose legal name was Novak, and subsequently Tragbauer/Novak in Austria of the late 1950s, he "no longer feared persecution," and he sought to end "this intolerable state of affairs" and live under his own name once again. In 1957 he filed a petition with the Bezirkshauptmannschaft (the district government office) Wolfsberg for restitution of his Austrian citizenship, of which he had been deprived because of his participation in the Naziputsch of 1934 and his subsequent escape. According to him, the change of identity of this former SS officer did not cause any problems in Wolfsberg.

> Nobody asked too many questions about the reasons for my forfeiture of citizenship. After all, half of Wolfsberg had taken part in that Putsch, too. . . . People in Wolfsberg and at the Bezirkshauptmannschaft knew me and knew perfectly well that I had taken an active part in it. . . . Obviously, they wanted to put the past behind them, and so they reinstated my Austrian citizenship.[9]

His registration with the police in Langenzersdorf near Vienna and a passport with the name Franz Novak completed his change of identity

Only one man of the group around Eichmann at the end of the war was arrested in the summer of 1945, in the Aussee area. Gendarmes jailed Anton Burger in late July for hiding a crate of weapons on an alpine dairy farm. Because he was a former member of the SS, the Austrian police transferred him to the United States occupation authorities in Salzburg, where they interned him as an SS member of unknown rank at Camp Marcus W. Orr in nearby Glasenbach. Not until spring 1947 did the U.S. authorities find out that Burger had been one of Eichmann's coworkers and commandant of Theresienstadt. Only after lengthy questioning by a member of the Army Counterintelligence Corps (CIC) and after being confronted with evidence did Burger admit to some details of his SS career.[10] Asked about his contacts with Eichmann at the end of the war, Burger claimed to have seen Eichmann for the last time in early May 1945, when he helped him transport large amounts of foodstuffs from the valley to some of the alpine dairy farms because Eichmann supposedly planned military action in the mountains around Altaussee. Since his return to Altaussee, Burger, who lived at Fischerndorf 38, had never heard from Eichmann again. No one asked him about his former Altaussee neighbor Vera Liebl at Fischerndorf 8 because the CIC officer interrogating Burger obviously did not notice that in December 1946 the CIC had questioned this woman, supposedly divorced from Eichmann, about the whereabouts of her former husband.[11]

In April 1947 the Czechoslovak government demanded Burger's extradition because of his activities as commandant of Theresienstadt. To indict Burger, the Landesgericht für Strafsachen in Vienna also asked the U.S. authorities for his transfer,[12] but none of this came about, for in mid-June 1947 Burger effortlessly escaped from Camp Marcus W. Orr through a hole in the fence. He left this written message: "To whomever would like to know! Because I consider myself unjustly deprived of my freedom in every way and have no desire whatsoever to remain penned up any longer, I had no other choice. As soon as affairs return to normal, I will contact Austrian authorities. Burger."[13] Of course he did no such thing: Austrian authorities contacted him. After living for four years in Germany and Austria without being recognized, the police arrested him in March 1951 in his native village of Neunkirchen in Lower Austria. After being transferred to Vienna's Favoriten jail of the Landesgericht für Strafsachen, he escaped again in early April after two weeks of detention. Even though Burger contacted his wife and parents in Neunkirchen after his escape, the search for him was unsuccessful.[14] For years neither German nor Austrian authorities were able to trace his whereabouts. By then, Burger, like so many of his "SS-comrades," probably had escaped to South America by way of Italy.

Alois Brunner, after concluding his manhunts in Slovakia, arrived in Vienna in the spring of 1945. According to the concièrge of his apartment building, he and his wife fled Vienna in March or April of that year. They went to Upper Austria, where they found refuge in Lembach, north of the Danube, between Passau and Linz.[15] From the days of the Umschulungslager für Juden, the retraining camps for Jews, in Doppl near Altenfelden, which had been administered by the Zentralstelle in Vienna, Alois Brunner had been acquainted with the innkeepers W., who then owned the largest hotel in Lembach. Brunner's wife and mother-in-law rented from a Mrs. R. in Lembach and stayed there until November 1945. After the war, Alois Brunner supposedly had been interned in an Allied prisoner-of-war camp in Wegscheid under a false name. Anton Brunner reported to have seen Alois Brunner at the end of 1945 "in the uniform of an ordinary infantry soldier" in a prisoner-of-war transport. Supposedly, he had altered his appearance "with a long black moustache."[16]

Apparently Alois Brunner soon moved to what later was to become the Bundesrepublik Deutschland (the Federal Republic of Germany, or BRD). He adopted several aliases, for example, "Alois Schmaldienst." Under this name, which he "borrowed" from a cousin born in 1910 in Hackenberg near Güssing in Burgenland, he was registered between 1947 and 1954 as a resident of Essen-Heisingen, Am Stauseebogen 114.[17] When in 1950 an Austrian passport with that name was sent to the Permit Office of the American occupation authorities in Vienna with the request for approval to enter West Germany, it was recognized as a forgery. Inquiries with the real Alois Schmaldienst revealed that the photograph on the forged passport was that of his cousin Alois Brunner. After his false identity became known to the police, Brunner operated under the name of Dr. Georg Fischer and in the early 1950s moved his field of operations to the Near East.

Despite some glitches, the former SS officers successfully evaded taking responsibility for their deeds. An efficient net of helpers enabled them to change their identities more than once, to live in Austria or West Germany, or to leave Europe altogether. Neither the fences of American internment camps nor the walls of a Viennese prison could contain them.

Defense Strategies

During the Nuremberg Trial, almost all of the top-level officials of the Third Reich presented themselves as the recipients of orders in regard to the roles they played in the destruction of European Jewry, or they pleaded ignorance.

> Schirach knew nothing, Funk knew nothing, Keitel knew nothing, Jodl knew
> nothing, Kaltenbrunner knew nothing.... And yet, all the defendants had an

excuse for their behavior: They had acted on orders, and Adolf Hitler was the man who had given the orders.[18]

Some pretended never to have harbored any antisemitic sentiments; others claimed to have disapproved of persecution measures. "Schacht had tried to help them emigrate. Streicher had been a Zionist. Von Schirach had believed that the deportations from Vienna to Poland 'really had been in the Jews' best interest.'" Kaltenbrunner, the former chief of the RSHA and Heydrich's successor, shifted responsibility to Himmler, Heydrich, and Müller: The decisive orders had passed from Himmler over Müller to Eichmann.[19] Independent of the testimonies of the leading National Socialists before the Nuremberg tribunal, Eichmann's men, whenever they were interrogated by police or in court, exculpated themselves the same way.

Anton Brunner was one of the first of Eichmann's subordinates to be arrested in Austria. After the conclusion of the mass deportations from Vienna in early 1943, the former Social Democrat had been transferred to the Protectorate of Bohemia and Moravia. In the Prague Zentralstelle für jüdische Auswanderung, an organization modelled upon the Vienna Zentralstelle, he was busy, mainly, administering the pilfered property of Czech Jews. After his escape from Prague in May 1945, he had been arrested in Upper Austria two months later and taken to the Vienna police headquarters. During the interrogation he insisted, "not to have held a leading position" at the Zentralstelle für jüdische Auswanderung in Vienna but "merely that of a Sachbearbeiter," a clerk in charge of the registration and "Kommissionierung," "picking," of Jews and the registration of their assets.[20] Only after additional questioning and after being confronted with contradictions did he make a partial confession that came close to the truth:

> In the course of my work at the Zentralstelle für jüdische Auswanderung, I handled about 48 *Kommissionierungen* (each involved the organization of a transport of 1,000 Jews). The transports I organized went to Riga, Minsk, Lublin, Auschwitz, Theresienstadt, and other places. From the accounts of the guard units who returned from these camps . . . I knew that a part of the Jews was liquidated in the camps. . . . I remember how once during [Alois] Brunner's absence a Schutzpolizei lieutenant from the transport escort reported that the Jews were liquidated in the camp. . . . According to my own observations, the Jews, too, must have been aware of what fate awaited them in Poland because they all wanted to go to Theresienstadt, if possible.[21]

In the course of this interrogation Anton Brunner also admitted to having mistreated people although, in doing so, he said, he had done only his "duty" and had tried to avoid brutality.

My immediate supervisor was [Alois] Brunner, the director of our office, to whom I had to report. I experienced Brunner as a brutal, ruthless man who didn't give an inch when it came to Jewish affairs. As was my duty, I followed his orders to the last detail. Sometimes I tried to soften his merciless rules and to intervene for people, but, unfortunately, always without success.[22]

Even before his first questioning session with the examining magistrate, Anton Brunner started revising his confession at the State Police headquarters. In handwritten notes, obviously meant to aid him in preparing additional testimony, he attempted to deny any connection between the Kommissionierungen in Vienna until the end of 1942 and the mass killings in the annihilation camps.

> I don't know to this day whether shootings, gassings, or other inhuman treatment of Jews took place in the reception camps before 1943. That some took place after 1942 I learned only after my arrest. Furthermore, I still question whether any such treatment also was meted out to those Jews who were evacuated through an assembly camp of the Zentralstelle für jüdische Auswanderung in Vienna. If so, I can't very well be held responsible for the deeds of persons whom I did not know and who did not work for me, especially since I . . . had no way of knowing their intentions or their actions.[23]

Then he compared the deportation of Jews from Vienna to the escape of Gestapo personnel and their families from Czechoslovakia, arguing that not just Jews but "the Aryan population" had been "evacuated" as well and "under infinitely worse conditions," as, for example, his own family from Prague. "My wife and my 3½-year-old child who had just been released from the hospital were evacuated just four hours later, destination unknown." Brunner even had the temerity to complain about not having been able to salvage the furniture in his Prague apartment, all of it probably the property of deported Czech Jews: "Our apartment, completely furnished, was seized by the Czechs. Who is going to answer for that in a court of law?"[24]

Before the examining magistrate he retracted his partial confession and justified himself during questioning by claiming not to have known the "ultimate fate of the evacuees in Poland" until 1944 when members of the SS in Prague had told him about "the large-scale annihilation devices, including the gas chambers." Until then he had been sure that the Jews were being sent to a reservation in Poland, where they "would erect a state within a state, replete with their own administrative organizations and social services." He emphasized that he, similar to the Zionists, had envisioned the "foundation of a sovereign Jewish state," although not in Palestine but "somewhere in Africa or America."[25] Brunner's defense strategy was a failure. After listening to more than fifty witnesses, the court pronounced him guilty of having "placed people into excruciating situations and having mistreated them severely because of political malice and through exploitation of his power." Furthermore, "by exploiting authoritative power, he had played a leading role in the resettlement of about 48,000 Austrians, and his activities had "caused the death of many... people."[26] He was sentenced to death by hanging and executed at the end of May 1946.

At the end of May 1945 Josef Weiszl arrived in Vienna from Prague by way of Plziň (Pilsen), Passau, and Lembach, his former "place of work," where he had been in charge of the Umschulungslager für Juden in Doppl. The Staatspolizei arrested him in Vienna in late August 1945. At his first interrogation he declared that he had joined the SD in 1938 through a referral by the state employment service. In the Palais Rothschild he had been responsible for sorting the passports and certificates Jews needed for emigration. He claimed not to have had anything to do with the later Transportverschickungen (transport deportations). He had assumed that "the Jews were sent to Poland for deployment as laborers."[27] When confronted with witness testimonies describing him as a bully and infamous manhunter, Weiszl defended himself by saying that he had mistreated Jews only when they had given him good reason to do so. He denied categorically ever to have done more than "his duty."

> Whenever I drove around in my car and saw someone whose looks resembled those of a Jew, I picked him up, as my duty required, and delivered him at the Sperl school for further processing.... When I left my place of work and I encountered Jews, I was required to turn them in, too. I really don't understand why I of all people am now accused of making Jews take to their heels upon encountering me.[28]

After France's demand for his extradition, Weiszl was turned over to French authorities in 1947. The military court in Paris accused him of having taken part in the deportation of Jews to Auschwitz during his tour of duty in Drancy. He shared the dock with O. R., a Viennese Jew who in 1938 had fled from Austria to France, had been interned in several camps in unoccupied France, and finally, at the end of 1943, had been sent to Drancy, where he worked in the SS-controlled camp police. In February 1949 this man, who under threat of being deported to Auschwitz had helped the SS perform its dirty work, was sentenced to death and executed on July 5, 1949, in Fort de Montrouge, in Arcueil, near Paris. Yet that same military court granted extenuating circumstances to the Viennese SS man who had categorized thousands as able to be transported, and so had aided and abetted their murder in the annihilation camps. He was sentenced to life imprisonment.[29] In 1952 the sentence was commuted to twenty years imprisonment, and in 1955 French authorities released him. In December 1955 Weiszl returned to Vienna and, according to his own testimony, was categorized by the State of Austria as a Spätheimkehrer, a late-repatriated prisoner of war, which entitled him to receive Heimkehrer-Fürsorge, special benefits and privileges. Moreover, even though Weiszl had been sentenced in Paris only for the crimes he committed in France, in 1956 the state prosecutor's office in Vienna granted him immunity from further prosecution in Austria "for having been sentenced by foreign courts already."[30]

Alfred Slawik was arrested in 1946 by the rural police in Mauerkirchen, Upper Austria, after his name appeared on a state police wanted-persons list. After a short internment in the Glasenbach detention camp, the occupation authorities turned him over to the Landesgericht in Vienna in March 1947. Before the interrogating magistrate he swore never to have "mistreated or robbed a Jew."[31] In 1949 the Landesgericht Wien sentenced Slawik, who had participated in the deportations from Vienna, Slovakia, Salonika, and Hungary, to five years in prison. The time of his detention in Glasenbach and his pretrial jail time were applied to the term. After he had served nine months at the correctional institution of Stein, the authorities released him in May 1950. He had completed his sentence.

Ernst Girzick, who in February 1947 had been arrested in the province of Salzburg and interned at Camp Marcus W. Orr in Glasenbach, explained in a written statement that in the course of his work at the Zentralstellen für jüdische Auswanderung in Vienna and Prague and as a member of the Sonderkommando Eichmann in Hungary in 1944 he had "never engaged in any activities or issued any orders in violation of human dignity or had been responsible for the death or mistreatment of Jews or other persons." He merely acknowledged that he had occasionally slapped Jews in the face, which, however, "had not happened more than ten times" in his entire SS career.[32] Girzick, who already in the mid-1930s had been arrested for illegal activities for the NSDAP and fire-cracker attacks in Austria, was turned over to Austrian authorities and in 1948 was sentenced to fifteen years in prison. In December 1953, however, the President of the Republic of Austria granted an amnesty to this recipient of the Nazis' coveted "Blood Order" medal.

Not a single one of the Eichmann men arrested in Austria after the war demonstrated dismay or pangs of conscience over having participated in the orchestrated murder of tens of thousands of people. Instead, they claimed to have known nothing about the annihilation camps, to have acted solely on orders, to have fulfilled their obligations, and never to having harbored any enmity against Jews. Not a single one of these former members of the "Black Order," the SS, owned up to the convictions he had espoused or the deeds he had committed.

From this arsenal of excuses, Adolf Eichmann also adopted important details for his own self-portrayal. Not just during his interrogation in Jerusalem but immediately after his apprehension in Argentina he already delineated the rationale for his lack of responsibility. He did this during his conversations with the Israeli Mossad agent who had apprehended him and guarded him before his removal to Israel. As he explained to Peter Malkin, he had never been an antisemite. Streicher and his newspaper *Der Stürmer* had been repulsive to him. He even trotted out the old stereotype of having had "Jewish friends" and claimed in all seriousness "always to have been fond of Jews."[33] As a participant of the Wannsee Conference, Eichmann did not even pretend to have known nothing about the mass killings but took refuge in his interpretation of obedience: He had been a soldier who had to follow orders. His real goal had been to resettle the Jews, but then the Führer's order for the destruction of the Jews came along. He had never killed a single person. He had not been involved with the concentration camps in any way; his responsibilities had been limited to gathering and transporting people.[34] Malkin could not discover even a trace of bad conscience in Eichmann: "Never, not once, did the man convey anything but the feeling that everything he had done was absolutely appropriate. Not nice necessarily, nor even reasonable, but within its context absolutely correct. There was a job to be done and he did it."[35]

Eichmann followed this same line of defense in Jerusalem. He built up and expanded his version in response to the details that came to the fore during his interrogation or appeared in the documents. When confronted with facts that clearly contradicted his self-characterization, Eichmann took refuge in lies or in denying the authenticity of the documents. That was his response when, during questioning, he was presented with Rademacher's note of September 1941 – "Eichmann suggests shooting."

> Well, then, I must have passed this matter on. Its content makes it perfectly clear to me that what was being said was "nothing else can be done but to shoot." In the interest of clarity I want to add here, though it is really quite unnecessary: Never did I give the order to shoot on my own authority. I always handled matters through official channels, and the information coming from my superiors had been: "Shoot!"[36]

That was an out-and-out lie. Before that telephone call, Eichmann's superiors had not even considered what was to happen to the Jews in Serbia. Even later, during deliberations between the RSHA and the Foreign Office, no order for shootings was issued. The decision was to send a commission of "experts" to Belgrade. When asked about the entire document during the trial, Eichmann, during the main examination (Session 83), as in the cross-examination (Session 97), accused Rademacher of falsifying the document. What the judges recorded in their summary of the Eichmann trial about the credibility of his statements is certainly correct: "The testimony of the accused in this trial was not truthful in spite of his constant protestations of having come to terms with his fate."[37]

After Eichmann's arrest, the whereabouts of other former SS men of Referat IV B 4 were investigated as well. Franz Novak, who since the beginning of the 1960s lived in Vienna once more under his real name, was tried in Vienna. During questioning about his part in the Eichmann Referat in Berlin, he presented himself as "a tiny cog" working "entirely with matters pertaining to transport, such as scheduling and registration."[38] He denied having been informed about the goings on in the extermination camps; as far as he knew, after the failure of the Madagascar Plan, Jews were sent to concentration camps for no reason other than to perform forced labor:

> At this point the expulsion of Jews to work camps and concentration camps, especially Auschwitz, Treblinka, and Lublin began. The justification for doing this went something like this: Because of the war, untold Germans at the front and at home lost their lives while the Jews, who were not drafted, got by unscathed. So, as far as I could tell at first, the plan was to make the Jews work, work for Germany, under the toughest conditions, until the Jewish Question would be solved through the death of these Jews, a death which, no doubt, occurred under the harshest conditions. At first I enjoyed my work at my post; later I lost that enjoyment.[39]

He did not elaborate on what exactly had made his work so enjoyable, but he too insisted that he had not been an antisemite but merely a victim of propaganda:

> I was not a Jew-hater as such, but it is important to call to mind the times, with the tremendous propaganda against the Jews directed from the top. Sure, I was not a friend of the Jews either, but I did not approve of these harsh measures. I couldn't even say whether Eichmann truly was a Jew-hater.[40]

Certainly it must have seemed totally unconvincing that Novak, who in the spring of 1942 had called Dannecker in Paris to tell him to go ahead and transport "all Jews (even the old and those unable to work)" to Auschwitz, had been convinced that those sent to the concentration camps with his assistance would be deployed exclusively in forced labor.[41] "I always supported the deployment

of Jews for hard labor, though later, when women, children, and people unable
to work were taken to the KZs in greater numbers, I wondered whether their
demise was perhaps also hastened by other means."[42] By focusing on German
war victims, however, Novak found it quite easy to dismiss such thoughts:

> Even though I occasionally did consider that those people might very well be
> getting killed there [in the camps], I pushed these thoughts aside since at home
> one witnessed such tremendous suffering. I mention only in passing that my
> wife was bombed out in Berlin and my child contracted smoke poisoning.
> Air raid alerts sounded day and night, and we were constantly on duty to
> recover victims buried in the ruins and remove the dead. Those were brutal
> times, and so people thought differently about brutal measures than they do
> now.[43]

Through other witnesses in this trial it soon became obvious that Novak's
statements were largely self-protective. Hartenberger, his and Eichmann's former coworker, already had been sentenced and, therefore, did not need to
fear further legal steps against him. As a witness in Franz Novak's preliminary
hearing, he stated that "already in 1941 or 1942" more and more particulars
surfaced,

> be it from people coming from the camps to our office, be it by reading the
> files in our office, that the Jews now were being killed outright. For example,
> as were all of us, I was aware of activities of the Einsatzkommandos such as
> Stahlecker's – that they liquidated Jews behind our eastern front. To all of us
> the term "Sonderbehandlung" meant killing. By 1942 we already knew that the
> Jews were being gassed in the camps, that crematoria were in operation, and
> that gold teeth were extracted from the corpses. I did not know anything about
> "Aktion Reinhard" as such but certainly was familiar with the factual details.
> Nothing was conveyed officially; still, all of us in Referat IV B 4, not just the
> members of the SS, knew that the Jews were being gassed. The women typists,
> for example, knew it too.

A female witness who had worked as an office apprentice at the Vienna Zentralstelle für jüdische Auswanderung, and later in Berlin as a secretary for
Eichmann, Günther, and others at Referat IV B 4, confirmed these statements.
   Hartenberger also assured the court emphatically that he had been
informed about the methods of mass destruction:

> I can only repeat that even though Eichmann never mentioned to me anything
> about such measures against the Jews, starting with the typists all the way to
> the top level, everyone in Referat IV B 4 knew about the systematic killing of
> the Jews. We also knew that Jews able to work often were separated from the
> rest and forced to work as long as they were able while the Jews who could not
> work were liquidated. So, if anyone from the Referat insists not to have known

anything about it, he does so for obvious reasons. It simply wasn't a secret at all.[44]

Hartenberger also commented on what some of Eichmann's men thought their fate might be as the end of the NS system was at hand: "The majority of us hoped to disappear or escape somehow by telling ourselves that we could not have acted differently and, after all, had only obeyed orders."[45]

The Secret Service Career of an Ardent Antisemite

At a time impossible to pinpoint precisely, Alois Brunner alias Schmaldienst alias Georg Fischer supposedly took up residence in Damascus as an employee of the CIA-financed "Gehlen Organization," the forerunner of the German Federal Republic's Bundesnachrichtendienst (BND-Intelligence Service), Federal located in Pullach near Munich.[46] Supposedly, the Austrian SS mercenary Otto Skorzeny recruited him in the 1950s to work for a CIA-funded training program for a new Egyptian secret service to be established in Cairo. Brunner also was rumored to represent the Orient Trading Company (OTRACO), an import-export business that, among other things, brokered weapons deals among Europe, North Africa, and the Near East. In Egypt he shared an office with the resident agent of the BND.[47] In Damascus, Brunner-Fischer continued his rise as an employee of the BRD's secret service and the OTRACO. In Syria he also met old acquaintances with good contacts to the Syrian secret service or who worked for the BND, such as Franz Rademacher who, as a senior government official in the Auswärtige Amt, had worked closely with Adolf Eichmann and the RSHA Referat IV B 4.[48] Brunner-Fischer acted as the BND representative for Syria and codirector of OTRACO.[49] In 1960, when confronted with the news that his former superior, Eichmann, had been captured by the Israelis and would stand trial in Jerusalem, he supposedly planned to kidnap Nahum Goldman, the former president of the World Jewish Congress, to force Eichmann's release and already had started preparations.[50]

Apparently, neither Brunner himself nor the CIA and the BND who employed him seemed particularly disturbed about two French military courts having sentenced him to death *in absentia* for a number of crimes. He continued his work for his clients. As long as he enjoyed, and may even continue to enjoy, the protection of the state of Syria, he did not need to worry about being on the "wanted list" of the Austrian Ministry of the Interior State Police since 1946 in connection with paragraphs 3 and 4 of the war crimes law, or about being on the "wanted list" of the Landesgericht für Strafsachen in Vienna since the early 1960s for suspicion of murder. After he narrowly escaped two letter-bomb attempts on his life, his residence, number 7 Ruc Haddad, was guarded around the clock by security forces. By advising the Syrian secret service and perhaps handling weapons deals, he had made himself useful to the political rulers of Syria. Nobody surrenders a bearer of secret information, especially if he is a tried-and-true enemy of those whom the Syrian regime also regards with enmity. When a British journalist queried Syrian government officials about whether Alois Brunner was in Damascus, an official government speaker replied: "I have made enquiries, and we have no such man in Syria." After a short pause he continued: "I think you want to keep good relations with Syria."[51]

Alois Brunner supposedly does not live in Damascus, yet he has given interviews to like-minded people and journalists there. For example, he supposedly spent several days in talks with the Austrian right-wing extremist Gerd Honsik. According to Honsik, whose comments are not necessarily to be taken at face value, Austrian diplomats had seen to Brunner's well-being for years. "Throughout the decades this man from Burgenland, devoured by homesickness, lived in Cairo and Damascus, he derived comfort not only from the friendship of the Syrians and the cordiality of Austrians stationed there professionally: More than anything he derived comfort through the efforts of the former Austrian ambassadors Baron von Waldstetten and Filz who, even without official instructions, looked after the SS officer in the most touching manner. The soirees that Brunner attended in the residences of the Austrian ambassadors were social events where leading representatives of important Austrian and German firms came together."[52] True or false, these statements do not change the fact that Eichmann's deportation specialist, this man who with his Viennese subordinates sent more than one hundred thousand men, women, and children from Austria, Germany, Greece, France, and Slovakia to the gas chambers, has lived more or less undisturbed in Damascus, without ever having been forced to answer for his deeds in a court of law. Syria has consistently refused all requests for extradition.

Pangs of conscience about his more than active contribution to National Socialist genocide policies have not troubled Alois Brunner. Quite the contrary: His stance has not wavered since his letter to his "dear Rudolf" of February 1943. *The Chicago Sun Times* claims that in answer to the question about his part in the persecution of Jews, he replied that the Jews deserved to die because they are "agents of the devil, human scum. I regret nothing and would do it all over again."[53]

Notes

Introduction

1. Raul Hilberg, *The Destruction of the European Jews* (Chicago: Quadrangle Books, 1961), 283. Hilberg coined the term by referring to the three commandants of Theresienstadt (Terezin) – Dr. Siegfried Seidl, Anton Burger, and Karl Rahm – as "all Eichmann's men and Austrians." See also Nora Levin, *The Holocaust: The Destruction of European Jewry 1933–1945* (New York: Schocken, 1973), 478, who also applies the term "Eichmann men" to Seidl, Burger, and Rahm.
2. Robert H. Jackson's Summation for the Prosecution, July 26, 1946.
3. Joe J. Heydecker and Johannes Leeb, eds. *Nuremberg Trial: A History of Nazi Germany as Revealed through the Testimony at Nuremberg* (Cologne: Kiepenheuer & Witsch, 1985).
4. Robert M. Kempner, *Eichmann und Komplizen* (Zurich: Europa Verlag, 1961).
5. Hannah Arendt, *Eichmann in Jerusalem: A Report on the Banality of Evil* (New York: Viking Press, 1963).
6. Hans Mommsen, "Die Realisierung des Utopischen: Die 'Endlösung der Juden-frage' im Dritten Reich," in *Geschichte und Gesellschaft* 9 (1983): n.p.
7. Primo Levi, *The Drowned and the Saved*, trans. Raymond Rosenthal (New York: Summit Books, 1986), 29. An exception was Dr. Hans Frank, the former Governor General of occupied Poland, and one of the defendants at the Nuremberg trial of the main war criminals. But Frank could not very well argue that he hadn't known anything or that he acted entirely in response to orders from above; the International Military Tribunal was in possession of his work diaries.
8. A copy of this letter is deposited at the Landesgericht für Strafsachen Wien, Vr 3388/61 (Lg. Wien). According to Franz Weiss, an expert in matters concerning the Gestapo in Vienna, "dear Rudolf" is probably Ebner's aide Rudolf Wagner, secretary of the Gestapo criminal branch, who functioned as a sort of liaison between the Gestapo in Vienna and the Central Bureau for Jewish Emigration.
9. Gerald Fleming, "It Is the Führer's Wish," extract reprinted from Fleming's *Hitler and the Final Solution* in Donald L. Niewyk, ed. *The Holocaust: Problems and Perspectives of Interpretation*, 2nd ed (Boston: Houghton Mifflin, 1997), 12–13.

10. Dan Diner, "Zwischen Aporie und Apologie: Über Grenzen der Historisierbarkeit des Nationalsozialismus," in Dan Diner, ed. *Ist der Nationalsozialismus Geschichte? Zu Historisierung und Historikerstreit* (Frankfurt: Fischer, 1987), 73.
11. Hilberg, *Destruction,* Quadrangle Books, 39.
12. Hilberg, *The Destruction of the European Jews,* 3rd ed. (New Haven and London: Yale University Press, 2003), 3: 1059.
13. Hilberg's contribution to this discussion is printed in Eberhard Jäckel and Jürgen Rohwer, eds. *Der Mord an den Juden im Zweiten Weltkrieg: Entschlußbildung und Verwirklichung* (Stuttgart: Deutsche Verlaganstalt, 1985), 187.
14. Ibid.
15. Saul Friedländer, "Vom Antisemitismus zur Judenvernichtung: Eine historiographische Studie zur nationalsozialistischen Judenpolitik und Versuch einer Interpretation," in Jäckel and Rohwer, 48.
16. Konrad Kwiet, "Judenverfolgung und Judenvernichtung im Dritten Reich: Ein historiographischer Überblick," in Diner, *Ist der Nationalsozialismus Geschichte?* 254 *ff.*
17. Gerhard Botz, "Stufen zur Ausgliederung der Juden aus der Gesellschaft: Die österreichischen Juden vom 'Anschluß' zum 'Holocaust,'" *Zeitgeschichte* 14 (1987): 359.
18. Günther Anders, *Besuch im Hades,* 2nd ed. (Munich: Beck, 1985), 184 *ff.*

1. Eichmann and the Development of the "Vienna Model"

1. Bundesarchiv Koblenz (BAK), R 58/486, fol. 28, RFSS Sicherheitsdienst, *Blitztelegramm,* SD-Hauptamt71014, 11.11.1938, 13:10, II-1, an SD-Führer des SS-Oberabschnitts Donau, z. Hd. v. SS-Staf. Stahlecker, i.V., signed SS-Sturmbannführer Ehrlinger.
2. Ibid.
3. Internationaler Militärgerichtshof, *Der Prozeß gegen die Hauptkriegsverbrecher vor dem Internationalen Militärgerichtshof Nürnberg,* (IMT), Nuremberg, 1948, 28: 499 *ff.,* doc. 1816 P. S., incomplete minutes of the "Besprechung über die Judenfrage unter Vorsitz von Feldmarschall Göring" on November 12, 1938; Bernhard Lösener, "Als Rassereferent im Reichsministerium des Inneren," *Vierteljahrshefte für Zeitgeschichte* 9 (1961): 264 *ff.*; Lösener participated in this conference.
4. Gerhard Botz, *Nationalsozialismus in Wien: Machtübernahme und Herrschaftssicherung 1938/39* (Buchloe: DVO, 1988), 96–97; and Karl Stuhlpfarrer, "Antisemitismus, Rassenpolitik und Judenverfolgung in Österreich nach dem Ersten Weltkrieg," in Anna Drabek et al. *Das österreichische Judentum* (Vienna: Jugend und Volk, 1974), 154, have discussed the efforts of the National Socialist rulers to subdue the wild excesses. For a discussion of the tradition of antisemitism, which from the last third of the 19th century constituted a part of Austrian political culture, see Wolfgang Häusler, "Toleranz, Emanzipation und Antisemitismus," in Anna Drabek et al., 83 *ff.*; Peter Pulzer, *Die Entstehung des politischen Antisemitismus in Deutschland und Österreich 1867–1914* (Gütersloh: S. Mohn, 1966); Ivar Oxaal et al., eds. *Jews, Antisemitism and Culture in Vienna* (London and New York: Routledge & Kegan Paul, 1987).

5. During an interrogation in Jerusalem, Eichmann presented himself as the inventor of the idea. See Jochen von Lang, ed. *Das Eichmann-Protokoll: Tonbandaufzeichnung der israelischen Verhöre* (Berlin: Severin & Siedler, 1982), 50. Heinz Höhne, among others, popularized this version in *Der Orden unter dem Totenkopf* (Frankfurt: Fischer, 1969), 310. "Untersturmführer [Eichmann] fell victim to an intoxication of organization: Suddenly he discovered that he could plan and give orders. He conceived an idea. He wanted to put an end to the confusion of police, state, and party organizations who were all involved in organizing the emigration of the Jews by centralizing them all – agencies and Jewish representatives alike."

6. Kurt Pätzold, "Von der Vertreibung zum Genozid," in Dietrich Eichholtz and Kurt Gossweiler, eds. *Faschismusforschung: Positionen, Probleme, Polemik* (Berlin: Akademie, 1980), 188, writes that "since spring 1938 the expulsion of the Jews from Vienna was handled in such a way as to represent a new level of persecution. . . . That the center of persecution [Eichmann's Zentralstelle] functioned as it did was mainly the result of brutal persecutions Jewish people were exposed to day by day through Gestapo, National Socialist organizations, and all other institutions of the fascist state."

   Susanne Heim and Götz Aly, "Die Ökonomie der 'Endlösung,'" in Götz Aly, ed. *Sozialpolitik und Judenvernichtung: Gibt es eine Ökonomie der Endlösung? Beiträge zur nationalsozialistischen Gesundheits- und Sozialpolitik* (Berlin: Rotbuch, 1987), 5:26–27, describe the "Vienna Model" for anti-Jewish policy as almost entirely the result of population and economic planning. "The de-Jewification of the Austrian economy was well planned and progressed quickly. Simultaneously, Eichmann's team saw to it that people who had been deprived of work, property, and social rights disappeared as quickly as possible through emigration."

7. Michael Geyer, *Deutsche Rüstungspolitik 1860–1980* (Frankfurt: Suhrkamp, 1984), 158, pointing to the connection between the National Socialist preparation and execution of the war that the "production" of an "altered social order by the National Socialists needs to be taken very seriously," which, in his opinion, was not "simply a matter of social-imperialist diversionary tactics or propagandistic window dressing to placate the man in the street." Part of the spaces, people, and objects conquered in the war immediately went to the armament industry. Another "was passed on in the form of chances for participation in building new social rule and as a chance for social advancement." Even when he cautions from referring too hastily to "the creation of an aristocracy of workers, bureaucrats, and soldiers" (167) since these "chances for authority" did not equal those of the "upper and propertied classes," he does refer the reader to a basic connection: "The place of participation in the political process and with it the openness of distribution and redistribution . . . was replaced by rule for everyone in a racist social order which produced its own forms of competition for power and corruption. These ultimately did connect the major and minor rulers with one another in spite of all differences." Geyer also discusses this connection of state, society, ideological politics in National Socialism and participation in "The Nazi State Reconsidered," in Richard Bessel, ed. *Life in the Third Reich* (Oxford and New York: Oxford University Press, 1987).

8. Botz, *Nationalsozialismus in Wien*, 463, summarizes a part of this connection, especially in respect to housing policies, as "negative social policy." Mommsen, "Die Realisierung des Utopischen," 400, emphatically cites "anti-Semitic excesses

in Austria immediately following the Anschluß" as examples of these material interests and argues that personal enrichment with Jewish property was a part of daily life in the Third Reich, which, consequently could be considered as a "system of publicly sponsored corruption."

9. Kwiet, "Judenverfolgung und Judenvernichtung im Dritten Reich," 249, however, differentiates between the NSDAP or rather its mass organizations, the state bureaucracy, and the police-administrative apparatus of repression.

10. Wolfgang Scheffler, *Judenverfolgung im Dritten Reich* (Berlin: Colloquium, 1964), 17 *ff.*; Uwe Dietrich Adam, *Judenpolitik im Dritten Reich* (Düsseldorf: Droste, 1972), 46 *ff.*; and Wolfgang Benz, ed. *Die Juden in Deutschland 1933–1945* (Munich: Beck, 1988), discuss anti-Semitic measures and the situation of the Jews in Germany during the first years of National Socialist rule.

11. Norbert Kampe, "'Endlösung' durch Auswanderung? Zu den widersprüchlichen Zielvorstellungen antisemitischer Politik bis 1941," in Wolfgang Michalka, ed. *Der Zweite Weltkrieg: Analysen, Grundzüge, Forschungsbilanz* (Munich: Piper, 1989), 827 *ff.*

12. For a discussion of the efforts and possibilities of transferring property, see Avraham Barkai, *Vom Boycott zur 'Entjudung': Der wirtschaftliche Existenzkampf der Juden im Dritten Reich 1933–1943* (Frankfurt: Fischer, 1988), 60 *ff.*

13. BAK R 7/3153, fol. 3, minutes of a meeting of the directors of foreign exchange offices and supervisory organizations within the Ministry of Economics on November 22, 1938.

14. About Heydrich and the establishment of the SD see Shlomo Aronson, *Reinhard Heydrich und die Frühgeschichte von Gestapo und SD* (Stuttgart: Deutsche Verlagsanstalt, 1984), 197; for a biography of Heydrich, see Günther Deschner, *Reinhard Heydrich: Statthalter der totalen Macht* (Esslingen: Bechtle, 1977).

15. Aronson, 61, quoting Paul Leffler, the former SD chief of staff.

16. See Hans Buchheim, "Die SS – das Herrschaftsinstrument," in Hans Buchheim, et al., eds. *Anatomie des SS Staates* (Munich: Deutscher Taschenbuch Verlag, 1982), 1: 37 *ff.* for a discussion of Himmler's assuming command of the political police in the German states.

17. See Max Gallo, *Der schwarze Freitag der SA: Die Vernichtung des revolutionären Flügels der NSDAP durch Hitlers SS im Juni 1934* (Vienna: F. Molden, 1972), for details on "The Night of the Long Knives," the murder of SA leaders and General Kurt von Schleicher.

18. Behrends led that office until 1937, followed by the economist and lawyer Dr. Otto Ohlendorf. The chief of the SD for matters abroad was Heinz Yost.

19. BAK R 58/544, fol. 34, note II-112–145/37, Wi.[sliceny], April 31 [sic], 1937 to II-1, Re: Guidelines and Requests to the Oberabschnitte, signed II-112.

20. See Eichmann's handwritten resumé of July 1937 in Jochen von Lang, ed. *Eichmann-Protokoll.*

21. BAK R 58/991, fol. 35, report on the status of work in Referat II-112 in combating Jews, August 28, 1936, signed Schröder.

22. Consult Leonard Baker, *Hirt der Verfolgten: Leo Baeck im Dritten Reich* (Stuttgart: Klett/Cotta Verlag), 280 *ff.* for details about Kareski, the President of the Reichsvertretung der deutschen Juden, and his disputes with Leo Baeck.

23. BAK R 58/991, fol. 56, II-112 Activities Report for October 1, 1936-February 15, 1937, signed Schröder.

24. BAK R 58/991, fol. 69, Situation Report for March 1–March 15, 1937, signed Eichmann, SS H'schaf.

25. Ibid., fol. 71.

26. For Six's biography, consult Aronson, 208.

27. BAK R 58/991, fol. 72, II-112 Activity Report, February 16-July 5, 1937.

28. BAK R 58/544, fol. 28, II-112 Note of April 7, 1937, signed SS-Hauptscharführer Wisliceny.

29. Ibid.

30. BAK R 58/544, fol. 35, II-112 Guidelines, April 21, 1937, signed Wisliceny. In this set of guidelines, Wisliceny also argues that because of "the prohibition of individual activities against Jewish economic enterprises," the Jews enjoyed a "degree of protection through Reichswirtschaftsministerium," (fol. 33).

31. BAK R 58/544, fol. 66, II-112 Hagen an II-1 z. H. SS-Sturmbannführer Dr. Six, June 8, 1937.

32. BAK R 58/954, fol. 1a, II-112 Hg/Pi, Top Secret Command Action! Report Re: Polkes, Feivel, Tel Aviv, June 16, 1937.

33. BAK R 58/623, fol. 22, II-112 memorandum from Eichmann to II-1 Re: Discussion of SS-Hpt. Scharf. Eichmann with SS-O'Scharf. Hagen with Dr. Reichert concerning travel to Palestine, September 2, 1937.

34. BAK R 58/623, fol. 23, Eichmann to II-1 Re: journey abroad, September 1, 1937.

35. BAK R 58/623, fol. 20, file entry of September 4, 1937, Re: journey Hagen and Eichmann, signed Six, SS-Sturmbannführer.

36. BAK R 58/954, fol. 11 ff., report on the Palestine-Egypt journey by SS-Hptscharf. Eichmann and SS-O'Scharf. Hagen, November 4, 1937.

37. BAK R 58/991, fol. 89, II-112, Hg/Pi, to II-1 Stbf. Re: Report on Department Reconstruction at II-1, December 7, 1937, signed Hagen.

38. BAK R 58/544, fol. 122, II-112 Hg/Pi, November 22, 1937, to II-1 Stbf., signed Hagen.

39. Carl Zuckmayer, *Als wär's ein Stück von mir* (Frankfurt: Fischer, 1966), 71–72.

40. Yad Vashem 0–1/ 208; Dr. Ludwig Wechsler's report "From Vienna to Dachau and Buchenwald," was written in Basle in 1939–1940.

41. Leo Lauterbach, "The Jewish Situation in Austria: A Report Submitted to the Executive of the Zionist Organization," April 29, 1938, cited by Herbert Rosenkranz, *Verfolgung und Selbstbehauptung: Die Juden in Österreich 1938–1945* (Vienna: Herold, 1978).

42. Botz, *Nationalsozialismus in Wien*, 98 ff.

43. Ibid., 94, quoting the *Wiener Zeitung*, March 14, 1938.

44. Allgemeines Verwaltungsarchiv, (AVA), Bestand (holdings) Reich Commissar for the Reunification of Austria with the German Reich (Rk, Box 103, folder 2010), memorandum from the Chief of the Security Police to the Special Party Commissar in Austria, SS-Gruppenführer Bürckel, March 17, 1938, Re: Excesses in Austria, signed Heydrich. Though on a smaller scale, before 1938 "wild" antisemitic excesses not sanctioned by the national party leadership in Germany were a problem for administrators in Germany as well. See Mommsen, "Der nationalsozialistische

Polizeistaat und die Judenverfolgung vor 1938," *Vierteljahrshefte für Zeitgeschichte* 10 (1962): 68 *ff.*

45. Ibid.

46. AVA, Rk 293 (4000); in a memorandum of the Gau leadership of the NSDAP Vienna dated March 22, 1938, Heydrich considered it "entirely reasonable if all sections of the party were to demonstrate their activist positions by drastically impressing on the former rulers and their backers the dawn of a new era through arrests, confiscations, and the like." He cautioned, however, about dissipation through individual actions and about upsetting the "harmonious cooperation of police executive order and political guidance of people."

47. Quoted by Botz, *Nationalsozialismus in Wien*, 97.

48. Heydrich to Bürckel March 17, 1938, AVA, Rk 103 (2010).

49. See Bürckel's response to lootings of March 19, 1938 in *Widerstand und Verfolgung in Wien 1934–1945* (Vienna: Dokumentationsarchiv des österreichischen Widerstandes, [DÖW]), 1976), 3: 204–05.

50. AVA, Rk 53, Gestapo – Gestapa, message transmission, telegram RMDI Berlin No. 527, March 21, 1938, to the Executive for Austria in Vienna, signed Reich and Prussian Minister of the Interior, Stuckart.

51. Quoted by Botz, *Nationalsozialismus in Wien*, 97.

52. *Völkischer Beobachter*, 26 April 1938.

53. Hans Witek, "'Arisierungen' in Wien: Aspekte nationalsozialistischer Enteignungspolitik 1938–1940," in Emmerich Tálos et al., eds. *NS-Herrschaft in Österreich* (Vienna: Verlag für Gesellschaftskritik, 1988), 199 *ff.*, traces the stages of Aryanization of the Austrian economy and its various types of beneficiaries.

54. *Völkischer Beobachter*, 16 April 1938.

55. Charles J. Kapralik, "Erinnerungen eines Beamten der Wiener Israelitischen Kultusgemeinde 1938/39," *Leo Baeck Institute Bulletin* 58 (1981): 8. I thank Doron Rabinovic for drawing my attention to this article.

56. Jürgen Egyptien, ed., *Herr Moriz Deutschösterreicher: Eine jüdische Erzählung zwischen Assimilation und Exil* (Graz: Drosche, 1988). The manuscript of this highly autobiographical anonymous story probably dates from 1939–1940.

57. Kapralik, 52 *ff.*

58. See the reconstructed minutes of a conference in the Reichsstatthalterei (Office of Under Secretary Keppler, Bureau of Counselor of State Eberhard) on May 17, 1938, signed Friedrich Neumann and Josef Rosental, Yad Vashem 0 30/9–3. The participants on the "National Socialist side were Fritz Kraus, Magister of Business Administration and leading specialist of the Counselor of State Otto Eberhardt, and Dr. Rajakovics of the law offices of lawyer Dr. Gallop." Representing the Jewish side were Dr. Alfred Neumann and other signatories. A main issue of this meeting was that many Austrian Jews did have exit permits to leave Vienna and entry permits for other countries but lacked the necessary travel funds. "All these people will immediately receive the necessary monies from a fund administered by Mr. Kraus. For this purpose a Jewish organization is to make a list of these persons and to submit it to the 'Aktion Gildemeester.' That organization, in turn, passes the list to the bureau of Counselor of State Eberhard, which transfers the necessary funds to the Bureau Gildemeester." In February 1939 the funds administered by Kraus were organized into the so-called Emigration Funds Wien. See Rosenkranz, 83 *ff.*, for details on Aktion Gildemeester and the emigration fund.

59. AVA, Rk 144 (2160, vol. 3), note concerning the Jewish Question in Austria, n.d. Since the Staatskommissar's memorandum on private enterprise, "Zweite Ergänzung zu den Vorschlägen für eine wirkungsvolle Durchführung der Entjudung" of October 21, 1938, AVA, Rk 145 (2160) refers to it, Bürckel's note must have been written earlier that fall.

60. BAK R 58/991, fol. 107 *ff.*, Activities Report of Section II-112, January 1-June 30, 1938.

61. Hannah Arendt, *Eichmann in Jerusalem: Ein Bericht von der Banalität des Bösen* (Reinbek: Rowohlt, 1963), 73.

62. BAK R 58/982, fol. 2, the materials Sonderkommando Hagen-Eichmann brought to Vienna consisted of lists of Jewish organizations and personal files. See file 11–112, Dr. Kn/SC, March 14, 1938, Re: Österreich, signed: SS-Obersturmführer Knochen; SD-Hauptamt, Sonderkommando II-112, Vienna, April 9, 1938, to II-1, Re: List of arrested persons on instruction of II-1112, signed Hagen, BAK R 59/982, fol. 13.

63. BAK R 58/982, fol. 4; in a note for SS-U'Stuf. Hagen dated March 23, 1938, Hagen was instructed to "once more expend all his energies concerning the Rothschild archives."

64. Lauterbach, 48.

65. Ibid., 49.

66. BAK R 58/544, fol. 153, note II-112, 18–1, Ech/Pi, April 19, 1938, Re: Consultation with SS-O'Stubaf. Six in matters of SD-Oberabschnitt Österreich, signed II-112 3 Eichmann.

67. BAK R 58/982, fol. 15, letter from Eichmann to Hagen, Vienna, April 23, 1938, signed: Adolf.

68. Ibid., fol. 16.

69. Ibid., fol. 20, letter from Eichmann to Hagen, Vienna, May 8, 1938, signed: Adolf.

70. Ibid., fol. 19; in a letter to Hagen, he stated: "In a sense it will become 'my' paper."

71. Ibid., fol. 20.

72. BAK R58/996, fol. 177, file entry II-112, HG/Pe., July 15, 1938, Re: Interrogation of prisoners in protective custody.

73. Kapralik, 57.

74. For the history of the Joint Distribution Committee, consult Yehuda Bauer, *American Jewry and the Holocaust: The American Joint Distribution Committee 1939–1945* (Jerusalem & Detroit: Wayne State University Press, 1982).

75. Letter to Hagen dated May 8, 1938, fol. 21.

76. BAK R 58/613, fol. 39, see Hagen's file entry concerning SS-Untersturmführer Eichmann, Oberabschnitt Österreich; Six's Memorandum from II-1 to SS-Oberführer Naumann, SD-Oberabschnitt Österreich, Re: SS-Untersturmführer Eichmann, May 16, 1938, BAK R 58/613, fol. 45.

77. BAK R 58/613, fol. 43, file entry by Dr. Six of June 30, 1938, Re: Jewish Department in Austria.

78. BAK R 58/613, fol. 42, memorandum by Hagen to I-1 Untersturmführer Gera of July 11, 1938; Section II-112 Activities Report January 1-June 30, 1938, BAK R 58/991, fol. 120.

79. Lang, document appendix, citing personnel report on SS-Untersturmführer Adolf Eichmann, Reichssicherheitshauptamt Department II-1, SD-Führer of SS-Oberabschnitt Donau, signed SD-Führer SS Oberabschnitt Donau.

80. Yad Vashem, O 30/9–4, "Entwurf des Aktionsprogramms einer zu gründenden 'Zentralstelle für die Auswanderung der Juden Österreichs,'" unsigned, undated; see also Rosenkranz, 121–22.
81. Stuhlpfarrer, 158.
82. BAK R 58/486, fol.1, SD-Führer of the SS-Oberabschnitt Donau, II-112, Ech./Ne., to the SD-Hauptamt, Re: Creation of a Zentralstelle für Jüdische Auswanderung in Vienna, Wien IV, Prince-Eugenstr. 22, undated.
83. Eichmann Trial document, (Police d'Israel PDI), 1521, telex of the RFSS Sicherheits-Dienst to SD-Führer of SS-Oberabschnitt Österreich, dated August 26, 1938, signed by authority of Ehrlinger.
84. BAK R 58/486, fol. 6, II-112, F 112 1, Hg/Pi, to I-112, September 12, 1938.
85. Ibid.
86. Ibid., fol. 7.
87. Franz Novak's testimony, during an interrogation, Landesgericht für Strafsachen, Wien, March 20, 1961, 27b Vr 529/61.
88. Lang, 55.
89. *Moriz Deutschösterreicher*, 77.
90. Ibid.
91. Ibid.
92. Ibid.
93. Ibid.
94. BAK R 58/486, fol. 26, from the Zentralstelle für Jüdische Auswanderung in Vienna, G1 Bbr. 952/38, Ech/R, October 21, 1938, to the SD-HauptmantII-112, Berlin, signed Eichmann.
95. According to the handwritten notes, paragraphs, and signatures in the margins, both Hagen and Six saw Eichmann's report.
96. Especially the Austrian Minister of Finance and Commerce Fischböck made recommendations based on the already advanced state of Aryanization in the Ostmark that were news to his counterpart in Germany but met with Göring's enthusiasm. See "Besprechung über die Judenfrage unter Vorsitz von Feldmarschall Göring," IMT, 28: 524 *ff.*
97. See Adam, 209; in answer to Göring's question what the assembled gentlemen expected in response to this "contribution," Reich Commissar Bürckel replied that "The Viennese Jews will be very much in favor of it," IMT, 28: 537.
98. IMT, 28: 532.
99. BAK R 58/276, fol. 195, Generalfeldmarschall Göring, the deputy in charge of the four-year plan, to the Reich Minister of the Interior in Berlin, January 24, 1939.
100. IMT, 26: 266–67.
101. Lg. Wien, Vr 2729/63, Franz Novak's testimony.
102. See Adam, 229; for a discussion of "Normenstaat" and "Maßnahmestaat," consult Ernst Fraenkel, *Der Doppelstaat* (Frankfurt: Europäische Verlagsanstalt, 1974).
103. BAK R 58/623, fol. 67 *ff.* II-112/27–3, dated June 15, 1939, "Das Judentum in Deutschland," initialed by Hagen.
104. BAK R 58/544, fol. 211, Director II, Sx/Scho. to SS-Gruppenführer Heydrich, June 26, 1939, signed: Six.

105. On this topic, see Witek, 199 *ff*; and Hans Safrian and Hans Witek, eds. *Und keiner war dabei: Dokumente des alltäglichen Antisemitismus in Wien 1938* (Vienna: Picus, 1988), 95 *ff*.

106. Staatskommissar in der Privatwirtschaft und Leiter der Vermögensverkehrsstelle, "Bericht über die Entjudung der Ostmark, *Stichtag* 1. Feber 1939," 43, (State Kommissar of Private Enterprise and Chief of the *Vermögensverkehrsstelle*, report on the de-Judaization of Austria as of February 1, 1939).

107. Though at first glance it may seem that the "Parteibuchwirtschaft," the exploitation of party membership, was an Austrian specialty, this was not the case. For details see Christoph Schmidt, "Zu den Motiven 'Alter Kämpfer' in der NSDAP," in Detlev Peukert and Jürgen Reulecke, eds. *Die Reihen fast geschlossen: Beiträge zur Geschichte des Alltags unterm Nationalsozialismus* (Wuppertal: Hammer, 1981), 21 *ff*. After analyzing 1936–37 Kampfberichte, reports of the so-called Alte Kämpfer from the Gau Hesse-Nassau, Schmidt concludes that for the majority of the Träger des Goldenen Ehrenzeichens, the golden badge of honor of the NSDAP had been worth their efforts and had paid off: "The description of the Kampfzeit, the struggle for political power especially in the last year or two before Hitler came to power, finds closure and fulfillment in the individual Reproduktionsbasis, basis of reproduction, guaranteed by the influence and protection of the party."

108. Quoted in Botz, *Nationalsozialsmus in Wien*, 227.

109. NSDAP personnel file of the Gau Wien No. 49.965, Karl Rahm's statement in the NSDAP personnel questionnaire for application for a temporary membership card and record of membership in Upper Austria, May 27, 1938.

110. Ibid., questionnaire of the Betreuungsstelle, Lower Austria signed by Karl Rahm on April 26, 1938.

111. Ibid., letter from Karl Rahm to the personnel office of the City of Vienna and questionnaire of the Magistratsdirektion der bundesunmittelbaren Stadt Wien (the director's office of the municipality of Vienna, personnel division) dated April 26, 1938.

112. Ibid., the chief of the NS-Betreuungsstelle for the Gau Wien, engineer Hanns Blaschke, dated May 25, 1938, Re: Preferential Employment of Alte Kämpfer, Group III.

113. Karl Rahm's Questionnaire of the R u. S [Rasse- und Siedlungshauptamt], Race and Settlement Headquarters, with handwritten resumé, April 30, 1940, Berlin Document Center (BDC), NSDAP central file, SS-Führer and R U. S-Headquarters, Karl Rahm.

114. NSDAP personnel file Vienna No. 49. 965 Letter from the State Criminal Police, Central Office Vienna, Department 1A, dated December 5, 1938, to the Gau leadership of the NSDAP, Re: Karl Rahm's application.

115. At the end of the war Rahm was arrested in Czechoslovakia, tried in 1947, sentenced to death and executed.

116. Personnel file of NSDAP-Gau Vienna No. 308. 876, Anton Zita's questionnaire from the Betreuungsstelle für die alten Parteigenossen und Angehörigen der Opfer der nationalsozialistischen Bewegung (Support Organization for Old Party Comrades and Families of Those Sacrificed for the National Socialist Movement) in the Gau Vienna, dated April 24, 1938.

117. For more details on the disputes and group in-fighting in which the members of the SS retained the upper hand, see Wolfgang Rosar, *Deutsche Gemeinschaft: Seyss-Inquart und der Anschluß* (Vienna: Europa, 1971); the point of view of an embittered SA Kämpfer who ended up empty handed when positions were handed out is recorded in Alfred Persche, "Erinnerungen aus der Geschichte der nationalsozialistischen Machtergreifung in Österreich 1936–1938," DÖW, unpublished manuscript.

118. See a detailed discussion of the National Socialist insurrection in Gerhard Jagschitz, *Der Putsch: Die Nationalsozialisten 1934 in Österreich* (Graz:Verlag Steiermark, 1976); for the military confrontations, especially the fighting in Carinthia, see Botz, *Gewalt in der Politik: Attentate, Zusammenstöße, Putschversuche, Unruhen in Österreich 1918–1938*, 2nd ed (Munich: W. Fink, 1983), 272.

119. Lg. Vienna, Vr 2729/63, interrogation of Franz Novak, February 1, 1961. "After being posted from Vienna to Prague and Katowice, I was posted to the RSHA Berlin on December 20, 1939." Franz Novak, handwritten resumé for his R. u. S. file, BDC, documents Franz Novak. He had followed Eichmann to the Reichszentrale für Jüdische Auswanderung, the Berlin Referat IV D 4, and finally joined Eichmann in Hungary in 1944. In September 1941 he described himself as a "senior clerk" in the RSHA Referat IV D 4. During the time when the RSHA-Referat IV B 4 was in charge of the deportations into concentration and extermination camps of Jews in much of Europe, Novak was responsible for setting up the timetables and coordinating rail traffic to guarantee that transportation to such places as Auschwitz functioned without a hitch.

120. See Jagschitz, 159 about the fights near Kollerschlag.

121. Lg. Wien, Vr 6300/58, copy of from Anton Burger's resumé, probably written in 1937.

122. The SA "legionnaires" housed at the Sterneck Plaza were infamous for their pogrom-like forays in Vienna's second municipal district, Vienna's old ghetto.

123. BDC records on Anton Burger; R.u..S. questionnaire, Burger Anton, SS membership application, signed February 12, 1939. In 1941–42 Burger directed the "Liaison Office of the Zentralstelle für jüdische Auswanderung Prague" in Brno, and then served for a time as commandant of the Theresienstadt camp. In early 1944 he was transferred to Greece to deport Greek Jews from the mainland and the islands to Auschwitz.

124. In Alois Brunner's handwritten resumé accompanying his R.u.S. questionnaire in BDC file Alois Brunner.

125. Personnnel file of the NSDAP Gau Wien No. 340. 051; NSDAP personnel questionnaire for application for a temporary membership card and record of membership in Upper Austria, signed Brunner, Alois, June 29, 1938.

126. BDC file Brückler.

127. BDC file Girzick, from Girzick's handwritten resumé in the R.u. S. personnel file dated November 11, 1938.

128. Instituted in March, 1934, this Nazi Party decoration had originally been designated as the *Ehrenzeichen vom 9. November 1923* to recognize the participants of Hitler's 1923 Munich *Putsch*. Beginning in 1938, it also honored "severely wounded Nazi members and those who had been sentenced to prison terms in Germany, Austria, and the Sudetenland."

129. Personnel file of the NSDAP Gau Wien No. 253.480, memorandum of the Betreu-
    ungsstelle to the tramway division of the municipality of Vienna dated December
    12, 1938. In the questionnaire of the Betreuungsstelle he listed "Student" as his
    profession until 1934; from 1934 to 1936 he had worked as a day laborer at a
    textile factory.

130. BDC personnel file Herbert Gerbing, in Gerbing's handwritten resumé dated
    October 27, 1938.

131. BDC personnel file Richard Hartenberger, in Hartenberger's handwritten resumé
    dated May 5, 1939.

132. Personnel file of the NSDAP Gau Wien No. 6578, political certificate for Josef
    Weiszl from the NSDAP Gau Wien.

133. Before 1938, in addition to studying history at the University of Vienna,
    Dr. Wilhelm Höttl had worked for the National Socialist news service and
    Kaltenbrunner; see Peter R. Black, *Ernst Kaltenbrunner: Ideological Soldier of
    the Third Reich* (Princeton: Princeton University Press, 1984). Höttl was chief
    of a section at the SD-Unterabschnitt Vienna in 1938 and later worked for the
    Department VI – the RSHA's news service abroad. Höttl's notarized deposition
    as a witness at the Nuremberg Trial is the source of the statement that six million
    Jews fell victim to the National Socialist genocide in Europe; see also Raul Hilberg,
    Die Vernichtung der europäischen Juden (Frankfurt: Fischer, 1990), 3: 1280. For
    details on Höttl's help, see the protocol of the accused Josef Weiszl of October 18,
    1946, Lg. Wien, Vr 658/46.

134. Lg. Wien, Vr 4574/45, Anton Brunner's statements during his interrogations in
    1945.

135. Lg. Wien, Vr 4969/47, see the testimony of witness E.G. in the protocol of the
    main session of the People's Court Vienna against Richard Hartenberger, March
    2, 1950.

2. The Unsuccessful Beginning: The Deportations to Nisko on the River San

1. Höhne, *Der Orden unter dem Totenkopf*, 322. In this matter Höhne also was
   taken in by Eichmann as he reiterates Eichmann's defense strategy during his
   interrogation in Jerusalem, claiming that the purpose of the Nisko operation was
   to give the Jews a territory of their own: "The two SS leaders [Stahlecker and
   Eichmann] proposed to establish a reservation for Jews in the extreme eastern
   part of German-occupied Poland where the Jews were to be concentrated. They
   went to Poland to look for a suitable large area. Southwest of Lublin, near the
   small town of Nisko, they found it. 'We encountered a huge area.' Eichmann's
   enthusiasm resembled the ecstasy of a prophet who has found the land of his
   dreams. 'We saw the San, hamlets, market towns, villages and realized: This is it.
   We thought, why not resettle Poles for a change and give the Jews a large territory
   right here?'" See also Arendt, *Eichmann in Jerusalem*, 105: "If Eichmann's version
   of the Nisko adventure is correct, and there is no reason not to believe him,
   he or...Franz Stahlecker must have anticipated this development months in
   advance."

2. At the end of 1941 or the beginning of 1942, the Israelitische Kultusgemeinde Vienna (IKG) created a statistical document about Jewish emigration from Austria. Entitled "Die Jüdische Wanderung aus der Ostmark," it is deposited in the Central Archive for the History of the Jewish People (CAHJP), A/W 2529/2. According to this document, in the spring of 1938, 180,000 Jews belonged to the Kultusgemeinden in Austria, 165,000 of them living in Vienna. Of those, approximately 105,000 had emigrated by the time World War II started. See, also in the library of the IKG Vienna, the English-language IKG Report concerning its activities from March 1938 until the end of 1939. How many of the 26,000 or so "non-Mosaic Jews" had been driven from Austria by that time remains unknown.

3. AVA, Rk. 31 (1710), memorandum from the Ortsgruppenleitung (local SA section office) Rossau to the Kreisleiter (district party leader) and Kreis-Geschäftsführung (district party management office), October 3, 1939, Re: Jewish Question, signed: "Heil Hitler!" Ortsgruppenleiter; the signature is indecipherable. See also Botz, *Wohnungspolitik und Judendeportationen in Wien 1938 bis 1945: Zur Funktion des Antisemitismus als Ersatz nationalsozialistischer Sozialpolitik* (Vienna: Geyer, 1975), 85–86.

4. Ibid.

5. Ibid.

6. See Helmut Krausnick and Hans-Heinrich Wilhelm, *Die Truppe des Weltanschauungskrieges: Die Einsatzgruppen der Sicherheitspolitzei und des SD 1938–1942* (Stuttgart: Deutsche Verlagsanstalt, 1981), for a detailed discussion of the Einsatzgruppen in general; about their deployment in Poland, see pp. 32 *ff.*

7. Krausnick and Wilhelm, 36, quoting "Richtlinien für den auswärtigen Einsatz der Sicherheitspolizei und des SD" (Guidelines for the external deployment of Sicherheitspolizei and the SD) drawn up by the Head of the Sicherheitspolizei in August 1939.

8. See Czesław Madajczyk, *Die Okkupationspolitik Nazideutschlands in Polen 1939–1945.* Berlin: Akademie, 1987, 18 *ff.*, for details on the practices of the Einsatzgruppen during the conquest of Poland; also Krausnick and Wilhelm, 42 *ff.*; also Ernst Klee and Willi Dreßen, eds., *Gott mit uns: Der deutsche Vernichtungskrieg im Osten 1939–1945* (Frankfurt: Fischer, 1989), 11 *ff.*

9. See Martin Broszat, *Nationalsozialistische Polenpolitik 1939–1945* (Frankfurt: Fischer, 1961); Krausnick and Wilhelm quoting Heydrich, 65.

10. See also Krausnick and Wilhelm, 79: "The cruel order of the Quartermaster General to push mainly the Jews from Upper Silesia across the River San without delay testifies to the readiness within the OKH to act in conformity with 'official' Jewish policy, or to the degree of agreement with it. That there could even be such a thing as a Jewish Question in occupied enemy territory, calling for immediate discriminating 'laws' on the part of the victor concerning the property, institutions, organizations, etc. of the Jewish citizens of a foreign country, most officers and civil servants apparently never questioned at all."

11. Krausnick and Wilhelm, 81. See also Hilberg, 198–199.

12. Krausnick and Wilhelm, 82. Krausnick assumes that the purpose of this amnesty was "to prevent unease on the part of the executors of the Flurbereinigungsmaßnahmen."

13. See Madajczyk for details about the German reign of occupation and "Germanization" in Poland.

14. Seev Goshen, "Eichmann und die Nisko-Aktion im Oktober 1939," *Vierteljahrshefte
für Zeitgeschichte* 29 (1981): 80, citing the memorandum of the meeting of September 21, 1939. Heydrich's other directives at this meeting applied to arrests of Polish
teachers, clergy, nobility, military officers, and their incarceration in concentration
camps. See also Krausnick and Wilhelm, 73–74, quoting Heydrich.

15. Krausnick quoting Heydrich in "Judenverfolgung," in Hans Buchheim et al.,
eds. *Anatomie des SS-Staates* (Munich: Deutscher Taschenbuch Verlag, 1967),
289.

16. BAK R 58/954, express letter to the Heads of all Einsatzgruppen of the Sicherheitspolizei, from the Chief of the Sicherheitspolizei, Berlin, September 21, 1939,
re: Jewish Question in the Occupied Territory, signed: Heydrich, reprinted in
*Faschismus-Getto-Massenmord: Dokumentation über Ausrottung und Widerstand
der Juden in Polen während des Zweiten Weltkrieges,* ed. Jüdisches Historisches
Institut Warschau (Berlin: Rütten & Loening, 1961), 37 *ff.*

17. Quoted in Krausnick and Wilhelm, 75; consult this source for further references
to similar statements Heydrich and Hitler made at that time.

18. Ibid.

19. Krausnick and Wilhelm, 76, quoting a note about the meeting of inspectors and
heads of Einsatzgruppen on October 3, 1939.

20. Quoted in Krausnick, "Hitler und die Morde in Polen," *Vierteljahrshefte für Zeitgeschichte* 11 (1963):196 *ff.*

21. BAK R 58/978, fol. 101, note II-112 of July 10, 1939, re: Jewish Emigration from
the Protektorat.

22. BAK R 58/978, fol. 64, telex from Stahlecker in Prague to the SD-Hauptamt Berlin
on July 24, 1939.

23. Dokumente des Eichmann Prozesses, PdI 1237; consult the June 19, 1944 report
of the Jewish Council of Elders in Prague about the bureaucratic organization
of the expulsions, emigration, and transports from the Protektorat Böhmen und
Mähren.

24. DÖW-file 17072/a, note by Eichmann, dated Berlin, October 6, 1939; the signatures
17017/a and 17072/b acknowledge copies of a file collection of the Gestapo in
Ostrava.

25. DÖW-file 17072/a, letter from the Gestapo Grenzkommissariat (Border Police
headquarters) in Ostrava to Executive Officer Hermann in Brno, re: Request for
administrative personnel.

26. DÖW-file 17072/a, see Eichmann's note dated Berlin, September 29, 1939, re:
Territory of Einsatzgruppe I.

27. DÖW-file 17072/a, according to Eichmann's note dated Berlin, October 6, 1939,
re: Preparations in Berlin, lists of "all registered Jews" were to be reorganized
under the headings of "Altreich," "Protektorat," and "Ostmark," and the "value
of the property owned by impecunious Jews to be expelled" was to be assessed. A
note from the Zentralstelle für Jüdische Auswanderung Vienna, dated October 17,
1939, re: Meeting of Eichmann, Dr. Ebner, and Dr. Becker, signed: [Alois] Brunner,
DÖW-file 17072/a, states that at this meeting Dr. Becker reported having informed
Reichskommissar Bürckel of his October 7 conversation with Eichmann.

28. DÖW-Document No. 9376, letter from SD-head and commander-in-chief of the Sicherheitspolizei in the office of the Reichsprotektor of Böhmen und Mähren, dated Prague, October 10, 1939, to Reichskommissar and Gauleiter Bürckel, at Neustadt, Weinstraße.

29. Ibid.

30. Iltis, Rudolf, and Rat der jüdischen Gemeinden in den böhmischen Ländern (Prague) and the Zentralverband der jüdischen Gemeinden in der Slowakei (Bratislava), eds, *Nazidokumente sprechen* (Prague: Kirchenzentralverband, 1965), 19–20, quoting a file entry by Danneker, dated Ostrava, October 11, 1939, re: work in Mährisch-Ostrau.

31. Concerning the negotiations in Katowice, see also Goshen, 85.

32. Note by Rolf Günther dated Ostrava, October 11, 1939, re: Conference with Gauleiter Wagner on October 10, 1939, in Katowice, quoted from *Nazidokumente sprechen*, 6.

33. "Umschichtung" is a German term for regrouping or shifting. Goshen, 85, notes that such an order listing specific numbers "cannot be documented in any other instance" and, therefore, considers it Eichmann's invention.

34. Quoted from *Nazidokumente sprechen*, 6.

35. DÖW-file 17072/a; note by Rolf Günther, dated Ostrava, October 13, 1939, re: Reconnaissance of a suitable territory for resettlement of Jews.

36. Ibid. Eichmann's telex addressed to Rolf Günther in Ostrava is dated Kraków, October 15.

37. Ibid., note dated October 17, 1939, re: Meeting of SS-Hauptsturmführer Eichmann, Dr. Ebner of the Gestapa, and Dr. Becker from the Staff of the Reichskommissar, signed [Alois] Brunner, to be sent to Eichmann, Ostrava, and SD office Vienna.

38. Ibid. See Safrian and Witek, 159 *ff.*, for a discussion of the particulars of the November pogroms.

39. Rosenkranz, p. 216.

40. Ibid., 217. Most members of these first transports signed up more or less out of their own volition. Construction and carpentry tools were to be brought along. See CAHJP, A/W 2465 for file entries about the summons of the leader of the Kultusgemeinde Vienna to Obersturmführer Günther's office on October 16 and 17, 1939.

41. DÖW-file 17072/a, telex from the SD-Hauptamt of October 13, 1939, to the Stapo branch office in Ostrava with the request that it be forwarded to SS-Hauptsturmführer Eichmann immediately. Nebe had called the SD-Hauptamt and was asked to wait for a few days until Eichmann's whereabouts would be known. Nebe pointed out that if the "expulsion of the Berlin Gypsies in particular" were to be delayed much longer, the City of Berlin would have "to build special camps specifically for Gypsies," which would involve exorbitant expenses and "even greater problems."

42. Ibid. Eichmann's telex is dated Vienna, October 16.

43. DÖW-file 17072/b, daily report for October 18, 1939, signed Brunner [Anton]. Of the original 916 Jews to be expelled, 5 did not appear; 901 persons were listed as members of the first transport to Nisko, (which leaves 10 persons unaccounted for).

44. Quoted from H. G. Adler, *Der verwaltete Mensch: Studien zur Deportation der Juden* (Tübingen: Mohr, 1974), 138.

45. Ibid.
46. Ibid., 139.
47. CAHJP A/W 2749, report of an anonymous member of the second Nisko transport from Vienna, "An den Joint in Warsaw," *Ulanow*, January 10, 1940.
48. Ibid. Some of those driven out escaped across the border into the Soviet Union; others moved in small groups to various places in Poland.
49. Lg. Wien,Vr 3967/61, Slawik's testimony, dated December 6, 1961, during his trial.
50. DÖW-file 17072/b, October 19, 1939-dated telex from the SD-Hauptamt to Einsatzgruppe VI via Schwerin; Inspector of Sicherheitspolizei (Sipo) and SD Donau; and to SS-Hauptsturmführer Eichmann, Ostrava.
51. Ibid., note by Rolf Günther, dated Ostrava, October 21, 1939, re: Transport of Jews to Poland.
52. Note dated Ostrava, October 24, 1939, re: Transport of Jews, *Nazidokumente sprechen*, 28–29.
53. It is fascinating to see how during his interrogation in Jerusalem, Eichmann recycled these same lies he had used to placate Löwenherz. This time he added some embellishments designed to prove his claims that all along he had intended to grant a territory to the Jews (see Lang, 56). As mentioned earlier, authors such as Höhne accepted this rehashed fairy tale without reservations; also see Rosenkranz, 219.
54. DÖW-file 17072/b, telex from Alois Brunner, dated Vienna, October 28, 1939, to Eichmann in Ostrava.
55. Ibid. See the daily reports of November 1 and 2, 1939, for Ostrava, dated November 3, 1939, signed: [Anton] Brunner.
56. This assertion that Eichmann made during his interrogation in Jerusalem also is disseminated in historical works such as Höhne's *Der Orden unter dem Totenkopf*, 323.
57. Reichskommissar Bürckel and his group suspected Seyss-Inquart of sabotaging the project. See Seyss-Inquart's letter to Himmler, dated November 4, 1939, IMT, vol. 32, 255–56, 3398-PS.
58. DÖW-document No. 9646, file note signed: Dr. Becker, Vienna, November 13, 1939, "presented to President Barth for acknowledgment."
59. BAK R 58/544, fol. 218, II/II-112, Dö., Berlin, December 12, 1939, to the Head of II, re: notes for subject Jewry for department head meeting, presented in a memorandum dated December 18, 1939, re: "Final Solution of the Jewish Problem in Germany" (underlined twice in the original), signed II/II-112, signed for – initials indecipherable.

3. The Development and Initial Activities of Referat IV D 4

1. See Adam, 250 *ff*. About German *Volkstumspolitik* in Poland, consult Benz, ed. "Der Generalplan Ost – Germanisierungspolitik in den besetzten Ostgebieten," in *Herrschaft und Gesellschaft im nationalsozilistischen Staat* (Frankfurt: Fischer, 1990). For Nazi resettlement policies in occupied Poland and for a closer examination of Eichmann's role in these policies, see Götz Aly's *"Final Solution": Nazi Population Policy and the Murder of the European Jews* (London: Arnold; New York: Oxford University Press, 1999).

2. See Buchheim vol. 1, 182 *ff.*, for a description of this office. Stuhlpfarrer's *Umsied-lung Südtirol 1939–1940* (Vienna: Löcker, 1985), 237 *ff.*, provides a detailed explanation of the appropriation and meaning of the title Reichskommissar.

3. Doc. PdI 1397, Reichsführer SS as Reichskommissar für die Festigung des deutschen Volkstums, official order 1/II of October 30, 1939, printed by Jüdisches Historisches Institut, 37 *ff.*; Uwe Dietrich Adam, 253, mistakenly refers to this order as the realization of the "Stahlecker-Eichmann Plan" because he bases his conclusion on the assumption that, in February 1940, 6,000 Jews had been expelled from Vienna, Ostrava, and Stettin (Szcezin). But at the time of Himmler's order, the Stahlecker-Eichmann Plan for expulsions from the Ostmark and the Protectorate across the line of demarcation with the Soviet Union had already run aground on account of unsolvable transportation problems.

4. Hilberg, *Die Vernichtung der europäischen Juden*, 205; 203 *ff.*, provides a short overview of the German administrative and SS offices in the parts of Poland annexed to the Reich and in the Generalgouvernement.

5. For details on the preparations in the Generalgouvernement, consult the minutes of a meeting at the office of the Governor General in Kraków on November 8, 1939, printed in Peter Longerich, ed. *Die Ermordung der europäischen Juden: Eine umfassende Dokumentation des Holocaust 1941–1945* (Munich: Piper, 1989), 53 *ff.*

6. Memorandum of HSSPF Koppe in the Warthegau of November 12, 1939, re: Expulsion of Jews and Poles from the Reichsgau Wartheland, printed in *Faschismus* by Jüdisches Historisches Institut Warschau, 44.

7. Dok. PdI 1460, telex from Heydrich to HSSPF and BdS (Krakau, Breslau, Posen, Danzig, and Königsberg (Kraków, Wrocław, Poznań, Gdansk, and Kaliningrad), re: Evacuations in the new eastern provinces, Dok. PdI 1459; and telex from Heydrich to HSSPF Kraków and Poznań, re: Evacuations in the Warthegau, both dated November 28, 1939.

8. Governor General Frank's speech at a meeting with Kreishauptmänner (District Governors) and Stadtkommissare (City Commissars) District Radom, Jüdisches Historisches Institut Warschau, 46.

9. IMT, vol. 30, 95.

10. Dok. PdI 1461, the higher SS and police leader attached to the Reichsstatthalter in Poznań in Defense District III as delegate of the Reichskommissar für die Festigung des deutschen Volkstums, office in charge of the resettlement of Poles and Jews, Poznań, January 26, 1940; Erfahrungsbericht for the resettlement of Poles and Jews from the Reichsgau Wartheland, signed: Rupp, SS-Sturmbannführer.

11. Report of civil servant Gschliesser, with the Division of Labor in the office of the Governor General, to the District Governor Kraków, dated December 29, 1939, Jüdisches Historisches Institut Warschau, 48; see also Madajczyk, 407 *ff.* on the disastrous conditions under which the deportations took place.

12. BAK R 58/276, fol. 246, Chief of the Sicherheitspolizei and SD, December 21, 1939, re: Evacuations in the eastern provinces, signed: Heydrich.

13. Dok. PdI 1399, file entry about the meeting in Berlin on January 4, 1940, "Concerning evacuations of Jews and Poles in the eastern provinces," signed: Abromeit, SS-Obersturmführer.

14. Dok. PdI 1400, note on meetings of SS-Hauptsturmführer Eichmann and SS-Hauptscharführer (Master Sergeant) Seidl on January 22–23, 1940, in Berlin; present: Eichmann, Rolf Günther, Dr. Rajakowitsch, and Seidl.

15. Report of HSSPF Krüger, in the Generalgouvernement, about a conference at Heydrich's office in Berlin on January 30, 1940, in *Faschismus*, Jüdisches Historisches Institut Warschau, 50.

16. Ibid., 52. Some German historians confuse the chronology of individual expulsions, as does Hermann Graml in *Reichskristallnacht, Antisemitismus und Judenverfolgung im Dritten Reich* (Munich: Deutscher Taschenbuchverlag, 1988), 191, when he states that "on February 13, 1940, the first mass deportations from the Reich, from Vienna, Ostrava, Teschen, and Stettin followed."

17. Jacob Toury, "Die Entstehungsgeschichte des Austreibungsbefehls gegen die Juden der Saarpfalz und Badens (22./23. Oktober 1940-Camp de Gurs)," *Jahrbuch des Instituts für Deutsche Geschichte* 15 (1986): 432, quoting a report by Arthur Abrahamson.

18. Report of a correspondent of the *Neue Zürcher Zeitung* quoted in Adler, *Der verwaltete Mensch*, 141.

19. Report of a Polish-Jewish aid committee, March 14, 1940, printed in Adler *Der verwaltete Mensch*, 144.

20. IMT, vol. 36, 302, Dok. 305-EC, minutes of a meeting on February 12, 1940, about matters concerning the East, chaired by Göring.

21. Ibid., 306.

22. Göring's original decree is not extant but can be reconstructed from a file entry describing an April 1, 1940, meeting of Greiser and representatives of the Chief of the Four-Year Plan, the Ministry of Finance, the Ministry of Nutrition, and the Main Trustee Office East; see also *Faschismus*, Jüdisches Historisches Institut Warschau, 54.

23. Memorandum from Regierungspräsident Uebelhör to Kalisch, dated December 12, 1939, re: Construction of a ghetto in the city of Łódź, *Faschismus*, Jüdisches Historisches Institut Warschau, 78 and 81. Longerich printed this memorandum, 59–60 and 81.

24. Wolfgang Scheffler, "Das Getto Łódź in der nationalsozialistischen Judenpolitik" in Hanno Loewy and Gerhard Schoenberger, eds. *"Unser einziger Weg ist Arbeit" Das Getto in Łódź 1940–1944"* (Vienna: Löcker, 1990), 12 *ff.*, and Florian Freund, Bertrand Perz, and Karl Stuhlpfarrer, "Das Getto in Litzmannstadt (Łódź)," in ibid., 17 *ff.*

25. Dok. PdI 1402, telex from the BdS in the Generalgouvernement, department "Resettlement," February 10, 1940, to the HSSPF in Posen (SS-Sturmbannführer Rapp confidential); and telex from IdS Posen, February 27, 1940, to the RSHA (SS-Hauptsturmführer Eichmann confidential), re: Transports of Poles and Jews, signed: Rapp, SS-Sturmbannführer.

26. Dok. PdI 1485, file entry, Posen, March 8, 1940, about a discussion between Rapp and Eichmann.

27. Madajczyk, Table 15: "Expulsion and Displacement of Poles by the Occupation Authorities," 411, does not differentiate between Jewish and non-Jewish citizens. The deportations also proved ever more difficult for their organizers because in

the spring and summer of 1940 many Poles targeted for expulsion either went into hiding or had fled.

28. Dok PdI 1403, telex: The Inspector of the Sicherheitspolizei and the SD at the Umwandererzentralstelle (Central Resettlement Office) Posen to the Umwandererzentralstelle Łódź, April 18, 1940.

29. Seidl, Dok. PdI 1404, file entry for SS-Hauptsturmführer Höppner, re: Conversation of SS-Hauptsturmführer Eichmann and SS-Untersturmführer Seidl on June 5, 1940, in Posen.

30. Dok. PdI 1406, IV D 4 note, re: Settlement of the 600–800 German-Galician upland peasants in the Saybusch district, Berlin, August 8, 1940, signed: Eichmann.

31. Telex from Łódź (Litzmannstadt) to the RSHA – to SS. Stubaf. Eichmann and to Chief of the Sicherheitspolizei and SD – SS-Staf Damzog – Posen, re: Transport of Poles, Operation Lithuania, dated December 17, 1940, in Adolf Diamant, *Getto Litzmannstadt: Bilanz eines nationalsozialistischen Verbrechens* (Frankfurt: Verlag Heimatland Sachsen, 1986), 76.

32. Madajczyk, Table 15.

33. Yad Vashem, 0–1/227, Ephraim Frank, "Die Vorladung der Repräsentanten der jüdischen Dachorganisationen in Berlin, Wien und Prag vor die Gestapo in Berlin (Eichmann) im März 1940.

34. For Rosenberg's and Himmler's comments on this subject, see Adam, 255–56; for discussions about Madagascar as a location for Jewish settlements – discussions conducted in France and Poland before the war and the December 1938 conversations between Ribbentrop and French Foreign Minister Georges Bonnet, also referring to Madagascar, consult Michael R. Marrus and Robert O. Paxton, *Vichy France and the Jews* (New York: Basic Books, 1983), 60 *ff.*

35. Concerning the role of the Auswärtige Amt in the National Socialist genocide program see Christopher R. Browning, *The Final Solution and the German Foreign Office: A Study of Referat D III of Abteilung Deutschland, 1940–1943* (New York: Holmes & Meier, 1978).

36. Hans-Jürgen Döscher, *Das Auswärtige Amt im Dritten Reich: Diplomatie im Schatten der "Endlösung,"* (Berlin: Siedler, 1987), 215, cites notes entitled "Gedanken über die Arbeiten und Aufgaben des Ref. D III" (considerations of the tasks and responsibilities of Section D III).

37. Adam, 256.

38. *Faschismus*, Jüdisches Historisches Institut Warschau, 56–58, cites the comments of Frank, Krüger, and Greiser in July 1940.

39. Döscher, 217, citing a letter from Heydrich to Ribbentrop dated June 24, 1940.

40. Döscher, 218.

41. Dok. PdI 1143, file entry about a discussion in the Reichssicherheitshauptamt with Jakob Edelstein, Prague; Franz Weißmann, Prague; Josef Löwenherz, Vienna, and Paul Eppstein, Berlin, on July 3, 1940.

42. For excerpts of this report see Adler, *Der verwaltete Mensch*, 75 *ff.*, and Döscher, 218; see also Döscher's brief comparison and summary of the drafts produced by the RSHA and the Auswärtige Amt: "It is important to realize that in the summer of 1940 the terms 'Solution to the Jewish Question' and 'Final Solution' referred to the expulsion of the Jews from Europe and their settlement on Madagascar. In this context the records do not support interpretations of homicide, much

less preparations for mass murder." This is accurate only to the extent that no organized plans for mass murder existed at the time. However, as was the case in the Reservatsplan in Galicia, an increased mortality rate based on climatic conditions, malnutrition, disease, and epidemics was very much part of the overall design.

43. Toury, 446. During a meeting of Hitler, Bürckel, Wagner, and Bormann in Berlin on September 28, 1939, Hitler demanded that ten years hence the two Gauleiter would have to be able to report that their area was "German, purely German." He would not inquire "what methods they employed to make it German."

44. Marrus and Paxton, 7.

45. Toury, 447 *ff.*

46. In the Saarpfalz the police notified people of their impending deportation by send-ing them an expulsion order (Ausweisungsbefehl) from the Gauleiter (see Adler, *Der verwaltete Mensch*, 160). Toury, 457 *ff.*, after examining pertinent sources, assumes that Gauleiter Wagner initiated these deportations. In the Pfalz the Gestapo dis-tributed instructions for officials appointed to participate in these operations, which, among other details, provided information about Jews to be expelled from the area, assembly locations, methods of arrest, regulations concerning cash, lug-gage, rations for the deportees, etc. Adler, *Der verwaltete Mensch*, 157, provides a copy of the document. On Section IV D 4 stationery Heydrich informed the Auswärtige Amt on October 29, 1940, about the expulsion of the Jews from Baden and Pfalz. See Paul Sauer, ed. *Dokumente über die Verfolgung der jüdischen Bürger in Baden-Württemberg durch das nationalsozialistische Regime 1933–1945* (Stuttgart: Kohlhammer, 1966) 2:2; see also Adler, *Der verwaltete Mensch*, 157, and Toury, 453.

47. Toury, 464, quotes pertinent documents.

48. BAK, NS 19/3979, memo "The Jewish Question," signed by Eichmann, Dec. 4, 1940, in a folder of material for a speech Himmler delivered Dec. 10, quoted in: Götz Aly, "*Endlösung*": *Völkerverschiebung und der Mord an den europäischen Juden* (Frankfurt: Fischer, 1995), p. 198.

49. IMT, vol. 39, 425 *ff.*, Bormann's file entry about his conversation on October 2, 1940, whose topic was the Generalgouvernement.

50. Yad Vashem, 018/213, copy of a letter from the Reich Minister and Chief of the Reich Chancellery to Gauleiter [Baldur] von Schirach, dated December 3, 1940.

51. For details about Heydrich's "Nahplan 3" see Aly, "*Endlösung*," p. 212 *ff.*, and the minutes of a work session in Kraków on January 15, 1941, which include Heydrich's directives, reprinted in *Faschismus*, Jüdisches Historisches Institut Warschau, 60–61. For particulars concerning the activities of RSHA Referat IV D 4 in relation to "Nahplan 3," see Eichmann's telexes of February 16, 1941 (Dok. PdI 1462), February 26, 1941 (Dok. PdI 1408), and February 27, 1941 (Dok. PdI 1409).

52. DÖW-Akt. 2562, Dr. Löwenherz's file note about his summons from Dr. Ebner and Brunner on February 1, 1941; see also Rosenkranz, 258, and Zentrale Stelle der Landesjustizverwaltung (Central Administrative Office of State Justice (ZStL) 415 AR 1310/63, E5, vol. 1, 29.

53. CAHJP, A/W 2750, instructions for officials and workers of the Israelitische Kultusgemeinde appointed to prepare resettlement transports.

54. A letter from deportees from Opole to their relatives and friends describes the conditions the people expelled from Vienna encountered in Polish small towns. See Ilse Behrend-Rosenfeld and Gertrud Luckner, eds. *Lebenszeichen aus Piaski: Briefe Deportierter aus dem Distrikt Lublin 1940–1943* (Munich: Deutscher Taschenbuch Verlag, 1970), 134 *ff.*

55. TsAMO (Tsentral'nyi arkhiv Ministerstva obonony RF-Central Archive of the Ministry of Defense), Fond 500, opis 12473, delo 104, Letter Army Group B to Army High Command, February 14, 1941, concerning resettlement of Jews and Poles. The whole folder contains captured German documents from Army Group B, Ib (Quartermaster) dealing with "resettlement" (Umsiedlung).

56. TsAMO, 500/12473/104, copy of a memo Army High Command, Quartermaster General, February 20, 1941, concerning resettlement of 800,000 Jews and Poles to Generalgouvernement.

57. TsAMO, 500/12473/104, Army Group B, Quartermaster, March 16, 1941, minutes of the conference.

58. TsAMO, 500/12473/104, conference minutes.

59. Dok. PdI 1395, telex from IV B 4, Müller to Posen, Łódź/Litzmannstadt, and Zentralstelle für Jüdische Auswanderung, Vienna, March 15, 1941.

60. Adler, *Der verwaltete Mensch*, 440, cites the results of a meeting on March 19, 1941.

61. Tone Ferenc, ed. *Quellen zur nationalsozialistischen Entnationalisierungspolitik in Slowenien 1941–1945* (Maribor: n.p., 1980) for details on germanization policies and the expulsion of Slovenes.

62. Dok. PdI 1079, Seidl's telexes to RSHA IV B 4 of June 7, 10, 13, 17, 20, and 24, 1941, announced the departures of deportation transports.

63. Lg. Wien, Vr 2729/63, interrogation of defendant Franz Novak.

4. From Expulsion to Mass Murder: 1941

1. Robert W. Kempner, *Eichmann und Komplizen* (Zurich: Europa, 1961), 98, citing the Reich Marshal of the Greater German Reich, Director of the Four-Year-Plan, and Chairman of the Cabinet for the Defense of the Reich, Berlin, July 31, 1941, to Chief of the Sicherheitspolizei and the SD, SS-Gruppenführer Heydrich, signed Göring.

2. Helma Kaden and Ludwig Nestler, eds. *Europa unterm Hakenkreuz, Dokumenten Edition: Die faschistische Okkupationspolitik in Österreich und der Tschecheslowakei* (Cologne: Pahl-Rugenstein, 1988), 177–178, citing Heydrich's speech in Prague on October 2, 1941, to the top occupation administrators.

3. Kempner, 99, for example, argues that with this appointment Heydrich and his coworkers were officially put in charge of state-administered murder; see also Krausnick, "Judenverfolgung," 306. One of the few historians who does not share this interpretation is Uwe Dietrich Adam, 308: "Surely this empowerment did not constitute a written order for committing what after the war would be summarily referred to by the term *Endlösung*." For a critical response to Adam, see Adler, *Der verwaltete Mensch*, xxvi *ff.*

4. See, for example, Helmut Krausnick's contribution to the discussion of the topic of "Entschlußbildung" (decision making) in Jäckel and Rohwer, 200–201. See also Christopher Browning, "Zur Genesis der Endlösung," *Vierteljahrshefte für Zeitgeschichte* 29 (1981): 100 *ff.*, and Krausnick's "Hitler und die Befehle an die Einsatzgruppen im Sommer 1941" in Jäckel and Rohwer, 139, which specifically refers to the interrogation in Jerusalem and adopts Eichmann's claim of having become acquainted with the specifics of the "Führerbefehl" in the late summer or early fall of 1941. Wolfgang Scheffler, "Wege zur 'Endlösung,'" in Herbert A. Strauss and Norbert Kampe, eds. *Antisemitismus: Von der Judenfeindschaft zum Holocaust* (Bonn: Bundeszentrale für Politische Bildung, 1984), 206 *ff.*, does point out that "generally dates were very imprecise" in Höß's testimonies, but he still accepts summer 1941 as the time when Höß supposedly was instructed to start preparations, in Auschwitz, for the destruction of European Jewry. Eichmann's statement of having been informed through Heydrich, approximately September 1941, of Hitler's order for the "physical annihilation of the Jews" September 1941 (Lang, 69–70) is questionable as well.
5. Adler, *Der verwaltete Mensch*, 152, cites the minutes of a meeting in the Ministry of Propaganda on March 21, 1941, Reichspropaganda Management, Main Office Reichsring. At this meeting Goebbels' representative reported on the lunch conversation with Hitler. In the summer of 1940, Goebbels occasionally had already stated his resolve to make Berlin "judenfrei," free of Jews; see Adler, *Der verwaltete Mensch*, 262.
6. Minutes of the meeting at the Ministry of Propaganda.
7. Adam, 290.
8. Adler, *Der verwaltete Mensch*, 211–12, citing the Reich Ministry of Labor directive dated March 14, 1941.
9. BAK R 58/954, fol. 189, Höppner's letter dated July 16, 1941, to the RSHA, Referat IV B 4, Attn: SS-Obersturmbannführer Eichmann, with attachment: file note. For information about Höppner's personality and career, consult Martin Pollack, "Jäger und Gejagter: Das Überleben der SS-Nr. 107 136," *Translatlantik*, November 1982, 17 *ff.*
10. Serge Klarsfeld, *Vichy-Auschwitz: Die Zusammenarbeit der deutschen und französischen Behörden bei der "Endlösung der Judenfrage" in Frankreich* (Nördlingen: Delphi Politik, 1985), 367–368, quotes Zeitschel's plan for Ambassador Abetz, Paris, August 22, 1941, Centre de Documentation Juive Contemporaine (CDJC) V-15.
11. Ibid.
12. Ibid. Whether Zeitschel's comment on Göring's interest in the Jewish problem was meant to refer to Heydrich's empowerment on July 31, 1941, to prepare the "organizational, factual, and material preconditions necessary to carry out the desired Endlösung of the Jewish Question" remains unclear. His letter of March 23, 1942, reprinted by Kempner, 148, reveals that he had at least cursory information about Göring's decree and the centralized discussions in Berlin.
13. Bräutigam's diary entry of September 14, 1941, printed in Hermann Langbein, *Wir haben es getan: Selbstporträts in Tagebüchern und Briefen 1939–1945* (Vienna: Europa, 1964), 42 *ff.*

14. Auswärtiges Amt, Deutschland. *Akten zur Deutschen Auswärtigen Politik 1918–1945.* Serie D (1937–1945). (Baden-Baden: Impr. Nationale, Vol. 5, 1950–1956).

15. Bernhard Lösener, "Als Rassereferent im Reichsministerium des Inneren," *Vierteljahrshefte für Zeitgeschichte* 9 (1961): 262 *ff.*; see also Jäckel, *Hitler's Herrschaft: Vollzug einer Weltanschauung* (Stuttgart: Deutsche Verlagsanstalt, 1986), 114, footnote 102, which contains notes about this Ministry of Propaganda meeting, confirming Lösener's commentaries about this conference.

16. Lösener, 303.

17. Martin Broszat, "Hitler und die Genesis der 'Endlösung,'" in Hermann Graml and Klaus-Dietmar Henke, eds. *Nach Hitler: Der schwierige Umgang mit unserer Geschichte* (Munich: Oldenbourg, 1986), 200, cites Goebbels' diary entry of August 20, 1941. "Although at this time it is not yet possible to make Berlin into a city free of Jews, at least the Jews can no longer parade about in the open with impunity. Beyond that, the Führer has assured me that immediately after the end of the eastern campaign I will be able to expel them to the East." Goebbels also found it "outrageous and scandalous that in the capital of the German Reich 70,000 Jews, parasites for the most part, are free to roam."

18. Lösener, 303.

19. The assumption that Hitler himself informed Rosenberg of the planned annihilation of the Jews as early as April 1941 is based on a rather cryptic entry in Rosenberg's diary on April 2, 1941, and is hardly convincing. This is because all Rosenberg says is that the Führer had revealed a plan he "does not want to commit to paper today." See also Graml, 221–222.

20. Consult Yitzhak Arad, "Alfred Rosenberg and the 'Final Solution' in the Occupied Soviet Territories," *Yad Vashem Studies* 13 (1979): 273–274. The contradiction between Rosenberg's directives and the content of Hitler's order to murder all Soviet Jews in the spring of 1941 and the order he issued in the summer of 1941 for the speedy physical annihilation of all European Jews, which many historians consider likely or even certain, raises almost insoluble problems of interpretation for the so-called Intentionalists. The Israeli historian Yitzhak Arad posits Hitler's decision for the total annihilation of all Soviet Jews in the course of the war as already having been part of the planning stages of Operation Barbarossa. After analyzing Rosenberg's directives in the Brown Folder of September 1941, Arad concludes that up to that time Rosenberg had not been privy to "the Führer's order to Himmler and the SS concerning the total destruction of the Jews of the USSR." This conclusion is questionable mainly in that a supposedly existing "Endlösungsbefehl" was kept secret or revealed only at a later time to the National Socialist functionary whom Hitler had only recently appointed Reich Minister responsible for the very areas where mass murder of Jews and other victims of the NS regime was already the order of the day.

21. Werner Präg and Wolfgang Jacobmeyer, eds. *Das Diensttagebuch des deutschen Generalgouverneurs in Polen 1939–1945* (Stuttgart: Deutsche Verlagsanstalt, 1975), 386.

22. Jüdisches Historisches Institut Warschau, 252, discussion between Rosenberg and Frank on October 13, 1941, in Berlin.

23. See Mommsen, "Die Realisierung des Utopischen," 408–409, and Broszat, "Hitler und die Genesis der 'Endlösung,'" 197 *ff.*, who arrive at similar conclusions.

24. The significance of the failure of the war aims for future policies of the NS-leadership in respect to the Jews is especially the subject of "Functionalist" interpretations such as Broszat's "Hitler und die Genesis der Endlösung," 203, who describes the situation as a cul-de-sac of one's own making.

25. Kempner, 289–290, telegrams of Edmund Veesenmayer, special representative of the Auswärtige Amt, and Ambassador Felix Benzler to the Auswärtige Amt, dated September 8 and September 12, 1941.

26. Kempner, 291, facsimile of Benzler's telegram and Rademacher marginal note.

27. See also Browning, *The Final Solution and the German Foreign Office*, 58–59; Luther to Weizsäcker, October 2, 1941, in Nuremberg Document NG 3354.

28. Kempner, 292, Ribbentrop's telegram of October 2, 1941.

29. Dok. PdI 1162, telex AA, D III 470 Ang. IIIg, October 15, 1941, to the Office of the special representative of the Auswärtige Amt Belgrade, Re: Expulsion of 8,000 Jews from Serbia, signed: Luther.

30. See *Akten der Deutschen Auswärtigen Politik*, 570 *ff.*, for Rademacher's travel report; see also Browning, "Wehrmacht Reprisal Policy and the Mass Murder of Jews in Serbia," in *Militärgeschichtliche Mitteilungen* 1 (1983): 31 *ff.*

31. Bundesarchiv/Militärarchiv (BA/MA), H 20/293, II./ANR 521 Major Duvigneau, October 5, 1941: "Based on a telephone report of the 714th Division and a written report of 4./ANR 521 ... about mutilations of casualties, the department ordered a forensic examination in the presence of Lt. Lockemann. A photographer from the propaganda department in Serbia was present to record the condition of the corpses and the wounded pictorially. According to the department physician, 'there is no proof of mutilations – the original statement is underlined – or mistreatment.' The department has attached the official report of the examination of the 22 dead soldiers.... The pictures have been requested directly by the AOK 12, Ic, 714, Military Commander in Serbia, and have already been delivered to the Commanding General [Böhme]." BA/MA, RH 24–18/213, telephonic order from General Böhme to the quartermaster department, October 10, 1941. For details about officers and men of the Wehrmacht units deployed in Yugoslavia, many of whom had been recruited in Austria, see Walter Manoschek and Hans Safrian, "Österreicher in der Wehrmacht," in Tálos, Hanisch, and Neugebauer, 331 *ff.*

32. Graml, 235, considers Eichmann's suggestion to shoot the Jews as "irrefutable" proof of the existence of a Führerbefehl for the murder of all Jews. "That functionaries of inferior rank belonging to a variety of organizations could routinely organize quantitatively important killing actions proves decisively that an order for killing all Jews without exception had already been issued by the regime's highest authority and had already been put into use." Graml's conclusion ignores several details: Neither Eichmann nor Rademacher were in a position to induce military commanders to organize such murders. The general of the Wehrmacht in Serbia had ordered the murder of the male Jews independently, without approval of the RSHA and the Auswärtige Amt (AA). Eichmann's and Rademacher's suggestions originated in their knowledge of the already wide-spread custom of murdering Jews in the occupied territories of the Soviet Union. The reports of the SS-Einsatzgruppen circulated in the RSHA and in Rademacher's department of the AA. See also Döscher, 245 *ff.*

33. For details on the use of gas vans in Serbia, see Browning, "The 'Final Solution' in Serbia: The Semlin Judenlager – A Case Study," *Yad Vashem Studies* 15 (1983): 55 *ff.*; about the Holocaust in Serbia and its perpetrators see Manoschek, "Gehst mit Juden erschießen? Zur Rolle von Österreichern in Wehrmacht und SS beim Holocaust in Serbien," Diss. Wien 1990; BA/MA, RW 40/32, Anlage 84 of the war diary of the general and commander in Serbia, chief of the military administration Dr. Turner's report to General Löhr, Wehrmacht Commander Southeast, on August 29, 1942.

34. BAK NS 19/2655, fol. 3, letter from Reichsführer-SS to Gauleiter Greiser, September 18, 1941.

35. Broszat, "Hitler und die Genesis der Endlösung," 201, quoting Goebbels' diary entry of September 24, 1941; only a month later, on October 24, Goebbels reports that thousands of Jews had already been sent to the East – "for the time being they go to Litzmannstadt."

36. These issues and decisions demonstrate that, during his interrogation in Jerusalem, Eichmann's claims of having the opportunity of choosing between two deportation sites (Litzmannstadt and the East) have to be dismissed. His testimony of having chosen to insist on Litzmannstadt, that is, having chosen the lesser evil after having informed himself about the preparatory decisions concerning the occupied Soviet Union, constitutes a means of self-protection.

37. Henry Friedlander, "Deportation of German Jews," *Leo Baeck Institute Yearbook* 29 (1984): 201 *ff.*, argues, "it is not clear why Łódź was chosen as the destination for the first deportations. It has been assumed that Hitler's sudden order prevented careful planning." However, because, according to Friedlander, the murder of German Jews already had been decided at that time, the deportation locations in the Baltic areas and Belorussia would have been a better choice because there the Einsatzgruppen already were prepared for the murder of the Jews whereas in the Warthegau the facilities for murder had not yet been completed. To resolve this contradiction, in Himmler's letter to Greiser, Friedlander interprets the passages that refer to the expulsion of Jews from Łódź to the East during the following spring to mean that Himmler "knew that Kulmhof (Chełmno) would be available for this purpose." Had the intentions for murder and the designs for killing facilities been as advanced as Friedlander assumes, Himmler's number of 60,000 Jews to be deported to Łódź to be murdered as speedily as possible would have prevailed. This, however, was not the case.

38. Memorandum from the mayor of Litzmannstadt to the district governor, re: Shipment of 20,000 Jews and 5,000 Gypsies to the Litzmannstadt ghetto, dated September 24, 1941. The memo was composed by the head of the German ghetto administration, Biebow, and signed by Mayor Ventzki. See Artur Eisenbach, ed. "Getto Lodzkie," *Dokumenty I Materialy do dziejow Okupacji niemieckiej w Polsce* (Warsaw: Centralna Zydowska Komisja Historyczna, 1946) 3:167 citing BAK NS 19/2655, fol. 4 *ff.* See also Freund, Perz, and Stuhlpfarrer, 17 *ff.*, about the controversies over the settlement of Jews in the districts of the Warthegau and the Łódź ghetto and about the history of the ghetto. I am indebted to the authors for valuable references to documents and discussions concerning the deportations to Łódź.

39. BAK NS 19/2655, letter from Regierungspräsident Uebelhör to the Reichsführer-SS, dated October 4, 1941.

40. Dok. PdI 1248 and BAK NS 19/2655, fol. 35.

41. See Freund, Pers, and Stuhlpfarrer, 27.

42. Dok. PdI 1544, letter from the Chief of the Sicherheitspolizei and the SD, IV B 4a, B. Nr. 2659/41 g (679), dated October 19, 1941, to the Reichsführer-SS, Führerhauptquartier, signed SS-Obergruppenführer Heydrich.

43. Dok. PdI 1545, memorandum from the Head of the Wehrwirtschaft-und Rüstungsamt im Oberkommando der Wehrmacht, Rü Via Nr. 26510/41 to Reichsführer-SS and Head of the German Police in the Reich Ministry of the Interior, dated October 11, 1941. General Georg Thomas signed with "Heil Hitler."

44. Himmler's letter to General Thomas, October 1941.

45. According to Uebelhör's letter to Himmler of October 9, 1941, Eichmann himself claimed to have conducted meetings in Litzmannstadt. Heydrich's letter to Himmler of October 19, 1941, also indicates Eichmann's presence at a meeting. The date emerges from the dates of Himmler's letter to Greiser and the Ventzki's memorandum to Uebelhör of September 24, 1941; see also the Litzmannstadt Stapo office report, which Heydrich cites in his letter to Himmler.

46. Whether the ghetto administrator agreed to this number during the discussion despite Uebelhör's protests, as Eichmann, according to Uebelhör's telex of October 9, 1941, and the Litzmannstadt Stapo office supposedly claimed, or whether he declared himself opposed to taking the deportees into the ghetto on principle, as Uebelhör insisted and as it is stated in Ventzki's memorandum to Uebelhör, cannot be established.

47. See Freund, Perz, and Stuhlpfarrer, 27.

48. Yad Vashem, DN/27–3, File: The President of Police, Vienna, Transports of Jews to the Generalgouvernement, fol. 1–2; this is a copy of the decree issued by the chief of the Ordnungspolizei and the Chief of the Higher SS and Police attached to the Reichsstatthalter in Vienna, Upper and Lower Austria in Military District 17/Inspector of the Ordnungspolizei, re: Evacuations of Jews from the Altreich and the Protectorate.

49. See Adam, 311; Graml, 232; Friedlander, 212; Rosenkranz, 282; see also ZStL., 415 AR 1310/1963, E 5, 1:3, for the comment of the Prosecutor's Office, Berlin, about the handling of the "Endlösung der Judenfrage" in the Altreich, including the Ostmark, 3, where this file number is cited from the records of the Stapo office in Würzburg.

50. Zentralstelle für jüdische Auswanderung, D10–2244/41- B/Rö, Vienna October 6, 1941, to SS-Brigadeführer Karl Scharizer, Deputy Gauleiter of Gau Vienna, re: resident permit for SS-Unterscharführer Richard Hartenberger, living with his parents in Vienna 5, Jahngasse 39/9, signed Head of the Zentralstelle für jüdische Auswanderung, Brunner [Alois], personnel file of the NSDAP-Gau Vienna, Nr. 86,359, Richard Hartenberger. Hartenberger's efforts were successful. He and his wife received permission to move into a Vienna 6th district apartment, the previous tenants of which had been Jews.

51. CAHJP A/W 3015, file entry about Dr. Löwenherz's appearance before SS-O'Stuf. Brunner on September 30, 1941, 10:30 AM, Vienna, October 2, 1941.

52. DÖW-Akt. E 18938/2, NSDAP, Gauleitung Vienna, the Deputy Gauleiter, memo-randum of October 25, 1941, signed Scharizer.

53. See Rosenkranz, 283.

54. CAHJP A/W 2735, Wirtschaftsstelle der Israelitischen Kultusgemeinde, Vienna, February 12, 1942, resettlement and emigration transports.

55. For a discussion of the Lackenbach camp, consult Erika Thurner, *Nationalsozialismus und Zigeuner in Österreich* (Vienna: Geyer, 1983).

56. Commando of the Schutzpolizei, Vienna, October 24, 1941, re: Provision of Transport Commando, File: President of Police, Vienna, fols. 4–5.

57. See the publication about Łódź/Litzmannstadt, "Unser einziger Weg ist Arbeit," *Das Ghetto in Łódź 1940–1944*, catalog for an exhibit of the same title by the Jewish Museum of Frankfurt/M., Vienna, 1990.

58. On this subject see Michael Zimmermann, *Verfolgt, vertrieben, vernichtet: Die nationalsozialistische Vernichtungspolitik gegen Sinti und Roma* (Essen: Klartext, 1989), 49–50, and "Unser einziger Weg ist Arbeit," 186–187.

59. Zimmermann, 61.

60. Diamant, 125, situation report of the State Police office, Litzmannstadt, department II B 4, dated June 9, 1942, signed: Fuchs.

61. Jüdisches Historisches Institut Warschau, *Faschismus – Ghetto – Massenmord*, 278, quotes Greiser's May 1, 1942, letter to Himmler; see also Broszat, "Hitler und die Genesis der 'Endlösung,'" 204, which ascribes an ad-hoc approach to the organization of the Chełmno/Kulmhof mass murders.

62. Freund, Perz, and Stuhlpfarrer, 28, discuss this issue in terms of a synchronization strategy.

63. Ernst Klee, *"Euthanasie" im NS-Staat: Die "Vernichtung lebensunwerten Lebens"* (Frankfurt/M.: Fischer, 1986), 191, includes a letter from Koppe, Höherer SS- und Polizeiführer in the office of the Reich Statthalter in Posen to the Höhere SS- und Polizeiführer Nord-Ost Sporrenberg, dated October 18, 1940. See also Mathias Beer, "Die Entwicklung der Gaswagen beim Mord an den Juden," *Vierteljahrshefte für Zeitgeschichte* 35 (1987): 406.

64. See Eugen Kogon, et al., eds. *Nationalsozialistische Massentötungen durch Giftgas: Eine Dokumentation* (Frankfurt/M.: Fischer, 1986), 110 *ff.*, and Adalbert Rückerl, ed. *Nationalsozialistische Vernichtungslager im Spiegel deutscher Strafprozesse: Bełzec, Sobibor, Treblinka, Chelmno* (Munich: Deutscher Taschenbuch Verlag, 1977), 262.

65. Beer, 406 and 409 *ff.* Whether the experiences of "Sonderkommando Lange" were applied in the development and construction of gas vans in the fall of 1941 cannot be determined, although Lange supposedly attended meetings at the RSHA in the summer of 1940 to "lead discussions concerning the appropriate type of gas van."

66. Rückerl, 250. A Hanover court of assizes sentenced Günther Fuchs, the former Head of the Judenreferat at the state police office Łódź, to life imprisonment for murder in nine cases, attempted murder in two cases, and aiding and abetting the murder of at least 15,000 persons.

67. Dok. PdI 1193. Notes from the October 10, 1941, meeting about the solution to the Jewish Question.

68. Browning, "Zur Genesis der Endlösung," 102. Based on these orders, Browning argues that for Heydrich the mass murder of deported Jews from Central Europe already had been determined, but Heydrich's statements render such certainty questionable.
69. Dok. PdI 1193.

5. Controversies over the Deportations to the Occupied Areas of the Soviet Union: 1941

1. YIVO Occ 3–29. Dr. Drechsler's file entry dated October 20, 1941, which he sent that same day to the Reichskommissar für das Ostland with the following explanation: "in the attachment I am sending you the requested note of my conversation with SS-Brigadeführer Stahlecker." The sources cited as YIVO Occ E 3 are original documents US forces recovered in September 1945 in Alfred Rosenberg's ministry, the former Soviet Embassy, in Berlin. Some of these documents were used as evidence at the Nuremberg trial of the major war criminals.
2. There are indications that Heydrich, in his new position as Reichsprotektor für Böhmen und Mähren, had received Hitler's permission to deport Czech Jews to the East while the war with the Soviet Union was in progress. On October 6, 1941, shortly before Heydrich's conference in Prague, Hitler, in one of his table talks, had discussed the necessity of removing all Jews from the Protectorate, "without their first being sent to the Generalgouvernement but farther east right away." Furthermore, Hitler was fully aware of the obstacles involved: "The only reason why it is impossible to do so right away is the military's extremely heavy need of transport facilities. All Jews from Berlin and Vienna should disappear at the same time as those from the Protectorate. Everywhere the Jews are the conduits for the immediate spread of every enemy newscast, even among the most isolated members of the population." Notes of Werner Koeppen, the permanent representative of the Reichsminister for the Occupied Eastern Territories at the Führer Headquarters, BAK R 6/34a cited in Martin Vogt, "Selbstbespiegelungen in Erwartung des Sieges: Bemerkungen zu den Tischgesprächen Hitlers im Herbst 1941," in Wolfgang Michalka, ed. *Der Zweite Weltkrieg: Analysen, Grundzüge, Forschungsbilanz im Auftrag des Militärgeschichtlichen Forschungsamtes* (Munich: Piper, 1989), 649.
3. Drechsler's file entry.
4. Longerich, 69, claims that the "systematic murder of Jews from the entire Reich," who since October 1941 "were being deported in increasing numbers," began in November 1941 with their being "shot immediately upon arrival in the occupied Eastern territories." Uwe Dietrich Adam, 311, describes the deportations to Riga as "entrapment for murder" because the Jews from Germany who were "unloaded there" were killed "in several mass executions." This faulty assumption leads him to conclude that "the final decision for the physical annihilation of European Jewry" was made in December 1941.
5. The only accounts providing specific information about the history of these ghettos, where deportees from Central Europe were imprisoned, come from survivors.

See Jeanette Wolff, *Sadismus oder Wahnsinn: Erlebnisse in den deutschen Konzentra-tionslagern im Osten* (Dresden: E. Bretfeld, 1946); Karl Löwenstein, "Minsk – Im Lager der deutschen Juden," in "Beilage" to *Das Parlament*, B 45/46, 7 November 1956; Gertrude Schneider, *Journey into Terror: The Story of the Riga Ghetto* (New York: Arc House, 1979); Bernhard Press, *Judenmord in Lettland 1941–1945* (Berlin: Metropol, 1988).

Helmut Heiber's annotated documentation entitled "Aus den Akten des Gauleit-ers Kube," *Deutsche Vierteljahrshefte für Zeitgeschichte* 4 (1956): 67 *ff.*, presents the exception by focusing on the differences of opinion between the SS and White Ruthenia (Belorussia) Generalkommissar Kube in Minsk concerning the treat-ment of Jews deported from Central Europe. The weakness of Heiber's approach lies in his limited view of Kube as a Nazi "heretic" who supposedly attempted to salvage "what still was salvageable" rather than a detailed exploration of the institutional backgrounds of these controversies.

6. By the end of 1942, according to a 1943 statistic entitled "Die Endlösung der europäischen Judenfrage," 217,748 Jews had been "evacuated," that is deported, from the "Altreich, Ostmark, Böhmen und Mähren." Because this number includes the number of people sent to Theresienstadt, and at the end of 1942 about 50,000 people lived in this "old folks ghetto," it is reasonable to assume that about 167,000 persons had been deported to the areas of Poland and the Soviet Union under German administration. This report of the "Inspector for Statistics" forms part of the appendix of Lang's *Das Eichmann-Protokoll.*

7. See Gerald Reitlinger, *Die Endlösung: Ausrottung der Juden Europas 1935–1945* (Munich: Kindler, 1964), 86 *ff.*; Raul Hilberg, *Die Vernichtung der europäischen Juden* (Frankfurt/M.: Fischer, 1982), 358 *ff.*; Gerald Fleming, *Hitler und die Endlösung: "Es ist des Führers Wunsch . . . "* (Wiesbaden: Limes, 1982), 89 *ff.* (Riga), 129 *ff.* (Minsk); H. G. Adler in *Der verwaltete Mensch*, 183, states that concern-ing the deportations to Riga and Minsk, much still needs clarification. Helmut Krausnik's and Hans-Heinrich Wilhelm's study provides the most detailed infor-mation on this topic. For additional information consult Andreas Hillgruber, "Der Ostkrieg und die Judenvernichtung," in Gerd R. Ueberschär and Wolfram Wette, eds. "*Unternehmen Barbarossa:*" *Der deutsche Überfall auf die Sowjetunion 1941* (Paderborn: F. Schöningh, 1984), 219 *ff.*; for details about the state of research concerning genocide in the Baltic territories, see Hans-Heinrich Wilhelm, "Offene Fragen der Holocaust Forschung: Das Beispiel des Baltikums," in Uwe Backes et al., eds. *Was heißt "Historisierung" des Nationalsozialismus?* (Berlin: Propyläen, 1990), 403 *ff.* See Alexander Dallin, *German Rule in Russia, 1941–1945: A Study of Occu-pation Policies* (London: Macmillan, 1981), 98 *ff.* about internal administrative conflicts.

8. Raul Hilberg, *Die Vernichtung der europäischen Juden*, 312, estimates that in the final six months of 1941 about half a million people, the vast majority of them Jews, fell victim to the ravages of the mobile SS killing units in the newly occupied areas of the Soviet Union.

9. See Omer Bartov, *The Eastern Front, 1941–45: German Troops and the Barbarisation of Warfare* (London: Macmillan in association with St. Anthony College Oxford, 1985), n.p., who labels the kind of warfare Germany practiced in that theater as "barbarization."

10. Chief of the Sicherheitspolizei and the SD, IV A 1-B. Nr. 1B/41 g. Rs., 11. 7. 1941, Operational Report USSR, No. 19, BDC, Stahlecker documents. Ibid. The degree of "spontaneity" of Lithuanian antisemites is hard to gauge because even in general terms the study of the importance of Lithuanian, Latvian, and Ukrainian volunteers still is at an early stage. See Wilhelm, 410 *ff.*, and Marger Vestermanis, "Der Lettische Anteil an der 'Endlösung,'" in Backes, et al., *Was heißt "Historisierung,"* 426 *ff.*

11. Historians differ in their reconstruction of the orders to the Einsatzgruppen. The majority believe that even before the attack on the Soviet Union the order to murder all Jews in the conquered areas already had been issued. Helmut Krausnick in "Judenverfolgung," 299–300, for example, states that according to testimonies, "the heads of the Einsatzgruppen, as they assembled their units in May of 1941, verbally received the secret order to shoot all Jews." See also Krausnick and Wilhelm, 159 *ff.*; Krausnick, "Hitler und die Befehle an die Einsatzgruppen im Sommer 1941," in Jäckel and Rohwer, 88 *ff.*; Jürgen Förster, "Das Unternehmen 'Barbarossa' als Eroberungs- und Vernichtungskrieg," in *Das deutsche Reich und der Zweite Weltkrieg*, 4, Militärgeschichtliches Forschungsamt (Stuttgart: Deutsche Verlagsanstalt, 1983); Andreas Hillgruber, in Überschär and Wette, 224 *ff.* Jurist Alfred Streim, on the other hand, perceives a step-by-step intensification and extension of the killing orders. He assumes the existence of orders to the Einsatzgruppen at the beginning of the campaign to incite pogroms by the indigenous Selbstschutzverbände ("Self-Defense Formations") and to kill "Jews in party and state offices" as promulgated in Heydrich's order of July 2, 1941, to the Higher SS and Police commanders for the conquered areas under civil administration. See Streim, *Die Behandlung sowjetischer Kriegsgefangener im "Fall Barbarossa:" Eine Dokumentation* (Heidelberg: Juristischer Verlag Müller, 1981), 74 *ff.*; "Zur Eröffnung des allgemeinen Judenvernichtungsbefehls gegenüber den Einsatzgruppen," in Jäckel and Rohwer, 107 *ff.*; and "Replik auf die Kritik von Krausnick," *Simon Wiesenthal Center Annual* 6 (1989): 331 *ff.* At first the Einsatzgruppen executed almost exclusively adult male Jews as part of "reprisals" or as "carriers of the Jewish-Bolshevik system." Yitzhak Arad, in "The 'Final Solution' in Lithuania," *Yad Vashem Studies* 11 (1976): 234 *ff.*, analyzes the course of various killing sprees in Lithuania and classifies the mass-murder actions of SS-Einsatzkommandos 2, 3, and 9 in July 1941, "in which the overwhelming majority of the victims were males" (241), as the second level. According to Streim, in this early stage, more extensive, explicit killing orders still met with lack of understanding from the army and even members of the SS-Einsatzgruppen. Streim's "Replik," 341, provides an example. Streim's contention of a certain caution on the part of the SS vis-à-vis the Wehrmacht would explain what Stahlecker meant by referring to a "stir" among Germans, quoted below, and is plausible because the SS never could predict the Wehrmacht's position. On that topic consult Christian Streit, *Keine Kameraden: Die Wehrmacht und die sowjetischen Kriegsgefangenen 1941–1945* (Stuttgart: Deutsche Verlagsanstalt, 1978), 126–127.

12. Einsatzgruppe A, Summary Report, October 15, 1941, Nuremberg Doc. 180-L, cited in *Schöne Zeiten: Judenmord aus der Sicht der Täter und Gaffer*, eds. Ernst Klee, Willi Dreßen, and Volker Rieß (Frankfurt/M.: Fischer, 1988), 34–35.

13. Ibid., 35. Details of this report repeat Heydrich's directives almost verbatim. In a telex to the heads of the Einsatzgruppen, dated June 29, 1941, a week after the start

of Operation Barbarossa, Heydrich referred to his verbal instructions of May 17 in Berlin, reminding them that the "self-cleansing efforts of anti-Communist or anti-Jewish circles" in the newly occupied territories of the Soviet Union were not to be restrained in any way. Rather, they were to be "incited, intensified if necessary and channeled appropriately" without leaving any traces to prevent "these local self-protection" groups from justifying their action later by being able to point to official orders;" quoted by Longerich, 118–19.

14. Ibid., 32.

15. On July 3, 1941, the official war diary of Heeresgruppe Nord (Army Group North) records that a general staff officer informed Colonel Schmundt, Hitler's personal adjutant, about the "outrages of the Lithuanian volunteer corps." Schmundt replied that the soldiers were not to burden themselves with "political issues." Moreover, according to Schmundt, this was a "necessary clean-up operation." See Krausnick and Wilhelm, 206 and 209.

16. Jürgen Förster, "Die Sicherung des 'Lebensraums:' Die Befriedung des eroberten Gebietes," in *Das deutsche Reich und der Zweite Weltkrieg*, vol 4, Militär-geschichtliches Forschungsamt, ed., 1045, quoting the diary of Field Marshal Wilhelm Ritter von Leeb, commander-in-chief of Heeresgruppe Nord: "We have no say in these measures. The only thing left for us to do is to keep our distance." In the very next sentence von Leeb opines that through pogroms "the Jewish Questions could not be solved;" therefore, he preferred the "sterilization of all male Jews." Christian Streit, *Keine Kameraden*, 118 *ff.*, describes similar attitudes among other generals. Manfred Messerschmidt, "Harte Sühne am Judentum: Befehlslage und Wissen in der deutschen Wehrmacht," in Jörg Wollenberg, ed. *"Niemand war dabei und keiner hat's gewußt": Die deutsche Öffentlichkeit und die Judenverfolgung* (Munich: Piper, 1989), 120–121, demonstrates that von Leeb's quite obvious anti-semitism was by no means unique among the generals of the eastern army. General Hoepner, for example, whose relationship to Stahlecker the latter praised as "quite cordial," as early as May 1941 had voiced the opinion that the imminent campaign was to be conducted as "the defense of European culture against a Muscovite-Asian flood" and "the repelling of Jewish Bolshevism."

17. Krausnick and Wilhelm, 80 *ff.*

18. Jürgen Förster, "Der historische Ort des Unternehmens 'Barbarossa,'" in Michalka, *Der Zweite Weltkrieg: Analysen*, 635.

19. Krausnick and Wilhelm, 116 *ff.* discuss the conversations between representatives of the Wehrmacht and the SS in preparation for the war against the Soviet Union. IMT, 26, 53 *ff.*, records the OKW's "Richtlinien auf Sondergebieten zur Weisung Barbarossa," the rules for special situations of authority regarding Barbarossa, issued on March 13, 1941. "In the field of the army's operations, the Reichsführer-SS, based on the Führer's authorization, will take on special duties that will result from the decisive combat between two diametrically opposed political systems. In carrying out these duties the Reichsführer-SS will act autonomously and on his own cognizance."

20. Hans-Adolf Jacobsen, "Kommissarsbefehl und Massenexekutionen sowjetischer Kriegsgefangener," in Buchheim, et al., *Anatomie des SS-Staates*, 2, 171, prints OKH, Gen. St. d. H./Gen. Qu., March 26, 1941. See Manfred Messerschmidt,

"Das Verhältnis von Wehrmacht und NS-Staat und die Frage der Traditionsbildung," in Manfred Messerschmidt, ed. *Militärgeschichtliche Aspekte der Entwicklung
des deutschen Nationalstaates* (Düsseldorf: Droste, 1988), 241–242, and Messerschmidt, "Harte Sühne am Judentum," in Wollenberg, 115 *ff.*, on the subject of the
army generals' "reorientation" in 1940 in response to "incisive measures" in the
"struggle of national and cultural survival in the East."

21. According to Jacobsen, 208, when Admiral Wilhelm Canaris, chief of military
intelligence, in September 1941 attempted to remind the Oberkommando der
Wehrmacht of the international laws regarding treatment of prisoners of war, Keitel demonstrated the Wehrmacht leadership's conscious and calculated break with
these regulations by writing on Canaris' letter that "such concerns reflect military
concepts of war as a chivalrous enterprise. Here [in the fight against the Soviet
Union] the aim is the annihilation of a world view. For this reason I approve and
defend them (the Kommisarsbefehl and the Gerichtsbarkeitserlaß)." On the subject
of Kommissarsbefehl and the treatment of Soviet prisoners, see also Jacobsen, 137
ff.; Streit, *Keine Kameraden*, 28 *ff.*; Krausnick, "Kommissarsbefehl und 'Gerichtsbarkeitserlaß Barbarossa' in neuer Sicht," *Vierteljahrshefte für Zeitgeschichte* 25
(1977): 682 *ff.*, traces the development of these directives.

22. Messerschmidt, "Der Reflex der Volksgemeinschaftsidee in der Wehrmacht,"
in *Militärgeschichtliche Aspekte*, 197 *ff.*, explores the "deutschvölkische" (German
nationalistic) and racist traditions within the Wehrmacht and their convergence
with NS-ideology. Jacobsen prints the OKW directives on pp. 187–188. See Keitel's directive, Attachment 2 to "Richtlinien für die militärische Sicherung und
für die Aufrechterhaltung der Ruhe und Ordnung im Ostland" (guidelines for the
military pacification and maintenance of peace and order in the East) issued by
the Wehrmachtsbefehlshaber Ostland, September 9, 1941, in YIVO Occ E 3–4 and
Jacobsen, 207–208.

23. Directive of October 10, 1941, re: "Troop Behavior in the East," cited from IMT,
Doc. 411-D, 34, 81 *ff.* Von Reichenau's view of the enemy was this: "Separate from
all political considerations concerning the future, the soldier has to accomplish
two tasks: 1. the total destruction of the Bolshevik heresy, the Soviet state and its
armed forces; 2. the merciless annihilation of alien treachery and cruelty to secure
the life of the German Wehrmacht in Russia. Only by doing this will we succeed
in our historic mission of liberating the German people once and for all from
the Asian-Jewish danger." See also the army directive of Generaloberst (General)
Hoth, commander-in-chief of the Seventeenth Army, dated November 17, 1941, or
that of Generaloberst von Manstein, commander-in-chief of the Eleventh Army,
of November 20, 1941, both printed in "Dokumentenanhang," in *Unternehmen
Barbarossa*, eds. Überschär and Wette, 341 *ff.*

24. See Klee, Dreßen, and Rieß, *Gott mit uns*, for a discussion of the massacre at
Babi Yar; Activity and Situation Report No. 6 of the Sicherheitspolizei and SD
Einsatzgruppen for October 1 to October 31, 1941, Nuremberg Doc. 102 R, IMT, 38,
292; Streit, *Keine Kameraden*, 114, and Förster, "Die Sicherung des 'Lebensraums,'"
1046 *ff.*, for a discussion of Babi Yar and other places where Wehrmacht units of
Heeresgruppe Süd (Army Group South) assisted SS-formations of Einsatzgruppe
C in mass murders of Jews.

25. On one of the decrees of the commanders-in-chief, consult Streit, *Keine Kameraden*, 113, and Förster, "Die Sicherung des 'Lebensraums,'" 1034. See Krausnick and Wilhelm, 274 *ff.*, and Hilberg, *Die Vernichtung der europäischen Juden*, 317–318, for Wehrmacht executions. Hilberg concludes that the number of Jews murdered by the army was "by no means insignificant." Quite the contrary: "The army was actively engaged in assisting Heydrich's troops in reducing the Jewish population."

26. IMT, 32, 71 *ff.*, 3257-PS, report of the Armament Inspector Ukraine to the head of the Office of War Economy and Armament at the OKW, December 2, 1941.

27. Rolf-Dieter Müller, "Von der Wirtschaftsallianz zum kolonialen Ausbeutungskrieg," in *Das Deutsche Reich und der Zweie Weltkrieg*, 4, 98 *ff.*, discusses the strategies of colonial exploitation employed previous to Operation Barbarossa. In April 1941 General Thomas' war-economic strategies were designed to achieve his aim of feeding the entire Wehrmacht with the resources of the conquered Soviet Union. Ibid., 147. This plan assumed that "without doubt, millions of people will starve to death as we extract what we need for our own use," as it was phrased during a meeting of state secretaries in May 1941; Förster, "Die Sicherung des 'Lebensraums,'" 1046, quotes from a report by a general of the 339th Infantry Division; the report demonstrates whom officers of the Wehrmacht considered "useless eaters." Complaining about the insufficient food supplies for his troops, he considered it appropriate to eradicate "all parasites and useless eaters (escaped and recaptured prisoners of war, vagrants, Jews, and 'Gypsies')."

28. Report of the Armament Inspector Ukraine.

29. Broszat, *Hitler und die Genesis der 'Endlösung,'* 209, cites Hitler's own statement revealing this barbarization through intentional mass destruction as, during his table talk of January 23, 1942, he claimed to limit himself to ordering the Jews to leave. "If they [the Jews] break their ribs during the trip, I can't help it. But if they refuse to leave of their own free will, I don't see any other way but their annihilation. Why should I look at a Jew differently than I do a Russian prisoner of war? Many die in prisoner camps. That's not my fault. I wanted neither this war nor prisoners of war. Why did the Jews provoke the war?"

30. Historians generally agree on the support of the Wehrmacht in the partial annihilation of the Jews of Eastern Europe. Krausnick and Wilhelm, 278, for example, summarize historical assessment as follows: "Partly as a result of the weakness and submissiveness of the army's highest leadership, partly as a result of increasing agreement among a growing number of officers and soldiers with the ideology and foreign policy goals of the National Socialist rulers, and more than likely as a result of (justified) fear of the consequences of open protest, though surely least of all as a result of a totally absolutistic military obedience, a widespread integration of the army into Hitler's annihilation program and annihilation policies, so terrifying in its extent, had taken place." Differences of opinion arise over the question of the importance of this cooperation in the subsequent processes of persecution and annihilation. Förster, "The German Army and the Ideological War Against the Soviet Union," in Gerhard Hirschfeld, ed. *The Policies of Genocide: Jews and Soviet Prisoners of War in Nazi Germany* (Boston: Allen & Unwin, 1986), 26, for example, argues against the opinion that the Holocaust was unleashed because the Wehrmacht's feared opposition to the murder of the Jews did not materialize.

Rather, Hitler's decision to destroy the Eastern European Jews was part and parcel of the military preparations for Operation Barbarossa without consideration of the response of the military. Streit, "The German Army and the Policies of Genocide," in Hirschfeld, 2, on the other hand, arguing an incremental intensification and spread of execution orders to the Einsatzgruppen, considers the campaign against the Soviet Union as the turning point in the development of the Holocaust, which, although in the planning stages conceived as a war of annihilation, did not aim for the total destruction of all Jews. In this context, the formulation of "criminal orders" by the political and military authorities of the Third Reich would have played a crucial role for the treatment of Soviet prisoners of war and the civilian population. These orders and their execution by the majority of the Wehrmacht in the East – decisive in Streit's opinion – contributed to the development of a situation that made the Holocaust possible.

31. The evacuees included Austrians. The Viennese family Rosenkranz, who had fled from the National Socialists to Riga in October 1938, was evacuated to Novosibirsk. There the parents and their two sons were interned in the camps Karaganda, Spask, and Kok-Uzek and returned to Vienna in 1947. See Mircia Rosenkranz's report in Yad Vashem, doc. 03/3358. For a discussion of the Perkonkrusts and Arajs see Schneider, 11; Krausnick and Wilhelm, 596–597; and Vestermanis, 429 ff.

32. Krausnick and Wilhelm, 535, quoting a fragment of a January 1942 report of Einsatzkommando 2.

33. Klee, Dreßen, and Rieß, 138, reprint of the report of Secretary Xaver Dorsch, OT, to Reichsleiter Rosenberg, July 12, 1941.

34. Krausnick and Wilhelm, 236, citing *Einsatzmeldungen* (action reports) 20 and 21; see also IMT 25, 81 *ff.*

35. Krausnick and Wilhelm, 539, citing Einsatzmeldung 32.

36. War diary of Police Battalion 322, DÖW doc. No. 17 057; ibid., entry of September 1, 1941.

37. Hilberg, *Die Vernichtung der europäischen Juden*, 347 *ff.*, provides a detailed description of this incident, based on the testimony of HSSPF Erich von dem Bach-Zelewski, a member of Himmler's entourage.

38. Krausnick and Wilhelm, 558 *ff.*, and Klee, 369–370, print sections of the sentence of the Stuttgart court of assizes in the trial of Dr. Albert Widmann.

39. See Kogon, et al., 83–84.

40. Krausnick and Wilhelm, 270, citing Einsatzmeldung 92, dated September 23, 1941; see also Hilberg, *Die Vernichtung der europäischen Juden*, 344.

41. Lang, *Das Eichmann-Protokoll*, 73.

42. Krausnick and Wilhelm, 283, provide a brief survey of Ehrlinger's SS career.

43. YIVO Occ E 3–18, Reichskommissar Ostland IIa 4, Provisional Guidelines for the Treatment of Jews in the Area Administered by the Reichskommissariat Ostland; similar formulations, but with more precise references to the "Solution of the Jewish Problem" in all of Europe, included in the directives of the "Brown Folder" of Lohse's superior Rosenberg, already have been quoted in chapter 4. See also Arad, "Alfred Rosenberg and the 'Final Solution,'" 273–274. In a response of August 6, 1941, Stahlecker criticized Lohse's guidelines because they were "appropriate for the situation created in the Generalgouvernement." Stahlecker proposed resettlements

as an immediate measure and proposed "certain areas be designated as reservations for Jews." See also Hans Mommsen and Dieter Obst, "Die Reaktion der deutschen Bevölkerung auf die Verfolgung der Juden 1933–1943," in Hans Mommsen and Susanne Willems, eds. *Herrschaftsalltag im Dritten Reich* (Düsseldorf: Schwann, 1988), 467 *ff.*, for a reprint of the response of the chief of Einsatzgruppe A – re: Proposal for the Establishment of Temporary Guidelines for the Treatment of Jews in the Territory of the Reichskommissariat Ostland – deposited at the State Historical Archives in Riga.

44. YIVO Occ E 3–27, letter from the Commissar General in Riga to the Reichskommissar Ostland, re: Establishment of Ghettos, Jewish Work Camps, and Labor Deployment of Jews, dated October 20, 1941.

45. YIVO Occ E 3–29, handwritten comment file entry Drechsler.

46. YIVO Occ E 3–30, the Reichkommissar Ostland, note concerning the meeting at the Reichkommissar's office on October 24, 1941, dated October 27, 1941, initialled by Heinz Wichmann, Lohse's personal assistant.

47. Ibid.

48. Krausnick, "Judenverfolgung," 337–338, cites Nuremberg Doc. NO 365 in its entirety: Dr. Erhard Wetzel, Senior Executive Clerk for the Reichsminister for the Occupied Eastern Territories, to the Reichskommissar Ostland, re: Your Report of October 4, 1941, Concerning the Solution of the Jewish Question.

49. Hilberg, *Die Vernichtung der europäischen Juden*, 938–939. In 1960 Dr. Helmet Kallmeyer testified that he did not travel to Riga in the fall and winter of 1941. Instead, he visited Bełżec, the soon-to-be-opened first annihilation camp in the Generalgouvernement equipped with permanent gas chambers. Ibid., 938. During his trial in Jerusalem, Eichmann denied having conferred with Wetzel about gas chambers.

50. Krausnick, "Judenverfolgung."

51. See Beer, 417, who assumes that at that time Viktor Brack and his men were working on the development of permanent gas chambers that were installed in the annihilation camps of Aktion Reinhard beginning in 1942.

52. YIVO Occ 3–31, Commander of the Sicherheitspolizei and SD, Einsatzgruppe A, to Reichskommissar Ostland, November 8, 1941, re: Transports of Jews from the Reich to Ostland, signed Lange.

53. YIVO Occ E 3–32, telex Reichskommissar Ostland, IIa, November 9, 1941, to Reichsminister for the Occupied Eastern Territories and Reichskommissar Lohse, Reich Ministry for the Occupied Eastern Territories at Hotel Adlon, signed: Trampedach.

54. YIVO Occ E 3–26, telegram from the Reichsministerium für die besetzten Ostgebiete, Dr. [Georg] Leibbrandt, November 13, 1941, to Reichskommissar Ostland, Riga, re: Telegram of November 9, 1941, received by the office of Reichskommissar Ostland, IIa, initialed by Trampedach on November 14, 1941. Whether at that time the sentence "The Jews will be sent farther east" already served as a euphemism for murder, as was the case in the spring of 1942, cannot be determined.

55. Yitzhak Arad, *Ghetto in Flames: The Struggle and Destruction of the Jews in Vilna in the Holocaust* (New York: KTAV Publishing House, 1982), 164 *ff.*, discusses the background of this intervention by Wehrmacht and civil administrative authorities in a chapter entitled "Suspension of the Massacres."

56. YIVO Occ E 3–33, note from Reichskommissar Ostland of November 7, 1941, signed Trampedach; the telex of the Reichskommissar Ostland office IIa 4, Riga of November 7, 1941, to the area commander of Vilnius (Wilno/Vilna) was initialed by Trampedach. The Wehrmacht Commander Ostland and Höhere SS und Polizeiführer Generalkommissar at Kauen (Kaunas/Kovno) received copies.

57. YIVO Occ E 3–28, letter from the Reichsminister für die besetzten Ostgebiete, October 31, 1941, to Reichskommissar Ostland, signed Dr. Leibbrandt; see Arad, "'The Final Solution in Lithuania,'" 249–250, for details about events in Liebau (Liepāja); Klee, Dreßen, and Rieß, Schöne Zeiten, 122 ff., contains a subchapter entitled "The Place of Execution Had Attracted Many Spectators," which also deals with the Liebau massacres.

58. IMT, 27, 2–3; Kube's letter is based on a report from the Gebietskommissar (area commissar) of Sluzk who informed Kube about the activities of a police battalion and Lithuanian volunteers at the end of October 1941, describing the massacres and outrageous pillage in graphic detail; see also Klee, Dreßen, and Rieß, 164 ff., for a reprint of the Gebietskommissar's report to the Generalkommissar in Minsk, re: Judenaktion.

59. YIVO Occ E 3–28 and Nuremberg doc. 3363 PS, IMT 32, 436 contain both the handwritten draft of a letter from Reichskommissar Ostland, IIa 4 No. 219/41 g to Reichsminister für die besetzten Ostgebiete, re: Execution of Jews in Reference to Directive of October 31, 1941, sender: Senior Executive Officer Trampedach, with Trampedach's initials, dated November 8, and Lohse's handwritten additions and initials dated November 15, as well as a copy of the letter of November 15 signed: Lohse.

60. See Arad, Alfred Rosenberg and the "Final Solution," 273 ff., about the content of the "Brown Folder," containing Rosenberg's directives concerning the structure and policies of the occupation apparatus in the Soviet Union, including measures to be enacted against Soviet Jews.

61. YIVO Occ E 3–35, letter from the Reichsminister für die besetzten Ostgebiete, I/293/41 Confidential!, dated December 4, 1941, to Reichskommissar Ostland, re: Solution of the Jewish Question, signed Leibbrandt.

62. YIVO Occ E 3–28, letter from the Reichsminister für die besetzten Ostgebiete, No. I/1/157/41, State Secret, dated December 18, 1941, to Reichskommissar Ostland, re: Jewish Question, Reply to Letter of November 15, 1941, signed: Bräutigam.

63. YIVO Occ E 3–26 contains Lange's letter: The Commander of the Sicherheitspolizei and the SD Einsatzgruppe A, Riga, November 20, 1941, to Reichskommissar Ostland, re: Transports of Jews from the Reich, signed Lange; YIVO Occ E 3–32, Lohse's handwritten note on the letter from the Reichsminister für die besetzten Ostgebiete, of November 13, 1941, with Lohse's initials, dated November 28.

64. See Martin Gilbert, The Holocaust: The Jewish Tragedy (London: Fontana, 1986), 228 ff.

65. YIVO Occ E 3–34, Wehrmachtsbefehlshaber Ostland, Ic, 82/41 secret, November 20, 1941, to Reichskommissar Ostland, Riga; BA/MA RH 26707/ vol. 1 contains the monthly reports for October and November 1941 from the Commander for Weißruthenien (Belorussia) to the Army Commander Ostland, which Förster

reprints in "Die Sicherung des 'Lebensraums,'" 1055 *ff.* The 707th Intantry Division had been stationed in Belorussia for some time and had proved itself especially zealous in combating "partisans." Within one month, two of its men had lost their lives and five had been wounded in the process of killing 10,431 "enemies" out of a total of 10,940 "prisoners," among them an unknown number of Belorussian Jews. Krausnick, "Judenverfolgung," 274, concludes from the records of the commander in Belorussia, which in reports about the "political situation" refer to activities relating to Jews as "eliminations," that most of these more than 10,000 murdered people must have been Jews.

66. Wehrmachtsbefehlshber Ostland, YIVO Occ E 3–34.

67. Ibid.

68. Klee, Dreßen, and Rieß, 171 *ff.*, Obersturmbannführer Dr. Strauch's report about Gauleiter Kube; Krausnick and Wilhelm, 554, draw extensive but inaccurate conclusions from this incident: Supposedly, Kube, upon the arrival of the first transports, assembled a list of "controversial cases" and threatened to make a report to Hitler. On November 30 this threat supposedly caused Himmler to cancel the annihilation of several transports already sent to Ostland until Heydrich examined the cases Kube had questioned. This interpretation seems hardly credible, if only because Kube did not demand this list until November 29 and Himmler's telephone conversation with Heydrich took place on November 30. Even if Kube had sent his protest by telegram, bypassing the official route of communication on November 29 – and there are no indications of his having done so – his protest is unlikely to have reached Himmler before noon of the following day to produce the supposed consequences. It is far more likely for Kube to have followed official routine by first contacting his superior, Reichskommissar Lohse, which he indeed did with the letter quoted here, before contacting Berlin. The speed of communications at that time precluded Himmler's reaction on the very next day. Furthermore, the telephone conversation did not refer to transports to Minsk, where no summary executions of deportees had yet occurred, but to a transport from Berlin to Riga. See also Broszat, "Hitler und die Genesis der 'Endlösung,'" 213.

69. YIVO Occ E 3–36, letter of Generalkommissar of Belorussia, Minsk, December 16, 1941, to Reichskommissar Hinrich Lohse, signed: Wilhelm Kube.

70. Ibid.

71. YIVO Occ E 3–37, Stadtkommissar Minsk, Geb 20 Ja/Wst., Minsk, January 5, 1942, to Reichsminister für die besetzten Ostgebiete, with copies to Reichskommissar in Riga and Generalkommissar in Minsk, re: Evacuations of Jews from Germany to Minsk.

72. YIVO Occ E 3–37, fol. 4, The Reichsminister für die besetzten Ostgebiete, No. I/1/730/41, January 16, 1941, to Reichskommissar Ostland, re: Evacuations from Germany to Minsk, signed: Dr. Wetzel.

73. Note, the Reichskommissar Ostland, Dept. IIa 4, Riga, January 13, 1942, signed: Trampedach.

74. YIVO Occ E 3–37, fols. 6–7, letter from Generalkommissar Belorussia to Reichskommissar Ostland, February 6, 1942, re: Evacuations of Jews from Germany to Minsk, signed: Kube.

75. See Arad, "The 'Final Solution' in Lithuania," 245–246; Klee, Dreßen, and Rieß, "*Schöne Zeiten,*" 59, cite the concluding statistics for the executions that took

place in the area of Einsatzkommando 3 until December 1, 1941, signed: SS-Standartenführer Jäger.
76. Ibid., 57.
77. Report of Events, UdSSR No. 151, January 5, 1942, fol. 14, BDC, Stahlecker documents.
78. Ibid.
79. Fleming, *Hitler und die Endlösung*, 88–89, bases his figures of the number of victims on legal investigations in the Federal Republic of Germany.
80. See Schneider, 23 *ff.*
81. Arad, *Ghetto in Flames,* 171. "The suspension of the massacres toward the end of December 1941 was the outcome of the conflict of interest among the different German authorities.... The Wehrmacht was the main factor in the decision to halt the *Aktionen* and leave the remnant of the Jews of Vilna alive. Reichskommissar for the Ostland Lohse decided to stop the extermination of Jews upon receiving urgent requests from the Wehrmacht.... The letter from the ministry in Berlin... did not change the substance of the order promulgated at the beginning of December, which suspended the slaughter of skilled Jewish workers." Wilhelm, 408, points to the assumption "that perhaps the systematic destruction of the Jews did not start for some time after the attack on the Soviet Union and without unequivocal directives from Berlin."

6. The Development of the Genocide Program: 1942

1. Kempner, 126–127; letter from the Chief of the Sicherheitspolizei and SD, IV B 4 -3076/41g, November 29, 1941, to State Undersecretary Luther at the Auswärtige Amt, signed Heydrich; Rückerl, 99–100, cites in its entirety an identical letter to SS-Gruppenführer Hofmann at the SS-Rasse- und Siedlungshauptamt, the Race and Settlement Headquarters.
2. Döscher, 222–223, Auswärtiges Amt, Referat D III. The suggestions of the Foreign Office referred to the expulsion of all Jews from the German Reich, of all Jews who had lost their citizenship from all occupied areas, and of all Jews from Serbia to the "East" to signal to the governments of Romania, Slovakia, Croatia, Bulgaria, and Hungary Germany's "willingness" to expel all Jews living in those states as well.
3. See Kempner, 129, for an assessment how the Japanese attack and U.S. response affected the planned Wannsee Conference; see Döscher, 224, and Arno J. Mayer, *Der Krieg als Kreuzzug: Das Deutsche Reich, Hitler's Wehrmacht und die "Endlösung,"* (Reinbek: Rowohlt, 1982), for a discussion of the impact of the failure of Operation Barbarossa.
4. For details on the impact on the war economy, consult Rolf-Dieter Müller, "Das Scheitern der wirtschaftlichen 'Blitzkriegsstrategie,'" in Militärgeschichtliches Forschungsamt, *Das Deutsche Reich und der Zweite Weltkrieg*, 4, 936 *ff.*; Streit, *Keine Kameraden*, 191 *ff.*, examines these events' consequences in the treatment of the hundreds of thousands of Soviet prisoners of war; Ulrich Herbert, *Fremdarbeiter: Politik und Praxis des "Ausländer Einsatzes" in der Kriegswirtschaft des Dritten Reiches* (Berlin: J. H. W. Dietz, 1985), 132 *ff.*, describes the impact on forced employment of foreign workers in Germany.

262	Notes to Pages 113–115

5. At the end of January 1942 Eichmann, in a memorandum, informed the state police offices and the Zentralstellen about progress "in locating new areas for placing" Jews, with the "purpose of expelling additional contingents." A short time later he issued "Guidelines for the Technical Implementation of Evacuations to the Generalgouvernement," cited in Adler, *Der verwaltete Mensch*, 188 *ff.*

6. Concerning the discussion within the German administrative apparatus in the Generalgouvernement about ghetto administration, antisemitic policies, and the level of importance of these controversies for the realization of National Socialist genocide policies, see Christopher R. Browning, "Nazi Ghettoization Policy in Poland: 1939–1941," *Central European History* 19 (1986): 343 *ff.*; Heim and Aly, 45 *ff.*, and Browning's "reply" to Heim and Aly, "German Technocrats, Jewish Labor, and the Final Solution," in *Remembering for the Future: Working Papers and Addenda* (Oxford: Pergamon, 1989). 2199–2208.

7. Jüdisches Historisches Institut Warschau, *Faschismus-Getto-Massenmord*, 262–263, quoting Frank at a government session on December 12, 1941.

8. Ibid.

9. Yitzhak Arad, *Bełzec, Sobibór, Treblinka: The Operation Reinhard Death Camps* (Bloomington: University of Indiana Press, 1987). Little is known about the history of Aktion Reinhard and its institutional backgrounds; Rückerl, 120, cites a June 23, 1942, letter from Brack to Himmler proving that quite some time earlier Brack, at the order of Reichsleiter Philipp Bouhler, had provided Brigadeführer Odilo Globocnik with personnel "for the execution of his special task."

10. See Lang, *Das Eichmann-Protokoll*, 69–70. Eichmann's report on his visit to Bełzec, which is not documented by any other source, cannot serve as proof for the assumption that he incriminated himself during interrogation even where irrefutable, documents would not put pressure on him to do so. The message of this passage – his status as a mere recipient of orders and self-portrayal as a person incapable of harming a fly – is crystallized in two supposedly psychic shocks: The first occurred at the supposed announcement of the Führerbefehl, the second upon hearing Wirth's account of the killing methods. "That was monstrous for me. I don't have a very robust nature. . . . When I see someone with a gaping cut, I can't stand looking at it. . . . "; Rückerl, 132 *ff.*, discusses Wirth and the construction of the annihilation camp Bełzec.

11. Kogon, 151 *ff.*; Lang, *Das Eichmann-Protokoll*, 69; dating this visit is important because, as Eichmann stated during his interrogation in Jerusalem, he had received Heydrich's order two or three months after the start of the war against the Soviet Union, in August or September 1941. But at that time there was no camp in Bełzec; hence, Eichmann's dates must be incorrect. Yet, a number of historians have accepted it, as, for example Fleming, *Hitler und die Endlösung*, 85, and Krausnick, "Diskussionsbeitrag," in Jäckel and Rohwer, 139.

12. Hilberg, *Die Vernichtung der europäischen Juden*, 460, note from OKW/Wi Rü IVc, October 23, 1941.

13. Döscher, 228, prints the entire protocol of the conference; Eichmann took the minutes; from Politisches Archiv des Auswärtigen Amtes, Inland II g 177.

14. Ibid., 229–231.

15. Ibid., 234.

16. Ibid. See Hilberg, *Die Vernichtung der europäischen Juden*, 450 *ff.*, for the background of the plan to send Jewish war veterans to Theresienstadt.

17. Ibid., 438 *ff.*, provides pertinent details about the Wannsee Conference discussion of the so-called Mischlinge; about another conference that took place on March 6, 1941, in Eichmann's offices at Kurfürstenstraße 116 (see Kempner, 170 *ff.*, for a reprint of the minutes), and for a conference held on October 27, 1943, consult Hilberg, *Die Vernichtung der europäischen Juden*, 438 *ff.*

18. Kempner, 147.

19. Ibid.

20. Jüdisches Historisches Institut Warschau, *Faschismus-Getto-Massenmord*, 268, express letter from Himmler to Richard Glücks, Chief of Amtsgruppe D (Konzentrationslager), January 26, 1942.

21. Adler, *Der verwaltete Mensch*, 188, memorandum IV B 4, signed: Eichmann.

22. Adler, *Die verheimlichte Wahrheit: Theresienstädter Dokumente* (Tübingen: Mohr, 1958), 12 *ff.*

23. Ibid., 9–10, reprint of Gestapo Düsseldorf, March 9, 1942, Report for the Conference of March 6, 1942, at the Reichssicherheitshauptamt-Office IV B 4.

24. Dok. PdI 1156, file note about the meeting with Obersturmbannführer Eichmann at the RSHA, IV B 4 on May 29 and 30, 1942, signed: Dr. Josef Löwenherz.

25. See Avner W. Less, ed. *Schuldig: Das Urteil gegen Adolf Eichmann* (Frankfurt/M.: Athenäum, 1987), 91 *ff.*, who reprints the judgment in Eichmann's trial.

26. CAHJP. A/W 2750, instructions for employees and workers of the Israelitische Kultusgemeinde to be employed in preparation for the emigration transports.

27. Rosenkranz, 259.

28. Rosenkranz, 231 *ff.*, discusses the origin and practices of the Verwaltungsstelle für jüdisches Umzugsgut der Geheimen Staatspolizei (Vugesta) in the summer of 1940.

29. Lg. Wien, Vr 4574/45, testimony of Max F.

30. Lg. Wien, Vr 435/47, testimony of S. K. in the trial of Alfred Slawik, March 12, 1948.

31. Lg. Wien, Vr658/46, written statement by Wilhelm B., Vienna, September 5, 1945.

32. Lg. Wien, Vr 658/46, see also testimonies from Lucie S. and Hermann K.

33. Lg. Wien, Vr 658/46, testimony of Gertrude H.

34. Lg. Wien, Vr 4574/45, testimony of Walter L.

35. Lg. Wien, Vr 435/47, testimony of S. K. in the trial of Alfred Slawik, March 12, 1948.

36. Lg. Wien, Vr 4574/45, testimony of Bruno F.

37. Lg. Wien, Vr 2729/63, testimony of Franzi D.

38. Rosenkranz, 261.

39. Lang, *Das Eichmann-Protokoll* reprints the Korherr Report, "Die Endlösung der Judenfrage: Statistischer Bericht für April 1943," Nuremberg Trial Doc. NO 5193, in the "Dokumentenanhang," the document section. According to this report, 8,100 Jews remained. Rosenkranz, 295, cites the Kultusgemeinde statistic, for 1942, listing 7,989 Jews.

40. Michael Zimmermann, "Die Deportation der Juden aus Essen und dem Regierungsbezirk Düsseldorf," in Ulrich Borsdorf and Mathilde Jamin, eds. *Überleben im Krieg: Kriegserfahrungen in einer Industrieregion 1939–1945* (Reinbek: Rowohlt, 1989), 138 *ff.*

41. CAHJP, A/W 2735; in mid-1943, the Jewish Community of Vienna (IKG Wien) assembled a list of departure dates and arrival stations for deportation transports; it lists these transports of April 9, May 12, May 15, and June 14, 1942; see also

Yad Vashem, DN/27–3, fol. 15, the Vienna 95th Police Precinct report for the transport of April 27, 1942, to Włodawa. It is in a file labeled "The Police President of Vienna, Transports of Jews to the Generalgouvernement;" see also Adler, *Der verwaltete Mensch*, 193.

42. Yad Vashem, DN/27–3, fol. 42, Report, 152nd Police Precinct, 27/II, Reichsbrückenstraße 46, Vienna, dated June 20, 1942, re: Transport commando unit for transport of Jews from Vienna-Aspang Station to Sobibor, June 14, 1942. For details on Franz Stangl, who before 1938 was a policeman in Linz and as a member of the so-called Euthanasie-Aktion ("euthanasia" program) served at Castle Hartheim and as camp commandant of the annihilation camps Sobibór and Treblinka in Aktion Reinhard, see Gitta Sereny, *Into that Darkness: From Mercy Killing to Mass Murder* (London: Deutsch, 1974).

43. Yad Vashem, DN/27–3, fol. 48. The requisition for a transport commando of July 8, 1942, listed five July transports destined for Theresienstadt. Yet for one scheduled to leave Vienna on July 17, this destination was scratched through and substituted with the handwritten comment "place of destination unknown." In Yad Vashem, DN/27–3, fol. 56, however, the Schutzpolizei transport expense account states that from July 17 to July 19 "one evacuation transport of Jews went from Vienna to Auschwitz, Upper Silesia."

44. Krausnick and Wilhelm, 586, Einsatzgruppe A Final Report.

45. Event Report UdSSR, No. 151, January 5, 1942, fol. 14, BDC Stahlecker Documents.

46. Adler, *Der verwaltete Mensch*, 414 *ff.*

47. Wilhelm and Krausnick, 586, Einsatzgruppe A Final Report.

48. According to Jeanette Wolff, 10, only 20 percent of those incarcerated at Salaspils survived; see also Schneider, 45.

49. Schneider, 43.

50. Kogon, et al., 88. At the end of 1944 a witness from Lithuania testified before a Soviet investigative commission that in February 1942 some 2,000 mainly elderly Jews, men and women from Germany, had been killed in gas vans; see also Gertrude Schneider's description, 42–43; she had been deported to Riga with this transport.

51. Schneider, 46–47.

52. Lg. Berlin, I Js 1/65, E 5, vol. 1, 26. According to Reichsbahn train schedules, on August 15 and 31; September 26; and October 3, 1942, transports with the designation DA 401, 403, 405, 407, and 486 were sent from Berlin to Riga and Raasiku.

53. Jeanette Wolff, 11, describes this "selection" as "relocation to Dünamünde;" see also Schneider, 53 *ff.*

54. Wolff, 13 *ff.*

55. Hilberg, *Die Vernichtung der europäischen Juden*, 377 *ff.*

56. Schneider, 81–82.

57. IMT, NO-1831, conference at the Ministry for the Occupied Eastern Territories, July 13, 1943: Vilnius 20,000; Kaunas 17,000; Riga 15,000; and Minsk 8,500 persons.

58. Krausnick, "Judenverfolgung," in Buchheim, 312, memorandum dated June 21, 1943, from Reichsführer-SS to the Höhere SS- and Polizeiführer Ostland and SS-WVHA, NO-2403.

59. Wolff, 21 *ff.*, and 41*ff.*; see also the names of the survivors in Schneider's appendix, which contradicts Hilberg's contention in *Die Vernichtung der europäischen Juden*, 371, that only a mere handful survived the German ghetto in Riga and the subsequently established camps.

60. Krausnick and Wilhelm, 547.
61. Raul Hilberg, *Sonderzüge nach Auschwitz* (Frankfurt/M.: Ullstein, 1987), 147 *ff.*, facsimile of *Fahrplanordnung Nr. 12*, train schedule No. 12, Deutsche Reichsbahn, Reichsbahndirektion Königsberg (Pr), 33 Bfp 9 Bfav, May 7, 1942.
62. See IKG Wien for departure dates and destinations of these transports; see Yad Vashem, DN/27–3, fol. 27–28 for details about this transport from the "Erfahrungsbericht for the completed evacuation transport (Jews)," reference: Vfg. S. Gk. Süd-1–6260, filed by the Vienna 95th Police Precinct on May 16, 1942.
63. DÖW-Akt 854, report of survivor deported from Vienna to Minsk on May 6, 1942.
64. Fritz Baade, et al., eds. *Unsere Ehre heißt Treue: Kriegstagebuch des Kommandostabes Reichsführer SS, Tätigskeitsberichte der 1. und 2. SS-Inf.-Brigade der 1. SS-Kav.-Brigade und von Sonderkommandos der SS* (Vienna: Europa, 1965), 236, reprint of the activity report of II. Zug, 1 Komp./Batl. d. Waffen-SS z.b.V. (2nd Platoon, 1st Company, Batallion of the Waffen-SS on special assignment), Minsk, May 17, 1942, signed: SS-Unterscharführer Arlt.
65. IMT, 26, 108, telex of BdSudSD Ostland, June 15, 1942, to RSHA II D 3A.
66. See IKG Wien, fol. 1–2 for departure dates and destinations; for details about the transport of May 27, 1942, see Hilberg, *Sonderzüge nach Auschwitz*, 158, which contains a facsimile of the wireless message from the Reichsbahn executive office, Vienna, of May 27 to the Reichsbahn offices Oppeln (Opole), Königsberg, Olmütz (Olomouc), Prague, Brünn (Brno), Kraków, and Minsk; activity report of June 18, 1942, in *Unsere Ehre heißt Treue*, 240–241.
67. Oral testimony by Johanna Braithwaite.
68. Erich Kulka, "The Annihilation of Czechoslovak Jewry," in *The Jews of Czechoslovakia: Historical Studies and Surveys*, vol. 3, ed. The Society for the History of Czechoslovak Jews (Philadelphia: Jewish Publication Society of America, 1983), 286.
69. Adler, *Der verwaltete Mensch*, 441.
70. Activity Report of August 3, 1942, in *Unsere Ehre heißt Treue*, 242.
71. YIVO Occ E 3–41, and Nuremberg Doc. 3428-PS, IMT 32, 280–81, report from Generalkommissar Weißruthenien to Reichskommissar Ostland, July 31, 1942, re: Combatting Partisans and Aktionen against Jews in the General District White Ruthenia, signed: Kube.
72. Ibid.
73. YIVO Occ E 3–41, fol. 3, and Nuremberg Doc. 3428-PS, IMT 32, 282.
74. See IKG Wien, fol. 2, and Kulka, 286, for dates of departure and destinations.
75. Adler, *Der verwaltete Mensch*, 442.
76. Kulka, 320, argues that Treblinka was the destination of the people deported from Terezin in October 1942; see also Adler, *Der verwaltete Mensch*, 443.
77. Kulka, 287.
78. DÖW Dok. No. 2563, certified witness testimony of Isak Grünberg, January 4, 1962; see also Kulka, 288.
79. Report, DÖW-Akt 854.
80. DÖW Dok. No. 2563, 3, Grünberg testimony.
81. Gilbert, *The Holocaust*, 698.
82. IMT, 38, 373, Nuremberg Doc. 135-R, letter from the court prison to the Generalkommissar for Weißruthenien, Minsk, May 31, 1943, re: Judenaktion, signed: Günther, prison director.

83. IMT, 38, 371, Nuremberg Doc. 135-R, Reichskommissar Ostland, Tgb. No. 3682/
43g, to the Reichsminister für die besetzten Ostgebiete, Riga, June 18, 1943.

84. Hilberg, *Die Vernichtung der europäischen Juden*, 405, comments on Kube's belated
"resistance" even though Kube's arguments with SS-organizations concerning the
murder of Jews scarcely were based on differences in fundamental principles.

85. Kogon, et al., 91.

86. CDJC, LXX-70, Report entitled "Das Leben der Juden in Berlin in den Jahren
1940–1943" (The Life of the Jews in Berlin during the Years 1940–1943), by an
anonymous writer who had worked as a nurse in a Berlin hospital operated by the
Jewish community.

87. Trial of Otto Bovensiepen and others, Kg. Berlin, 1 Js 9/65, Indictment, fol. 205,
Leo Baeck Institute [LBI], microfilm R 239.

88. LBI, microfilm R 66, fr. 47, file entry by Philipp Kozower, November 14, 1942,
meeting at the office of the Geheime Staatspolizei with Hauptsturmführer Brunner,
records of the Reichsvereinigung der Juden in Deutschland; and LBI R 66, fr. 71, and
file entry of the directions concerning the retirement home at Große Hamburger
Straße.

89. Ibid., fr. 69, file entry by Philipp Kozower, November 17, 1942, about session at
HSTF. Brunner.

90. Ibid., fr. 67, file entry by Philipp Kozower, November 18, 1942.

91. Adler, *Der verwaltete Mensch*, 395–396, quoting a report by Dr. Martha Mosse.

92. LBI, microfilm R 66, fr. 70, file entry by Philipp Kozower, November 17, 1942.

93. Anon., "Das Leben der Juden in Berlin in den Jahren 1940–1943."

94. Martha Mosse, "Report" at the trial of Otto Bovensiepen and others, fol. 203; see
also Hilberg, *Die Vernichtung der europäischen Juden*, 485.

95. Anon. "Das Leben der Juden in Berlin in den Jahren 1940–1943."

96. LBI, R 66, fr. 20, file entry by Moritz Henschel.

97. Anon., "Das Leben der Juden in Berlin in den Jahren 1940–1943."

98. See Mosse, fol. 204, and Hilberg *Die Vernichtung der europäischen Juden*, 484–485.

7. Collaboration and Deportations: 1942

1. Kempner, 141, quoting the minutes of the Wannsee Conference.

2. See the document appendix of Serge Klarsfeld's *Vichy-Auschwitz: Die Zusammenarbeit der deutschen und französischen Behörden bei der "Endlösung der Judenfragen
in Frankreich,"* trans. Ahlrich Meyer (Nördlingen: Delphi Politik, 1989), 356–357,
for a reprint of notes from the Administrative Staff of the Chief of the Military
Administration in France, Department of Administration, Paris, August 19, 1940.

3. See Jacques Adler, *The Jews of Paris and the Final Solution: Communal Response
and Internal Conflicts, 1940–1944* (New York: Oxford University Press, 1987),
15 *ff.*; Marrus and Paxton, 152 *ff.*; and Hilberg, *Die Vernichtung der europäischen
Juden*, 649 *ff.*, for details on aryanizations.

4. Hilberg, *Die Vernichtung der europäischen Juden*, 642, provides a description of the
distribution of Vichy government offices and their jurisdictions. See Marrus and
Paxton, 3–4, and 12 *ff.*, and Klarsfeld, *Vichy-Auschwitz*, 22, for details about the
two laws. See also Marrus and Paxton, 7, and the chapter "The Roots of Vichy
Antisemitism," 25 *ff.*

5. Klarsfeld, *Vichy-Auschwitz*, document appendix, 362, prints Dannecker's file entry of January 21, 1941.

6. Ibid., 364–65, Klarsfeld's reprint of a note from the Military Commander in France, Administrative Staff, Department of Administration, about a meeting on January 30, 1941, concerning further handling of the Jewish Question in France and another meeting at the German embassy on February 28, 1941.

7. Marrus and Paxton, 81–82; CDJC, LXXXIX-14, copy of a situation report from the Military Commander in France, Command Staff, Department Ia, for February 1941.

8. Marrus and Paxton. 223; Dr. Best from the Military Administration had "encouraged" the Vichy Interior Ministry's representative in Paris to instruct the French police to expel or intern non-French Jews in the Occupied Zone. See Marrus and Paxton, 165 *ff.*, for details about the internment camps in the Occupied Zone and all of France; about Drancy, consult Jacques Darville and Simon Wichene, *Drancy la Juive ou la deuxième Inquisition* (Cachan: A. Breger Frères, 1946), and George Wellers, *L'Étoile jaune à l'heure de Vichy: De Drancy à Auschwitz* (Paris: Fayard, 1973).

9. Klarsfeld, *Vichy-Auschwitz*, 35.

10. Marrus and Paxton, 83 *ff.*, discuss the arguments within the Vichy government about the Commissariat General for Jewish Affairs and its first director, Xavier Vallat.

11. See Jacques Adler, 81 *ff.*, on the establishment of the UGIF and the internal discussions of the Jewish community; see Maurice Rajsfus, *Des Juifs dans la collaboration: L'UGIF. 1941–1944* (Paris: Études et documentation internationales, 1980), and Richard I. Cohen, *The Burden of Conscience: French Jewish Leadership during the Holocaust* (Bloomington: Indiana University Press, 1987), on the controversial assessment of the conduct of the functionaries of Jewish organizations.

12. Klarsfeld, *Vichy-Auschwitz*, document appendix, 370, cites Zeitschel's telex of December 16, 1941, informing the Auswärtige Amt about the wave of arrests and the subsequent internments at the Compiègne camp, and announcing that the internees' "further transport to the East" would take place "in the next few days." See also Zeitschel's note dated Paris, March 11, 1942, in Klarsfeld's document appendix, 375.

13. Kempner, 182–183, cites Dannecker's file entry dated Paris, March 10, 1942, re: Expulsion of 5,000 Jews from France; see also Klarsfeld, *Vichy-Auschwitz*, document appendix, 374.

14. Ibid.

15. Ibid., 376. Klarsfeld cites Dannecker's telex to the RSHA IV B 4 of March 12, 1942, re: Deportations of Jews–reception camp Auschwitz. In his document appendix, 378, Klarsfeld cites a directive of the Supreme Command of the Army of May 13, which charged the commander of Greater Paris to avoid the term "deportation" for the "forced expulsion of citizens" because it "still conjured up the expulsions to Siberia during the tsarist régime in Russia." The term "dispatch for forced labor" was to be used instead.

16. Kempner, 186, memorandum from IV B 4a-3233/42g (1550), of March 9, 1942, to Legationsrat Rademacher, Auswärtiges Amt, re: Evacuation of 1,000 Jews from France, signed: Eichmann.

17. Ibid., 189, memorandum from IV B 4a, March 11, 1942, to the Auswärtige Amt, signed: Eichmann.
18. Kempner, 192, cites the reply from the Foreign Office, DIII 265 g, to RSHA IV B 4, confidential to SS-Obersturmführer Eichmann, re: Evacuation of 6,000 Jews from France, signed: Rademacher. See Döscher, 239 *ff.*, for a discussion of Weizsäcker's role in the AA's consent to the deportations from France. During the Nuremberg trials Weizsäcker was found guilty mainly because of this record of consent. See Kempner, 193 *ff.*, for sections of the judgment.
19. Klarsfeld, *Vichy-Auschwitz*, 46.
20. Ibid., document appendix, 459, quoting a telex from the German embassy in Paris, dated September 11, 1942, signed: Schleier. The offer to deport interned foreign Jews from the Unoccupied Zone almost certainly came from the French. During talks involving Heydrich, Karl Oberg, Helmut Knochen, and René Bousquet, the chief of the French police in early May 1942, the French representative learned about the plans for deporting Jews interned in the Occupied Zone "to the East for work details." Bousquet responded by asking Heydrich "whether the Jews who already had been interned in the Unoccupied Zone for eighteen months could not be sent along as well." At the time there was no follow-up on Bousquet's offer, due to transportation problems. See Klarsfeld, 57, for the motives of the Vichy government.
21. Klarsfeld, *Vichy-Auschwitz*, document appendix, 379, Dannecker's file entry of June 15, 1942, re: Additional transports of Jews from France.
22. Ibid., 383, Dannecker's file entry of June 18, 1942.
23. Ibid., 385–387, contain the minutes of Dannecker's and Jean Leguay's meetings on June 25 and 26, 1942. On p. 390 Klarsfeld reprints Dannecker's file entry of June 26, 1942, re: Additional transports of Jews from France.
24. Klarsfeld, *Vichy-Auschwitz*, 131 *ff.*, points out that the SS leadership in France depended on French police not only in arresting Jews but also in combating growing political resistance and maintaining public law and order.
25. Ibid., document appendix, 389, Legationsrat Dr. Zeitschel, Paris, "Notes for Ambassador Abetz," June 27, 1942.
26. Ibid., 387. Eichmann, in a telex of June 26, 1942, announced his arrival to the commander of the Sicherheitspolizei in Paris, justifying his trip by saying that "here [in Berlin] no further problems exist concerning the smooth, speedy execution of the planned evacuations" and that he would be coming at the request of his superior, Müller, and would arrive, probably on June 30, 1942, to "discuss the final details." Obviously, Eichmann considered Paris as the source of complications.
27. Kempner, 206, RSH IV B 4, Paris, July 1, 1942, re: Meeting for imminent evacuations from France, with SS-Hauptsturmführer Dannecker, Paris, signed: Dannecker and Eichmann; see also Klarsfeld, *Vichy-Auschwitz*, document appendix, 390–391; for quotes, see Kempner, 205–206.
28. Klarsfeld, *Vichy-Auschwitz*, document appendix, 396, file entry, by the leader of the Higher SS and Police in the area of the military commander in France, about conference of July 2, 1942, dated July 4, 1942, signed: Hagen, SS-Sturmbannführer.
29. Ibid., 408.
30. For more details on this raid, consult Claude Lévy and André Tillard, *La Grande Rafle du Vel d'Hiv* (Paris: R. Laffont, 1967).

31. Kempner, 212, quoting a facsimile of Dannecker's file entry dated July 21, 1942, re: Jewish expulsions; see also Klarsfeld, *Vichy-Auschwitz*, document appendix, 416.

32. Czech, Danuta, *Kalendarium der Ereignisse im Konzentrationslager Auschwitz-Birkenau 1939–1945* (Reinbek: Rowohlt, 1989), 250–51; see Hilberg, *Die Vernichtung der europäischen Juden*, 987, for details on the IG-Farben installations, the "IG-Auschwitz."

33. Klarsfeld, *Vichy-Auschwitz*, 412, and Czech, *Kalendarium*, 241–42.

34. See Marrus and Paxton, 265 *ff.*, for details about the efforts of US chargé d'affaires H. Pinkney Tuck in France to provide entry visas to the United States for some of the children, and Laval's refusal to agree to this arrangement.

35. Klarsfeld, *Vichy-Auschwitz*, document appendix, 469, telex from Dr. Knochen, commander of the Sicherheitspolizei, to RSHA IV B 4, dated Paris, September 25, 1942; see Klarsfeld, 132–133, about Dannecker's removal at Knochen's instigation.

36. Ibid., 516, quoting Heinz Röthke's note of March 27, 1943.

37. Susan Zuccotti, *The Italians and the Holocaust: Persecutions, Rescue, and Survival* (New York: Basic Books, 1987), 82 *ff.*, discusses the policies of the Italian occupation administration in France concerning the Jews.

38. Klarsfeld, *Vichy-Auschwitz*, document appendix, 489–490, citing a memorandum from the commander of the Sicherheitspolizei to RSHA, Department IV, SS-Gruppenführer Müller, February 12, 1943.

39. Ibid., 513–514, Röthke's note of March 23, 1943; see p. 515 for Hagen's file entry of March 25, 1943, re: Refusal of French police to participate in removal of Jews with French citizenship from Drancy to Germany.

40. Lg. Wien, Vr 3967/61, interrogation of the accused Alfred Josef Slawik, June 12, 1961.

41. BAK, R58/859, fol. 99–100; a letter of the RSHA IG 6, Berlin, February 28, 1941, clarifies that the Adviser for Jewish Questions was attached to the German embassy in Bratislava (Preßburg) but received his instructions from the RSHA, Referat IV B 4. His original title was Sonderbeauftragter des Reichsführers SS bei der Deutschen Gesandschaft in Preßburg (Special Envoy of the Reichsführer-SS at the German Embassy in Bratislava).

42. Lang, *Das Eichmann-Protokoll*, document appendix, cites a facsimile of the report from the inspector for statistics: "Die Endlösung der europäischen Judenfrage," dated March 23, 1943, Nuremberg Trial documents NO 5193 & NO 5194. According to the Korherr Report, 56,691 people were deported from Slovakia; the Slovak ministry of transportation lists 57,752. Consult Hilberg, *Die Vernichtung der europäischen Juden*, 1283 *ff.*, for genesis and various versions of the Korherr Report.

43. Ladislav Lipscher, *Die Juden im Slowakischen Staat 1939–1945* (Munich: Oldenbourg, 1979), 1.

44. Lipscher, 33–34. In contrast to the Nuremberg racial laws, the Slovak government directives of April 18, 1939, defined as Jews all persons who had committed themselves to the "Israelite faith," even if they had converted to Christianity after October 30, 1918, and all persons without religious affiliations who were descendents of "at least one parent of Israelite faith."

45. Kulka, 306, and Lipscher, 69 *ff.*

46. Lipscher, 60.

47. Ibid., 70.
48. Ibid., 80.
49. Yad Vashem, M5/162, Interrogation of Dieter Wisliceny, May 6 and 7, 1946.
50. YIVO Occ E 7(b)-8, report on the Jewish work camps and labor centers in Slovakia.
51. YIVO Occ E 5f-1, confidential memorandum from the Foreign Office D III, 661 g, December 1, 1941, to RSHA, IV B 4, Obersturmbannführer Eichmann.
52. Lipscher, 100, assumes that the Slovak government proposal was intended to serve as a sort of barter to fend off German demands for an increase in the allotments of Slovak workers for the Reich. Kulka, 307, comes to a similar conclusion.
53. Kempner, 229, prints a facsimile of an August 1942 telex from State Undersecretary Luther; see also Hilberg, 776, and PdI 1271, Luther's March 20, 1942, telex to the German embassy in Bratislava.
54. Lipscher, 104, comments bitterly that "during the entire existence of the Slovak state, the officials never were able to discharge duties of such extent with such focus and precision as they handled this one."
55. Dok. PdI 1270, telex, Berlin, March 13, 1942, to the German embassy Bratislava.
56. YIVO Occ E 7(b)-8, report on the Jewish work camps and labor centers in Slovakia; during the deportations, the work camps for Jews also served as collection and transit camps.
57. Yad Vashem, M5/162, Interrogation of Dieter Wisliceny, May 6 and 7, 1946; see also Lipscher, 108.
58. Yad Vashem, M5/162, Interrogation of Dieter Wisliceny. May 6 and 7, 1946.
59. Danuta Czech, *Kalendarium*, 190 *ff.*, discusses the arrival of the Slovak women in Auschwitz. Krajowa Agencja Wydawnicza, ed. *Majdanek: Dokumente und Fotografien* (Lublin: n.p., 1980), 51, provides a facsimile of a copy of a telex dated March 27, 1942, from the Stapo headquarters in Katowice, announcing the imminent arrival of the deported men at the concentration camp Lublin, which at that time did not have facilities for murdering people with poison gas. The telex is addressed to RSHA-IV B 4, Berlin; Economic-Administrative Office of Department D in the Oranienburg concentration camp; and Kommandant of Sipo and SD in Kraków; KL. Lublin, re: Work detail of 20,000 Jews from Slovakia. For information on the concentration camp Lublin/Majdanek, see Jósef Marszalek, *Majdanek: Geschichte und Wirklichkeit eines Vernichtungslagers* (Reinbek: Rowohlt, 1982).
60. Kulka, 308, cites the report by Katerina Singerova.
61. Lipscher, 107, 109.
62. Ibid., 109.
63. Kulka, 311.
64. Lipscher, 189, quoting Tiso's speech of August 16, 1942, in Halič.
65. Ladislaus Hory and Martin Broszat, *Der kroatische Ustascha Staat 1941–1945* (Stuttgart: Deutsche Verlagsanstalt, 1964), 13 *ff.*, explain the origin of the *Ustasha* and its ideology. The term itself means "rebel."
66. Holm Sundhaussen, *Wirtschaftsgeschichte Kroatiens im nationalsozialistischen Großraum 1941–1945: Das Scheitern einer Ausbeutungsstrategie* (Stuttgart: Deutsche Verlagsanstalt, 1983), 99–100, and 249 *ff.*; Hilberg, *Die Vernichtung der europäischen Juden*, 757, provides a comparison of Croat and German definitions of the term "Jew."

67. Sundhaussen, *Wirtschaftsgeschichte Kroatiens*, 249 *ff.*

68. Ibid., 248–49, quoting a the report on the aryanizations in Croatia. Dated February 24, 1942, the document was issued by the head of the German Volksgruppe's main office for economic management.

69. Hory and Broszat, 93 *ff.*, base their report of these mass murders mainly on reports from German offices and organizations in Croatia and Serbia. See also Edmond Paris, *Genocide in Satellite Croatia, 1941–45: A Record of Racial and Religious Persecutions and Massacres* (Chicago: American Institute for Balkan Affairs, 1962).

70. Hory and Broszat, 108, quoting from Dr. Turner's report to the Militärbefehlshaber Südost on September 3, 1941.

71. Gert Fricke, *Kroatien 1941–1944: Der "Unabhängige Staat" in der Sicht des Deutschen Bevollmächtigten Generals in Agram, Glaise von Horstenau* (Freiburg: Rombach, 1972), 69, cites von Horstenau's report to the OKW, dated February 25, 1942.

72. Holm Sundhausen, *Geschichte Jugoslawiens 1918–1980* (Stuttgart: Kohlhammer, 1982), 123.

73. BA/MA, RH 31 III/13, report from Arthur Haeffner to Glaise von Horstenau, dated January 1, 1944. Due to the lack of documentation, the exact number of victims at Jasenovac cannot be determined. The report von Horstenau received from Haeffner cites information from a former camp inmate who estimated that by the end of 1943 the Ustasha had murdered between 300,000 and 400,000 persons there.

74. Franz Theodor Csokor, *Als Zivilist im Balkankrieg* (Vienna: Ullstein, 1947), 181 *ff.*

75. Ibid., 183–184.

76. Ibid., 186–187.

77. Hilberg, *Die Vernichtung der europäischen Juden*, 760.

78. Bauer, 281.

79. ZStL. 415 AR 1310/63, vol. 3, section B, 315; confidential telex from RSHA, IV B 4a, August 14, 1942, to KL Auschwitz, with exact copy to the police attaché at the German embassy in Agram, Hauptsturmführer [Franz] Abromeit, signed: Günther.

80. Consult Daniel Carpi, "The Rescue of Jews in the Italian Zone of Occupied Croatia," in Israel Gutman and Efraim Zuroff, eds. *Rescue Attempts during the Holocaust: Proceedings of the 2nd Yad Vashem International Historical Conference* (Jerusalem: Yad Vashem, 1977), 465–507, and Zucotti.

8. The Destruction of the Jewish Community of Salonika: The Cooperation of the SS and the Wehrmacht

1. For the history of the Jews of Salonika, consult Joseph Nehama, *Histoire des Israélites de Salonique*, 7 vols. (Salonika & London: World Sephardi Federation, 1937–1978).

2. See Julio Caro Baroja, *Los Judios en la España Moderna y Contemporánea* (Madrid: Ediciones Arión, 1961) for a history of the Jews in Spain and their expulsion. Béatrice Leroy, *L'Aventure séfarade: De la Péninsule ibérique à la Diaspora* (Paris: A. Michel, 1986) discusses the history of the Sephardim in Spain and the Sephardic diaspora in general.

3. Cecil Roth, "The Last Days of Jewish Salonica," *Commentary*, July 1950, 50.

4. Martin Gilbert, *Endlösung: Die Vertreibung und Vernichtung der Juden–Ein Atlas* (Frankfurt/M.: Büchergilde Gutenberg, 1983), 138.

5. These population estimates come from Hagen Fleischer's manuscript "Die nazis- tische Verfolgung und Vernichtung der Juden im besetzten Griechenland," which the author graciously made available before the contribution was printed in an anthology to be published by the Institut für Zeitgeschichte, Munich; see also Roth, 49.

6. The order for this cooperation of Wehrmacht and SD-Sonderkommandos was issued on April 2, 1941, even before the attack on Yugoslavia and Greece; see Regulations for the deployment of the Sicherheitspolizei and the SD in Operations "Marita" and "Twenty-Five," Oberkommando des Heeres, Gen St d H/Gen Qu. Abt. Kriegsverwaltung, April 2, 1941, signed: Halder, BA/MA, RH 311, vol. 23. Within the individual general staffs, the Ic officers were responsible for cooperation with the Sonderkommandos: "Within the area of each army, a deputy of the chief of the Sicherheitspolizei and SD will be appointed to take charge of the central coordination of these Kommandos. . . . They will be dependent on constant, close cooperation with the Ic. . . . The Ic is responsible for coordinating the tasks of the Sonderkommandos with military intelligence, the activities of the GFP [Geheime Feldpolizei, Wehrmacht secret field police], and the necessities of the various operations."

7. Nuremberg Trial, document NOKW 1382, Directive of the Quartermaster of the Kommandant rückwärtiges Armeegebiet 560 (Army Group A, Twelfth Army, 560th Army Rear Area Security Command), of May 21, 1941.

8. Michael Molho et al., eds. *Israelitische Gemeinde Thessalonikis: In Memoriam*, trans. Peter Katzung (Essen: Jüdische Gemeinde Thessalonikis, 1981), 69, report that now and then members of the Wehrmacht "let themselves be swayed to attack individual Jews" but stress that "such activities were few and by no means are there orders from above for attacking the entire Jewish population, which lives in relative calm."

9. Hildegard von Kotze, ed. *Gerhard Engel, Heeresadjudant bei Hitler 1938–1943* (Stuttgart: Deutsche Verlagsanstalt, 1974), 111. Most of the time Engel's dates are unreliable; see Hilberg, *Die Vernichtung der europäischen Juden*, 417.

10. ZStL. 415 AR 1310/63, vol. 3, section B, 332 *ff.*; letter RSHA/IV B 4 b-2427/42 g (1148), July 11, 1942, to the German Foreign Office, signed: Suhr.

11. Ibid.

12. Ibid.

13. See Molho et al., 70 *ff.*, and victim testimonies at Eichmann's trial in Jerusalem, session 47, May 22, 1961.

14. Roth, 51.

15. IMT 4, Wisliceny's witness testimony at the trial of the main war criminals before the International Military Tribunal. The documents cited below about Günther Altenburg, the Plenipotentiary of the Reich, refute the claim that in January 1943 Eichmann personally travelled Greece to prepare the deportations, a claim that originated with Reitlinger, p. 334, who in his description of the deportations from Salonika confuses Alois Brunner with Anton Brunner. Nevertheless, Eichmann's appearance in Greece is being reiterated even in later publications, as, for exam- ple, in Hanspeter Born, *Für die Richtigkeit: Kurt Waldheim* (Munich: Schneek- luth, 1987), 119–120: "When Adolf Eichmann as head of Referat IV B 4 in the Reichssicherheitshauptamt in mid-January 1943 undertook a whirlwind trip to Salonika. . . . Eichmann came to light a fire under people. He called a meeting for January 15 with the leaders of Heeresgruppe E [Army Group E], the German

military administration of Salonika, and the police to inform all present, among them Oberstleutnant Hans Behle, then the head of group Ic/AO, that very soon he would send a delegation from the Sicherheitsdienst to Salonika to deport the Jews. He charged Generaloberst Löhr as Oberbefehlshaber of Heeresgruppe E with the responsibility of "helping with whatever that group required of him." *Wochenpresse* 49, December 1987, 24, relates a similar account of these events.

16. Altenburg's letter of January 13, 1943, Politisches Archiv des Auswärtigen Amtes (PAAA), Inland IIg/190, and Auswärtiges Amt telex of January 22, 1943, signed: Luther, to Diplogerma Rom No. 294, which cites sections of Altenburg's telex; see copy at Lg. Wien, Vr 3388/61.

17. ZStL. V 508 AR 1314/68.

18. Telegram dated January 23, 1943, from the Auswärtige Amt to Consugerma Athen No. 205, signed: v. Hahn; copy at Lg. Wien Vr. 3388/61.

19. Chief of the Sicherheitspolizei and SD, IV B 4–2427/42g (1148), January 25, 1943, to Auswärtiges Amt, re: Measures against Jews in Greece, signed: Günther; copy at Lg. Wien, Vr 3388/61.

20. Institut für Zeitgeschichte, Munich, MA 688 (National Archives Washington, Microfilm T 501, roll 252) frames 1116 *ff*. In January 1943, several persons served in the position of "Befehlshaber Saloniki-Ägäis." On January 1, 1943, v. Krenski, who was transferred to the Führer reserve, was replaced by Generalleutnant v. Studnitz who died on January 13 in a rail accident. From January 13 to January 20, 1943, Generalmajor Herrmann, general of the engineers at the supreme command of Heeresgruppe E, filled in until Generalleutnant Haarde took over.

21. BAK, All. Proz. 21/242, 3. Dr. Max Merten's written statement of September 9, 1958, to the *Landesgericht* (state court) Berlin. Merten's testimony needs to be handled with extreme caution. Because in 1959 a court in Athens sentenced him to twenty-five years imprisonment as one of the main participants in the deportations from Salonika and that same year handed him over to the Federal Republic of Germany, he tried to reduce his own responsibility by shifting blame to others. The content of his letter, however, does coincide in part with Günther's statements from 1943 cited above and, as far as the group of participants is concerned, the roster includes officers customarily involved in meetings of this nature at that time. To mention an example from occupied France, for a "conference on the subsequent treatment of the Jewish Question in France" on January 30, 1941, hosted by the military commander of France in Paris, the leaders of his own administrative staff; the RHSA members and Eichmann coworkers Lischka and Dannecker representing the head of the Sicherheitspolizei and SD in Belgium and France; Major Crome, the Ic of the military commander; and Oberleutnant Grüninger of the Ic department were in attendance; see CDJC, XXVI-13.

22. BA/MA, RW 40/32, Appendix 84 of the war diary of the commanding general and commander in Serbia, Dr. Turner's presentation on August 29, 1942, to Generaloberst Löhr, Wehrmachtsbefehlshaber Südost.

23. BA/MA, RH 31 III/7, Note for the Führer, re: Situation in Croatia, dated October 1, 1942, signed: von Löhr, Generaloberst; Glaise von Horstenau, Generalleutnant; S. Kasche [German ambassador to the Ustasha state]; Peter Broucek, ed. *Ein General im Zwielicht: Die Erinnerungen Edmund Glaises von Horstenau, Deutscher Bevollmächtigter General in Kroatien und Zeuge des Untergangs des "Tausendjährigen Reiches,"* vol. 3 (Vienna: Böhlau, 1988), 162. From recent discussions with

Hitler, v. Horstenau knew that the "note" was to serve as an aid in Hitler's negotiations with Mussolini: "In Winnica the Führer decided . . . to initiate a discussion of this matter with the Duce."

24. ZStL. 505 AR 983/61, Witness testimony, Dr. Theodor P., June 13, 1961.

25. Molho et al., 94–95.

26. Lg. Wien, Vr 183/53, interrogation of Alfred Slawik.

27. See the memorandum cited in note 19; Döscher, 296, quoting a facsimile of a memorandum of Reichsführer-SS, IV B 4–3433/42 g (1446) to Reichsaußenminister v. Ribbentrop November 30, 1942, signed: Himmler, shows that in November 1942 Himmler already had suggested Wisliceny's reassignment from Bratislava, although at that time not to Salonika but to Budapest: "In light of Hungarian efforts it seems useful soon to send to the German embassy in Budapest one of my specialists, perhaps SS-Hauptsturmführer Wisliceny, who is taking care of the technical assistance for freeing Slovakia of Jews in perfect harmony with your men in Bratislava. There he could work at the German embassy as a scientific specialist or specialist of Jewish affairs." See also a copy of a telex from the Auswärtige Amt to Consugerma Athen no. 217, dated January 25, 1943, signed: Luther, Lg. Wien, Vr 3388/61.

28. Copy of telegram no. 276 from Altenburg dated January 26, 1943, to the Auswärtige Amt, Lg. Wien, Vr 3388/61.

29. IMT, Wisliceny's witness testimony.

30. Slawik's testimony identified in note 26.

31. Molho et al., 95.

32. Ibid., 96, quotation from a copy of the directive issued by the Befehlshaber Saloniki-Ägäis, Department of Military Administration, February 6, 1943, re: Marking and resettlement of the Jews of Salonika, signed: Kriegsverwaltungsrat Dr. Merten.

33. Ibid., 97.

34. See "Excerpts from the Salonika Diary of Lucillo Merci (February-August 1943)," *Yad Vashem Studies* 18 (1987): 300–301. "In recent days, the consulate offices have been besieged by Italian nationals of Jewish faith seeking to exempt their relatives holding Greek citizenship from the restrictions imposed on the Jews. I accompanied our consul, Mr. Zamboni, on his visit to Dr. Merten. We submitted the requests we had received for exemptions from the restrictions against the Jews. . . . 'There is nothing I can do here,' replied Merten. 'These directives have been issued in Berlin on behalf of Reichsführer-SS Himmler. They are clear: everyone is required to wear the Star of David and reside in the ghetto. This applies also to Italian Jewesses married to Greek nationals.'"

35. Molho et al., 98, citing the directive from the field office of Sipo and SD in Salonika IV B 4 to the Jüdische Kultusgemeinde of Salonika, signed: SS-Hauptsturmführer Wisliceny.

36. ZStL. 508 AR-Z 26/1963, vol. 3, testimony of Jitzak N.

37. Molho et al., 99, Befehlshaber Saloniki-Ägäis, Department of Military Administration, to the president of the Jüdische Kultusgemeinde Salonika, February 13, 1943, signed: Kriegsverwaltungsrat Merten.

38. "Salonika Diary," 300.

39. Molho et al., 100.

40. Ibid., 110–11.

41. Ibid., 113.

42. Lg. Wien, Vr 3388/61, copy of Dieter Wisliceny's notarized statement given in Bratislava, dated June 27, 1947.

43. Molho et al., 104.

44. Ibid.

45. Lg. Wien, Vr 3388/61, copy of a letter from the German Consulate General Salonika to the Auswärtige Amt Berlin, February 26, 1943. This letter proves without doubt that the German Foreign Office was not merely informed on issues demanding diplomatic intervention but also about concrete details concerning the organization of deportations.

46. Roth, 52. "If the Jews were isolated, they could be despoiled with greater ease; and having been despoiled, they could be exterminated."

47. Akt. Lg. Wien, Vr 3388/61, copy of a memorandum from the Befehlshaber Saloniki-Ägäis, Department of Military Administration, February 25, 1943, re: Membership of Jews in organizations, signed: Kriegsverwaltungsrat Dr. Merten.

48. Molho et al., 107.

49. Ibid., 107–108.

50. "Salonica Diary," 302.

51. Molho et al., 119; see also the report from Hella Cougno in Miriam Novitch, *Le Passage des Barbares: Contribution à l'Histoire de la Déportation et de la Résistance des Juifs Grecs* (n.p.: Ghetto Fighters House Publications, 1982), 57–58.

52. ZStL. 508 AR-Z 26/1963, vol. 3, Walter St., witness testimony.

53. Molho et al., 120.

54. Ibid., 121.

55. Ibid., 122; see also Hella Cougno's report in Novitch, *Le Passage des Barbares*, 58.

56. Akt. Lg. Wien, Vr 3388/61, copy of the directive of the Befehlshaber Saloniki-Ägäis, Department of Military Administration, March 13, 1943, signed: Dr. Merten.

57. Molho et al., 116.

58. Ibid.

59. Roth, 53.

60. Consult Wisliceny's notarized statement identified in note 42.

61. See Slawik's testimony, note 26.

62. Molho et al., 123; see Albert Menasche, *Birkenau* (New York: Saltiel, 1947), 12, for a similar description.

63. Roth, 53. The cars were loaded "to twice their capacity.... Soon the cargo of human misery began its journey to the Polish slaughterhouses. Four hundred and fifty-one years earlier, their ancestors had been the victims of one of the greatest tragedies in the history of medieval Europe when they had been driven out of Spain, hoping in vain for a miracle that would save them at the last moment."

64. Danuta Czech's "Deportation und Vernichtung der griechischen Juden im KL Auschwitz," *Hefte von Auschwitz* 11 (1970), is the source of these figures. Only the count of the people "received" into the camp is relatively well known because they had consecutive numbers tattooed into the left forearm and were registered in Auschwitz's camp inmate record. No statistics exist about the victims who, on their arrival, were murdered in the gas chambers. The figures stated here represent the difference between the numbers of deportees listed for the individual transports in Salonika and those entered in the camp inmate registers.

65. PAAA, Inland IIg/190, Deutsches General-Konsulat via Bevollmächtigte des Reiches für Griechenland (Greece), Athen, to Auswärtiges Amt Berlin, No. 103-J, March 15, 1943, signed: Schönberg; see Hilberg, *Die Vernichtung der europäischen Juden*, 745–746; in the summer of 1944, the representatives of the Ministry of Transport, the Ministry of Finance, the German Foreign Office, and the Supreme Command of the Army still were arguing about payment of transport expenses.

66. Schönberg's letter to the Foreign Office, March 15, 1943.

67. Molho et al.,131 *ff.*

68. The numbers of deportees listed below are based on an unidentified Transportübersicht (Transport Summary), a copy of which is deposited at Akt Lg. Wien Vr 4574/45. The missing entry of the number of deportees for train Da 19 on August 11, 1943, has been added from data provided by Molho et al., the editors of *Israelitische Gemeinde Thessalonikis: In Memoriam*, 140, which lists 1,800 passengers.

Individual Transport Train Data

Train Designation	Departure from Salonika (in 1943)	No. of Deportees Based on Furnished Data a)	b)	c)	Arrival at Auschwitz	Admitted to Auschwitz KL	Gassed in Auschwitz
Da 1	March 15	2,400	2,400	2,800	March 20	609	1,800
Da 2	March 17	2,635	2,500	2,800	March 24	814	1,800
Da 3	March 19	2,800	2,500	1,901	March 25	695	2,100
Da 4	March 23	2,800	2,800	2,501	March 30	453	2,300
Da 5	March 27	2,800	2,800	2,800	April 3	592	2,200
Da 6	April 3	2,800	2,800	2,500	April 9	479	2,300
Da 7	April 5	2,800	2,800	2,750	April 10	783	2,000
Da 8	April 7	2,800	2,800	2,800	April 13	864	1,900
Da 9	April 10	2,800	2,800	3,000	April 17	729	2,100
Da 10	April 13	2,800	2,800	2,501	April 18	605	2,200
Da 11	April 16	2,818	2,800	2,800	April 22	668	2,150
Da 12	April 20	2,800	2,800	2,700	April 26	638	2,200
Da 13	April 22	2,600	2,800	3,070	April 28	541	2,100
Da 14	April 28	2,800	2,600	2,930	May 4	538	2,300
Da 15	May 3	2,500	2,600	2,500	May 7/8	883	1,600
Da 16	May 9	1,805	1,700	4,500	May 16	677	1,100
Da 17	June 1	766	no info	880	June 6	308	460
Da 18	August 2	441	no info	no info	August 13	(Bergen-Belsen)	
Da 19	Aug. 11	no info	no info	1,800	August 18	271	1,500
TOTAL		45,324 Auschwitz; 441 Bergen-Belsen				11,147	34,000

Train designations, departure dates, and numbers of deportees

a). Data originate from an unidentified, undated, unsigned transport summary statistic the place of origin of which is also unknown. How it became part of the state prosecutor's documents in the trial against "Brunner II" (Anton) cannot be determined. That the original was an SS internal table that probably originated with the Sonderkommando in Salonika is supported by the figures of deported Jews it provides for March 1943, which are identical to the number of "evacuees" the Korherr Report lists for Greece for the first quarter of 1943. Both documents list a total of 13,435 persons for the quarter ending at the end of March.

b). The numbers of deportees reflect the Greek rail management office data quoted by Hagen Fleischer, 32.

c). Arrival dates of the trains in Auschwitz and the number of deportees delivered to the camp come from Danuta Czech's article "Deportation und Vernichtung," 24. I have corrected one obvious error in Czech's figures; she lists two trains as having arrived in Auschwitz on May 7 and 8, 1943, respectively. There was only one train, Da 15, which left Salonika on May 3, 1943. The files of the German Federal Republic prosecutor's investigation contain the same figures because they too are based on the 1943 Auschwitz Kalendarium; see ZStL. 415 AR 1310/63 E5, vol. 3, section B, 381–382.

The numbers of victims who were murdered in the gas chambers immediately after the initial selections are rough estimates based on the difference between the number of deportees listed in column a) and the number of men and women actually taken into the camp. Czech's assumption that Jews from Salonika also were deported to the Treblinka extermination camp and murdered there probably is incorrect; see also ZStL. 415 AR 1310/63 E5, vol. 5, section C, for similar statements. In "Deportation und Vernichtung," 21, Czech cites as proof train Da 101, which arrived in Treblinka on March 28, 1943, allegedly transporting "resettlers" from Salonika. But the victims on this train probably were Thracian Jews whom the Bulgarian occupation administration of northern Greece had arrested in Alexandróupoli, Komotiní, Xánthi, Kala, Dráma, and Serres during the night of March 3–4 and then had taken them to the Danube port of Lom; see Molho et al., 152–153. Lg. Wien, Vr 3388/61, cites the Final Report of the police attaché at the German embassy in Sofia, dated April 5, 1943, which states that from there these Jews were sent to Vienna: "I can now announce the removal of 11,343 Jews [the Korherr Report provides almost the same number, of 11,364 Jews 'evacuated' from Bulgaria during the first quarter of 1943]. Of these, 4,221 Jews from Thrace were shipped by water from Lom to Vienna while 7,122 Macedonian Jews went there by train from Skopje." The transport on the Danube involved four ships, one of which, the *Saturn*, belonged to the Donaudampfschiffartsgesellschaft (DDSG), the Austrian Danube Steamship Company. According to the Reichsbahn headquarters in Vienna (see ZStL. Dokumentensammlung Polen, vol. 264), on March 25–26, 1943, train Da 101 transported these deportees in freight cars to the "reception station" Treblinka. Hilberg, *Die Vernichtung der europäischen Juden*, 480–481, discusses the negotiations between Spanish and German officials concerning the fate of Salonika Jews who were Spanish citizens; see *In Memoriam*, 140, on the subject of "privileged" Jews.

69. Gilbert, *The Holocaust*, 577. "The first experiments, intended to provide evidence about the effects and consequences of sterilization, were carried out on a number of young Jewish girls between the ages of fifteen and eighteen. All were from Greece. First, they were sterilized by X-rays. Then their ovaries were removed. Or, three months after the sterilization, parts of their reproductive organs would be removed

and sent to the Research Institute in Breslau. Such experiments were performed two to three times a week. Each experiment would 'use up' about thirty women. Hundreds of women, having been mutilated by these experiments, were then sent to Birkenau and to its gas-chambers."

70. ZStL. 508 AR-Z 26/63, vol. 6. Report of Ruth K.

71. Menasche, 12; see also ZStL. 415 AR 1310/63 E5, vol. 4, section C, citing Kalendarium Auschwitz.

72. Lg. Wien, Vr 3388/61, contains Burckhardt's testimony. See also ZStL. V 508 AR 1314/68; at the instigation of the German plenipotentiary, Günther Altenburg, Dr. Burkhardt was expelled from Greece a short time after this incident. Altenburg, in a telegram of March 15, already had demanded that the Auswärtige Amt take action against Burkhardt: "Representative of the International Red Cross in Salonika, Dr. Burkhardt, Switzerland, about whose anti-German stance the consulate general has received numerous reports, lately attempted to involve himself in Judenaktionen. Please now, through competent authority, probably the Committee of the International Red Cross in Geneva, effect Burkhardt's immediate recall"; consult Lg. Wien, Vr 3388/61, which contains a copy of Dr. Marten's memorandum to the Jüdische Kultusgemeinde in Salonika, re: Escape of the Jew Dr. Cuenca on March 21, 1943. Hilberg's incorrect discussion of Cuenca's "escape," in *Die Vernichtung der europäischen Juden*, 743, is based on this document.

73. Akt Lg. Wien, Vr 3388/61 contains the testimonies of Lisa Blumenfeld; Molho et al., 137, report that Blumenfeld was murdered in the Baron-Hirsch camp.

74. ZStL. 415 AR 1310/63, vol. 3, section B, 335–36, letter from RSHA IV B 4 b-2427/42g to the Foreign Office concerning measures against Jews in Greece, February 2, 1943, signed: Eichmann.

75. Ibid.

76. Daniel Carpi, "Nuovi Documenti per la Storia dell'Olocausto in Grecia: L'atteggiamento degli Italiani (1941–1943)" in *On the History of the Jews in the Diaspora*, vol. 7 (Tel Aviv: University of Tel Aviv Research Institute, 1981); the AA's written response on February 18 informed Eichmann that the cabinet chief of the Italian Foreign Ministry doubted that Jews holding citizenship of other countries had been awarded Italian citizenship at Italian consulates. Accordingly, the Foreign Office asked Eichmann "for proof at his disposal" to provide the German embassy in Rome with more specific instructions and more specific details. See Lg. Wien, Vr 3388/61 for a copy of this confidential letter signed v. Hahn to the RSHA, for Obstbf. Eichmann. See ZStL., V 508 AR 1314/68 for a copy of an AA file entry of February 24, 1943: "Until now the efforts of Ambassador [Hans Georg von] Mackensen [in Rome] and envoy Altenburg to establish cooperation with the Italian commander in Greece in the planned execution of measures against the Jews in Salonika have not produced any concrete results."

77. Merci, 305. "April 5: I am extremely busy working on Jewish affairs. Everyone with any sort of ties to Italy – family, business, or any other – applies to us. From morning till night our offices are packed with people wearing the Star of David on their chest and with others."

78. Carpi, "Nuovo Documenti."

79. Merci, 303.

80. Ibid., 308–309.

81. PAAA, Inland IIg/190, Befehlshaber Saloniki-Ägäis, Department of Military Administration, MV 2165/43, to the German Consulate General, Salonika, April 26, 1943, signed: Dr. Merten, re: Departure of Jews holding Italian citizenship to southern Greece–Ital. occupied area.

82. Ibid.

83. Merci, 311.

84. Lg. Wien, Vr 3388/61, Henke's notes from June 3, 1943.

85. PAAA, Inland, IIg/190, Schönberg's memorandum to the Auswärtige Amt, dated June 21, 1943.

86. Henke's notes of June 3, 1943.

87. Ibid.

88. PAAA, Inland IIg/190, memorandum from the Sonderkommando of the Sicherheitspolizei for Jewish Affairs, Salonika-Ägäis, to the German Consulate General, Salonika, June 21, 1943, re: Trip to Athens to locate escaped Jews, signed: Wisliceny.

89. Wisliceny's testimony.

9. Manhunts in France and Greece: 1943–1944

1. See CDJC, CCXVII-29, "Rapport sur l'Equipe Brunner," and CDJC, CCXVIII-25-b, report about the personnel at Drancy.

2. See Klarsfeld, *Vichy-Auschwitz*, 330–331, for a list of all deportation transports from France, and Klarsfeld's *Le Mémorial de la Déportation des Juifs de France* (Paris: Klarsfeld, 1978), for the deportations in general.

3. Marrus and Paxton, 323 *ff.*, discuss the debates over the "denaturalization laws."

4. YIVO, UGIF-Collection, fr. 92, Compte-Rendu de la Réunion du Conseil d'Administration du Juin 8, 1943.

5. Klarsfeld, *Vichy-Auschwitz*, document appendix, 532–533, IV B, Paris, June 14, 1943, meeting at the office of Sturmbannführer Hagen with Brunner and Röthke about the application of the French government's then-pending repeal of the post-1927 naturalization of Jews.

6. Ibid., 538, IV B, Paris, June 28, 1943, to the RSHA, SS-Gruppenführer Müller, re: Judenaktion in France, signed: Dr. Knochen.

7. Ibid., 540, Telex from Müller to the BdS Paris, Dr. Knochen, July 2, 1943.

8. YIVO, UGIF-Collection, fr. 111 *ff.*, Procès-verbal de la Séance du 30 Juin 1943.

9. CDJC, CCXXI-19, Report: Situation, July 15, 1943; see also CDJC, CCXVI-55, Report André Cohen, March 1, 1945.

10. CDJC, CXCIV-101, telex dated July 18, 1943, signed: Brunner, SS-Hauptsturmführer.

11. CDJC, CCXXI-19, Report: Situation au 15. Juillet, 1943.

12. Wellers, 187.

13. Darville and Wichené, 80–81, describe several incidents involving Brückler; see also Wellers, 187.

14. CDJC, DLXXIX-5, receipt, Judenlager Drancy near Paris.

15. Wellers, 253.

16. CDJC, CCXIII-1, letter to Laval, July 13, 1943, signed: Le Président du Consistoire Central, Le Grand Rabbin de France.

17. Marrus and Paxton, 326 *ff.*, discuss various Vichy leaders' motives for refusing to pass the "denaturalization laws."
18. Ibid., 325.
19. Ibid., 321.
20. Jean-Louis Panicacci, *Les Juifs et la question juive dans les Alpes-Maritimes de 1939 à 1945* (Nice: Archives départmentementales des Alpes-Maritimes, 1983) gives a description of the situation of the Jews in this region; Albert Drach's *Unsentimentale Reise* (Munich: Müller, 1988) is a literary presentation of the realities of life in southern France from the perspective of an Austrian refugee; see also Klarsfeld, *Vichy-Auschwitz* for Röthke's reports and Eichmann's and Müller's interventions; see also Marrus and Paxton, 315 *ff.*
21. Kempner, 334, reprints a note from Eberhard von Thadden, dated September 30, 1943, from a facsimile.
22. CDJC, CCCLXVI-64, report about Nice, written by members of a Zionist youth organization in early 1944.
23. CDJC, CCXVI-66, Témoignage du Dr. Drucker, February 15, 1946. Dr. Drucker was at Drancy from May 1943 until August 1944. He describes the differences between the French administration of the early period and Brunner's régime, which changed Drancy from an internment camp into a "veritable gare de triage," a train-switching station.
24. CDJC, CCXVI-55, Report Sala Hirth, March 16, 1945.
25. Klarsfeld, *Vichy-Auschwitz*, 284–285, describes how he and his mother managed to escape the raids whereas his father was captured and deported.
26. Klarsfeld, *The Children of Izieu: A Human Tragedy* (New York: H. Abrams, 1985) provides biographies of the children and their caregivers and describes efforts to save Jewish children. On p. 94 he cites from a facsimile of a telex Kdr. Sipo und SD Lyon, IV B 61/43, April 6, 1944, to Commander of the Sicherheitspolizei, Abt. IV B Paris, re: Jewish children's home in Izieu-Ain, signed: Barbie, SS-Ostuf, Nuremberg Document RF 1235; the original is in CDJC.
27. Klarsfeld, 94; in 1942–1943, with Röthke's permission, children whose parents had been arrested and who were in the custody of the French police or the Gestapo had been turned over to the care of the UGIF. Most of these "blocked" children were housed in children's homes administered by the UGIF; see also CDJC, CDXXX-30, "Note sur les Maison d'enfants de l'UGIF"; Jacques Adler, 154 *ff.*, discusses the role the children's homes played in the internal UGIF discussions about possibilities and limits of collaboration.
28. CDJC, CDXXXIV-10, IV B 4, Paris, April 14, 1944, signed: Dr. Knochen, SS-Standartenführer und Oberst der Polizei, Brunner, SS-Hauptsturmführer; Klarsfeld reprints this memorandum in *Vichy-Auschwitz*, document appendix, 574 *ff.*
29. Ibid.
30. Marrus and Paxton, 332.
31. Klarsfeld, *Vichy-Auschwitz*, 306; in February 1944 the Gestapo asked the police prefecture to surrender the lists but was unable to obtain them.
32. CDJC, CCXXI-27, Dr. Schendel's report about the arrest of children in July 1944; see Klarsfeld, *Vichy-Auschwitz*, 315–316, and Jacques Adler, 159, for the backgrounds of the UGIF leaders' decision to leave the children in homes known to the SS;

also consult Jean-François Chaigneau, *Le dernier wagon* (Paris: Julliard, 1982), for details about the last transport from Drancy, which left Paris on August 17, 1944, with 51 deportees.

33. CDJC, CCXVII-26, report on Drancy's liberation; CDJC, DLXXIX-5, probably the last SS report on the number of internees at Drancy, "Situation on September 17, 1944."

34. Wellers, 250.

35. Daniel Carpi, "Notes on the History of the Jews in Greece during the Holocaust Period: The Attitude of the Italians (1941–1943)," in George Schneiweis Wise, ed. *Festschrift in Honor of Dr. George S. Wise* (Tel Aviv: Tel Aviv University Publications, 1983), 25 *ff.*

36. See Kasimierz Moczarski, *Gespräche mit dem Henker: Das Leben des SS-Gruppenführers und Generalleutnants der Polizei Jürgen Stroop aufgezeichnet im Mokatów Gefängnis zu Warschau* (Düsseldorf: Droste, 1978), for details about the life of Stroop, who after crushing the Warsaw Ghetto rebellion, entered history as "the executioner of the Warsaw Ghetto."

37. BAK, R 70 Griechenland, vol. 2, fol. 31, provides a personnel roster of the BdS Greece, Dept. IV b; BAK, R 70 Griechenland, vol. 3, fol. 14, Befehlshaber of the Sicherheitspolizei und SD for Greece in Athens, office personnel roster as of July 15, 1944.

38. Molho et al., 2:217.

39. Ibid.

40. Yad Vashem, M-5/162, notarized statement of Elias Barsilai, Greek National Office for War Crimes, Athens, May 8, 1946.

41. Hagen Fleischer, *Im Kreuzschatten der Mächte: Griechenland 1941–1944* (Frankfurt/M.: and New York: Peter Lang, 1986), and John Louis Hondros, *Occupation and Resistance: The Greek Agony 1941–1944* (New York: Pella, 1983), 95 *ff.*, discuss Greek resistance groups and Greek collaboration.

42. Molho et al., 2: 227–28.

43. Molho et al., 2: 229–30, reprint the text of Stroop's directive; BA/MA, RW 40/147, fol. 256, Situation Report from the chief of the military administration, office of the Militärbefehlshaber Griechenland, for November 1943, dated December 18, 1943, point 4e – Jewish Question.

44. ZStL., 415 AR 1310/63, vol. 3, section B, 339, file entry von Thadden, Auswärtiges Amt, January 26, 1944.

45. Errikos Sevillias, *Athens – Auschwitz*, trans. Nikos Stavroulakis (Athens: Lycabettus Press, 1983), 6 *ff.*, gives a detailed description of the arrest of the people who came to the synagogue on March 24 and of their internment in the Chaidari concentration camp; see Molho et al., 2:257, for quotation.

46. BA/MA, RH 24–68/36, according to the Ic daily report of March 25, 1944, issued by the Ic, LXVIII Army Corps, the SD arrested 70 Jews in Pátra during that day's raid conducted jointly by Wehrmacht units and the SD. See also Sevillias, 15–16, and Molho et al., 2:259.

47. NARA, T 311/179/1410, copy of the monthly situation assessment, wireless transmission from the 1st Mountain Div. on August 15, 1943, to the German general staff at the Italian Eleventh Army High Command, copy certified correct:

Waldheim, Oberleutnant. This Oberleutnant is Kurt Waldheim who at that time served as adjutant at the German liaison general staff at the high command of the Italian field army headquartered in Athens.

48. BA/MA, RH 24–22/16, fol. 315. 1st Mountain Division, Ic, minutes of the meeting on September 10, 1943; NAW, T 1119/26/480, intelligence unit 377 to Gen. Kdo. XXII. Geb. AK., Ic, re: Aktion against Communist elements in Ioánnina, March 5, 1944.

49. NARA, T 311/180/777, war diary of Heeresgruppe E, entry of March 14, 1944, subject: Transport of Jews.

50. BA/MA, RH 24–22/23, fol. 50–51, Geheime Feldpolizei Group 621 Kommando at the XXII. Geb. AK, March 27, 1944, report, re: Evacuation of the Jews from Ioánnina, signed: Bergmayer, Unteroffizier, to Ic, XXII. Geb. AK. Circulated for on-site information.

51. Ibid.

52. Ibid.

53. Ibid.

54. ZStL., 508 AR-Z 26/1963, vol. 4, fol. 848, interrogation transcript for witness F. S., March 14, 1966.

55. Because in March 1944 a large number of units of the XXII Army Corps had left Greece to participate in the occupation of Hungary, the Corps Group Ioánnina carried out occupation duties in the Epirus and on Corfu; BA/MA, RH 24–22/20, fol. 240, daily report for March 26, 1944, of Corps Group Ioánnina Ia to Okdo. Heeresgr. Ia & Ic; BA/MA RH 24–22/21, fol. 31, Abt. Ic, Ic-situation report, for April 4, 1944.

56. ZStL., V 508 AR 1314/68, fol. 78, Graevenitz's report to the Auswärtige Amt, April 18, 1944.

57. BA/MA, RH 24–22/21, fol. 81 ff., Geheime Feldpolizei Group 621, Corfu Field Office, situation report to Corps Group Ioánnina, Ic, April 27, 1944, signed: Härtel, Feldpolizei Inspector.

58. BA/MA, RH 24–22/21, fol. 85, Ic, Corfu Field Office, No. 6/44, Secret Command Item, April 25, 1944, signed: König, Oberleutnant.

59. BA/MA, RH 24–22/21, fol. 88–89, Corps Group Ioánnina, dept. Ic 781/44 (confidential), to Obkdo. Heeresgruppe E, Ic/AO, April 28, 1944, report about the island of Corfu in connection to an Ic service trip, April 23–24, 1944, signed: Oberstleutnant i. G., signature indecipherable.

60. Ibid.; NARA, T 311/181; according to the duties-assignment roster of group Ic/AO in the operations branch of Heeresgruppe E of December 1, 1943, "cooperation with the SD, Sich.[erheits] Pol [izei]" was part of the duties of the Ic officer.

61. NARA, T 311/177/47, war diary of Heeresgruppe E, entry for May 12, 1944, re: Deportation of Jews.

62. NARA, T 1119/25/957, also Nuremberg doc. NOKW 1915, Oberst Jäger's memorandum to Gen. Komm. XXII. (Geb.) AK., May 14, 1944, re: Deportation of the Jews from Corfu.

63. Ibid., 958.

64. NARA, T 1119/25/956, Generalkommando XX. (Geb.) AK., Ic No. 5564/44, to Oberkommando Heeresgruppe E, May 18, 1944, re: Deportation of Jews, signed: Chief of the General Staff, signature undecipherable.

65. NARA, T 1119/25/953, file entry about the Jewish Question, undated, probably May 30, 1944, signed: Magnus, Kapitän zur See und Seekommandant Westgriechenland (Captain and Marine Commander for Western Greece), Oberst Jäger, Inselkommandant.

66. Ibid.

67. NARA, T 311/177/120, war diary Heeresgruppe E, entry of May 30, 1944, re: Deportation of Jews from Corfu.

68. ZStL., 508 AR-Z 26/1963, vol. 3, fol. 479, interrogation of Burger's translator, C. R., July 20, 1964.

69. See the report of Joseph Vitale in Novitch, 100 ff.

70. ZStL., 508 AR-Z 26/1963, vol. 4, fol. 753; see witness testimony of Mrs. R. N., a deportee from Corfu, July 21, 1965, who stated that Burger murdered the victim by shooting him in the base of the skull; ZStL., 508 AR-Z 26/1963, vol. 3, fol. 475; according to Burger's translator, C. R., the priest wanted to give the man a package.

71. BA/MA, RM 35 III/204, war diary Transport Office Pátra, entry dated June 17, 1944; see also the report of Estir Pitzon in Novitch, 104.

72. BA/MA, RH 24–22/23, fol. 59, Befehlshaber der Sicherheitspolizei und SD f. Griechenland, field office Ioánnina, IV B to the Gen. Kom. XXII (Geb.) A. K. Ic, June 17, 1944, re: Judenaktion on Corfu, signed: SS-Hptstuf. u. Krim. Kom., signature indecipherable.

73. Field Command Post 606, diary no. Ic 781/41, Chania August 4, 1941, orders the listing of all persons "belonging to the 'Jewish race' (without regard to religious affiliation)." I thank Hagen Fleischer, of the University of Athens, who provided a copy of this document.

74. Letter of the mayor of Chania to the GFP, February 20, 1943. Again, Hagen Fleischer furnished a copy of this document.

75. ZStL., 508 AR-Z 26/1963, vol. 6, fol. 1239, witness deposition J. J.; see also Molho et al., 2:279; and ZStL., 508 AR-Z 26/1963, vol. 4, fols. 803–804, for witness testimony of W. L., a former member of GFP Group 611.

76. ZStL., 508 AR-Z 26/1963, vol. 6, fol. 1242, testimony of A. M., a former member of GFP Group 611 in Iráklio.

77. BA/MA RM 35 III/193, fols. 13–14, war diary of the chief of Sea Transport Ägäis from June 1 to June 30, 1944.

78. NARA, T 311/177/178, war diary of Heeresgruppe E, entry for June 9, 1944, daily report with activity table.

79. ZStL., V 508 AR 1314/68, fol. 78; Graevenitz's report to the Auswärtige Amt, June 28, 1944.

80. ZStL., 508 AR-Z 26/1963, vol. 1, fol. 26; Ulrich Kleemann's undated written response to the preliminary legal proceedings against him, written probably in 1957.

81. Ibid., fol. 38, witness testimony of K. G.; fol. 48, testimony of C. K.; and fol. 66, testimony of R. R.

82. Ibid., fol. 476, interrogation of C. R.

83. BA/MA, RH 26–1007. The activity report for July 1–September 15, 1944, of the Department Ic of the Kommandant Ostägäis, states, "the expulsion of the Jews who were not citizens of Turkey," which was to be carried out by the SD-Greece, took place "at the order of Oberkommando Heeresgruppe E, Ic/AO." Because

cooperation with the SD and the Sicherheitspolizei was the responsibility of the Ic officer (see note 60), the order to Kleemann must have come from Ic officer Oberstleutnant Herbert Warnstorff, his adjutant Oberleutnant Kurt Waldheim, or the Ic officer's deputy, the Abwehr (intelligence) officer Major Hammer. Because by that time the cooperation of Wehrmacht units and SS in the deportation of Jews had become routine for the staff of Heeresgruppe E, Kleemann's orders more than likely were sent by the officer who happened to be on duty.

84. BA/MA, RH 26–1007/14, Directive No. 30, Registration on the Island of Rhodes, July 13, 1944, signed: Kleemann, Kommandant Ost-Ägäis.

85. Ibid., Sturmdivision Rhodos, Commander, Br. B. No. 5236/44, confidential, July 16, 1944, signed: Kleemann.

86. Abraham Galanté, *Appendice à l'Histoire des Juifs de Rhodes, Chio, Cos, etc. et Fin Tragique des Communautés Juives de Rhodes et de Cos, Œuvre du Brigandage Hitlerien* (Istanbul: Kâgit ve Basim I, sleri, 1948), 41; see also the report of Monsieur Soriano in Novitch, 108–109.

87. ZStL., 508 AR-Z 26/1963, vol. 3, fol. 477, interrogation of C. R.

88. See Galanté, and Soriano's report in Novitch, 108–109.

89. Fleischer, 29, speaks of 1,673 victims; Molho et al., 2:288, cite 1,700 victims of the deportations from Rhodes. Consult Galanté's report in Novitch, 106; and Soriano's report in Novitch on the mistreatments during the march to the harbor and the embarkation.

90. ZStL., 508 AR-Z 26/1963, vol. 6, fols. 1239 and 1241, for the testimonies of H. E. and H. B., respectively, both former members of the Feldgendarmerie; Fleischer, 32, cites between 1,790 and 1,846, whereas Soriano, 109, cites 2,000 deportees.

91. NARA, T 501/260/477, Kommandant Ost-Ägäis, Dept. Ic to Okdo. Heeresgruppe E, Gr. Ic/AO, Ic situation report, August 11, 1944.

92. ZSt.L., 508 AR-Z 26/1963, vol. 1, fol. 35, witness testimony K. G., January 6, 1958.

10. Manhunts in Hungary and Slovakia: 1944–1945

1. Randolph L. Braham, *The Politics of Genocide: the Holocaust in Hungary* (New York: Columbia University Press, 1981), 77; Hilberg, *Die Vernichtung der europäischen Juden*, 864, provides a synopsis of definitions in Hungary's anti-Jewish laws of 1938, 1939, and 1941.

2. During the so-called White Terror of 1919, thousands of Hungarian Jews became victims of pogroms and shootings. In 1920 the Hungarian government passed the Numerus Clausus Law, limiting the number of Jewish university students to 6 percent of the total student body. See Braham, *The Politics of Genocide*, 39 ff., for a discussion of antisemitism in Hungary during the 1920s and 1930s.

3. Hilberg, *Die Vernichtung der europäischen Juden*, 866 and 867 ff., details the entire process of step-by-step aryanizations in Hungary.

4. Mária Schmidt, "Provincial Police Reports: New Insights into Hungarian Jewish History, 1941–1944," *Yad Vashem Studies* 19 (1988): 233 ff., evaluated police reports from various Hungarian districts and discovered that, especially in the recently acquired provinces of northern Transylvania and Felvidék (southern Slovakia) and in Carpatho-Ukraine, senior police officials favored persecution measures above

and beyond the laws already established; Braham, *The Politics of Genocide*, 56 *ff.*, gives an overview of the antisemitism of the various factions among the right-wing extremists, especially that of the Pfeilkreuzler (Hung. Nyilas), the fascist Arrow Cross Party.

5. Doc. PdI 1646, contains a May 23, 1962, notarized statement from Leslie Gordon, describing the arrests in Budapest, the expulsions to Galicia, and the massacres the SS Einsatzgruppen and their Ukrainian assistants committed in the Kolomea region; see also Braham, *The Politics of Genocide*, 199 *ff.*, and "The Kamenets-Podolsk and Delvidek Massacres," *Yad Vashem Studies* 9 (1973): 133 *ff.*

6. Braham, *The Politics of Genocide*, 316.

7. Ibid., 207 *ff.*

8. Ibid., 241–242.

9. György Ránki, *Unternehmen Margarethe: Die deutsche Besetzung Ungarns* (Vienna: Corvina, 1984) discusses the policies of Prime Minister Miklós Kállay, German preparations, and the course of the occupation of Hungary.

10. Doc. PdI 584, Dieter Wisliceny's affidavit, Nuremberg November 29, 1945, also is reprinted in *Nazi Conspiracy and Aggression*, vol. 8, (Washington: USGPO,1947), 606 *ff.* Consult "Die Entwicklung der 'Judenreferate' des SD und der Gestapo," ZStL. 415 AR 1310/3, E 5, vol. 1, for changes in the organization of the RSHA.

11. First as an employee of State Secretary Wilhelm Keppler and later as Sonderbeauf-tragter (special commissioner), Edmund Veesenmayer became active whenever "diplomatic" preparations or the organization of expansions of the Third Reich in Central Europe were at stake, for example, in Austria in 1938, in Slovakia and Poland in 1939, and Yugoslavia in 1941. Veesenmayer wrote reports about Hungary as early as 1943, claiming, among other things, that the Hungarian Jews were responsible for "sabotage of the common war aim;" see Kempner, 411 *ff.*

12. Braham, *The Politics of Genocide*, 401–402.

13. Ibid., 403–404 for László Baky's and László Endre's biographies.

14. Ibid., 492–493.

15. Doc. PdI 813 contains Hermann Krumey's and Wisliceny's guidelines to the Jewish community of Budapest of March 20, 1944; see Braham, *The Politics of Genocide*, 422 *ff.*, about Samuel Stern, the long-time president of the Jewish community of Pest.

16. Jenő Lévai, ed. *Eichmann in Ungarn: Dokumente* (Budapest: Pannonia, 1961), 80, reprints a stenographic copy of Eichmann's March 31, 1944, speech to the Central Council.

17. Ibid., 81; also, Lang, *Das Eichmann-Protokoll*, 187. When in the course of the inter-rogation in Jerusalem Avner Less asked Eichmann whether during this session he had explained to the Jewish representatives that there were no plans for deporta-tion, Eichmann replied: "Captain, since I was sent to Hungary to deport Jews, I did not tell these officers that there would be no deportations. I never lied to Jewish representatives. Among the Jewish representatives I dealt with for so many years, you will not find a single one [sic!] who will accuse me of lying to him."

18. Braham, *The Politics of Genocide*, 481.

19. Braham, Randolph, ed., *The Destruction of Hungarian Jewry: A Documentary Account* (New York: Pro Arte, 1963), 2:539, copy of Veesenmayer's telegram to Ambassador Karl Ritter, March 31, 1944.

20. Braham, *The Politics of Genocide*, 482–483; Marsálek, 283; according to the statistics of KL Mauthausen, in May 1944 more than 2,000 Hungarian Jews were imprisoned there.

21. Braham, *The Destruction of Hungarian Jewry*, 834 *ff.*, pertinent Foreign Office documents reveal the tensions that arose among German and Hungarian organizations over the takeover of this industrial complex; consult Braham's *The Politics of Genocide*, 514 *ff.*, about the entire transaction, and Hilberg, *Die Vernichtung der europäischen Juden*, 892 *ff.*; see Bertrand Perz, *Projekt Quarz: Steyr-Daimler-Puch und das KZ Melk* (Vienna: Verlag für Gesellschaftskritik, 1991), about the "cooperation" of the Steyr-Daimler-Puch Co. with the Donau Flugzeugwerke in the production of airplane motors and the relocation of the factory in 1944.

22. Lg. Wien, VR 2729/63, Novak's interrogation of March 30, 1961.

23. Lévai, 82–83, and Braham, *The Politics of Genocide*, 529 *ff.*, directive signed by Baky.

24. Lg. Wien, Vr 529/61, interrogation of Ernst Girzick, September 14, 1961.

25. Lg. Wien, Vr 770/46, interrogation of the accused Dr. Siegfried Seidl, June 27, 1946. Allegedly "politically suspect persons" were arrested with "the closest cooperation of the Hungarian authorities" in Debrecen, and dwellings or household furnishings belonging to Jews were confiscated.

26. Braham, *The Politics of Genocide*, 547.

27. Lévai, 100–101, petition of the Jewish Council to Eichmann, May 3, 1944.

28. Braham, *The Politics of Genocide*, 547–548.

29. Braham, *The Destruction of Hungarian Jewry*, 2:560 reprints Veesenmayer's telegram to Ambassador Ritter, Budapest, April 28, 1944, announcing under the heading "Jews" that the "total of arrests from Sonderaktionen is 194,000."

30. Braham, *The Politics of Genocide*, 369 *ff.*, details the negotiations between German and Hungarian organizations in March 1944. Even though Hitler himself had approved the employment of 100,000 Hungarian Jews as forced laborers in Germany, only a small number of the more than 400,000 deportees from Hungary to Auschwitz-Birkenau were actually deployed. For example, 520 women had to perform heavy labor for Krupp in Essen; see also Hilberg, *Die Vernichtung der europäschen Juden*, 998 *ff.*

31. Braham, *The Destruction of Hungarian Jewry*, 357 reprints Veesenmayer's telegram.

32. Ibid., 356, reprint of Veesenmayer's telegram to the Foreign Office.

33. Braham, *The Politics of Genocide*, 551.

34. Ibid., 558 and 598.

35. Braham, *The Destruction of Hungarian Jewry*, 361, reprints Veesenmayers' telegram to the Auswärtige Amt, April 27, 1944.

36. Braham, *The Politics of Genocide*, 599.

37. Braham, *The Destruction of Hungarian Jewry*, 368, reprint of a note from Rolf Günther to Thadden about the train scheduling conference, and a reprint of Thadden's note in a memorandum to the German embassy in Bratislava, May 5, 1944.

38. Ibid., 373, reprint of Veesenmayer's telegram to the Foreign Office, May 12, 1944.

39. Braham, *The Politics of Genocide*, 601–602, cites the minutes of the meeting.

40. Lévai, 110–111, citing Thadden's report of May 26, 1944, Nuremberg doc. NG 2190.

41. Ibid., 383–384.

42. Braham, *The Destruction of Hungarian Jewry*, 380 *ff.*, reprint of Thadden's travel report, May 25, 1944, Nuremberg doc. NG 2980.
43. Braham, *The Politics of Genocide*, 570; reportedly most of the "Christian" Hungarians of northern Transylvania stood by passively, though many cooperated with the authorities. Likewise in every populous locality there were persons who betrayed Jews in hiding; few helped the persecuted victims.
44. Ránki, 308, cites a report of May 6, 1944, from Szekszárd.
45. Braham, *The Destruction of Hungarian Jewry*, 2:617; reprint of the June 30, 1944, report of the Höhere SS- und Polizeiführer, and Veesenmayer's July 6, 1944, telegram to Ritter.
46. The information about the number of Hungarian Jews deported to Straßhof is contradictory: Braham, in *The Politics of Genocide*, 652, cites 20,787 people, whereas Rezső Rudolf Kasztner (Kasztner, *Der Kastner-Bericht über Eichmann's Menschenhandel in Ungarn* (Munich: Kindler, 1961), lists at one time 18,000 and at other times 15,000 persons. According to a August 3, 1944, memorandum from the Reich Economics Minister to the Foreign Office, under the heading "maintenance of Hungarian Jews," 14,700 Hungarian Jews were listed as employed "in the Gaue of Vienna and Lower Austria;" see reprint in Braham, *The Destruction of Hungarian Jewry*, 2:465; see also Werner Eichbauer, "Die 'Judenlager' von Wiener Neustadt, Felixdorf und Lichtenwörth," unpublished project report, 1987. Braham, *The Destruction of Hungarian Jewry*, 415–416, reprints an express letter with the letterhead IV A 4b-3433/42g, the letterhead of the Eichmann Referat in the RSHA, in which Kaltenbrunner responded to Mayor Karl Blaschke's June 7, 1944, request for an "allotment of workers for important war production in the city of Vienna," by informing him that "within the next few days 4 transports of about 12,000 Jews" would arrive as a first installment; according to the statements of Seidl and witnesses in the investigations against him, a "detachment of the Special Action Kommando Hungry" established a field office under Krumey's and Seidl's direction.
47. A number of contradictory representations about the progress and possible motives for the negotiations between Eichmann ("blood in exchange for goods") and Kurt Becher representing the SS on one side, and leading members of the Jewish aid society "Vada" such as Rezső Kasztner, Joel Brand, and Andreas Biss on the other, as well as the background to the Brand mission have been advanced by the participants; see the Kastner Report of 1945–1946, Nuremberg doc. 4824, published as *Der Kastner-Bericht über Eichmann's Menschenhandel in Ungarn*; Joel Brand and Alex Weißberg, *Die Geschichte von Joel Brand* (Cologne: Kiepenhauer & Witsch, 1956), Brand's recollections recorded by Weißberg; and Andreas Biss, *Der Stopp der Endlösung: Kampf gegen Himmler und Eichmann in Budapest* (Stuttgart: Seewald, 1966), reissued under the title *Wir hielten die Vernichtung an: Kampf gegen die "Endlösung" 1944* (Hemsbach über Weinheim: n.p., 1985). Yehuda Bauer, 380 *ff.*, and Hilberg, *Die Vernichtung der europäischen Juden*, 909 *ff.*, offer divergent evaluations of the entire issue as well; Braham, *The Politics of Genocide*, 932 *ff.*, provides the most detailed and plausible analysis of these negotiations and the Brand mission, as well as the Kastner Report, 952 *ff.*, and the murder of almost all Hungarian deportees from Hungary, 674 *ff.*, See Biss, 98 *ff.*, who negotiated the amount of the ransom with Becher and other SS officers, for details on the payments.

48. Braham, *The Politics of Genocide*, 611–612.
49. Horthy had several reasons for halting the deportation program: Protests from the Vatican, the president of the United States, the king of Sweden, and from Switzerland arrived in Budapest. Hungarian intelligence posts were listening in on the transmissions of detailed information about mass murders of Hungarian Jews in Auschwitz – these messsages sent from British and American diplomatic personnel in Switzerland to their governments. The Hungarian intelligence service informed their government about these transmissions. (The telegram in question is reprinted in Kempner, 421–422.) Horthy also feared a government takeover by the Hungarian national socialists through a putsch by State Secretary Baky and for that reason the Regent dismissed the police- and gendarmerie units concentrated in Budapest; see Veesenmayer's telegrams to Ribbentrop of July 6, 1944, reprinted in Braham, *The Destruction of Hungarian Jewry*, 2: 419 *ff.*, and 425 *ff.*, and *The Politics of Genocide*, 743 *ff.*; see also Hilberg, *Die Vernichtung der europäischen Juden*, 916 *ff.*
50. Braham, *The Destruction of Hungarian Jewry*, 2:444 *ff.*, reprints Veesenmayer's telegrams of July and August 1944 to Ribbentrop and the Foreign Office.
51. Braham, *The Politics of Genocide*, 771 *ff.*, discusses details of the deportation from Kistarcsa; as Less, 158, reports, the sentence of the Jerusalem court referred to Eichmann's handling of the Kistarcsa transport as symptomatic: "This incident is of great importance as proof of the position of the accused in Hungary and his insistence and underhandedness, which are characteristic of his deeds."
52. Lévai, 146, reports that Franz Novak handled the Kistarcsa deportation while Otto Hunsche organized the one from Sárr; Lg. Wien, Vr 2729/63. The minutes of the main session of November 16 to December 17, 1964, however, show that during the deliberations against Franz Novak at the Landesgericht für Strafsachen in Vienna, the defendant denied having organized the deportation from Kistarcsa.
53. Braham, *The Destruction of Hungarian Jewry*, 2:443, reprints Veesenmayer's July 11, 1944, telegram to the Foreign Office. In it he reports that the sum of persons deported from Zones I to V, including the Aktion in the Budapest suburbs, "now stands at 437,402." This figure did not include the victims of Einzelaktionen, individual raids, and deportations that Eichmann conducted even in July 1944, some of whose victims were transported to Mauthausen.
54. Ibid., 480, reprint of Veesenmayer's August 24, 1944, telegram to the Foreign Office.
55. Braham, *The Politics of Genocide*, 797; *The Destruction of Hungarian Jewry*, 2: 481, reprints Veesenmayer's August 25, 1944, telegram to Ribbentrop. It is about a discussion with SS-Obergruppenführer Otto Winkelmann.
56. Braham, *Destruction*, 2: 492, reprint of a note from Horst Grell, dated September 29, 1944, which Veesenmayer passed on to the Foreign Office.
57. See Ránki, 385 *ff.*, about Hungary's situation in domestic and foreign policy in August and September of 1944; Braham, *The Politics of Genocide*, 820 *ff.*, discusses the Arrow Cross coup preparations and Veesenmayer's and SS interventions; Glenn B. Infield, *Skorzeny: Hitler's Commando* (New York: Military Heritage Press, 1981), 65 *ff.*, presents a racy account of Skorzeny's kidnapping of Horthy's son.
58. Braham, *The Destruction of Hungarian Jewry*, 2: 506–507, reprints Veesenmayer's October 17 and 18, 1944, telegrams to the Foreign Office.
59. Biss, 195.

60. Braham, *The Politics of Genocide*, 830.
61. Lévai, 167 *ff.*; Braham, *The Politics of Genocide*, 836 *ff.*, discusses the forced labor of Jews for the defense of Budapest, and the murder of those men by Arrow Cross members retreating to Budapest in November 1944.
62. Lévai, 187 *ff.*, provides the reports of representatives of the Swiss and Swedish legations.
63. Braham, *The Destruction of Hungarian Jewry*, 527 and 532, reprints Veesenmayer's November 13 and November 21, 1944, telegrams to the Foreign Office. Because of "obvious inadequacies" during these treks, Szálasi insisted on permitting deportation "only if transport devices would be furnished," which in light of the impossibility of procuring rail cars for all practical purposes means the cessation of deportations." Furthermore, during a visit to Budapest, SS-Obersturmbannführer Hoess, who directed the deployment of Jews in Lower Austria, made it clear that he "could use only men in 'prime working condition,' no older than forty," who "would be able to perform the especially heavy subterranean labor in the Reich for a considerable length of time." He was already considering "rejecting unsuitable contingents on the march."
64. Yad Vashem, M-5/167, contains an unsigned, undated report of the situation in Slovakia from April 1944 until the end of that year, written by one or several members of the Slovak Jewish aid committee.
65. YIVO, Occ E7(b)-8; report about the Jewish labor camps and labor centers in Slovakia until June 30, 1943.
66. Lipscher, 61–62, discusses the establishment of the Judenzentrale in September 1940; see 85 *ff.*, for details about its duties and activities; Lipscher, 122 *ff.*, also provides information about the aid committee, "illegally" established in the spring of 1942, which scholarly studies sometimes refer to as an Arbeitsgruppe, a work group, or Nebenregierung, shadow government. Oskar Neumann, *Im Schatten des Todes: Ein Tatsachenbericht vom Schicksalskampf des slowakischen Judentums* (Tel Aviv: Edition "Olamenu," 1956), and Joan Campion, *In the Lion's Mouth: Gisi Fleischmann and the Jewish Fight for Survival* (Lanham, MD: University Press of America, 1987), study the individual members of the aid committee and their activities.
67. Rudolf Vrba and Alan Bestic, *I Cannot Forgive* (New York: Bantam, 1964), and Josef Lanik, *Co Dante nevidel* – What Dante Did Not See – (Bratislava: Obzor, 1946). Rosenberg received counterfeit papers bearing the name Rudolf Vrba, a name he retained. He and Wetzler (Josef Lanik) had been deported to Auschwitz, but in early April 1944 both were able to escape. See Braham, *The Politics of Genocide*, 696 *ff.*, about the spread of the "Auschwitz Protocols" in Hungary, Switzerland, and the Vatican, as well as the level of information among Allied organizations. Martin Gilbert, *Auschwitz und die Alliierten* (Munich: Beck, 1982), and David S. Wyman, *Das unerwünschte Volk: Amerika und die Vernichtung der europäischen Juden* (Frankfurt/M.: Fischer, 1989) investigate the level of information in the USA and the lack of military response on the part of the Allies.
68. Kaden and Nestler, 243, summarize a September 22, 1944, file entry by the Bratislava SD's SS-Hauptsturmführer Albrecht for SS-Obergruppenführer Gotlob Berger. Among other reasons for the widespread support of the rebellion, it comments on the extreme social differences among segments of the population. As laborers and white-collar workers were suffering severe hardships because of high inflation

and insufficient distribution of food, the population was enraged about "ministers and party leaders who just a few years earlier had been poor but now earned high salaries and who, moreover, had taken over Jewish businesses, doing so under assumed names or through straw men." In the opinion of the reporter, "in these circumstances anyone thinking to defeat by purely military means the rebellious workers and soldiers entrenched in the forests is a fool." See Yeshayahu Jelinek, "The Role of the Jews in Slovakian Resistance," *Jahrbücher für Geschichte Osteuropas* 15 (1967):415–422, and Lipscher, 169 *ff.*

69. Lipscher, 179–180.
70. Yad Vashem M5/163, Protocol about Brunner's activities in Slovakia from September 1944 to March 30, 1945, signed by Dr. Oscar Neumann, Dr. Tibor Kovac, and Dr. Winterstein, Bratislava, October 27, 1945; see also Neumann, 225.
71. Yad Vashem M5/163,1.
72. Ibid., 2.
73. Yad Vashem O-33/198, 3, "Jüdisches Los," report by Jitzchak H., and report about the situation in Slovakia, 14.
74. Yad Vashem M5/163, 3–4.
75. Ibid., 4.
76. Ibid., 5.
77. See Neumann, 246–248, and Campion, 120; consult the Kastner Report, 188–189, and Biss, 177, about the unsuccessful appeals to Eichmann and Brunner on Gisi Fleischmann's behalf.
78. Yad Vashem M5/163, 6.
79. Ibid., 7.
80. ZStL. 415 AR 1310/63 E5, vol. 3, section B; see also Lipscher 179–180, and Hilberg, *Die Vernichtung der europäischen Juden*, 504–505. Reportedly, five transports went to Auschwitz between August 22, 1944, and November 3, 1944.

11. The Postwar Era

1. Leo Frank, "Ein 'heimlicher Besuch' in der Alpenfestung – und seine Folgen," *Salzkammergut-Zeitung Bad Ischler Stadt-Zeitung,* 14 March, 1991. "Leo Frank" is the pen name of retired police officer Leo M., who writes articles for local newspapers.
2. Ibid.
3. See Safrian and Witek, 193 *ff.*, for a discussion of how Austrian politicians after 1945 sought to shift the blame for National Socialist crimes exclusively to Germany; Robert Knight, *Ich bin dafür, die Sache in die Länge zu ziehen: Die Wortprotokolle der österreichischen Bundesregierung von 1945 bis 1952 ber die Entschädigung der Juden* (Frankfurt/M.: Athenum, 1988) examines the perfidy of Austrian government representatives in response to Jewish organizations' demands for restitution and redress.
4. Frank.
5. See Peter R. Black's study of Ernst Kaltenbrunner, Heydrich's successor as director of the Reichssicherheitshauptamt.

6. Lang, 235–236.
7. Simon Wiesenthal, *Doch die Mörder leben* (Munich: Droemer, 1967), 132–133.
8. Sereny, 354, spoke with Anton Weber.
9. Lg. Wien, Vr 2729/63, interrogation of Franz Novak, March 16, 1961.
10. NARA, Record Group 319, Dossier H 8212602, interrogation report, Anton Burger, interned in Camp Marcus W. Orr, Salzburg, March 7, 1947; Wiesenthal, 131, reports that the gendarmerie, looking for Eichmann in Altaussee, found Burger instead.
11. NARA, RG 319, Dossier XE 004471, Army Counterintelligence Corps (CIC), 430th Det., United States Forces in Austria [U.S.F.A], Oberoesterreich Section, Bad Ischl, December 12, 1947, Subject: Liebl, Vera, Ex-wife of Eichmann, Alleged War Criminal.
12. Headquarters U.S.F.A., Legal Division, to Lg. Wien, Lg. Wien Vr 3069/47.
13. NARA, RG 319, Dossier H 8212602, CIC, 430th Det., U.S.F.A, Land Salzburg Section Province of Salzburg, June 20, 1947, Subject: Burger, Anton, Suspected War Criminal.
14. Lg. Wien, Vr 122/51; Lg. Wien. Vr 110/51, report of the district court Neunkirchen to Lg. Wien, February 19, 1952.
15. Yad Vashem, 0–5/26, fol. 19, investigative report of February 4, 1946; NAW, RG 319, XE 004471, Dossier Adolf Eichmann, report about Lembach, Linz, February 14, 1947, without author.
16. Yad Vashem, 0–5/26, fol. 18, report about the interrogation of Anton Brunner about Alois Brunner, Vienna, January 30, 1946.
17. Lg. Wien, Vr 5387/45, notification from the Federal Police headquarters, Vienna, Department of Safety, to Lg. Wien, June 23, 1954.
18. Hilberg, *Die Vernichtung der europäischen Juden*, 1130–1140.
19. Ibid.
20. Lg. Wien, Vr 4574/45, record of the interrogation of the accused, October 1, 1945.
21. Lg. Wien, Vr 4574/45, Police headquarters, Vienna, State Police Ref. I/e, record of the interrogation of Anton Brunner, October 12, 1945.
22. Ibid.
23. Lg. Wien, Vr 4574/45, Anton Brunner's handwritten undated notes, probably written in the fall of 1945.
24. Ibid.
25. Lg. Wien, Vr 4574/45, interrogation of the accused, Anton Brunner, February 25, 1946.
26. Lg. Wien, Vr 4574/45, sentence of the Lg. Wien in the case of Anton Brunner.
27. Lg. Wien, Vr 658/46, record of the interrogation of the accused, Josef Weiszl, August 31, 1945.
28. Lg. Wien, Vr 658/46, interrogation of Weiszl, September 4, 1945.
29. Record of the execution, Préfeture de Police, Direction de la Police Judiciaire, Commissariat de Police de la Circonscription de Choisy-le-Roi, Procès-Verbal Executions Capitales, July 5, 1949. I thank Serge Klarsfeld for the information about the fate of O. R. and the opportunity to consult the appropriate documents. Lg. Wien, Vr 658/46 contains a translation of the sentence the permanent military court in Paris, pronounced in the case of Josef Weiszl.

30. Lg. Wien, Vr 658/46, interrogation of Josef Weiszl, February 3, 1956; Lg. Wien, Vr 871/55, decision of the council chamber of the Landesgericht für Strafsachen Wien, May 24, 1956.

31. Lg. Wien, Vr 435/46, interrogation of the accused.

32. NARA, RG 319, Dossier H 8212620, written statement, Salzburg, February 10, 1947, signed: Girzick, Ernst.

33. Peter Z. Malkin, and Harry Stein, *Eichmann in My Hands* (New York: Warner, 1990), 213.

34. Ibid., 218.

35. Ibid., 216.

36. Lang, 125.

37. Less, 145 and 321.

38. Lg. Wien, Vr 2729/63, Novak's interrogation, April 21, 1961.

39. Lg. Wien, Vr 2729/63, Novak's interrogation, February 2, 1961.

40. Ibid.

41. Kempner, 212, reprints a facsimile of Dannecker's file note dated July 21, 1942, re: Judenabschub; see also Klarsfeld, *Vichy-Auschwitz*, document appendix, 416.

42. Novak's interrogation.

43. Ibid.

44. Ibid.

45. Lg. Wien, Vr 3388/61, examination of witness Richard Hartenberger, September 22, 1961; Hartenberger confessed quite openly because he could not be tried again after already having served a nine-month sentence in a penitentiary in 1950 on a conviction for torture and maltreatment (§3 KVG 1947), and for crimes against humanity and human dignity (§4 KVG 1947); see also Lg. Wien, Vr 4969/47.

46. See Heinz Höhne, *Krieg im Dunkeln: Macht und Einfluß des deutschen und russischen Geheimdienstes* (Frankfurt/M.: Ullstein, 1988), 484 *ff.*, about the U.S. Army and the CIA hiring the former chief of the OKH's Department Fremde Heere Ost (Foreign Armies East). After 1945 it was the rule rather than the exception for secret services to hire former members of the SS and SD as agents and employees. Apparently, the American CIC took all who offered their services, but Gehlen's "Org" was not choosy either. "Actually, Gehlen had Krichbaum [a former SS-Standartenführer and friend of Heydrich] send him one SD-man after another; speedily the offices and field offices of the Org were manned by former members of the SS." Ibid., 505.

47. See Christopher Simpson, *Der amerikanische Bumerang: NS-Kriegsverbrecher im Sold der USA* (Vienna: Ueberreuter, 1988), 294 *ff.*; E. H. Cookridge, *Gehlen: The Spy of the Century* (New York: Random House, 1971), 352 *ff.*; and Roger Faligot and Rémi Kauffer, *Le Croissant et la Croix Gammée: Les secrets de l'alliance entre l'Islam et le nazisme de Hitler à nos jours* (Paris: Albin Michel, 1990), 174–175.

48. Hilberg, *Die Vernichtung der europäischen Juden*, 1177; Tom Bower, *Blind Eye to Murder* (London: Granada, 1981); and Faligot and Kauffer, 162 *ff.*, trace Rademacher's career after 1945, which led from the Reemtsma tobacco company in Hamburg and a trial in the Federal Republic of Germany to Syria in the early 1960s and then back again to West Germany.

49. Faligot and Kauffer, 183 and 262–263.
50. Simon Wiesenthal, *Recht, nicht Rache* (Frankfurt/M.: Ullstein, 1988), 290–291.
51. Citation from Robert Fisk, "Syria protects Eichmann aide," *London Times*, 17 March, 1983.
52. Gerd Honsik, *Freispruch für Hitler?* (Vienna: Burgenländischer Kulturverband, 1988), 18.
53. Citation taken from Bernhard Harthoff, "7, Rue Haddad, Damaskus, Syrien," *Tribüne* 27 (1988): 20.

References

Unpublished Sources

Allgemeines Verwaltungsarchiv Wien (General Administrative Archives Vienna)
Bestand Reichskommissar für die Wiedervereinigung Österreichs mit dem Deutschen Reich (Collection Reichskommissar for the Reunification of Austria with the German Reich)

Berlin Document Center (BDC)
Unterlagen NSDAP Zentralkartei, SS-Führer und Rasse- und Siedlungshauptamt (RuSHA) (Records of the NSDAP Central Card Index; SS-Leaders; and the Race and Settlement Central Office)

Ernst Brückler	Richard Hartenberger
Alois Brunner	Franz Novak
Anton Brunner	Karl Rahm
Anton Burger	Siegfried Seidl
Theo Dannecker	Walter Stahlecker
Herbert Gerbing	Franz Stuschka
Ernst Girzick	Josef Uschan
Hans Günther	Josef Weiszl
Rolf Günther	Anton Zita

Bundesarchiv Koblenz (BAK) Federal Archives Koblenz
NS 19 neu – Persönlicher Stab Reichsführer-SS (Personal Staff Reichsführer-SS)
R 7 – Reichswirtschaftsministerium
R 58 – Reichssicherheitshauptamt
R 70 – Griechenland (Greece)
Various Trial Records
21/242 (Max Merten)

Bundesarchiv – Militärarchiv Freiburg (BA/MA) (Federal Archives – Military Archives Freiburg, Germany)
Befehlshaber Südost – Kommandierender General und Befehlshaber in Serbien
Befehlshaber der deutschen Truppen in Kroatien
Kommandant Ost-Ägäis

XVIII. Armeekorps
XXII. (Gebirgs) Armeekorps
LXVIII. Armeekorps

Bundesministerium für Inneres, Wien (Federal Ministry of the Interior, Vienna)
Öffentliches Denkmal und Museum Mauthausen Archiv (Public Memorial and
Museum Mauthausen Archive)
    Documents of the Eichmann Trial
Staatspolizei: Personalakten des NSDAP-Gaues Wien (State Police Personnel Files of
the NSDAP Gau Vienna)

Ernst Brückler (Gau file No. 99 674)	Karl Rahm (No. 49 965)
Alois Brunner (No. 340 051)	Siegfried Seidl (No. 337 472)
Anton Burger (No. 272 042)	Alfred Slawik (No. 22 523)
Herbert Gerbing (No. 337 048)	Dr. Walter Stahlecker (No. 150 407)
Ernst Girzig (No. 253 480)	Franz Stuschka (No. 136 601)
Richard Hartenberger (No. 86 359)	Josef Weiszl (No. 6578)
	Anton Zita (No. 308 876)

Central Archive for the History of the Jewish People, Jerusalem (CAHJP)
Bestand Archiv der Israelitischen Kultusgemeinde Wien 1784–1945 (Vienna)

Centre de Documentation Juive Contemporaine, Paris (CDJC) (Center for Contemporary
Jewish Documentation)
    Documents of the Eichmann Trial, Police d'Israel (PdI)
    Individual documents about Drancy, Deportations

Dokumentationsarchiv des österreichischen Widerstandes (DÖW) Document Center of
the Austrian Resistance)
    Copies of Gestapo Records from Ostrava – Mährisch-Ostrau: 17072 a & b

Landesgericht für Strafsachen Wien (Vienna) *(Lg. Wien)*
    Vr 4574/45, Proceedings against Anton Brunner
    Vr 6995/46, Proceedings against Franz Stuschka
    Vr 658/46, Proceedings against Josef Weiszl
    Vr 770/46, Proceedings against Siegfried Seidl
    Vr 8881/46, Proceedings against Ernst Girzick
    Vr 435/47, Proceedings against Alfred Slawik (reopened under Vr 3967/61)
    Vr 4969/47, Proceedings against Richard Hartenberger
    Vr 8689/50, Proceedings against F. K. (for forging of a passport in the name of "Alois
        Schmaldienst")
    Vr 6300/58, Proceedings against Anton Burger
    Vr 3388/61, Proceedings against Alois Brunner
    Vr 2729/63, Proceedings against Franz Novak

Leo Baeck Institute, New York
    Bestand Reichsvereinigung der Juden in Deutschland (Documents of the Reich
    Association of Jews in Germany)
        Microfilm R 65
        Proceedings of the Kammergericht Berlin (Superior Court) against Otto
        Bovensiepen and others
        Microfilm R 239

National Archives and Records Administration (NARA), Washington, D.C.
  Record Group 319
  File H 8212602, Anton Burger
  File H 8212620, Ernst Girzick

  Captured German Documents (Microfilms)
    T 311/177
    T 311/180
    T 501/260
    T 1119/25
    T 1119/26

Yad Vashem, Archives, Jerusalem
  0–1 Collection K. J. Ball-Kaduri
  0–3 Collection of Oral Witness Testimonies
  0–5 Collection T. Frydman
  0–8 Germany Collection
  0–30 Austria Collection
  0–51 Collection of NS Documents (DN)
  DN/27–3, File: Der Polizeipräsident in Wien, "Judentransporte ins General-
    gouvernement" (The President of Police, Vienna, "Transports of Jews to the
    Generalgouvernement")
  M-5 Collection Jewish Community Bratislava

YIVO Institute for Jewish Research, New York
  Occ E3, Documents of the Reich Ministry for the Occupied Eastern Territories
  Occ E7, Documents from Slovakia
  Collection Union Générale des Israélites de France (Association of the Jews in
    France)

Published Sources and Document Collections

Adler, H. G. *Die verheimlichte Wahrheit: Theresienstädter Dokumente.* Tübingen: Mohr,
  1958.
Auswärtiges Amt, Deutschland. *Akten zur Deutschen Auswärtigen Politik* 1918–1945,
  Serie D (1937–1945). Baden-Baden: Impr. Nationale, 1950–1956.
Baade, Fritz et al., eds. *Unsere Ehre heißt Treue: Kriegstagebuch des Kommandostabes
  Reichsführer SS, Tätigkeitsberichte der 1. und 2. SS-Inf.- Brigade, der 1. SS-Kav.-Brigade
  und von Sonderkommnandos der SS.* Vienna: Europa, 1965.
Behrend-Rosenfeld, Else, and Gertrud Luckner, eds. *Lebenszeichen aus Piaski: Briefe
  Deportierter aus dem Distrikt Lublin 1940–1943.* Munich: Deutscher Taschenbuch
  Verlag, 1970.
Braham, Randolph L., ed. *The Destruction of Hungarian Jewry: A Documentary Account.*
  2 vols. New York: Pro Arte, 1963.
Broszat, Martin, ed. *Rudolf Höss, Kommandant in Auschwitz: Autobiographische Auf-
  zeichnungen.* Munich: Deutscher Taschenbuch Verlag, 1963.
Broucek, Peter, ed. *Ein General im Zwielicht: Die Erinnerungen Edmund Glaises von
  Horstenau, Deutscher Bevollmächtigter General in Kroatien und Zeuge des Untergangs
  des "Tausendjährigen Reiches."* Vol. 3. Vienna: Böhlau, 1988.

Carpi, Daniel. *Nuovi Documenti per la Storia dell' Olocausto in Grecia: l'atteggiamento degli Italiani (1941–1943).* Vol. 7. Tel Aviv: University of Tel Aviv Research Institute, 1981.

Diamant, Adolf, ed. *Getto Litzmannstadt: Bilanz eines nationalsozialistischen Verbrechens.* Frankfurt/M.: Steinmann und Boschen, 1986.

Dokumentationsarchiv des österreichischen Widerstandes. *Widerstand und Verfolgung in Wien 1934–1945.* 3 vols. 2nd ed. Vienna: Österreichischer Bundesverlag für Unterricht, Wissenschaft und Kunst, 1984.

Eisenbach, Artur, ed. *Getto Łódzkie. Vol. 3, Dokumenty I Materiały do dziejów Okupacji niemieckiej w Polsce.* Warsaw: Centralna Żydowska Komisja Historyczna, 1946.

Ferenc, Tone, ed. *Quellen zur nationalsozialistischen Entnationalisierungspolitik in Slowenien 1941–1945.* Maribor: Obzorja, 1980.

Heiber, Helmut. "Aus den Akten des Gauleiters Kube." *Vierteljahrshefte für Zeitgeschichte* 4 (1956): 67–92.

Iltis, Rudolf, and Rat der jüdischen Gemeinden in den böhmischen Ländern und vom Zentralverband der jüdischen Gemeinden in der Slowakei, eds. *Nazidokumente sprechen.* Prague and Bratislava: Kirchenzentralverband, 1965.

Internationaler Militärgerichtshof. *Der Prozeß gegen die Hauptkriegsverbrecher vor dem Internationalen Militärgerichtshof.* 42 vols. Nuremberg: 1947–1949.

Jüdisches Historisches Institut Warschau, ed. *Faschismus-Getto-Massenmord: Dokumentation über Ausrottung und Widerstand der Juden in Polen während des Zweiten Weltkrieges.* Berlin: Rütten & Loening, 1961.

Kaden, Helma, and Ludwig Nestler, eds. *Europa unterm Hakenkreuz: Die faschistische Okkupationspolitik in Österreich und der Tschechoslowakei: Dokumentationsedition.* Berlin: Deutscher Verlag der Wissenschaften, 1988.

Klarsfeld, Serge. *Le Mémorial de la Déportation des Juifs de France.* Paris: Klarsfeld, 1978.

Klee, Ernst, and Willi Dreßen, eds. *Gott mit uns: Der deutsche Vernichtungskrieg im Osten 1939–1945.* Frankfurt/M.: Fischer, 1989.

Klee, Ernst, Willi Dreßen, and Volker Rieß, eds. *Schöne Zeiten: Judenmord aus der Sicht der Täter und Gaffer.* Frankfurt/M.: Fischer, 1988.

Knight, Robert. *Ich bin dafür, die Sache in die Länge zu ziehen: Die Wortprotokolle der österreichischen Bundesregierung von 1945 bis 1952 über die Entschädigung der Juden.* Frankfurt/M.: Athenäum, 1988.

Kotze, Hildegard von, ed. *Gerhard Engel, Heeresadjudant bei Hitler 1938–1943.* Stuttgart: Deutsche Verlagsanstalt, 1974.

Lang, Jochen von, ed. *Das Eichmann-Protokoll: Tonbandaufzeichnung der israelischen Verhöre.* Berlin: Severin & Siedler, 1982.

Langbein, Hermann. *Wir haben es getan: Selbstportraits in Tagebüchern und Briefen 1939–1945.* Vienna: Europa, 1964.

Less, Avner, ed. *Schuldig: Das Urteil gegen Adolf Eichmann.* Frankfurt/M.: Athenäum, 1987.

Lévai, Jenő, ed. *Eichmann in Ungarn: Dokumente.* Budapest: Pannonia, 1961.

Loewy, Hanno, and Gerhard Schönberner, eds. *Unser einziger Weg ist Arbeit: Das Getto in Łódź 1940–1944.* Vienna: Löcker, 1990. Exhibition Catalog, Jüdisches Museum Frankfurt am Main.

Longerich, Peter, ed. *Die Ermordung der europäischen Juden: Eine umfassende Dokumentation des Holocaust 1941–1945*. Munich: Piper, 1989.

Lösener, Bernhard. "Als Rassereferent im Reichsministerium des Inneren." *Vierteljahrshefte für Zeitgeschichte* 9 (1961): 262–316.

Majdanek: Dokumente und Fotografien. Lublin: Krajowa Agencja Wydawnicza, 1980.

Marsálek, Hans. *Die Geschichte des Konzentrationslagers Mauthausen: Dokumentation*. 2nd ed. Vienna: Österreichische Lagergesellschaft Mauthausen, 1980.

Merci, Lucillo. "Excerpts from the Salonika Diary of Lucillo Merci (February–August 1943)." *Yad Vashem Studies* 18 (1987): 293–323.

Mommsen, Hans. "Der nationalsozialistische Polizeistaat und die Judenverfolgung vor 1938: Dokumentation." *Vierteljahrshefte für Zeitgeschichte* 10 (1962): 68–94.

Pätzold, Kurt, ed. *Verfolgung, Vertreibung, Vernichtung: Dokumente des faschistischen Antisemitismus 1933–1942*. Leipzig: Reclam, 1983.

Präg, Werner, and Wolfgang Jacobmeyer, eds. *Das Diensttagebuch des deutschen Generalgouverneurs in Polen 1939–1945*. Stuttgart: Deutsche Verlagsanstalt, 1975.

Rückerl, Adalbert, ed. *Nationalsozialistische Vernichtungslager im Spiegel deutscher Strafprozesse: Belzec, Sobibor, Treblinka, Chelmno*. Munich: Deutscher Taschenbuch Verlag, 1977.

Safrian, Hans, and Hans Witek, eds. *Und keiner war dabei: Dokumente des alltäglichen Antisemitismus in Wien 1938*. Vienna: Picus, 1988.

Sauer, Paul, ed. *Dokumente über die Verfolgung der jüdischen Bürger in Baden-Württemberg durch das nationalsozialistische Regime 1933–1945*. 2 vols. Stuttgart: Kohlhammer, 1966.

Streim, Alfred. *Die Behandlung sowjetischer Kriegsgefangener im "Fall Barbarossa:" Eine Dokumentation*. Heidelberg: Juristischer Verlag Müller, 1981.

United States Office of Chief Counsel for the Prosecution of Axis Criminality. *Nazi Conspiracy and Aggression*. Vol. 8. Washington, DC: USGPO, 1947.

Secondary Sources

Adam, Uwe Dietrich. *Judenpolitik im Dritten Reich*. Düsseldorf: Droste, 1972.

Adler, H. G. *Theresienstadt 1941–1945: Das Antlitz einer Zwangsgemeinschaft*. 2nd ed. Tübingen: Mohr, 1960.

———. *Der verwaltete Mensch: Studien zur Deportation der Juden*. Tübingen: Mohr, 1974.

Adler, Jacques. *The Jews of Paris and the Final Solution: Communal Response and Internal Conflicts 1940–1944*. New York: Oxford University Press, 1987.

Anders, Günther. *Besuch im Hades*. 2nd ed. Munich: Beck, 1985.

Arad, Yitzhak. "Alfred Rosenberg and the 'Final Solution' in the Occupied Soviet Territories." *Yad Vashem Studies* 13 (1979): 263–86.

———. *Belzec, Sobibor, Treblinka: The Operation Reinhard Death Camps*. Bloomington: Indiana University Press, 1987.

———. "The 'Final Solution' in Lithuania." *Yad Vashem Studies* 11 (1976): 234–72.

———. *Ghetto in Flames: The Struggle and Destruction of the Jews in Vilna in the Holocaust*. New York: KTAV Publishing House, 1982.

Arendt, Hannah. *Eichmann in Jerusalem: A Report on the Banality of Evil.* New York: Viking Press, 1963.

———. *Eichmann in Jerusalem: Ein Bericht über die Banalität des Bösen.* Reinbek: Rowohlt, 1978.

Aronson, Shlomo. *Reinhard Heydrich und die Frühgeschichte von Gestapo und SD.* Stuttgart: Deutsche Verlagsanstalt, 1971 and 1984.

Backes, Uwe, Jesse Eckhard, and Rainer Zitelmann, eds. *Die Schatten der Vergangenheit: Impulse zur Historisierung des Nationalsozialismus* Berlin: Propyläen, 1990.

———. "Was heißt 'Historisierung' des Nationalsozialismus?" In *Die Schatten der Vergangenheit,* 25–58.

Badia, Gilbert. *Les Barbelés de l'exil: Études sur l'émigration allemande et autrichienne (1938–1940).* Grenoble: Presses Universitaire de Grenoble, 1979.

Baker, Leonard. *Hirt der Verfolgten: Leo Baeck im Dritten Reich.* Stuttgart: Klett-Cotta, 1982.

Barkai, Avraham. *Vom Boycott zur 'Entjudung': Der wirtschaftliche Existenzkampf der Juden im Dritten Reich 1933–1943.* Frankfurt/M.: Fischer, 1988.

Baroja, Julio Caro. *Los Judíos en la España Moderna y Contemporánea.* Madrid: Ediciones Arión, 1961.

Bartov, Omer. *The Eastern Front 1941–1945: German Troops and the Barbarisation of Warfare.* London: Macmillan, 1985.

Bauer, Yehuda. *American Jewry and the Holocaust: The American Joint Distribution Committee 1939–1945.* Detroit, MI: Wayne State University Press, 1981.

Beer, Mathias. "Die Entwicklung der Gaswagen beim Mord an den Juden." *Vierteljahrshefte für Zeitgeschichte* 35 (1987): 403–417.

Benz, Wolfgang, ed. "Der Generalplan Ost – Germanisierungspolitik in den besetzten Ostgebieten." In *Herrschaft und Gesellschaft im nationalsozialistischen Staat: Studien zur Struktur-und Mentalitätsgeschichte.* Frankfurt/M.: Fischer, 1990. 72–82.

———. *Die Juden in Deutschland 1933–1945.* Munich: Beck, 1988.

Biss, Andreas. *Der Stopp der Endlösung: Kampf gegen Himmler und Eichmann in Budapest.* Stuttgart: Seewald, 1966. 2nd ed. entitled *Wir hielten die Vernichtung an: Kampf gegen die "Endlösung" 1944.* Hemsbach/Weinheim: Herbstein, 1985.

Black, Peter R. *Ernst Kaltenbrunner: Ideological Soldier of the Third Reich.* Princeton, NJ: Princeton University Press, 1984.

Born, Hanspeter. *Für die Richtigkeit: Kurt Waldheim.* Munich: Schneekluth, 1987.

Botz, Gerhard. *Gewalt in der Politik: Attentate, Zusammenstöße, Putschversuche, Unruhen in Österreich 1918–1938.* 2nd ed. Munich: W. Fink, 1983.

———. *Nationalsozialismus in Wien: Machtübernahme und Herrschaftssicherung 1938/39,* Buchloe: DVO, 1988.

———. "Stufen zur Ausgliederung der Juden aus der Gesellschaft: Die österreichischen Juden vom 'Anschluß' zum 'Holocaust.'" *Zeitgeschichte* 14 (1987): 359–378.

———. *Wohnungspolitik und Judendeportationen in Wien 1938 bis 1945: Zur Funktion des Antisemitismus als Ersatz nationalsozialistischer Sozialpolitik.* Vienna: Geyer, 1975.

Bower, Tom. *Blind Eye to Murder.* London: Granada, 1983.

Braham, Randolph L. "The Kamenets-Podolsk and Delvidek Massacres." *Yad Vashem Studies* 9 (1973): 133–56.

———. *The Politics of Genocide: The Holocaust in Hungary.* New York: Columbia University Press, 1981.

Broszat, Martin. "Hitler und die Genesis der 'Endlösung.'" In Hermann Graml and Klaus-Dietmar Henke, eds. *Nach Hitler: Der schwierige Umgang mit unserer Geschichte.* Munich: Oldenbourg, 1987, 187–229.

———. *Nationalsozialistische Polenpolitik 1939–1945.* Stuttgart: Deutsche Verlagsanstalt, 1961.

Browning, Christopher R. *The Final Solution and the German Foreign Office: A Study of Referat D III of Abteilung Deutschland, 1940–1943.* New York: Holmes & Meier, 1978.

———. "The 'Final Solution' in Serbia: The Semlin Judenlager, A Case Study." *Yad Vashem Studies* 15 (1983): 55–90.

———. "German Technocrats, Jewish Labour and the Final Solution." In *Remembering for the Future: Working Papers and Addenda.* Oxford: Pergamon, 1989, 2199–2208.

———. "Nazi Ghettoization Policy in Poland: 1939–1941." *Central European History* 19 (1987): 343–368.

———. "Wehrmacht Reprisal Policy and the Mass Murder of Jews in Serbia." *Militärgeschichtliche Mitteilungen* 1 (1983): 31–47.

———. "Zur Genesis der Endlösung: Eine Antwort an Martin Broszat." *Vierteljahrshefte für Zeitgeschichte* 29 (1981): 97–109.

Buchheim, Hans et al., eds. *Anatomie des SS Staates.* 2 vols. Munich: Deutscher Taschenbuch Verlag, 1967.

———. "Die SS – das Herrschaftsinstrument." In Hans Buchheim, et al., eds. *Anatomie des SS Staates,* 1: 15–215.

Campion, Joan. *In the Lion's Mouth: Gisi Fleischmann & the Jewish Fight for Suvival.* Lanham, MD: University Press of America, 1987.

Carpi, Daniel. "Notes on the History of the Jews in Greece during the Holocaust Period: The Attitude of the Italians (1941–1943)." In *Festschrift in Honor of Dr. George S. Wise.* Tel Aviv: Tel Aviv University Publications, 1983, 25–62.

———. "The Rescue of Jews in the Italian Zone of Occupied Croatia." In Israel Gutman and Efraim Zuroff, eds. *Rescue Attempts during the Holocaust: Proceedings of the 2nd Yad Vashem International Historical Conference.* Jerusalem: Yad Vashem, 1977, 465–507.

Chaigneau, Jean François. *Le dernier wagon.* Paris: Julliard, 1982.

Cohen, Richard I. *The Burden of Conscience: French Jewish Leadership during the Holocaust.* Bloomington: Indiana University Press, 1987.

Cookridge, E. H. *Gehlen: The Spy of the Century.* New York: Random House, 1971.

Csokor, Franz Theodor. *Als Zivilist im Balkankrieg.* Vienna: Ullstein, 1947.

Czech, Danuta. "Deportation und Vernichtung der griechischen Juden im KL Auschwitz." *Hefte von Auschwitz* 11 (1970): 5–38.

———. *Kalendarium der Ereignisse im Konzentrationslager Auschwitz/Birkenau 1939–1945.* Reinbek: Rowohlt, 1989.

Dallin, Alexander. *German Rule in Russia, 1941–1945: A Study of Occupation Policies.* London: Macmillan, 1957.

Darville, Jacques, and Simon Wichené. *Drancy la Juive, ou la deuxième Inquisition.* Cachan: A. Breger Frères, 1945.

Deschner, Günther. *Reinhard Heydrich: Statthalter der totalen Macht.* Esslingen: Bechtle, 1977, in English as *Reinhard Heydrich: A Biography.* Briarcliff Manor, NY: Stein and Day, 1981.

Diner, Daniel. "Austreibung ohne Einwanderung: Zum historischen Ort des '9. November.'" *Babylon* 5 (1989): 22–28.

_____, ed. *Ist der Nationalsozialismus Geschichte? Zu Historisierung und Historikerstreit.* Frankfurt/M.: Fischer, 1987.

_____. "Zwischen Aporie und Apologie: Über Grenzen der Historisierbarkeit des Nationalsozialismus." In Diner, *Ist der Nationalsozialismus Geschichte?* 62–73.

Döscher, Hans-Jürgen. *Das Auswärtige Amt im Dritten Reich: Diplomatie im Schatten der "Endlösung."* Berlin: Siedler, 1987.

Drabek, Anna et al., eds. *Das österreichische Judentum: Voraussetzungen und Geschichte.* Vienna and Munich: Jugend und Volk, 1974.

Drach, Albert. *Unsentimentale Reise.* Munich: Müller, 1988.

Egyptien, Jürgen, ed. *Herr Moriz Deutschösterreicher: Eine jüdische Erzählung zwischen Assimilation und Exil.* Graz: Drosche, 1988.

Eichbauer, Werner. "Die 'Judenlager' von Wiener Neustadt, Felixdorf und Lichtenwörth." Unpublished project report, 1987.

Faligot, Roger, and Rémi Kauffer. *Le Croissant et la Croix Gammée: Les secrets de l'alliance entre l'Islam et le nazisme de Hitler à nos jours.* Paris: Albin Michel, 1990.

Fleischer, Hagen. *Im Kreuzschatten der Mächte: Griechenland 1941–1944.* Frankfurt/M.: Peter Lang, 1986.

_____. "Die nazistische Verfolgung und Vernichtung der Juden im besetzten Griechenland." Manuscript.

Fleming, Gerald. *Hitler und die Endlösung: Es ist des Führers Wunsch. . . .* Wiesbaden: Limes, 1982.

_____. "It Is the Führer's Wish." In Donald L. Niewyk, ed. *The Holocaust: Problems and Perspectives of Interpretation* 2nd ed. Boston: Houghton Mifflin, 1997, 12–26.

Förster, Jürgen. "The German Army and the Ideological War against the Soviet Union." In Hirschfeld, *The Policies of Genocide*, 15–29.

_____. "Der historische Ort des Unternehmens 'Barbarossa.'" In Michalka, *Der Zweite Weltkrieg*, 626–40.

_____. "Die Sicherung des 'Lebensraums': Die Befriedung des eroberten Gebietes." In Militärgeschichtliches Forschungsamt, *Das Deutsche Reich und der Zweite Weltkrieg*, 4: 1030–1078.

_____. "Das Unternehmen 'Barbarossa' als Eroberungs- und Vernichtungskrieg." Ibid., 417–447.

Fraenkel, Ernst. *Der Doppelstaat.* Frankfurt/M.: Europäische Verlagsanstalt, 1974.

Frank, Leo. "Ein 'heimlicher Besuch' in der Alpenfestung – und seine Folgen." *Salzkammergut-zeitung und Bad Ischler Stadt-zeitung,* March 14, 1991.

Freund, Florian, Bertrand Perz, and Karl Stuhlpfarrer. "Das Getto in Litzmannstadt (Łódź)." In Loewy and Schönberner, *Unser einziger Weg ist Arbeit*, 17–31.

Fricke, Gerd. *Kroatien 1941–1944: Der "USK" in der Sicht des Deutschen Bevollmächtigten Generals in Agram Glaise v. Horstenau.* Freiburg: Rombach, 1972.

Friedlander, Henry. "Deportation of German Jews." *Leo Baeck Institute Yearbook* 29 (1984): 201–226.

Friedländer, Saul. "Vom Antisemitismus zur Judenvernichtung: Eine historiographische Studie zur nationalsozialistischen Judenpolitik und Versuch einer Interpretation." In Jäckel und Rohwer, *Mord an den Juden*, 18–60.

Galanté, Abraham. *Appendice à L'Histoire des Juifs de Rhodes, Chio, Cos, etc. et Fin Tragique des Communautés Juives de Rhodes et de Cos, Œuvre du Brigandage Hitlerien.* Istanbul: Kâgit ve Basim I, sleri, 1948.

Gallo, Max. *Der schwarze Freitag der SA: Die Vernichtung des revolutionären Flügels der NSDAP durch Hitlers SS im Juni 1934.* Vienna: F. Molden, 1972.

Geyer, Michael. *Deutsche Rüstungspolitik 1860–1980.* Frankfurt/M.: Suhrkamp, 1984.

———. "The Nazi State Reconsidered." In Richard Bessel, ed. *Life in the Third Reich.* Oxford and New York: Oxford University Press, 1987, 57–67.

Gilbert, Gustave M. *Nürnberger Tagebuch: Gespräche der Angeklagten mit dem Gerichtspsychologen.* Frankfurt/M.: Fischer, 1962.

Gilbert, Martin. *Auschwitz und die Alliierten.* Translated by Karl Heinz Silber. Munich: Beck, 1982.

———. *Endlösung: Die Vertreibung und Vernichtung der Juden – Ein Atlas.* Translated by Nikolaus Hansen. Frankfurt/M.: Büchergilde Gutenberg, 1983.

———. *The Holocaust: The Jewish Tragedy.* London: Fontana, 1986.

Goshen, Seev. "Eichmann und die Nisko-Aktion im Oktober 1939." *Vierteljahrshefte für Zeitgeschichte* 29 (1981): 74–96.

Graml, Hermann. *Reichskristallnacht, Antisemitismus und Judenverfolgung im Dritten Reich.* Munich: Deutscher Taschenbuch Verlag, 1988.

Harthoff, Bernhard. "7, Rue Haddad, Damaskus, Syrien." *Tribüne* 27 (1988): n.p.

Häusler, Wolfgang. "Toleranz, Emanzipation und Antisemitismus: Das österreichische Judentum des bürgerlichen Zeitalters (1782–1918)." In Drabek et al., *Das österreichische Judentum*, 83–140.

Heim, Susanne, and Götz Aly. "Die Ökonomie der 'Endlösung.'" In Götz Aly, ed. *Sozialpolitik und Judenvernichtung: Gibt es eine Ökonomie der Endlösung? Beiträge zur nationalsozialistischen Gesundheits- und Sozialpolitik.* Berlin: Rotbuch, 1987. 5:11–90.

Herbert, Ulrich. *Fremdarbeiter: Politik und Praxis des "Ausländer-Einsatzes" in der Kriegswirtschaft des Dritten Reiches.* Berlin: J. H. W. Dietz, 1985.

Heydecker, Joe J., and Johannes Leeb, eds. *Der Nürnberger Prozeß.* Cologne: Kiepenheuer & Witsch, 1985.

Hilberg, Raul. *The Destruction of the European Jews.* Chicago: Quadrangle Books, 1961.

———. *The Destruction of the European Jews.* 3 vols. 3rd ed. New Haven and London: Yale University Press, 2003.

———. *Sonderzüge nach Auschwitz.* Frankfurt/M.: Ullstein, 1987.

———. *Die Vernichtung der europäischen Juden.* Frankfurt/M.: Fischer, 1982.

Hillgruber, Andreas. "Der Ostkrieg und die Judenvernichtung." In Gerd R. Überschär and Wolfram Wette, eds. *"Unternehmen Barbarossa": Der deutsche Überfall auf die Sowjetunion 1941.* Paderborn: F. Schöningh, 1984, 219–236.

Hirschfeld, Gerhard, ed. *The Policies of Genocide: Jews and Soviet Prisoners of War in Nazi Germany.* Boston: Allen & Unwin, 1986.

Höhne, Heinz. *Krieg im Dunkeln: Macht und Einfluß des deutschen und russischen Geheimdienstes.* Frankfurt/M.: Ullstein, 1988.

———. *Der Orden unter dem Totenkopf: Die Geschichte der SS.* Frankfurt/M.: Fischer, 1969.

Hondros, John Louis. *Occupation and Resistance: The Greek Agony 1941–44.* New York: Pella, 1983.

Honsik, Gerd. *Freispruch für Hitler?* Vienna: Burgenländischer Kulturverband, 1988.

Hory, Ladislaus, and Martin Broszat. *Der kroatische Ustascha Staat 1941–1945.* Stuttgart: Deutsche Verlagsanstalt, 1964.

Infield, Glenn B. *Skorzeny: Hitler's Commando.* New York: Military Heritage Press, 1981.

Jäckel, Eberhard. *Hitlers Herrschaft: Vollzug einer Weltanschauung.* 3rd ed. Stuttgart: Deutsche Verlagsanstalt, 1986.

Jäckel, Eberhard, and Jürgen Rohwer, eds. *Der Mord an den Juden im Zweiten Weltkrieg: Entschlußbildung und Verwirklichung.* Stuttgart: Deutsche Verlagsanstalt, 1985.

Jacobsen, Hans-Adolf. "Kommissarbefehl und Massenexekutionen sowjetischer Kriegsgefangener." In Buchheim et al., *Anatomie des SS-Staates*, 2: 166–169.

Jagschitz, Gerhard. *Der Putsch: Die Nationalsozialisten 1934 in Österreich.* Graz: Verlag Steiermark, 1976.

Jelinek, Yeshayahu. "The Role of the Jews in Slovakian Resistance." *Jahrbücher für die Geschichte Osteuropas* 15 (1967): 415–422.

Kampe, Norbert. "'Endlösung' durch Auswanderung? Zu den widersprüchlichen Zielvorstellungen antisemitischer Politik bis 1941." In Wolfgang Michalka, ed. *Der Zweite Weltkrieg*, 827–843.

Kapralik, Charles J. "Erinnerungen eines Beamten der Wiener Israelitischen Kultusgemeinde 1938/39." *Leo Baeck Institute Bulletin* 58 (1981): 52–78.

Kasztner, Resző R. *Der Kastner-Bericht über Eichmanns Menschenhandel in Ungarn.* Munich: Kindler, 1961.

Kempner, Robert M. *Eichmann und Komplizen.* Zurich: Europa Verlag, 1961.

Klarsfeld, Serge. *The Children of Izieu: A Human Tragedy.* New York: H. Abrams, 1985.

———. *Vichy-Auschwitz: Die Zusammenarbeit der deutschen und französischen Behörden bei der "Endlösung der Judenfrage" in Frankreich.* Translated by Ahlrich Meyer. Nördlingen: Delphi Politik, 1989.

Klee, Ernst. *"Euthanasie" im NS Staat: Die "Vernichtung lebensunwerten Lebens."* Frankfurt/M.: Fischer, 1985.

Kogon, Eugen et al., eds. *Nationalsozialistische Massentötungen durch Giftgas: Eine Dokumentation.* Frankfurt/M.: Fischer, 1986.

Krausnick, Helmut. "Hitler und die Befehle an die Einsatzgruppen im Sommer 1941." In Jäckel und Rohwer, *Der Mord an den Juden*, 88–106.

———. "Hitler und die Morde in Polen," *Vierteljahrshefte für Zeitgeschichte* 11 (1963): 196–209.

———. *Hitlers Einsatzgruppen: Die Truppe des Weltanschauungskrieges 1938–1942.* Frankfurt/M.: Fischer, 1985.

———. "Judenverfolgung." In Buchheim et al., *Anatomie des SS-Staates*, 1: 235–366.

———. "Kommissarsbefehl und 'Gerichtsbarkeiterlaß Barbarossa' in neuer Sicht." *Vierteljahrshefte für Zeitgeschichte* 25 (1977): 682–738.

Krausnick, Helmut, und Hans-Heinrich Wilhelm. *Die Truppe des Weltanschau-ungskrieges: Die Einsatzgruppen der Sicherheitspolitzei und des SD 1938–1942.* Stuttgart: Deutsche Verlagsanstalt, 1981.

Kulka, Erich. "The Annihilation of Czechoslovak Jewry." In *The Jews of Czechoslovakia: Historical Studies and Surveys.* Edited by the Society for the History of Czecheslovak Jews. Philadelphia: Jewish Publication Society of America, 1983. 262–328.

Kwiet, Konrad. "Judenverfolgung und Judenvernichtung im Dritten Reich: Ein historiographischer Überblick." In Diner, *Ist der Nationalsozialismus Geschichte?* 237–264.

Lánik, Jozef. *Co Dante nevidel.* Bratislava: Obzor, 1946.

Leroy, Beatrice. *L'aventure séfarade: De la Péninsule ibérique à la Diaspora.* Paris : Albin Michel, 1986.

Levi, Primo. *The Drowned and the Saved.* Translated by Raymond Rosenthal. New York: Summit Books, 1986.

Levin, Nora. *The Holocaust: The Destruction of European Jewry, 1933–1945.* New York: Schocken, 1973.

Lévy, Claude, and André Tillard. *La Grande Rafle du Vel d'Hiv.* Paris: R. Laffont, 1967.

Lipscher, Ladislav. *Die Juden im Slowakischen Staat 1939–1945.* Munich: Oldenbourg, 1979.

Loewy, Hanno, and Gerhard Schönberner, eds. *"Unser einziger Weg ist Arbeit": Das Getto in Łódź 1940–1944.* Vienna: Löcker, 1990.

Löwenstein, Karl. "Minsk – Im Lager der deutschen Juden." *Das Parlament* (Beilage, 45–46), 7 November 1956.

Madajczyk, Czeslaw. *Die Okkupationspolitik Nazideutschlands in Polen 1939–1945.* Cologne: Pahl-Rugenstein, 1988.

Malkin, Peter Z., and Harry Stein. *Eichmann in My Hands.* New York: Warner Books, 1990.

Manoschek, Walter. "'Serbien ist judenfrei': Die Ermordung der Juden in Serbien durch Wehrmacht und SS unter besonderer Berücksichtigung von Österreichern." PhD diss., University of Vienna, 1990, subsequently published as *"Serbien ist judenfrei": Militärische Besatzungspolitik und Judenvernichtung in Serbien 1941/42.* Munich: R. Oldenbourg, 1993.

Manoschek, Walter, and Hans Safrian. "Österreicher in der Wehrmacht." In Tálos, Hanisch, and Neugebauer, *NS-Herrschaft in Österreich,* 331–360.

Marrus, Michael R., and Robert O. Paxton. *Vichy France and the Jews.* New York: Basic Books, 1983.

Marszalek, Jósef. *Majdanek: Geschichte und Wirklichkeit eines Vernichtungslagers.* Reinbek: Rowohlt, 1982.

Mayer, Arno J. *Der Krieg als Kreuzzug: Das Deutsche Reich, Hitlers Wehrmacht und die "Endlösung."* Reinbek: Rowohlt, 1989.

Menasche, Albert. *Birkenau.* New York: Saltiel, 1947.

Messerschmidt, Manfred. "Harte Sühne am Judentum: Befehlslage und Wissen in der deutschen Wehrmacht." In Jörg Wollenberg, ed. *Niemand war dabei und keiner hat's gewußt: Die deutsche Öffentlichkeit und die Judenverfolgung 1933–45.* Munich: Piper, 1989. 113–28.

————. "Der Reflex der Volksgemeinschaftsidee in der Wehrmacht." In Messerschmidt, *Militärgeschichtliche Aspekte*, 197–220.

————. "Das Verhältnis von Wehrmacht und NS-Staat und die Frage der Traditionsbildung." In Messerschmidt, *Militärgeschichtliche Aspekte*, 233–55.

————, ed. *Militärgeschichtliche Aspekte der Entwicklung des deutschen Nationalstaates.* Düsseldorf: Droste, 1988.

Michalka, Wolfgang, ed. *Der Zweite Weltkrieg: Analysen, Grundzüge, Forschungsbilanz, im Auftrag des Militärgeschichtlichen Forschungsamts.* Munich: Piper, 1989.

Militärgeschichtliches Forschungsamt, ed. "Der Angriff auf die Sowjetunion." *Das Deutsche Reich und der Zweite Weltkrieg.* Vol. 4. Stuttgart: Deutsche Verlagsanstalt, 1983.

Moczarski, Kasimierz. *Gespräche mit dem Henker: Das Leben des SS-Gruppenführers und Generalleutnants der Polizei Jürgen Stroop aufgezeichnet im Mokatów Gefängnis zu Warschau.* Düsseldorf: Droste, 1978.

Molho, Michael, et al., eds. "*Israelitische Gemeinde Thessalonikis: In Memoriam.*" Translated by Peter Katzung. Essen: Jüdische Gemeinde Thessalonikis, 1981.

Mommsen, Hans. Introduction to *Eichmann in Jerusalem: Ein Bericht von der Banalität des Bösen* by Hannah Arendt. Munich: Piper, 1986. i–xxx.

————. "Die Realisierung des Utopischen: Die 'Endlösung der Judenfrage' im Dritten Reich." In *Geschichte und Gesellschaft* 9 (1983): 381–420.

Mommsen, Hans, and Dieter Obst. "Die Reaktion der deutschen Bevölkerung auf die Verfolgung der Juden 1933–1943." In Hans Mommsen and Susanne Willems, eds. *Herrschaftsalltag im Dritten Reich.* Düsseldorf: Schwann, 1988, 374–421.

Moser, Johnny. *Die Judenverfolgung in Österreich 1938–1945.* Vienna: Europa, 1966.

Müller, Rolf-Dieter. "Das Scheitern der wirtschaftlichen Blitzkriegstrategie." In Militärgeschichtliches Forschungsamt, *Das Deutsche Reich und der Zweite Weltkrieg,* 4: 936–1029.

————. "Von der Wirtschaftsallianz zum kolonialen Ausbeutungskrieg." Ibid., 98–189.

Nehama, Joseph. *Histoire des Israélites de Salonique.* 7 vols. Salonika and London: World Sephardi Federation,1937–1978.

Neumann, Oskar. *Im Schatten des Todes: Ein Tatsachenbericht vom Schicksalskampf des slowakischen Judentums.* Tel Aviv: Edition "Olamenu," 1956.

Novitch, Miriam. *Le Passage des Barbares: Contribution à l'Histoire de la Déportation et de la Résistance des Juifs Grecs.* Israel: Ghetto Fighters House Publications, 1982.

Oxaal, Ivar, Michael Pollak, and Gerhard Botz, eds. *Jews, Antisemitism and Culture in Vienna.* London and New York: Routledge & Kegan Paul, 1987.

Panicacci, Jean Louis. *Les Juifs et la Question Juive dans les Alpes-Maritimes de 1939 à 1945.* Nice: Archives départementales des Alpes-Maritimes, 1983.

Paris, Edmond. *Genocide in Satellite Croatia 1941–1945: A Record of Racial and Religious Persecutions and Massacres.* Translated by Lois Perkins. Chicago: American Institute for Balkan Affairs, 1962.

Pätzold, Kurt. "Von der Vertreibung zum Genozid." In Dietrich Eichholtz and Kurt Gossweiler, eds. *Faschismusforschung: Positionen, Probleme, Polemik.* Berlin: Akademie, 1980, 181–208.

Persche, Alfred. "Erinnerungen aus der Geschichte der nationalsozialistischen Machter-greifung in Österreich 1936–1938." DÖW. Unpublished manuscript.

Perz, Bertrand. *Projekt Quarz: Steyr-Daimler-Puch und das KZ Melk.* Vienna: Verlag für Gesellschaftskritik, 1991.

Pollack, Martin. "Jäger und Gejagter: Das Überleben der SS-Nr.107 136." *Transatlantic,* November 1982.

Press, Bernhard. *Judenmord in Lettland 1941–1945.* Berlin: Metropol, 1988.

Pulzer, Peter. *Die Entstehung des politischen Antisemitismus in Deutschland und Österreich 1867–1914.* Gütersloh: Mohn, 1966.

Rajfus, Maurice. *Des Juifs dans la Collaboration: L'U.G.I.F. 1941–1944.* Paris: Études et documentation internationales, 1980.

Ránki, György. *Unternehmen Margarethe: Die deutsche Besetzung Ungarns.* Vienna: Corvina, 1984.

Reitlinger, Gerald. *Die Endlösung: Ausrottung der Juden Europas 1935–1945.* Munich: Kindler, 1964.

Romano, Jasa. *Jevreji Jugoslvije 1941–1945: Zrtve genocida i ucesnici narodnooslobodi-lackor rata* [Jews of Yugoslavia 1941–1945: Victims of Genocide and Freedom Fighters]. Belgrade: Jewish Historical Museum Belgrade & the Federation of Jewish Communities in Yugoslavia, 1980.

Rosar, Wolfgang. *Deutsche Gemeinschaft: Seyss-Inquart und der Anschluß.* Vienna: Europa, 1971.

Rosenkranz, Herbert. *Verfolgung und Selbstbehauptung: Die Juden in Österreich 1938–1945.* Vienna: Herold, 1978.

Roth, Cecil. "The Last Days of Jewish Salonika." *Commentary,* July 1950.

Scheffler, Wolfgang. "Das Getto Łódź in der nationalsozialistischen Judenpolitik." In Loewy and Schönberner, *Unser einziger Weg ist Arbeit,* 12–16.

———. *Judenverfolgung im Dritten Reich.* Berlin: Colloquium, 1964.

———. "Wege zur 'Endlösung.'" In Strauss and Kampe, *Antisemitismus: Von der Judenfeindschaft,* 186–214.

Schleunes, Karl A. *The Twisted Road to Auschwitz: Nazi Policy toward German Jews.* London: Deutsch, 1972.

Schmidt, Christoph. "Zu den Motiven 'alter Kämpfer' in der NSDAP." In Detlev Peukert and Jürgen Reulecke, eds. *Die Reihen fest geschlossen: Beiträge zur Geschichte des Alltags unterm Nationalsozialismus.* Wuppertal: Hammer, 1981. 21–43.

Schmidt, Mária. "Provincial Police Reports: New Insights into Hungarian Jewish History, 1941–1944." *Yad Vashem Studies* 19 (1988): 233–267.

Schneider, Gertrude. *Journey into Terror: Story of the Riga Ghetto.* New York: Arc House, 1979.

Schramm, Hanna. *Menschen in Gurs: Erinnerungen an ein französisches Internierungslager (1940–1941).* Worms: Heintz, 1977.

Sereny, Gitta. *Am Abgrund: Eine Gewissensforschung. Gespräche mit Franz Stangl.* Frankfurt/M.: Ullstein, 1980.

———. *Into That Darkness: From Mercy Killing to Mass Murder.* McGraw-Hill, 1974.

Sevillias, Errikos. *Athens – Auschwitz.* Translated by Nikos Stavroulakis. Athens: Lyca-bettus Press, 1983.

Simpson, Christopher. *Der amerikanische Bumerang: NS-Kriegsverbrecher im Sold der USA.* Vienna: Überreuter, 1988.

Strauss, Herbert A. "Der Holocaust: Reflexionen über die Möglichkeit einer wissenschaflichen und menschlichen Annäherung." In Strauss and Kampe, *Antisemitismus: Von der Judenfeindschaft,* 215–233.

Strauss, Herbert A., and Norbert Kampe, eds. *Antisemitismus: Von der Judenfeindschaft zum Holocaust.* Frankfurt/M.: Campus, 1985.

Streim, Alfred. "Zur Eröffnung des allgemeinen Judenvernichtungsbefehls gegenüber den Einsatzgruppen." In Jäckel and Rohwer, *Der Mord an den Juden im Zeiten Weltkrieg,* 107–119.

————. "Replik auf die Kritik von Krausnick." *Simon Wiesenthal Center Annual* 6 (1989): 331–343.

Streit, Christian. "The German Army and the Policies of Genocide." In Hirschfeld, *The Policies of Genocide,* 1–14.

————. *Keine Kameraden: Die Wehrmacht und die sowjetischen Kriegsgefangenen 1941–1945.* Stuttgart: Deutsche Verlagsanstalt, 1978.

Stuhlpfarrer, Karl. "Antisemitismus, Rassenpolitik und Judenverfolgung in Österreich nach dem Ersten Weltkrieg." In Drabek et al., *Das österreichische Judentum,* 141–164.

————. *Umsiedlung Südtirol 1939–1940.* Vienna: Löcker, 1985.

Sundhaussen, Holm. *Geschichte Jugoslawiens 1918–1980.* Stuttgart: Kohlhammer, 1982.

————. *Wirtschaftsgeschichte Kroatiens im nationalsozialistischen Großraum 1941–1945: Das Scheitern einer Ausbeutungsstrategie.* Stuttgart: Deutsche Verlagsanstalt, 1983.

Tálos, Emmerich, Ernst Hanisch, and Wolfgang Neugebauer, eds. *NS-Herrschaft in Österreich 1938–1945.* Vienna: Verlag für Gesellschaftskritik, 1988.

Thurner, Erika. *Nationalsozialismus und Zigeuner in Österreich.* Vienna: Geyer, 1983.

Toury, Jacob. "Die Entstehungsgeschichte des Austreibungsbefehls gegen die Juden der Saarpfalz und Badens (22./23. Oktober 1940 – Camp de Gurs)." *Jahrbuch des Instituts für deutsche Geschichte* 15 (1986): 431–464.

Überschär, Gerd R., and Wolfram Wetter, eds. "*Unternehmen Barbarossa*": *Der deutsche Überfall auf die Sowjetunion 1941.* Paderborn: F. Schöningh, 1984.

Vestermanis, Margers. "Der Lettische Anteil an der 'Endlösung'." In Backes, Eckhard, and Zitelmann, *Im Schatten der Vergangenheit,* 426–449.

Vogt, Martin. "Selbstbespiegelungen in Erwartung des Sieges: Bemerkungen zu den Tischgesprächen Hitlers im Herbst 1941." In Michalka, *Der Zweite Weltkrieg,* 641–651.

Vrba, Rudolf, and Alan Bestic. *I Cannot Forgive.* New York: Bantam Books, 1964.

Weißberg, Alex. *Die Geschichte von Joel Brand.* Cologne: Kiepenheuer & Witsch, 1956.

Wellers, Georges. *L'Étoile Jaune à l'heure de Vichy: De Drancy à Auschwitz.* Paris: Fayard, 1973.

Wiesenthal, Simon. *Doch die Mörder leben.* Munich: Droemer, 1967.

————. *Recht, nicht Rache.* Frankfurt/M.: Ullstein, 1988.

Wilhelm, Hans-Heinrich. "Offene Fragen der Holocaust Forschung: Das Beispiel des Baltikums." In Backes, Eckhard, und Zitelmann, *Im Schatten der Vergangenheit,* 403–425.

Witek, Hans. "'Arisierungen' in Wien: Aspekte nationalsozialistischer Enteignungspolitik 1938–1940." In Tálos, Hanisch, and Neugebauer, *NS-Herrschaft in Österreich*, 199–216.

Wolff, Jeanette. *Sadismus und Wahnsinn: Erlebnisse in den deutschen Konzentrationslagern im Osten.* Dresden: E. Bretfeld, 1946.

Wyman, David S. *Das unerwünschte Volk: Amerika und die Vernichtung der europäischen Juden.* Frankfurt/M.: Fischer, 1989.

Zimmermann, Michael. "Die Deportation der Juden aus Essen und dem Regierungsbezirk Düsseldorf." In Ulrich Borsdorf and Mathilde Jamin, eds., *Überleben im Krieg: Kriegserfahrungen in einer Industrieregion 1939–1945.* Reinbek: Rowohlt, 1989.

———. *Verfolgt, vertrieben, vernichtet: Die nationalsozialistische Vernichtungspolitik gegen Sinti und Roma.* Essen: Klartext, 1989.

Zuccotti, Susan. *The Italians and the Holocaust: Persecution, Rescue, and Survival.* New York: Basic Books, 1987.

Zuckmayer, Carl. *Als wär's ein Stück von mir.* Frankfurt/M.: Fischer, 1966.

Index

Abetz, Otto, 76, 135, 139
Abromeit, Albert, 64, 148, 196, 201
Afritsch, Josef, 211
Agudas Jisroel-Weltorganisation (Agudas Yisroel World Organization), 17, 18, 28
Aktion Gildemeester, 26
Allgemeine Treuhandstelle für jüdische Auswanderung (Altreu – General Trusteeship Office for Jewish Emigration), 19
Alte Kämpfer (Austria), 39, 41
Altenburg, Dr. Günther, 151, 153–154, 158, 185
Altreu, 19
American Jewish Joint Distribution Committee (Joint), 30
Anders, Günter, 12
Anschluß (annexation of Austria), 2, 20–21
Antal, István, 196
antisemites, activities in post-Anschluß Austria, 21–26
antisemitism
  in Austria, 44–45
  in Hungary, 194–195
  in Slovakia, 143
Arad, Yitzhak, 110
Arajs, Victor, 97
Arendt, Hannah, 6, 27
Arrow Cross (Hungary), 196, 205–206
aryanization
  in Croatia, 146 ff.
  in Salonika, 162–164
  in Slovakia, 143
  of Hungarian Jewish properties, 197 ff.
  of Jewish property in Austria, 20, 23–26, 39
Asoziale ("asocials"), 3, 73, 78, 92
Austrian Legion (organization of Austrian SA and SS members in pre-Anschluß Germany), 41–44, 211

B'nai B'rith, 27
Babi Yar, 95
Baky, László, 196, 198, 203–204
Baldoni, Corrado, 170–171
Barbie, Klaus, 178
Barsilai, Rabbi Elias, 181–182
Barth, Regierungspräsident, 57
Becher, Kurt, 198, 287n47
Becker, Dr. 53, 57
Behr, Dr. Kurt von, 178
Benzler, Felix, 79–80
Best, Dr. Werner, 17, 31, 135
Betreuungsstelle für die alten Parteigenossen und Angehörigen der Opfer der nationalsozialistischen Bewegung im Bereich des Gaues Niederösterreich (Support Organization for Old Party Comrades and the Families of Those Sacrificed for the National Socialist Movement in the NSDAP Province Lower Austria), 40–41, 44
Biebow, Hans, 84
Bilartz, 177
Biss, Andreas, 287n47
Blumenfeld, Alex, 168
Blumenfeld, Lisa, 168
Bodurian, Jakob, 157
Böhme, Franz, 80–81
Bonczo, Miklós, 205

Bosel, Siegmund, 123
Botz, Gerhard, 12
Bousquet, René, 140
Brack, Viktor, 101, 104, 113–114
Brand, Joel, 287n47
Brauchitsch, Field Marshal Walther von, 49
Bräutigam, Otto, 76–77
Brückler, Ernst, 40, 43, 56, 119, 142, 157, 159, 174–177
Brunner, Alois, 4–5, 7–9, 39, 42–43, 57, 65, 85–86, 118, 120–123, 130–133, 142–143, 157–158, 161–163, 165, 167–169, 171–172, 174 ff., 194, 206, 208–210, 212, 214–217, 223–224
    in Syria, 223–224
    pseudonyms,
        Fischer, Dr. Georg, 215, 223
        Schmaldienst, Alois, 215, 223
Brunner, Anton, 45, 52, 124, 212, 215–217, 276
Bundesnachrichtendienst (Federal Intelligence Service, West Germany), 223
Bürckel, Josef, 22–23, 26–27, 31, 51–51, 53, 57, 67, 68, 117
Burckhardt, Dr. René, 168
bureaucracy, role of in the Holocaust, 11–12
Burger, Anton, 5, 9, 33, 39, 42, 51, 120, 181, 183, 186, 188–189, 190–192, 194, 212, 214, 225

Calmes, Dr. Albert, 151, 154, 168
Central Council of Hungarian Jews, 196–197
Central Intelligence Agency, 223
Chorin, Ferenc, 197–198
Ciano, Galeazzo, 148
Commissariat Général aux Questions Juives, 136
Concentration camps
    Auschwitz, 117
    Beaune-la-Rolande, 136, 138
    Belgrade, 80
    Bergen-Belsen, 167–168
    Chaidari (Greece), 189, 192
    Compiègne, 136, 138
    Dachau, 34
    Djakovo, 148
    Drancy, 136, 138, 140, 142, 174–176, 178–180, 208, 218
    Gurs, 67, 140
    Jasenovac, 147–148
    Jungfernhof, 109, 122–123

Kaiserwald (Riga), 124
Lackenbach ("Gypsy" camp), 86
Les Milles, 67, 140
Lublin, 117
Mauthausen, 196–197
Oranienburg, 175
Pithiviers, 136, 138
Ravensbrück, 168
Rivesaltes, 67, 140
Šabac (Serbia), 80
Sachsenhausen, 210
Salaspils (Riga), 102, 108, 122–123
Stara Gradiška, 147
Stutthof, 124
Theresienstadt (Terezin), 41, 115, 118, 121, 122, 126–127, 131, 181, 210, 214, 216
Vernet, 140
Zarzecze, 55
Csany, Josef, 174
Csokor, Franz Theodor, 147–148
Cuenca, Dr. Leon, 168

Dagatsch, Gesar, see Takasch, Gesar
Danneker, Theodor, 9, 18, 52, 55, 58, 65–67, 135–137, 139–141, 196, 201, 212, 221
Darquier de Pellepoix, Louis, 136, 140
Daurach, Ferdinand, 40
Deedes, Sir Wyndham, 27–28
Deportations, 46 ff.
    from Alsace and Lorraine, 67
    from Austria, 15–16, 19, 25–40, 36–37
    from Baden and Saarpfalz to unoccupied France, 67
    from Berlin, 73–74, 82
    from Central Europe to occupied USSR territory 1941–42, 91–92
    from Croatia, 148–149
    from France, 137 ff., 179–180, 268n20
    from Gau Wartheland, 64
    from Greater Germany (the Reich), 36–37, 46, 126
    from Greece, 183 ff.
        conflict between Italy and Germany over, 168–170
    from Salonika to Auschwitz, 163 ff.
    from Slovakia, 144 ff.
    from Corfu, Rhodes, Crete, and Cos, 185 ff.
    from Protektorat, 89–90
        to Galicia, 51–5
    from Theresienstadt, 126–128
    from Vienna, 126–128
        to Poland, 51–52, 68–69

in the Balkans, 71
of Hungarian Jews, 200 *ff.*
  to Strasshof, 287n46
  to Generalgouvernement, 67–71
  to Łódź, 86–87
Dodecanese Islands, Jews in, 150, 190–193
Doriot, Jacques, 179
Dosch, 129
Drechsler, Dr. Otto Heinrich, 91, 100
Drucker, Dr. Abraham, 177

EAM-ELAS (National Liberation
    Front-National Peoples Liberation
    Army in Greece), 182
Eberhard, Kurt, 95
Ebner, Dr. Karl, 53
Ehrlinger, Dr. Erich, 14, 99
Eiche, Heinrich, 129
Eichmann, Adolf, passim
  in Jerusalem, 220–221
  pseudonyms
    Alfred Barth, 213
    Otto Eckmann, 213
    Ricardo Klement, 213
  trip to Egypt, 19
Einsatzgruppe A, 89, 93, 97, 99, 105, 122, 138
Einsatzgruppe B, 89, 98–99
Einsatzgruppe C, 95
Einsatzgruppen, 48–49, 51, 92, 94–95, 195
Einsatzkommando II, 108
Einsatzstab Reichsleiter Rosenberg, 151–152
Endlösung, various meanings of, 73
Endre, László, 196, 198–199, 201, 203–204
Eppstein, Dr. Paul, 132
"euthanasia" program, 78, 88, 113
expulsion from and murder of Serbs in
    Croatia, 147
extermination centers and sites
  Auschwitz-Birkenau, 10, 121, 137–138,
      140–141, 144–145, 149, 167, 174, 178,
      180, 201–202, 207
  Bełżec, 101, 113–114, 117, 121
  Chełmno (Kulmhof), 78, 87–88, 113, 111,
      130
  Fort IX (Kaunas/Kovno), 108, 123
  Maly Trostinets, 4, 121, 124–130
  Majdanek (Lublin), 144–145
  Rumbula Forest, 122
  Sobibór, 117, 121, 174
  Treblinka, 117

Feketehalmy-Czeydner, Ferenc, 195

Feldblum, Léa, 178
Ferenczy, László, 198–199
"Final Solution Machine," 12
Final Solution to the Jewish Question, 3, 66,
    72, 114–118
Fleischmann, Gisi, 208–209
forced labor
  of Jews, 114, 123–124
  of Jews in Greece, 153–154
  of Jews in occupied USSR territories, 100,
      103, 105
Frank, Hans, 57, 60, 63, 66, 68, 77–78, 113,
    115–116, 225
Friedländer, Saul, 11–12
Friedmann, Desider, 27, 29
Fuchs, Günter, 87–88
Führerbefehl (Hitler's order to kill the Jews),
    10–11, 73, 114, 247n32
functionalist school, see structuralist school
Funk, Walter, 215

Gallop, Heinrich, 26
gas chambers, 113, 121, 141
  statistics of victims, 276–277n68
gas vans, 88, 99, 110, 113, 116, 123–124, 126,
    128, 130
Gehlen Organization, 223
Generalgouvernement (General Government,
    German-occupied Poland), 3
Gerbing, Herbert, 40, 44, 119, 142, 157–158,
    165, 175, 177
Giericke, Major, 70
Gestapa (Geheimes Staatspolizeiamt, Gestapo
    headquarters in Berlin), 19
Gestapo (Geheime Staatspolizei, Secret State
    Police), 17
Ghettos
  "German ghetto" in Minsk, 105–106, 110
  Kaunas, 102, 107
  Łódź (Litzmannstadt), 63–65, 72, 75–76,
      81–88, 90, 110
  Lublin, 76
  Minsk, 98, 100, 105, 122, 126–127,
      129–130
  Riga, 97, 108–110, 122–123, 124
      (social life)
  Sjauliai (Schaulen), 105, 107, 109
  Vilnius (Vilna), 105, 107
  Warsaw, 76
ghettoization
  in Hungary, 198 *ff.*
  in Salonika, 160 *ff.*

Ghigi, Pellegrino, 153–154
Girzick, Ernst Adolf, 40, 43–44, 121, 196, 199,
    219
Glaise-Horstenau, Edmund, 147, 156
Globocnik, Odilo, 114
Goebbels, Joseph, 14, 73–74, 77–78, 81
Goertz, Colonel, 70
Goldman, Nahum, 223
Göring, Hermann, 14, 36–37, 63, 72–74, 76,
    114
Graevenitz, Dr. Kurt von, 185, 190
Greiser, Arthur, 63, 66–67, 74–75, 81–84,
    88
Grünberg, Isak, 128–129
Günther, Hans, 9, 31, 37–38, 41, 65, 66, 212
Günther, Rolf, 8–9, 31, 37–38, 52, 56–57,
    61–62, 89, 132, 148–149, 154–155,
    158, 212, 222
Gypsies, see Roma and Sinti

Ha'avara Agreement, 16, 19, 25
Hagen, Herbert, 18, 19, 27, 29, 30, 32–33, 37,
    138, 140
Hartenberger, Richard, 40, 44–45, 85, 196,
    212–213, 222–223
Hasselbacher, Friedrich, 28
Helm, Hans, 148
Hencke, Andor, 170–171
Henschel, Moritz, 132
Hermann, Dr. (Regierungsrat), 51, 56
Heuser, Dr., 126
Heydrich, Reinhard, 2, 14, 16, 22, 35–38,
    48–50, 53, 60–63, 66, 68–69, 71–73,
    77–78, 81, 83–84, 88–90, 91, 99, 100,
    104, 114–117, 134, 137, 216
Hilberg, Raul, 10–11
Hilfsverein der Juden in Deutschland (Relief
    Organization of Jews in Germany), 28
Himmler, Heinrich, 16, 53, 59, 61, 63–64, 67,
    81–84, 87–88, 98, 114, 116, 138–141,
    152, 216, 205
Hitler, Adolf, 48–49, 53, 66, 68–69, 70, 73, 75,
    77–78, 81–82, 114, 152
    on deportations to the east in 1941, 251n2
Hlinka Guard, 142–143, 145, 208–209
Hoepner, Generaloberst Erich, 93
Höppner, Rolf-Heinz, 64, 71, 75, 82, 88–89
Horthy, Miklós, 194–196, 204–205
Höß, Rudolf, 7, 175
Höttl, Wilhelm, 44–45
Hunsche, Otto, 196, 212

intentionalist school, 9
International Committee of the Red Cross,
    174
internment camps
    for Hungarian Jews
        Csepel, 197
        Kistarcsa, 197, 201, 204
        Sárn, 205
        Topolya, 197, 201
        Sered' (Slovakia), 208–210
Israelitische Kultusgemeinde (Jewish
        Community Center in Vienna),
        27–30, 32, 34, 51, 54, 56, 58, 69,
        85–86, 118–119
Israelitische Kultusgemeinde Ostrava, 52
Italian occupation
    in Croatia, 156
    in Greece, 152–153
Izieu, 177–178

Jackson, Robert H., 6
Jäger (Army colonel in command on Corfu),
    187–188, 193
Jäger, Karl (Jäger Report), 107–108
Jarosz, Andor, 202
Jeckeln, Friedrich, 102, 105, 108
Jewish Agency, 207
Jewish Community in Athens, 181–183
Jewish Council Budapest, 204–205
Jewish Councils, 106
Jewish property in Vienna, disposition of,
        53–54, 85–86
Jodl, Alfred, 215
Judenabgabe (post-Kristallnacht tax on Jews),
        34–35
Judenpolizei (JUPO – Jewish Police), 118–119
Jüdische Kultusgemeinde Salonika, 159–160,
        163
Jüdische Kultusvereinigung (Berlin), 131–132

Kállay, Miklós, 195
Kallmeyer, Dr. Helmut, 101
Kaltenbrunner, Ernst, 196, 212, 215–216
Kareski, Georg, 17
Kasztner Transport, 204
Kasztner, Rezső (Rudolf), 287n46–47, 290n77
Keitel, Wilhelm, 95, 215
Kempner, Robert M. W., 6
Keren Hayesod, 18
killing centers, see "extermination centers"
Kleemann, Ulrich, 190–193

Knochen, Dr. Helmut, 138–141, 174, 176, 178
Koch, Erich, 68
Kommissarbefehl (order to kill Soviet political commissars in the Red Army), 94
Koppe, Wilhelm, 59
Koppel, Max, 174
Koretz, Chief Rabbi Zvi (Salonika), 151, 154, 159–161, 163, 165
Kovac, Tibor, 208
Kozower, Philipp, 132
Kreindler, Leo, 132
Kristallnacht, 14
Krumey, Hermann, 64, 82, 196–197
Kube, Wilhelm 103, 106–107, 127, 129
Kuchmann, Otto, 28
Kvaternik, Slavko, 77
Kwiet, Konrad, 12

Lange, Dr. Rudolf, 28, 88, 100–102, 105, 108, 116, 123
Lauterbach, Leo, 21, 27
Laval, Pierre, 139, 142, 174, 176
Leeb, Wilhelm Ritter von, 254n16
Leguay, Jean, 139
Leibbrandt, Dr. Georg, 102, 104
Levi, Primo, 1, 7
Liebl (Eichmann), Vera, 214
Lischka, Kurt, 28, 37, 136, 140
Löhr, Alexander, 81, 147, 154–155, 181
Lohse, Hinrich, 99–101, 103–105, 107, 127, 129
Lösener, 114
Löwenherz, Dr. Josef, 27, 29–30, 31, 56, 85, 125
Lueger, Karl, 143
Luther, Martin, 112

Madagascar Plan, 3, 58, 65–67, 73, 76–77, 116, 221
Magnus (Navy captain on Corfu), 187–188
Malkin, Peter Z., 220
Menasche, Albert, 167
Merci, Lucillo (Italian Consulate Salonika), 163, 169–170
Merten, Dr. Max, 154–155, 160, 162, 168–170
Mildenstein, Leopold Itz Elder von, 17
Mischehen (mixed marriages), 119–120, 168, 181, 185
Mommsen, Hans, 6
Movarek, 143

Müller, Heinrich, 51, 52, 56, 70, 141, 174, 212, 216
Mussolini, Benito, 66

Nationalsozialistische Deutsche Arbeiterpartei (NSDAP), 16
Navarro, Sam, 170
Nebe, Artur, 54, 57, 89, 99
Neubacher, Hermann, 182
Novak, Franz, 9, 33, 37, 39, 40–42, 44, 51, 71, 139–140, 182, 196, 198, 202, 212–213, 221
Nuremberg Laws, 8, 56, 143

Oberg, Karl, 138, 140, 142
ODESSA (Organisation der ehemaligen SS-Angehörigen), 213
Operation Barbarossa, 3, 75, 77, 92–94, 112, 195
    failure of as reason for the postponement of the Wannsee Conference, 112
Operation Margarethe (German occupation of Hungary), 195–196
Operation Nisko, 2, 46 ff., 55 ff.
Operation Reinhard, 101, 111, 114 ff., 117, 222, 262n9
Order police, Jewish (Salonika), 161–162
Organisation Todt, 98, 167, 180
Orient Trading Company (OTRACO), 223
Österreich-Auswertungskommando (Austria Evaluation Task Force), 27
Ousiel, Salomon, 161

Palästina-Treuhandstelle zur Beratung deutscher Juden (Paltreu-Palestine Trusteeship for Advice to German Jews), 16, 19
Paltreu, 16, 19
Parti Populaire Français, 179
Pavelić, Ante, 146, 148
Pavlou Mela (SIPO and SD prison camp in Greece), 151
Permilleux, Charles, 179
Pétain, Henri-Philippe, 134
Poison gas, 116
Poland
    occupation of, 48 ff.
    resettlement of populations, 62–63
    SS conflict with the army in, 50
    treatment of Jews in, 49 ff.
Polkes, Feivel, 19

Rademacher, Franz, 65–67, 79–80, 82, 112, 220–221
Raffelberger, Walter, 39
Rahm, Karl, 33, 40, 41, 51, 212, 225
Rajakowitch, Erich, 26, 56, 62, 66
Rapp, Albert, 64
Rassenschande ("racial defilement"), 46
Referat II-112 (Eichmann's first SS office), 15–19, 27, 29, 30, 58
Referat IV D 4, later IV B 4 (Eichmann's SS organization to enforce the Final Solution), 3, 38, 58, 62, 64–66, 71 and passim
Reichenau, Walther von, 95
Reichsbahn (German national railway), 2
Reichsbund jüdischer Frontsoldaten (Reich Association of Jewish War Veterans), 17
Reichsfluchtsteuer (departure tax), 34–35
Reichskommissar für die Wiedervereinigung Österrreichs mit dem Deutschen Reich (Reich Commissar for the Reunification of Austria with the German Reich), 22
Reichssicherheitshauptamt (Reich Security Main Office), 2, 38 and passim
Reichsstelle für das Auswanderungswesen, 16
Reichsvereinigung der Juden in Deutschland (Reich Association of Jews in Germany), 37, 62, 66–67, 117–118, 132
Reichszentrale für jüdische Auswanderung (Reich Center for Jewish Emigration), 36–37, 51
Ribbentrop, Joachim von, 66, 79–80
Roma and Sinti, 4, 10, 57, 71, 78–79, 80–87, 90, 92, 95, 110, 147, 155
    deportation from Austria and Berlin to Poland, 54, 238n41
    deportation from the Reich, 62
Rosenberg, Alfred, 76–78, 99, 129
Rosenberg, Dragutin, 148
Rosenberg, Walter, 207
Röthke, Heinz, 141–142, 174

SA (Sturmabteilung, Storm Troops), 15
    in Austria, 20, 23–26
Salonika, 4, 7–8, 150 ff.
San River, 2, 46 ff., 55

Saul, Moises, 170–171
Schacht, Hjalmar, 216
Scharizer, Karl, 85–86
Schefe, Robert, 83–84
Schefczig, Mathias, 157, 159
Schimana, Walter, 181
Schirach, Baldur von, 68, 215
Schmidt, Friedrich, 60
Schmund, Rudolf, 77
Schönberg, Fritz, 162, 166, 168
Schröder, Kuno, 17
Schwerin von Krosigk, Johann Ludwig (Lutz), 63
Seidl, Siegfried, 9, 62, 64, 71, 82, 122, 181, 196, 199, 201, 203, 212, 225
Seyß-Inquart, Arthur, 57, 60
Siberia as reservation for Jews, 116
Six, Franz Adolf, 18, 19, 28–29, 30, 32, 37
Skorzeny, Otto, 223
Slave labor, 116, 125
Slawik, Alfred, 40, 55, 119–120, 142, 157, 159, 165, 181, 196, 212–213, 219
Slovak National Uprising, 5, 207
Söllner, Anton, 174
Soviet POWs, 92, 128–129
Soviet Union as "reservation" for European Jews, 76–79
Speer, Albert, 77
Spiegel, Else, 126
Spiegel, Jona Jakob, 126
SS-Sicherheitsdienst (SD, Security Service), 2, 16 ff.
Staatszionistische Organisation in Deutschland (State Zionist Organization in Germany), 17
Stahlecker, Franz Walter, 14, 31, 32, 50–53, 89, 91, 93, 97, 100, 138, 222
Stangl, Franz, 121
Star of David, 7, 159–162, 278n77
Statut des juifs, 135
Stern, Samuel, 197
Steuerunbedenklichkeitsbescheinigung (certificate of paid taxes), 25
Streicher, Julius, 216, 220
Stroop, Jürgen, 181–182
structuralist school, 9–10
Stuckart, Wilhelm, 23
Stuschka, Franz, 40, 44, 51, 80
Suhr, Friedrich, 80
Szálasi, Ferenc, 196, 205–207
Sztójay, Döme, 196, 200–202

Takasch (Takacs), Gesar, 157, 159, 181
Thadden, Eberhard von, 182, 203
Tiso, Dr. Josef, 142, 145
Trampedach, Friedrich, 102–104
Turner, Dr. Harold, 81, 147, 155

Uebelhör, Friedrich, 63, 75, 82–84
Ullmann, Josef, 174, 177
Umschulungslager für Juden in Doppl
   ("Retraining" Camp for Jews, in
   Doppl), 215, 218
Unbedenklichkeitsbescheinigung (certificate
   of no restrictions), 35
Union Générale des Israélites de France
   (UGIF), 136, 174–175, 179
Ustasha 4, 146 ff.

Vallat, Xavier, 136
Veesenmayer, Dr. Edmund, 196–197,
   200–206, 285n11
Veil, Simone, 178
Vélodrome d'Hiver, 140
Verwaltungsstelle für jüdisches Umzugsgut
   der Gestapo (Vugesta – Gestapo
   Administrative Office for Jewish
   Property Removals, Vienna), 86,
   118–119
Vienna Model, 2, 14 ff., 121

Wagner (Army colonel), 48
Wagner, Josef, 51–53
Wagner, Robert, 67
Wagner, Rudolf, 225
Walcher, Robert, 142
Waldheim, Kurt, 281–282n47, 284n83
Wannsee Conference, 3, 14, 112 ff., 134, 220
Weber, Anton, 213
Wehrmacht (German armed forces)
   persecution of Jews in Greece, 183–193
   priorities over transport of Jews, 56–57
   resistance to deportations to Poland, 69–70

role in deportations from France, 137–138
role in killing Jews, 79–81
role in killings in occupied territories of
   USSR, 93 ff., 256–257n30
Weiss, Manfred (Industries), 197–198
Weiszl, Josef, 40, 44–45, 119, 131, 174,
   218–219
Weizsäcker, Ernst von, 137
Wellers, Georges, 176, 180
Wetzel, Dr. Erhard, 100–101
Wetzler, Alfred, 207
Westerkamp, Eberhard, 70
Winkelmann, Otto, 196–197, 203
Wirth, Christian, 114
Wisliceny, Dieter, 17, 18, 142–143, 157–160,
   164–165, 171–172, 181–183, 197–197,
   201, 212
World ORT, 17

yellow star, see Star of David

Zamboni, Guelfo (Italian consul in Salonika),
   160, 169–170
Zeitschel, Dr. Karl-Theodor (Carl-Theodor
   and Carltheo), 76, 139
Zentralstelle für jüdische Auswanderung
   (Central Bureau for Jewish
   Emigration, Vienna), 2, 8, 15, 27,
   31–35, 38–45, 51–53, 55–57, 68–70,
   85–86, 118–121, 216–219, 222
Zentralstelle für jüdische Auswanderung
   (Prague), 38, 41–42, 50–51, 216, 219
Zionistische Landesverband für Österreich
   (Zionist Association for Austria),
   28–29
Zionistische Rundschau, Die (newspaper
   controlled by Eichmann), 28–29
Zita, Anton, 40–41, 44, 55–56, 119, 157, 159,
   174–175, 177
Zöldi, Márten, 195
Zuckmayer, Carl, 20